5th Edition

The Trustee's Legal Companion

**Attorneys Liza Hanks and
Carol Elias Zolla**

FIFTH EDITION	MARCH 2019
Editor	DAVID GOGUEN
Cover Design	SUSAN PUTNEY
Book Production	SUSAN PUTNEY
Proofreading	ROBERT WELLS
Index	RICHARD GENOVA
Printing	BANG PRINTING

Names: Hanks, Liza Weiman, 1961- author. | Elias Zolla, Carol, 1971- author.
Title: The trustee's legal companion / Attorneys Liza Hanks and Carol Elias Zolla.
Description: 5th edition. | Berkeley, CA : Nolo, 2019. | Includes index.
Identifiers: LCCN 2018042915 (print) | LCCN 2018048332 (ebook) | ISBN 9781413325980 (ebook) | ISBN 9781413325973 (pbk.)
Subjects: LCSH: Living trusts--United States--Popular works. | Executors and administrators--United States--Popular works.
Classification: LCC KF734 (ebook) | LCC KF734 .H36 2019 (print) | DDC 346.7305/2--dc23
LC record available at https://lccn.loc.gov/2018042915

This book covers only United States law, unless it specifically states otherwise.

Please note

We believe accurate, plain-English legal information should help you solve many of your own legal problems. But this text is not a substitute for personalized advice from a knowledgeable lawyer. If you want the help of a trained professional—and we'll always point out situations in which we think that's a good idea—consult an attorney licensed to practice in your state.

Get Updates and More on Nolo.com

Go to this book's companion page at:

www.nolo.com/back-of-book/TRUG.html

When there's an important change to the law affecting this book, we'll post updates. You'll also find articles and other related materials.

More Resources from Nolo.com

Legal Forms, Books, & Software

Hundreds of do-it-yourself products—all written in plain English, approved, and updated by our in-house legal editors.

Legal Articles

Get informed with thousands of free articles on everyday legal topics. Our articles are accurate, up to date, and reader friendly.

Find a Lawyer

Want to talk to a lawyer? Use Nolo to find a lawyer who can help you with your case.

NOLO
LAW for ALL

⚖ NOLO　**The Trusted Name**
(but don't take our word for it)

"In Nolo you can trust."
THE NEW YORK TIMES

"Nolo is always there in a jam as the nation's premier publisher of do-it-yourself legal books."
NEWSWEEK

"Nolo publications…guide people simply through the how, when, where and why of the law."
THE WASHINGTON POST

"[Nolo's]…material is developed by experienced attorneys who have a knack for making complicated material accessible."
LIBRARY JOURNAL

"When it comes to self-help legal stuff, nobody does a better job than Nolo…"
USA TODAY

"The most prominent U.S. publisher of self-help legal aids."
TIME MAGAZINE

"Nolo is a pioneer in both consumer and business self-help books and software."
LOS ANGELES TIMES

Dedications

To my wonderful family: Howie, Aaron, and Abby.

—Carol Elias Zolla

To Marjorie Baer, in loving memory, for creating a generous and loving legacy with her living trust, and to her brother, Philip Baer, for being a fabulous trustee and making his sister's last wishes come true. Together they taught me everything I'll ever need to know about the power of estate planning and trust administration.

—Liza Hanks

Acknowledgments

I would like to thank Barbara A. Beck and John F. Hopkins, amazing mentors who taught me nearly everything I know about trust administration and estate planning; the members of TEXCOM and EPLAC, who make estate planning fun; my mother, Emilie H. Elias, who personifies the ethical and responsible practice of law; and my father, Charles A. Elias, who reminds me that it's possible to be a lawyer and still maintain a healthy work-life balance.

—Carol Elias Zolla

I would like to thank the following people:

My family, Steven, Kate, and Sam, for putting up with yet another writing project.

All of my Nolo editors, for always making the book better.

My partners at GCA Law Partners LLP, for being great colleagues, my paralegal, Susie Granata for everything, and my estate planning friends and mentors: Tish Loeb, Carol Elias Zolla, Michael Carney, Julie Lanz, Barbara Wright, and all of the members of the Bay Area Estate Planning study group, for keeping me honest, answering my endless questions, and inspiring me, always.

—Liza Hanks

And, finally, we both would like to give our most heartfelt thanks to Mary Randolph, whose persistent advocacy for our readers made this book much better than it ever would have been without her.

About the Authors

Liza Hanks is a partner at GCA Law Partners LLP in Mountain View, California, where she practices estate planning, trust administration, and probate law. She is a certified specialist in Estate Planning, Trust and Probate Law by the State Bar of California Board of Legal Specialization and taught Estate Planning and Taxation at Santa Clara University Law School as an adjunct lecturer. She is a graduate of Stanford Law School, the host of the podcast Life/Death/Law, a former magazine editor, and the mother of two children (neither of whom has any interest in becoming an attorney). She's also the author of *Every Californian's Guide to Estate Planning* (also published by Nolo).

Carol Elias Zolla is an attorney who practices only in the field of estate planning and administration. She is certified as a Specialist in Estate Planning, Trust and Probate Law by the State Bar of California Board of Legal Specialization. Carol has an AV Preeminent rating from Martindale-Hubbell and has been named a Northern California Super Lawyer since 2012. Carol graduated from the University of California at Berkeley and the UCLA School of Law. She frequently speaks about estate planning to attorney organizations and parent groups. Carol and her family live in Los Gatos, California.

Table of Contents

The Trustee's Companion

Someone who trusted you very much gave you the job of administering a living trust. That's no small thing. It's your job to carry out that person's last wishes, pay their remaining debts and taxes, and distribute their property to their favored relatives and friends.

In the old days, only wealthy families created trusts. Those were the folks with the family attorney who knew everyone's names and could be counted on to give advice at every turn. These days, all sorts of people create trusts, many of whom don't have the luxury of a family lawyer and who don't know the first thing about what will happen when the trust actually has to be wrapped up someday. As a result, every single day people just like you find themselves stuck with a job that they don't know much about, aren't sure that they can handle, and yet, for many reasons, feel honor bound to take on. That's why we wrote this book.

We don't blame you if right now you are wondering how on earth to get this done properly, efficiently, and with a minimum of drama. Consider this book your trusty companion (pun absolutely intended). It's full of practical advice that will help you handle it smoothly, whether you are administering a trust that's going to get settled quickly or one that lasts for years. We'll show you how to:

- Decide whether or not to take on the job of trustee
- Understand your legal duties
- Develop good relationships with the trust beneficiaries
- Get organized
- Identify and collect trust assets
- Deal with life insurance, retirement assets, and other nontrust assets
- Find and work effectively with expert advisers
- Set up ongoing trusts for the benefit of the surviving spouse, children, or someone with a disability
- Invest trust assets properly

- Handle income tax returns for the deceased person and for the trust (and get help with estate tax returns)
- Prepare proper trust accounting reports
- End the trust and distribute assets to the beneficiaries.

As estate planning attorneys with nearly 40 years of collective experience, we've counseled trustees on all aspects of trust administration, from beginning to end. We've seen what works well, what can go wrong, and how to avoid some of the most dangerous mistakes. We've taken our best advice, our most illustrative war stories, and our best practices and put them here for you.

You can read this book from beginning to end, or just skip to the specific chapters that you need help with. You can use this book as a do-it-yourself guide so you can do much of the work without hiring help. You can also use it as a way to work effectively with attorneys, accountants, and financial advisers. However you choose to use it, we hope it will help you along the way.

Get Updates and More Online

When there are important changes to the information in this book, we'll post updates online, on a page dedicated to this book:
www.nolo.com/back-of-book/TRUG.html

1

Should You Serve as Trustee?

t's an honor to be chosen as a successor trustee of a loved one's trust. The person who chose you considered you trustworthy and responsible—someone who pays attention to detail and gets along with others. But do you want the job? You don't have to take on the responsibility of serving as trustee—you can decline.

Most of our clients agree to act as successor trustee because they feel a sense of loyalty to the person who asked them. In many cases, the trustee is a beneficiary of the trust, the deceased person's accountant or other adviser, or a close friend or relative.

Sometimes, however, the best thing you can do for all involved is to politely decline. If you are overwhelmed by demands on your time and energy or don't get along with one or more of the beneficiaries, you may not in fact be the best person for this added responsibility. No one will be happy if you take on the job but are unable to give it the time and attention it requires. Accept the position only if you have the time, the patience, the organizational skills, and the sense of humor required to juggle a thousand administrative details and a few anxious beneficiaries at the same time.

> **EXAMPLE:** Karen names her friend Marjorie as the successor trustee of her living trust. Marjorie is close to both Karen and Karen's brothers, Pete and Josh. She is married, living nearby, and working as an accountant.
>
> When Karen dies 15 years later, Marjorie is no longer on speaking terms with either Pete or Josh, is raising three children as a single mother, and has moved across the country. When Marjorie is notified that she's been named as successor trustee, she doesn't accept the job. Although she loved Karen dearly, she knows that it would be difficult for her to act as successor trustee because of her limited free time, the distance, and because she does not get along with Karen's brothers.

What about accepting, with the idea that you can quit later if serving as trustee gets to be too much work and hassle? We don't recommend it. If you are worried that the responsibility is going to require too much of your time or put you in an uncomfortable position with respect to your relatives, our advice is not to accept in the first place. It's true that you can always resign later on, but when you act as trustee for any period of time, you expose yourself to some personal liability that you might rather avoid altogether. Also, before you can resign you'll have to take a number of steps to protect yourself and the beneficiaries. That all can be avoided if you decline the job now.

Think twice about taking the job if:

You don't get along with the beneficiaries. If you don't like the people you're managing the trust for, you probably won't have an easy time doing it.

You don't know what the settlor owned and think it will be hard to find out. If you don't have the time for massive detective work, perhaps this just isn't the right job for you at this time.

Lawsuits are threatened or already in progress. As trustee, you'll have a duty to defend the trust against a lawsuit that could reduce its value; you will also have to collect money owed to the trust. Trust money can be used to pay for the legal expenses, but this may take up a lot of your time and energy.

You're named along with a cotrustee. This complicates everything, because generally all cotrustees must sign off on everything. And chances are that one of you will end up doing all the work.

Getting the Big Picture

Before you decide whether or not to serve as a successor trustee, you really need to understand what a trust is and why someone would create one in the first place.

On the legal side, a trust is an agreement in which one person, the *settlor*, agrees to transfer property to another, the *trustee*, who will manage that property for the benefit of someone else, the *beneficiary*. For the whole plan to work, the settlor must legally transfer ownership of the assets to the trustee of the trust. A deed transfers a house; other documents are used to transfer brokerage and bank accounts. These documents notify the county, the bank, or the brokerage firm that the settlor used to own the asset and is now transferring it to the care of the trustee. The trust, in the person of the trustee, becomes the new legal owner, and the trustee becomes the new manager.

With a living trust, usually the settlor is also the first trustee and beneficiary. So the person who puts the property into the trust continues to use and manage that property during his or her lifetime. There's a flurry of paperwork, but nothing actually changes in real life with respect to how the settlor can use or invest the assets. When the settlor dies (or becomes unable to manage the trust assets), the next trustee steps up to manage and distribute the assets. That's you, if you accept the job.

When you are the trustee, you are responsible for the trust's assets. Your job is to manage those assets and distribute them as the trust document directs. Your actual duties will vary enormously depending on what kind of trust you are in charge of and what the trust document instructs you to do. But no matter what kind of trust you've got on your hands, you'll have certain common challenges and issues.

In general, your job is to:
- identify and protect the trust's assets
- figure out what the trust instrument (the document that created the trust) requires you to do
- be scrupulously honest
- communicate regularly with the trust beneficiaries
- manage the assets long-term or distribute them to the beneficiaries right away, and
- end the trust when it's time (as determined by the trust instrument).

The chief benefit of this arrangement is that the assets can be distributed to the people who inherit them without the need for a probate court proceeding. That saves the beneficiaries time and money. If the trust is designed to stay in existence for a while, it can also provide a way to manage assets for young beneficiaries or provide tax savings.

Environmental Problems: A Really BIG Red Flag

If the trust includes real estate that has possible environmental liability, such as a gas station, an urban lot bordered by old factories, or even farmland that was treated with pesticides, get an environmental risk assessment from a qualified expert right away. If the problems are big, think very carefully about accepting the job.

You may have to accept the trusteeship in a limited scope just to hire and supervise a general inspector. But you are well within your rights to demand that the trust foot the bill for an inspection before you agree to take on the job of trustee. If the inspection turns up problems and you decline to serve as trustee, you must tell any prospective successor trustees what you know, and let them determine for themselves whether to accept the position.

Do not transfer title to the property to your name until you have an idea of whether clean-up will be required; once you're in the public record as owner, you can be personally on the hook.

If you do accept the trusteeship, you can authorize an in-depth inspection that will show the scope of the damage and the work needed to prepare the property for sale or transfer. The trust may be required, under local, state, or federal law, to clean up any environmental problems before the beneficiaries receive their share of trust assets. That kind of clean-up can be time-consuming, complicated, and costly—and beneficiaries may disagree with you on the proper way to proceed. But if you don't prevent environmental damage that you should have, you could become personally liable for the cost of clean-up.

Trustees and Executors: What's the Difference?

Even when you're dealing with a trust, there's almost always a will, too. That's a good thing, because wills do two things that trusts can't:

they nominate guardians to raise minor children in case there are no surviving parents, and they distribute property that was owned by the settlor but was not placed in the trust.

As trustee, you are legally responsible only for assets that are held in the trust. Most often these are the assets that the settlor transferred to the trust by recording a new deed or by filling out forms at a bank or brokerage house. But life is messy, and it often happens that people leave some things out of their trusts. These can range from small everyday checking accounts to large brokerage accounts, stock, or even real estate. The job of collecting, protecting, and distributing nontrust assets falls instead to the executor (also called personal representative) of the person who has died.

It's common for the same person to be named as trustee and executor. If the deceased person's will names you as the executor, then you are the person in charge of assets governed by the will. An executor steps into the shoes of the settlor and finishes up all the odds and ends that get left behind after a death. Among other things, the executor goes through the settlor's mail, cancels credit cards and utility bills as necessary, notifies creditors, and files the settlor's last tax returns.

If the will gives someone else the executor's job, then you'll need to work together and communicate closely to get debts paid, tax returns filed, and assets distributed. You'll probably always be in the loop anyway. It is common practice for most attorneys to draft living trusts along with a special kind of will, called a "pour-over" will. This will directs the executor to transfer any property owned by the settlor at death into the living trust. The goal is to prevent having two separate sets of instructions about who should get what. If all the property is poured into the trust, then only one set of instructions (those in the trust instrument) need to be followed. This is a sensible way to arrange things, and it means that you, as trustee, will ultimately be in charge of everything the settlor owned.

Before assets outside of the trust are transferred into the trust, there might have to be a probate proceeding. It depends upon what assets are outside of the trust and what the laws of your state say. In many states, small assets, such as checking accounts, can be transferred into the trust without a formal probate proceeding. (Chapter 5 helps you figure this out.) Whether it's the executor or the trustee who transfers the assets to the trust will depend on the value of the asset and state law. Until the process is complete, the trust assets cannot be completely distributed.

> EXAMPLE 1: Ethan was the successor trustee of his father's living trust. After his father died, Ethan discovered that his father had left a brokerage account worth $20,000 outside of his trust. Because it wasn't held in the trust, Ethan had no authority over it as the successor trustee. But under the terms of his father's pour-over will, the trust inherited the brokerage account. As a result, Ethan could claim it on behalf of the trust. (He didn't have to go to probate court, because the account's value was low enough to qualify for a simple, out-of-court transfer process under state law.) Once the account was in the trust, Ethan divided it into equal thirds and distributed it to his siblings, as the trust document directed.

> EXAMPLE 2: Felix was the successor trustee of his mother's living trust and nominated as her executor in her pour-over will. After his mother died, Felix discovered that her recently purchased vacation home, worth $200,000, was not held in her trust. So Felix had to initiate a probate court proceeding to request that the judge appoint him as executor, follow his state's probate procedures, and wait for the court's approval to distribute the property.
>
> After about a year, the judge ordered the property to be distributed to Felix, in his position as successor trustee of his mother's trust. Only then could Felix distribute the vacation home to the trust beneficiaries, as the trust document directed.

What Kind of Trust Do You Have?

You don't know what you're getting yourself into until you figure out what kind of trust you've got on your hands. Some trusts are relatively simple to administer, and your job would be wrapped up quickly. Others might take time and effort for years to come.

How can you tell whether you've got an easy trust or a hard one? Look at the trust instrument—specifically, the section that states what is to happen when the person who created the trust (called the settlor, grantor, or trustor) dies. If the trust was made by a couple, find where it says what will happen when the first settlor dies. Usually you'll see a section heading that says something like "Trust Distribution Upon the Death of Settlor."

If the trust says that the trust assets are to be handed over (distributed) to certain people outright, you've got a simple trust to administer. If, however, the trust says that certain assets are to be held in trust for beneficiaries, you've got a more complicated trust, one that could last a while.

If you've been named trustee of an ongoing trust, it may make sense to ask an attorney or a CPA to review the trust instrument. An expert might be able to identify potential issues that would make your job as trustee especially difficult—for example, commercial real estate that would require a lot of your time to manage, or complicated distribution requirements that would require you to balance the needs of several beneficiaries over a long period of time.

Simple Living Trusts

A simple living trust is designed to end soon after the settlor's death, so there will be no ongoing trust for you to manage. You will collect all the trust assets, pay the debts, expenses, and taxes of the trust, and distribute what's left to the beneficiaries. Because trust assets don't need to go through probate, you can wrap everything up and give property to the beneficiaries without the time and delay of a court proceeding. In six months or so, you should be done.

> **EXAMPLE:** Joshua established a living trust to hold his assets and named his close friend, Adam, to serve as the successor trustee. The trust instrument directed Adam, at Joshua's death, to distribute half of the trust assets to Joshua's sister, Mary, and half to his cousin, Leopold.

When Joshua died, Adam collected the trust's assets and paid the debts, expenses, and taxes due. Then he distributed half of the trust's remaining assets to Mary and half to Leopold. When he'd done that, the trust administration was finished.

This kind of basic, probate-avoidance living trust is a substitute for a will. Traditionally, people used wills to direct what should happen to their property after death. Most of us know from movies, books, and plays that a person's last will and testament is the document that gets read in front of the family, by the lawyer, after a death. (That's the part where Junior finds out that he's been disinherited and his sister discovers that she's the new owner of the manor house.) That's still a perfectly legal way to get the job done, though sadly nobody does a big dramatic will reading anymore.

Wills are legal and effective, but they have a big drawback: Property left through a will generally has to go through probate court after a person dies. Probate is a court process that was designed to make sure that a person's wishes were followed. There's nothing inherently evil or wrong about probate. In some situations it's useful to have a judge make sure that a will is valid, identify the property owned by the deceased person, ensure valid bills are paid, and make sure that the property is distributed as directed by the will. The problem with probate is simply that for many families, court supervision of this process isn't necessary—and in many states, the process can take more than a year and can cost thousands of dollars.

That's why living trusts are very popular, especially in states where probate is time-consuming and expensive. They allow a person to transfer assets to loved ones without the time and expense of a probate court proceeding.

> EXAMPLE: Rebecca establishes a living trust during her lifetime. That makes her the settlor, and the trust instrument also names her as trustee. It names her grown daughter Erin as the successor trustee.

She transfers the title to her house, her brokerage account, and her savings account to herself as the trustee of her living trust. Now, the name on her deed and accounts is "Rebecca Durham, Trustee of the Rebecca Durham Revocable Living Trust." During her lifetime, she manages and uses trust assets however she wants.

When Rebecca dies, her daughter takes over as the successor trustee. The trust instrument directs her to distribute the trust assets in three equal shares to herself and her two siblings. After notifying certain people as required by state law and paying all of Rebecca's last expenses, debts, and taxes, Erin distributes the trust assets in equal thirds. No probate court proceeding is required.

Ongoing Trusts

Although probate avoidance (as discussed above) is the main benefit of a simple living trust, settlors can get additional benefits if they set up a more complicated trust, designed to last for years or even decades. For example, couples in second marriages can control assets left to the surviving spouse or ensure that children from prior marriages will inherit. The very wealthy can do sophisticated tax planning.

There are many kinds of ongoing trusts. For example, if the trust was created by a couple and one of them has died, the trust instrument might state that assets are to be placed in trust for the benefit of the surviving spouse. Or it might direct that certain assets are to be held in trust for young children until they grow up, or in trust for other family members indefinitely.

If you are trustee of an ongoing trust of this kind, you'll be in charge of filing tax returns, investing trust assets, and choosing how to spend trust funds for beneficiaries. You will likely work with an accountant and an attorney. You could wear your trustee's hat for a lengthy period of time.

EXAMPLE: Martina and Steven established a living trust. Upon the death of the first spouse, the trustee was directed to hold trust assets in two trusts, both for the benefit of the surviving spouse. One trust was to hold the amount of money that the first spouse to die could pass estate tax-free; the other was to hold the assets owned by the surviving spouse.

Martina and Steven named Steven's younger brother, Todd, to serve as successor trustee after both of them had either died or resigned as trustees. After Martina died, Steven was in ill health and overwhelmed by grief; he asked Todd to take over management of the trust and resigned. Todd reviewed the trust and realized that he would be managing Steven's two trusts for the rest of Steven's life. After consulting an attorney and a CPA, he decided that he could do the job and accepted the position of successor trustee.

Is There a Cotrustee?

Remember having to do a group project in high school? Every group seemed to include one slacker who made big promises but never followed through, one member who brought the pizza, and one responsible person who pulled an all-nighter to actually finish the project. If you serve with someone else as a cotrustee, you may find yourself recalling those school projects.

The settlor probably named you and another person as cotrustees in hopes that your skills would complement each other's and that together you would make a perfect trustee. Or maybe the settlor just didn't want to hurt anyone's feelings and named you and all of your siblings. The truth is that when you work with another person, you have many more obstacles than when acting alone.

Most trusts require cotrustees to act unanimously. In an ideal world, you will get together and delegate tasks. One of you will meet with the real estate agent to discuss listing the house, while the other talks with the financial adviser about investments. Once you've each done your legwork, you will get together, discuss the pros and cons of a particular action, and then both sign the papers to move the trust administration process along.

But most of the time, one person does most of the work. There can be lots of reasons—maybe a cotrustee is overwhelmed by other aspects of life or can't stand the idea of selling the settlor's house. In any case, if you're the responsible cotrustee you'll end up with more work than if you were sole trustee. Not only will you have to research the options and figure out what needs to be done, you will have to corral the cotrustee to meet and sign documents. If the cotrustee decides to be stubborn and object to your preferred action, you're back to square one.

You might also be legally liable for actions that the cotrustee takes on behalf of the trust. If the cotrustee promises to file the trust tax return but doesn't, for example, both of you will be on the hook.

Finally, most of the trusts we've seen say that cotrustees must share the trustee's fee. As a result, the responsible cotrustee could end up doing 125% of the work for 50% of the fee. Perhaps the other cotrustee will recognize that you're doing the bulk of the work and agree to take less, but it isn't guaranteed.

You can guess what our advice is here: If you're named as a cotrustee, don't do it! Talk with the other named cotrustee and see whether that person will resign. If not, you should consider resigning before the two of you miss important deadlines. If you must continue to act as cotrustee, make sure your cotrustee reads this book and understands the work involved. Then create a task sheet with deadlines and inform the cotrustee that you expect that both of you will share information and cooperate.

Is the Settlor Incapacitated?

If a trust document names you as a successor trustee, it's most likely that you'll take over management of the trust when the settlor dies. But most trusts are written so that you could step in sooner, if the settlor became unable to manage the trust assets. In that situation, you would manage the trust assets until the settlor died, and then, depending on the kind of trust you're dealing with, either wrap up the trust quickly or manage it over the long term.

You'll step in to manage a trust for a living settlor in one of two circumstances:

- the settlor asks you to, or
- the settlor is incapacitated and unable to manage trust assets.

If you've been asked to step in, the trustee should formally resign in writing, and you should formally accept in writing. That way, no one will be confused about who is managing the trust. Examples of resignation and acceptance statements are shown below.

Resignation of Trustee of the Susan L. Woods Living Trust

I, Susan L. Woods, settlor and trustee of the Susan L. Woods Living Trust, executed on May 12, 20xx, resign as trustee, pursuant to Section 1.8, which provides that I may resign at any time during my lifetime by a signed writing delivered to the successor trustee.

This resignation shall be effective as of the date on which I sign it.

Signed:

_____   _____
Signature: Susan L. Woods, Trustee   Date

_____   _____
Accepted: Susan L. Woods, Settlor   Date

[NOTARY]

Agreement to Act as Trustee

I, Manuela Woods, agree to serve as trustee of the Susan L. Woods Living Trust, dated May 12, 20xx, and to abide by the terms of the trust instrument as of the date that this document is signed.

_____   _____

Manuela Woods, Successor Trustee   Date

[NOTARY]

If you are replacing a settlor who is gradually losing the ability to manage the trust, it can be a more difficult process. It's best, if you can, to work with the settlor during this process, which is a time of major suffering and loss. Be patient. Listen to the settlor's concerns. It may be helpful to emphasize that as the successor trustee, you are simply managing the assets. The trust assets still belong to the settlor, and your job is only to follow instructions. Try to understand the settlor's fear of losing control and make it clear that you're trying to help.

If the settlor has already lost the capacity to manage financial matters, you've got to read the trust document to see how it defines incapacity. You can't step in as the new trustee until the settlor resigns or is declared incapacitated. So carefully document that the settlor is in fact incapacitated before you take over as trustee.

Whatever the trust instrument says about proving incapacity, follow its instructions. Some trusts require a statement from one, two, or even three doctors. Others require a statement from a specialist, such as a neurologist or psychiatrist. Some trust instruments specifically define the tasks a settlor must be unable to do, while others state generally that a settlor who is unable to manage the affairs of daily living is incapacitated. Almost no trust will require that you get a court order of incapacity.

EXAMPLE: Johnny's trust defined incapacity this way:

Definition of Incapacity. As used in this instrument, "incapacity" or "incapacitated" means operating under a legal disability such as a duly established conservatorship, or a person who is unable to do either of the following:

(a) Provide properly for that person's own needs for physical health, food, clothing, or shelter; or

(b) Manage substantially that person's own financial resources, or resist fraud or undue influence.

The determination of incapacity shall be made by the physician of the person whose capacity is at issue.

Johnny's grandson Rob is the successor trustee. In order to take over as trustee, he must get a written statement from Johnny's physician that states that Johnny is unable to provide for his needs or manage his finances. Because Johnny has been unable to properly feed and clothe himself and has been hospitalized as a result, Rob has no trouble getting the doctor to write the statement.

Getting a Doctor's Statement

If you think the settlor isn't capable of managing the trust, start by approaching the settlor's primary, general care physician. Doctors with a lot of elderly patients are familiar with this request and can quickly have a written statement ready for you, stating that the settlor is incapacitated. Medical doctors have a duty to act in the best interest of their patients, which should include cooperating in your efforts to take care of a patient who needs help.

If the doctor won't cooperate, you can approach another doctor who sees the settlor regularly. If that doctor won't help either, you may need to have the settlor's mental capacity determined by a neurologist or other specialist. You may have to pay for this evaluation and then, if the settlor is determined to be incapacitated, reimburse yourself with trust money.

A doctor may be reluctant to provide a statement because of medical privacy laws such as the federal Health Insurance Portability and Accountability Act (HIPAA) and its state equivalents. These laws require a patient's consent before a doctor can release personal health care information.

If you run into this, see whether the settlor signed a consent form authorizing the doctor to release information to the person named as the settlor's "health care agent" under a valid durable power of attorney for health care or health care directive. Many attorneys routinely draft these documents, which give the health care agent authority to make medical decisions on behalf of the settlor if it's necessary, as part of an estate plan. (The power of attorney is called "durable" because it stays in effect even if the person who made it becomes incapacitated. Conventional powers of attorney end if the person becomes incapacitated.)

Even if the settlor didn't sign a consent form, doctors may still communicate with you if you are the settlor's attorney-in-fact or agent, named in the settlor's durable power of attorney (DPOA) for health care or finance. These documents almost always state that the agent may communicate with doctors on the settlor's behalf. Of course, there is a chicken-and-egg problem here: they can't talk to you until you're appointed; and you're not appointed until the settlor is determined to be incapacitated. Still, in practice, many doctors will cooperate with you if it's clearly in the interest of their patients.

> **EXAMPLE:** When Barbara created her will and living trust, she also signed a durable power of attorney for health care. She named her nephew Benjamin as executor of her will, successor trustee of her living trust, and attorney-in-fact under the durable power of attorney.
>
> When Barbara becomes ill with Alzheimer's disease and can no longer manage daily tasks without help, Benjamin shows her doctor the DPOA, which gives him authority to make health care decisions for Barbara should she be unable to make them herself. Seeing this evidence of Barbara's wishes, the doctor feels comfortable sharing her medical information with Benjamin.

If a doctor doesn't think the settlor is incapacitated, you'll have to get help to meet the settlor's urgent needs. If the settlor is in physical danger, being abused by a caretaker, or living in squalor, call in the adult protective services in your area to get the settlor moved to a safer place. You may need to initiate protective proceedings in court, such as a temporary restraining order (to remove an abusing caregiver, for example) or an adult guardianship (also called a conservatorship), which makes a court-appointed conservator or guardian legally responsible for the settlor.

Managing the Settlor's Trust Assets

If the settlor resigns or you get the required statements of incapacity, then you can take over management of the trust assets. Notify all of the trust's account holders that you're now the trustee and start keeping careful records (even if the settlor did not) so that you can prepare an accounting of the trust's assets for the trust beneficiaries. (See Chapter 11.) If the trust owns real estate, record an affidavit (sworn statement) with the county land records office, stating that you are now the successor trustee. (See Chapter 4.)

You won't have authority over assets that aren't in the trust, such as retirement accounts, life insurance policies, or everyday checking accounts, unless the settlor named you as attorney-in-fact in a document called a durable power of attorney (DPOA) for finances. (This is a different document from the DPOA for health care discussed above.) A DPOA for finances should be part of the settlor's estate plan; commonly, it is drawn up at the same time as a living trust. An attorney-in-fact has the legal authority to manage an incapacitated person's financial affairs.

It can get confusing to keep track of which document gives you authority and over which assets. As successor trustee you have authority over the assets that the trust owns, but not over anything else. You can't turn off the settlor's cell phone or write a check on the settlor's personal checking account. The bank, the phone company, the retirement account holder, and any other financial institution want proof that you are the properly appointed attorney-in-fact before they will deal with you about nontrust assets. After all, how do the people at the bank know the settlor is really incapacitated, not just away on vacation? Why should they let you, a stranger to them, have access to the settlor's accounts?

> **EXAMPLE:** Scott's sister, Penelope, has terminal brain cancer. Scott is both the successor trustee of her living trust and her attorney-in-fact for finances. Taking over as trustee, he moves $20,000 from her brokerage account, which is held in the trust's name, into her everyday checking account, which is not in her trust. As her attorney-in-fact, he uses this money to pay her telephone and utility bills, to pay her caregivers, and to hire housecleaners. He signs these checks, "Penelope Thompson, by Scott Smythe, attorney-in-fact." When Penelope wants to make a change to the beneficiaries of her life insurance policy, Scott can do that for her, acting as her attorney-in-fact.

Are the Records a Mess?

Before you sign on for the job, take a moment and consider whether you'll be working with the legacy of an organized person or a whirlwind. It will make your job considerably harder if you're trolling through the wreckage of someone's financial life or if the settlor never even got around to transferring assets to the trust. (You may be able to get assets into the trust, even now; but it will take months and a lot of effort. See Chapter 5 for details.)

One of your threshold jobs as trustee will be to identify and collect trust assets. It can be easy, if the settlor left good records and was an organized person. Or it can be a nightmare, if the settlor didn't keep good records or simply left you with a house full of seemingly random scraps of paper. (If you serve as trustee, you'll need to keep excellent records of every dollar of trust assets that you spend or give to a beneficiary, so you can report to the beneficiaries how and where the assets were invested. We cover this in detail in Chapters 4 and 11.)

Most likely, you'll have some detective work to do. A good starting place is the trust document itself, which should have a list of trust assets (called a schedule) attached to it.

At a minimum, you'll be searching through account statements, looking at the settlor's mail, and going over old tax returns. Assets that are owned by a trust are usually identified pretty clearly. For example, the deed for a house or the statement for a brokerage account will say that the asset is owned by the "Smith Family Trust." (Chapter 5 goes into more detail on how to figure out what the trust does and doesn't own.)

Can You Get Along With Beneficiaries?

You may be dealing with the beneficiaries for just five or six months or for decades, depending on the kind of trust. A long-term relationship is fraught with more potential problems. But even if your job is to distribute the trust property quickly, your job will probably be stressful if the beneficiaries don't like what you're doing. In fact, if you know up front that your relations with beneficiaries will be difficult, it's one very good reason not to accept the job in the first place.

To avoid conflict, we advise you to communicate frequently and clearly to the beneficiaries from the get-go. You can do a lot to reassure people by being open about what's happening and how you're making decisions. (See Chapter 3 for more on how to do that gracefully.)

If beneficiaries become truly unhappy, they have a few legal options. They can:

- **Demand frequent accountings.** Beneficiaries may ask for reports showing how trust assets are being managed and distributed. (See Chapter 11.) State law may limit how often beneficiaries can demand formal accountings, but they always have the right to be kept reasonably informed about the assets being managed for their benefit.

- **Ask a court to remove you as trustee.** Whether or not the court will grant this request depends on the terms of the trust and state law. Some trusts allow beneficiaries to choose a new trustee if the current one isn't doing a good job of managing trust assets. If the trust doesn't say anything about this issue, a court can act, but rules vary from state to state. In some places, beneficiaries must prove that you acted in bad faith; in others, judges will remove a trustee just because the beneficiaries request it.

- **Sue you for violation of your legal duties to them.** If you don't send beneficiaries the accountings required by the trust document, or if you mismanage assets, you can get sued. For example, say you kept all the trust money invested in one mutual fund for years, despite its dismal performance. The beneficiaries could sue you for the losses they've suffered, and you could end up reimbursing the trust out of your own pocket.

We are not trying to scare you, but you need to know that if beneficiaries aren't happy with their share of the trust (they hardly ever think that they got too much), you'll be the one that they complain to and about. If a beneficiary complains to you about the terms of the trust, you can be sympathetic, but there isn't much you can do to help. You have no power to equalize benefits or reward a beneficiary who had, for example, been especially attentive to an elderly settlor. You'll just have to explain to beneficiaries that you must follow the terms of the instrument and can't do anything except what it authorizes you to do.

Other Issues You May Be Concerned About

If you've gotten past the red flags discussed above and are seriously considering accepting the job of trustee, you probably have lots of questions about the responsibility you might be taking on. Here are some of the big ones.

Your Responsibility for Paying Trust Debts

You are not personally responsible for the debts on trust property, such as mortgages on property that the trust owns or loans that were taken out in the trust's name during the settlor's lifetime. In other words, you don't have to use your own money to pay them. You must use trust assets to make payments on these debts, though, until you distribute the assets to the beneficiaries. For example, you must continue to pay the mortgage on a house until it's transferred to the beneficiaries or sold. (Or, in unusual circumstances, until you decide to stop making payments and let the lender foreclose.)

If there is cash in the trust, you can use it to make payments. If there isn't enough cash, you'll need to figure out how those payments will be made. Commonly, a trustee or beneficiary will pay these costs and then get reimbursed after the asset is sold and the trust has enough cash to pay them back.

> EXAMPLE: Lee's trust had just one asset: her house, which was fully paid for. The trust instrument stated that at Lee's death, her adult daughters Sarah and Caitlin would receive all the trust's assets equally. Sarah was the successor trustee. Both daughters wanted to sell the house because they lived far away, but the place needed some maintenance work before it would bring a good price. Sarah, with Caitlin's consent, spent $12,000 of her own money to have it painted and landscaped and to pay the property tax that was due. She kept excellent records to document her expenditures.
>
> When the house sold for $112,000, Sarah reimbursed herself the $12,000 that she'd spent on the house. Sarah and Caitlin then split the remaining $100,000 equally and amicably.

What Happens If You Mess Up

If you're thinking about taking on the responsibility of serving as a trustee, you probably wonder about the consequences of a mistake on your part. Don't worry. As long as you act reasonably and in good faith, you shouldn't run into any liability problems. For example, you wouldn't be liable for investing trust money in a stock that simply doesn't do well, if the initial purchase was reasonable and you regularly reviewed the holding as part of an overall investment strategy. Similarly, you wouldn't be liable for selling a property for less than its asking price in a down market, as long as you did your best under the circumstances and made reasonable choices.

You'll be all right if you follow one simple rule: Always put the interests of the trust beneficiaries before your own. When a new client comes into our offices to discuss becoming a trustee, we put it this way: *The trustee serves the trust.*

Trustees are held to a high standard of honesty and faithfulness. If beneficiaries can prove that you acted in bad faith and breached your duties under the trust, a court could remove you as trustee and order you to compensate the beneficiaries for their losses. For example, you might have to pay the beneficiaries (out of your own pocket) the lost income or lost appreciation that resulted from your improper actions.

The liability we're talking about here is for trustees who do really bad things, like stealing trust money and spending it on themselves. Or investing trust assets in extremely risky stocks. Or hiring their friends to do jobs that they're clearly not qualified to do and damaging trust property. Honestly, if your kids were the beneficiaries of a trust, you'd want your trustees not to do these things—and to be held accountable if they did.

RELATED TOPIC

Communication is key. You'll head off most troubles with beneficiaries by keeping them very well informed about what you're doing. See Chapter 3.

Getting Paid for Your Work as Trustee

Most trustees are entitled, under the terms of the trust or state law, to "reasonable" compensation for their work. If the trust instrument states what you are to be paid, that's what you get, though if it were clearly unreasonable (say, $1 a year), you could ask a court to authorize something more reasonable.

Should You Take a Fee?

If you are both the trustee and a beneficiary, you might decide not to pay yourself compensation at all. One reason is that any fee you collect is earned income, subject to income tax. If you instead just inherit your distribution from the trust, it won't be taxed.

> EXAMPLE: Hendrick is the trustee of his father's trust and its only beneficiary. Although he could pay himself reasonable compensation for administering his father's trust, which he determines is $5,000, there's no need to, because he'll inherit everything anyway (after debts, taxes, and gifts are paid). If he received $5,000 from the trust for his work as trustee, he would have to report it as income. His inheritance, however, is not reported as income and so is free of income tax.

Family dynamics might also prompt you to forgo compensation, even if it means you'll end up with a little less money. Let's say you agree to be the trustee—you're the oldest, after all, and your siblings know that Mom always trusted you with financial matters. You do some work, but it's nothing very onerous. Will your siblings think it's fair for you to be compensated for your time, or will they consider your work just a family obligation that you shouldn't expect to be paid for? The tax hit you'll incur by taking compensation might be the factor that leads you to skip the fee altogether.

In our experience, trustees named in the trust instrument who are also beneficiaries typically do not take compensation. Maybe it's because they don't think it's fair that they were already singled out as the "most responsible kid" and now get more money, too. Or maybe the amount of money, seen in the larger context of a decent inheritance, isn't worth the family aggravation.

What's a Reasonable Fee?

If you decide to take a fee, you are in charge of paying yourself for your work. (You're in control of trust assets.) What's a reasonable amount? Well, for starters, you should always be able to justify what you've paid yourself if you were challenged.

We advise clients to keep track of the time that they spend administering the trust and pay themselves a reasonable hourly rate for their services. If you're not a professional, charge a rate that you can justify by comparing it to the going rate for bookkeeping or similar services. If you are an accountant or a lawyer, you are expected to use your special skills and training as you administer the trust. So it would be reasonable for you to charge the trust what you would charge a client.

To compare, it's helpful to know that professional trustees usually charge fees based on a percentage of the trust assets, plus an additional yearly fee. Small trusts might be charged 1.5% of the assets for administrative costs, while larger ones might be charged 0.75% or less. Most nonprofessional trustees, who don't offer comparable expertise or services, charge less than this.

Getting Expert Help

You won't be on your own. As trustee, you can hire financial advisers, attorneys, accountants, and other professionals to assist you in administering the trust—and you can use trust assets to pay their bills. But you'll still be responsible for the decisions that they advise you to make. (Chapter 7 will help you figure out whom you need and how to find them.)

If You Decide to Say No

If the trust names you as the successor trustee and you don't want to serve, you need to formally decline, in writing. Notify each of the trust beneficiaries that you have done so. Notifying the beneficiaries in writing is the best way to protect yourself against any future charges that they had "no idea" that you weren't taking care of business.

You should also notify the person identified in the trust as the next successor trustee, who must then decide whether or not to take the job. With luck, the next trustee in line will accept. For example, a first choice trustee who lives far away from where the settlor lived might resign so that a sibling who lives closer can take over.

If there's no named successor trustee, or the named one doesn't want the job either, you'll need help from an attorney to fill the vacancy. The trust may say who gets to choose the next trustee—sometimes it falls to the adult trust beneficiaries to take a vote. Or the trust may simply be silent as to what happens next. If so, your state's law may permit a trust company to act as trustee if the beneficiaries agree; otherwise, any person interested in the trust (like a beneficiary or someone acting on their behalf) or any person named as trustee in the trust, may ask the probate court to appoint a trustee.

Declination to Act as Trustee

I, Genevieve Harmon, decline to act as trustee of the Jones Revocable Trust, dated January 1, 20xx.

Pursuant to Section 7 of the Jones Revocable Trust, Arthur Harmon shall act as sole trustee of the trust.

This declination to serve shall be effective as of the date on which all adult beneficiaries receive a copy of this instrument.

_____   _____
Genevieve Harmon   Date

[NOTARY]

If the next trustee is ready to step in and take over, this is what he or she would sign.

Agreement to Act as Trustee

I, Arthur Harmon, agree to act as the trustee of the Jones Revocable Trust, dated January 1, 20xx, and to abide by the terms of the trust instrument as of the date that this document is signed.

_____   _____

Arthur Harmon   Date

[NOTARY]

Thinking Like a Trustee

We want your trusteeship to be a happy one. In our ideal world, the trust will be easy to understand, the assets will be simple to identify and collect, the beneficiaries will be thrilled about their shares, and the whole thing will roll along smoothly.

Ironically, probably the easiest way to achieve this ideal is to keep the opposite scenario in mind. As distasteful as it sounds, you'll do a better job as trustee if you imagine that a disgruntled beneficiary could sue you at any time for any decision. A modicum of paranoia is healthy because it will nudge you to be sure to follow the trust's instructions carefully. And if you're always looking over your shoulder, you'll remember to be meticulous about documenting your actions. If, before you do anything, you ask yourself how you could justify your actions to an unhappy beneficiary and convincingly explain that you did the reasonable thing given the circumstances, you will avoid many of the conflicts that could make your job difficult.

Most trust administrations, in fact, do end happily and don't end up in the news or in court. The key to making sure that your administration is one of those happy ones is for you to clearly understand your legal responsibilities and how to fulfill them. We don't want you to make any easily avoidable missteps in your trust administration. So our focus here is in highlighting your essential trustee duties and explaining how they work in practice.

First, you must follow the instructions in the trust instrument. So you will need to read it carefully. Unfortunately, trusts can be hard to read, and we recommend that you hire an attorney to explain the document to you, or at least any part of it that confuses you. At a minimum, your trust instrument should identify what the trust property is, who the beneficiaries are, and how and when you are to make distributions to them.

In addition to the explicit instructions in the trust, you must also follow state law. These laws, which vary from state to state but are similar in their important provisions, govern every action you take as trustee.

It's kind of like a contract an individual or business makes. The contract sets out the specific terms of the deal—it may name the goods to be sold, the price, and when the buyer will pay. But the buyer and seller are also subject to the state's laws about business conduct—contracts would be as thick as books if they had to include all of them, and so they don't. The parties to the contract have to follow both the contract's specific rules and conduct their business in a legal manner under state law. It's the same with your trust: you have to follow the trust's specific rules, and you have to do so in a way that's legal under state laws that spell out how trustees must act.

Fiduciary Duty: It's All About the Beneficiaries

Once you are the trustee, you take on what's called a *fiduciary duty* to the trust beneficiaries. That's a fancy legal term for the idea that your job is to take even better care of trust property than you might of your own. You are to always act in the best interests of the beneficiaries and never in your own self-interest. Trust is the key to the relationship—the settlor entrusted you with the job of managing his or her money, and the beneficiaries are trusting you to act solely in their best interests at all times.

"Fiduciary" is an all-encompassing term, but a rather vague one. It's like being a parent—you know that you have to always take care of your children and keep them safe, but that alone doesn't provide much guidance on what to do in specific situations. So here are some more specific pointers.

Act in the Best Interests of the Beneficiaries, Not Your Own

As a trustee, you must administer the trust solely in the interests of the trust beneficiaries and not use trust assets to benefit yourself. If you just keep repeating, "It's not my money," you'll do a better job with this.

Obviously, you can't use trust money for your own needs. You can't borrow trust money, even if you fully intend to repay it later. You can't place it in an account that you own. You can't forget to keep careful records. You certainly cannot take advantage of your position as trustee to benefit yourself by, for example, investing trust money in your own company. All of the above are obvious conflicts of interest. And incredible as it may seem, trustees have done ALL of them—newspapers are full of such stories.

Some trusts do permit you to do certain things that might otherwise appear to be a conflict of interest. For example, a trust instrument might specifically allow you to invest trust funds in your own company or borrow funds from the trust. But most trusts still have safeguards to make sure that the trustee acts in the trust beneficiaries' best interest. For example, if the trust authorizes you to borrow from the trust, it might also require that you pay appropriate interest and provide adequate security (collateral). Or if you are allowed to use trust assets to buy stock in your company, the trust might restrict the investment to a small part of the trust's diversified portfolio.

You can't do things that aren't in the best interests of the beneficiaries, even if these actions don't benefit you directly. For example, you can't hire a friend who is a general contractor to do work for the trust for an inflated price. It also means that you cannot sell trust real estate to a friend at a discount.

What about hiring a your general contractor friend at what you think is a fair price, but without bothering to get bids from other contractors? Or selling trust real estate to a friend at what you think is a good price, but without putting the real estate on the open market? The answer is that you always need to focus on the beneficiaries, not your friends. Do what's best for the beneficiaries, and be prepared to defend your actions. If you have any reason to think a transaction might look fishy, let the beneficiaries know what you plan to do *before* you do it.

The trust instrument may allow you to "self-deal," meaning that you, as trustee, can sell property to yourself, individually, provided you pick a fair price. By extension, you could sell the property to a close friend at that price as well. But how do you know the price is fair and the transaction will not be criticized in the future? If you make any deals with someone who is associated with you, *always* document your actions. For example, if you're selling property, get an appraisal and notify the beneficiaries ahead of time. This avoids any appearance of partiality and gives the beneficiaries the chance to request additional estimates of value before the sale.

EXAMPLE: Tonya and her husband Josh had been looking for a house in a certain good school district for well over a year. Every weekend they scoured the listings and went to open houses. One day, they saw a listing for a house well below the market rate, in exactly the right neighborhood. Astonished, they quickly made an offer. It turned out that the house was owned by the deceased owner's living trust, and the trustee, who lived in another state, had told her real estate agent to sell to the first offer that was over a certain amount because she was too busy to spend time on selling the house.

The fact that the offer was made less than 24 hours after the house was listed raised red flags to the trustee's attorney, who advised the trustee that she had a duty to get the best possible price for the house. Following her lawyer's advice, the trustee then made a counteroffer of $50,000 more. Tonya and Josh still bought the house, and it was still a good deal.

The busy trustee wasn't trying to help herself or hurt the beneficiaries— she was just trying to get the house sold and wasn't thinking about getting the most money for the beneficiaries. Her attorney spotted the problem: A quick sale, done for the convenience of the trustee, would violate her duty to act in the beneficiaries' best interest.

Your duty to act in the beneficiary's best interest extends beyond money. It means that you are obligated in all your trust dealings to place the interests of the beneficiaries first in every possible way. For instance, you can't withhold information from the beneficiaries that could affect their rights in the trust's property. If, for example, you are selling a house in a falling property market, you should tell the beneficiaries about each offer you receive and your response to each.

EXAMPLE: Ted was the trustee of his brother Cliff's trust. After Cliff passed away, Cliff's daughters were eager to sell their father's house and receive their inheritance. Ted, though, decided to fix up the house before placing it on the market, hoping to get a higher price. The house went on the market six months after Cliff died. By then, the local housing market was swamped by a wave of foreclosures, and prices were falling steeply.

Cliff's daughters were angry at their uncle, who they felt had waited too long to sell and hadn't kept them informed. They didn't know the asking price, what commission the agent was getting, what offers were being received, or whether offers were being rejected. Uncle Ted thought his nieces were being impossible and intrusive, and he refused to give them any of that information. Finally, he sold the house for much less than the original asking price and distributed the proceeds to his nieces. They then filed a lawsuit, alleging that Ted had breached his fiduciary duty to them by not acting in their best interest, and requested all the records relating to the transaction.

Keep Beneficiaries Informed

A lack of communication is what starts many conflicts between beneficiaries and trustees and eventually gets lawyers involved. Even trustees who are doing a skillful and honest job of managing assets violate one of their key duties if they don't keep the beneficiaries reasonably informed.

We advise clients to communicate regularly with the beneficiaries from the very beginning of the administration process all the way through to the end. It's always good to show the beneficiaries the work you're doing on their behalf, without raising their expectations of a lightning-quick administration.

If you want to take any action that beneficiaries might object to, it's a good idea to notify the beneficiaries who will be affected by the action in writing.

Unless the trust says otherwise, you should also send a written financial report, called an accounting, to the beneficiaries once a year. Also send one if you resign as trustee or the trust ends. (Chapter 11 gets into this in detail.) This accounting would normally include information about:

- how you invested and spent the trust's principal and income
- the trust's assets and liabilities
- the amount of compensation that you received, and
- the amount you paid to advisers, such as attorneys and accountants.

Obviously, in order to create that kind of detailed accounting, you're going to have to keep comprehensive and accurate records of all transactions involving the trust. You don't want to be shuffling through a shoebox full of receipts at the end of year, or worse, paying an accountant to do it. (Chapter 4 can help you set up a simple record-keeping system to prepare for the necessary accountings.)

Act and Invest Prudently

When you are the trustee, you have to make decisions. These may be short-term or long-term decisions, depending on the kind of trust you're administering. For example, you might need to decide whether to sell or keep a house, sell or hold stock, or settle a lawsuit or fight on. The beneficiaries may second-guess you. If you're challenged, you need to be able to prove that you understood what the trust instrument required you to do, that you gathered the best possible information about the decision at hand, and that you made a reasonable and cautious choice. In other words, you need to show that you acted the way a prudent person would in your circumstances.

> EXAMPLE: Margaret was the trustee for her friend Sharon's living trust. The trust beneficiary was Sharon's cousin Elaine, who lived in Germany. When Sharon died, it was Margaret's job to sell Sharon's house. Margaret hired contractors who helped her to clean out the house, landscape it, and put it on the market. She invested $15,000 to repaint the outside and plant a nice garden in the front yard.
>
> The house sold for the asking price the first weekend it was on the market. Margaret kept records showing that the amounts she paid to the contractors were reasonable for the area and that the asking price for the house was fair, given a professional appraisal and recent sales of comparable houses in the neighborhood. In the month leading up to the sale, Margaret kept Elaine informed about each major decision and kept notes of their conversations, so that she could document that she'd done so.

If you're just wrapping up a simple revocable trust, you shouldn't have to make any major investment decisions. But if the trust will probably go on for years—for example, a child's trust—then investment strategy will be a big part of your job. (See Chapter 9 for a detailed discussion of "prudent investor" rules.)

Be Fair

If a trust has more than one beneficiary, and doesn't direct you to treat one differently than another, you must treat them all fairly in the light of the purpose and terms of the trust itself. Treating them fairly doesn't necessarily mean that you must treat them equally. If one child, for instance, requires more money for medical treatment than another child, and the trust's stated purpose is to provide for what each child needs, then you may spend more on that one child than another. What you can't do, though, is pay for one child to go to Harvard if as a result there isn't enough money for the others to go to college at all. Similarly, unless you have a very good reason, you couldn't let one beneficiary live rent-free in the settlor's house while forbidding another beneficiary from doing the same thing. Of course, if one child had druggy, destructive friends, you would be perfectly justified in forbidding that child use of the house.

The trust instrument tells you how you can use trust money and whether or not you must treat all of the beneficiaries equally.

EXAMPLE 1: Fred and Wilma establish a living trust. After their deaths, the trust is to benefit their three children in a single "pot" trust. The trust says that the trustee should, if possible, distribute the amount each child needs for medical care and living expenses. That means that the trustee can use reasonable discretion to take care of each child's needs and does not need to worry about treating each child exactly the same, just fairly. For example, if one child has cancer and needs expensive treatment, the trustee can use more than one-third of the trust's assets to pay for her care.

EXAMPLE 2: Roger and Lucy establish a living trust during their lifetime. After their deaths, the trust is to divide into three separate trusts, one for each of their children. The trustee is supposed to pay, out of each child's trust, whatever the child needs for medical care and living expenses. In this situation, the trustee must spend money for each child only out of that child's trust. If one child has greater needs, the trustee cannot take money out of the other children's separate trusts to assist the needy child. If the need were really critical, however, the trustee could ask the probate court for permission to do so and get the consent of the other beneficiaries.

If you are administering a trust that has both current beneficiaries, who receive income from the trust, and future beneficiaries, who will receive the trust's principal later, then your duty to be fair extends to being fair to both groups (classes) of beneficiaries. As always, your first source of guidance is the trust instrument itself. The trust might direct you to favor one group over another. Sometimes a trust specifically says that the trustee must invest all trust funds in income-producing assets like certificates of deposits and Treasury bills, even though these investments will not keep pace with inflation. Some trusts instruct the trustee to invest most of the trust assets for growth, which would mean that the investments might not generate much if any income. If your trust simply leaves it up to you, which is common, you must be sure that trust investments are balanced between those that provide a current benefit in the form of dividends and those that provide a future benefit in terms of growth.

> **EXAMPLE:** Matt established a trust that after his death will provide income to his wife, Matilda, for the rest of her life. That means that any dividends, interest, and rent earned by trust assets will go to Matilda. Following Matilda's death, Matt's two daughters from a prior marriage will get the remaining trust assets.
>
> One of those children, Isabella, is the successor trustee. She has a difficult job: she has to make sure her stepmother, Matilda, has adequate income to maintain her lifestyle and take care of her needs, but also protect the trust principal, which should grow over time and ultimately benefit herself and her sister. How she invests the trust's money will affect how much income it produces. Matt's trust gives Isabella authority over how to invest the money. That flexibility may be overwhelming to Isabella, even if she wants to do the right thing for Matilda as well as for herself and her sister.
>
> The first thing Isabella can do is hire a competent financial adviser who understands her job as trustee and can put together a balanced investment portfolio. If Isabella is uncomfortable with this balancing act or is challenged by Matilda or her sister on the investments she's made in consultation with the adviser, she can go to court and ask for help deciding how much of the trust assets should be invested for income and how much for growth. If Isabella feels she cannot be impartial, because she is an interested party, she should resign as trustee.

For more on investing in a way that's fair to both current and future beneficiaries, see Chapter 9.

Protect Trust Property

As soon as you're the trustee, you have to figure out what the trust owns and collect and protect it for the benefit of the beneficiaries. If there's a house, you may need to change the locks. You'll certainly have to catalog personal items and keep them safe, either in the house or in storage. You'll also have to take possession of bank and brokerage accounts to ensure that no one else fraudulently takes over the accounts. You need to maintain any insurance policies that are in place for the house and its contents, and continue paying any mortgage. If the trust is going to last more than a few months, you should begin inventorying the assets to decide whether money is invested prudently. (Chapters 4, 5, and 6 discuss in detail how to go about all of this.)

Keep Trust Property Separate

You must be careful to keep all trust property separate from your own property. Never put trust funds in your personal bank account. Instead, open a bank account in your name as trustee. If you must pay for trust-related expenses out of your own pocket because there's some kind of emergency, keep good records of what you've spent and how you reimburse yourself. Don't be greedy. Remember that you owe the beneficiaries a careful and accurate accounting of how the trust funds are spent. Don't get sloppy about where the money is going.

> **EXAMPLE:** David was the trustee of his mother's trust. After her death he couldn't get access to her main brokerage account for a few weeks because he had to wait for his mother's death certificate. He had to pay for her hospice care and for her caretakers, so he used his own money to do so. When he got access to the trust account, he wrote himself a reimbursement check.

Many trusts allow trustees to keep trust property in their own names or to merge funds from different trusts into one account for convenience. Avoid this at all costs! If you are great at keeping records, you may be able to separate the accounts at the end of the year. But for most of us, including many attorneys and professional trustees, it is very difficult to keep the trusts straight if they aren't maintained in separate accounts. You do not want anyone to think that you've borrowed—or worse, stolen—trust money. Even if all of the money is there at the end of the year, it can be impossible to attribute growth or income to the appropriate trust. You will not save any expense by merging trusts to avoid bank fees. The administration and bookkeeping costs will astound you and the ambiguity will likely cause a lot of animosity between you and the beneficiaries.

Enforce Claims and Defend Actions

Thankfully, it's unlikely that you'll have to deal with a lawsuit during your trust administration. Still, it can happen. For example, you might have to start legal actions on behalf of the trust to collect debts or bring a wrongful death claim. It is also your duty to defend the trust if it gets sued, if a defense is reasonable under the circumstances. You'll need to decide (almost certainly in consultation with a lawyer) whether to settle or go to trial. You can use trust funds to pay for all of the expenses of resolving such disputes.

What if a beneficiary sues you because they think you've breached your duties as trustee? In that unhappy (and unlikely) event, you can probably use trust funds to defend yourself, though your state might require you to get a judge's approval before you do. If the court finds that you irresponsibly caused the beneficiaries to lose money, you might have to reimburse the trust. Needless to say, if you get sued, quickly see a lawyer who knows your state's rules on these issues.

Get Help When You Need It

As trustee, you aren't expected to be a master of all trades; you can hire experts to help you out. In fact, it is virtually certain that you'll need expert help during a trust administration. But you are responsible for the decisions that get made and for the actions taken in the name of the trust. In other words, the buck stops with you.

Prudent trustees will seek professional help for trust matters that are difficult, specialized, or complex—anything from coming up with a trust investment strategy to rewiring a house. You need to be able to justify your decision to hire help, and you need to know what your advisers are doing and why they're doing it. You can't just hire someone and then wash your hands of the task itself. These rules makes sense if you think about them. The trustee is the person in charge. It's fine to get help—you just can't ever evade responsibility for taking someone else's bad advice.

If you're not numbers-oriented, you won't get sued if you hire a bookkeeper to keep track of your spending instead of spending hours each week wrestling with a spreadsheet. But if you hire assistants for every aspect of trust administration, and if you fail to oversee their work or you double-bill the trust, by charging your rate and the rate of your hired help for mundane tasks, the beneficiaries may have a legal claim against you for wasting trust money. This sounds a bit frightening. But if you just act reasonably in hiring advisers and act in the best interest of the trust beneficiaries at all times, you'll be okay. What you shouldn't do is stop paying attention to what's going on. You are responsible for your decisions, whether you made them alone or consulted or relied on professionals.

> **EXAMPLE:** Carolyn is the successor trustee of her aunt Marilyn's living trust. More than 50% of the value of the trust consists of 10,000 shares of the Xilax corporation, where Carolyn's uncle worked in the 1960s. After Marilyn died, Carolyn spoke to her accountant about the stock, but the accountant told her not to worry about diversification, and Carolyn sold none of it.

Two years later, when it's finally time to distribute the trust's assets to Marilyn's cousins, Xilax is worth significantly less than it was at Marilyn's death.

If the beneficiaries sue Carolyn, she could be found liable for the losses they suffered due to the decline in value of the stock. Carolyn isn't expected to be a financial whiz, but she is expected to act prudently. Here, she should have diversified the investments and monitored the portfolio as the stock declined in value. Though Carolyn was just heeding the advice someone she trusted, she is ultimately responsible for her decision.

(There's lots more on hiring, paying, and supervising experts in Chapter 7.)

Working With Beneficiaries

At their most obvious, trusts are about money—investing it, managing it, and distributing it. But at a more fundamental level, they are about people. Your job as trustee will be infinitely easier, and you'll be far more effective, if right from the start you can do a good job of managing the money *and* deal well with the trust beneficiaries.

Settlors create trusts because they want to manage money for the people they love. After the settlor's death comes the disclosure of the financial arrangements, including the details of who is to inherit the trust assets and who is to control those assets. Often these arrangements reflect the settlor's honest opinions about his or her children and spouse's ability to manage money. It's not always a nice surprise for the survivors, which means you might be dealing with some unhappy people.

As we've said many times, your experience as a trustee is determined in large part by the kind of trust that you're administering. But whether the trust is going to last for years or only a few months, the personal dynamic is the same.

Communicate Well and Often

Beneficiaries are often anxious about their lack of control and unfamiliar with the trust administration process. This combination is the perfect recipe for fear and paranoia. You may be doing everything right from a technical standpoint, but if the beneficiaries don't know what you're doing or why you're doing it, you're not likely to get their cooperation or support. And without it, your trust administration is likely to be longer and more difficult than it needs to be.

Beneficiaries are often fearful and uncertain about the trustee's role in administering the trust. The more you understand their feelings, the better you'll be able to work productively with them, regarding their questions as opportunities to engage them, rather than as annoying intrusions.

Put yourself in the beneficiaries' shoes for a moment and imagine that someone else, possibly someone you know very little about, has suddenly taken over your checking account, your mortgage, and your brokerage account. This person promises to do an honest and careful job managing these assets for you, but there's nothing you can do about the fact that you are no longer in charge of your finances. This has never happened to you before, so it's all new territory. For most of us, it would be frightening and uncomfortable. Now imagine that those assets weren't yours to begin with, but instead were your parents' beloved home and everything that they'd saved during their lives, and it might feel even worse. If you're controlling assets that belonged to the beneficiaries' parents, that's almost exactly the situation they find themselves in.

In our experience, the best way to allay beneficiaries' fear and concern is to:

- get in touch with them early
- educate them about your role
- help them to form realistic expectations of how long it will take to administer the trust, and
- don't hide the trust document or assets from them.

You're required, by law, to keep beneficiaries reasonably informed about how trust assets (their assets, remember) are being managed. Some states require you to send specific kinds of notices and information. (See Chapter 4.) Please think of these requirements as the minimum you should do. You'll do better if you exceed them and make sure that all the beneficiaries know exactly what the trust owns and what you're doing with the assets. The more transparency there is during a trust administration, the happier the beneficiaries should be.

Getting in Touch

If the beneficiaries all live nearby, calling a family meeting and sitting down together to go over the process of trust administration can be a good way to start. You can answer beneficiaries' basic questions about the trust and its terms and give them an overview of the steps necessary before the trust assets can be distributed. You can review the trust's terms, its assets, and whether or not an estate tax return will be filed for the trust.

This meeting may be more amicable if only blood relatives are included—excluding spouses can sometimes make it simpler for family members to have honest discussions about the trust. Of course, if beneficiaries feel strongly about bringing their spouses, you're likely to accomplish more if you include them.

Consider having the attorney at the first meeting to answer questions about the trust and your responsibilities. (You might even hold the meeting at your attorney's office.) Make sure that the attorney explains to the beneficiaries that he or she is there to represent you in your capacity as trustee and cannot give the beneficiaries legal advice. Be careful to limit the scope of the meeting to a discussion of what the trust instrument says and how trust administration works. Unhappy beneficiaries can get their own attorneys to help them advocate for them in the trust administration process—though your efforts to keep them informed and engaged will, we hope, make that unnecessary.

If a face-to-face gathering isn't practical, send each beneficiary a letter (even if your state does not require it) that notifies them that you are the trustee, gives them your contact information, and provides an overview of the trust administration process. This letter may be sent in addition to whatever notices your state law requires.

There's a sample letter below. It would work for a simple trust administration, in which no ongoing trusts are created and you don't need to file an estate tax return.

Staying in Touch

Whenever you take an action or discover information that the beneficiaries should know about, follow up with reports to the beneficiaries. You have an ongoing duty to the beneficiaries to keep them informed of information that they need to protect their interests. For example, if you find that a rental unit owned by the trust is riddled with black mold that will be expensive to eradicate, let them know about the problem and how you intend to fix it. Or if you decide to liquidate an investment in one stock and invest the money in a diversified mutual fund, let them know what you're doing and why. You'll be providing regular written accountings

Sample Letter to Trust Beneficiaries

Lillian Debartalo
4588 Center Court
Springfield, CA

Dear Lillian,

I am serving as the trustee of the Jay Shah Trust, following Jay's death in July. Upon his death, the trust became irrevocable. As trustee, it is my job to distribute the trust assets in accordance with its terms. It is also my job to act in accordance with state law, which requires, among other things, that I act only in your best interests, that I be fair to all beneficiaries, that I avoid any conflicts of interest that may result in any profit to myself, and that I keep you informed about the trust's administration.

I have been meeting with an attorney and accountants to inventory trust property, file tax returns, and pay any debts owed by the trust. This process will take at least four months, and I ask you to be patient. It is to everyone's advantage that I wait to distribute the trust assets until I am sure that all trust property has been identified and that all debts and taxes have been paid. If I distributed assets and then creditors came forward with valid debts, they could look to beneficiaries for payment.

I will do my best to answer your questions concerning the trust. You are also entitled to an annual accounting report that details what assets the trust owns and any income or expenses that flowed in or out of the trust during that time. If you would like to receive a copy of the trust instrument, please contact me to request it.

Sincerely,

Evelyn Montalvo

Evelyn Montalvo, Trustee
44 Sunrise Dr.
Oakland, CA 95887
emontalvo2400@yahoo.com
510-555-1234

that detail all financial transactions (see Chapter 11), but it's a good idea to keep informal lines of communication open, too. A simple phone call or note that tells the beneficiaries what happened during an open house or the troubles you've been having with liquidating a brokerage account will let the beneficiaries know of your progress and also that you have them in mind.

Many of our trustees give beneficiaries informal updates via email. Unlike phone conversations, email gives everyone a written trail. If you do talk in person or over the phone, we suggest that you follow up with a written note, so that the beneficiary will be less likely to misinterpret what's going on. In our experience, if a trustee tells a beneficiary that the real estate agent thinks the house will sell within one to three months, the beneficiary will hear "one" and will start calling on the 32nd day. But if the beneficiary receives a note with the same information, the trustee can remind the beneficiary—if those calls start coming in on the 32nd day—that the sale date was just the agent's estimate.

Should You Share the Trust Document With Beneficiaries?

Beneficiaries need to know the terms of the trust, at least insofar as those terms relate to their shares. In many states that require you to send a special notice to beneficiaries when the settlor dies, they have the right to see a copy of the trust itself. In other states, beneficiaries don't have a legal right to see the whole trust instrument; if you wish, you can give them only enough information for them to safeguard their interests. You might decide to disclose only the provisions that apply directly to a particular beneficiary. (See Appendix A to see what your state requires.)

In many cases, such as when all siblings are receiving an equal share of the trust, it may make sense to give each one a full copy of the trust instrument itself, even if it's not required by state law.

But in some situations, sharing the whole trust document with all the beneficiaries can trigger bad feelings. If one beneficiary's share is being kept in a trust because of that beneficiary's past inability to manage money, or if one beneficiary is receiving more than others, you might not want to offer the entire trust instrument. You can provide it if a beneficiary asks you for it.

> **EXAMPLE 1:** Louise left her trust assets in equal shares to her three children. Upon her death, her daughter, Elizabeth, who was the successor trustee, gave each of her siblings a copy of the trust instrument. There was no reason not to, and this way everyone would be equally informed and would feel confident she was treating them all in exactly the same way.

> **EXAMPLE 2:** Peter's trust left his three sons money equally, but Peter was concerned that his youngest son might gamble away his inheritance. So he directed, in the trust document, that the trustee was to use that son's share to buy an annuity that would give him an annual payment, but never a lump sum. After Peter died, his successor trustee notified the sons that they were the beneficiaries of an irrevocable trust—and that they could request a copy of the trust instrument if they wanted to see it.

What Beneficiaries Need to Know

Don't assume the beneficiaries understand how the trust administration will proceed. Because most people have never been beneficiaries (or trustees), they don't know what your job entails or what they can expect while they're waiting for their inheritance. Here are some threshold issues to make clear early on.

They'll Need to Wait for Their Money

Beneficiaries deserve a reasonable expectation of when they will receive their shares of the trust assets. Many beneficiaries think that they should receive their money immediately, so it's critically important to explain that that isn't going to happen. Make sure that they know that before you can give any money to them, you first have to identify and collect all of the trust's assets and pay all the settlor's outstanding debts and taxes.

> **EXAMPLE:** Alfonso is the successor trustee of his mother's trust. He has eight brothers and sisters. One of them, Tony, insists that he needs his 1/9 of the assets immediately. Alfonso, after consulting a trust administration attorney, tells Tony that it will take at least four to six months to pay all of their mother's last bills and taxes, and that only then will he be able to distribute trust funds to the siblings. Once Tony understands why it will take a while before Alfonso can distribute any of the trust's assets, he calms down.

Give them a reasonable timeline. It will take four to six months to settle even a simple trust, and at least a year and a half if an estate tax return needs to be filed. (More than 99% of estates *don't* have to file a federal estate tax return.) Once beneficiaries know that you really can't distribute the money until you've paid debts and taxes, the timeline should make sense to them. After all, they don't want anyone coming after them for unpaid taxes or debts.

If beneficiaries had to put up their own money for an immediate postdeath expense like a funeral or last payment to a caregiver, encourage them to submit claims to you, so you can reimburse them promptly. You can pay those claims sooner rather than later, which can take some pressure off you.

You're in Charge

Beneficiaries must understand that if the trust gives you discretion to make decisions, then it's your responsibility to make them, even if the beneficiaries do not agree with you. Of course, you need to keep good records and be able to justify your decisions, but you should not defer to vociferous beneficiaries who want to second-guess or overrule you. That's not what the settlor intended.

> **EXAMPLE:** When Joyce dies, her brother Doug becomes the trustee of her living trust. Over the objections of the beneficiaries, Joyce's two adult children, Doug uses trust assets to fix the roof on Joyce's house before placing the house on the market. He gives the beneficiaries notice of the repair job and keeps detailed records of the bids he receives for it, as well as

receipts for what he spends to get the job done. He brings in three different real estate agents to discuss the issue with the beneficiaries—and all three agree that the house would sell for more with a new roof. Although the beneficiaries disagree with his decisions regarding the preparation for the sale, as trustee, Doug has the last word on how to invest and manage the trust's assets.

You Can't Go Against the Trust

Even if beneficiaries aren't happy with what they've inherited, your hands are tied—you can't change the terms of the trust. But they may very well vent their frustration at you, because you are now the one in charge. All you can really do is listen patiently, while making it clear that your legal obligation is to carry out the settlor's wishes. You may find, however, that lending a sympathetic ear goes a long way to help people come to terms with their disappointment.

> EXAMPLE: When Jasmine died, it fell to Sylvia, Jasmine's friend and trustee, to tell Jasmine's only sister Kimberley that Jasmine had left almost all of her trust assets to their first cousin instead of to her. Kimberley was shocked, but Jasmine's trust was quite clear on this point. After several tearful conversations with Sylvia, Kimberley understood that there was nothing that Sylvia could do to change the situation. She accepted the small gift that Jasmine had left to her and came to terms with what had happened.

You Can't Favor Anyone

Beneficiaries need to understand that your job is to be fair to all of them and that you are not allowed to benefit one of them at another's expense. You couldn't, for example, allow one of them to stay rent-free in the settlor's house before it was sold, unless the rest of the beneficiaries agreed. Be respectful and considerate, but make it clear that your job as trustee requires you to act independently, and that your duty to the beneficiaries requires that you be fair to all of them.

You're Being Paid for Your Work

If you are paying yourself for your work as trustee, let the beneficiaries know. The trust instrument should say what this compensation can be—though many trusts simply say that the trustee is entitled to "reasonable" compensation. If that's what your trust says, explain to the beneficiaries how you've determined what's reasonable in your situation. (See Chapter 1 for more on how to figure out what's reasonable for you.)

The Attorney Works for You, Not Them

You might well hire a lawyer to guide you through the administration process, and if you do, the beneficiaries need to know that your attorney isn't their attorney. There's a lot of confusion about this.

Your lawyer's job is to make sure that you understand what the trust and your state's law require you to do. Beneficiaries who call your lawyer with questions about the trust will probably be surprised, and possibly upset, to be told that the attorney just can't speak with them. But it's true. An attorney who's hired to represent you as the trustee owes loyalty to you alone, and your conversations with the lawyer are confidential. Beneficiaries who have questions about their rights with respect to the trust will have to get their own attorneys to advise them.

What Unhappy Beneficiaries Can Do

If you keep the lines of communication open and treat everyone as fairly as you can, you'll greatly reduce the chances of having unhappy beneficiaries. But some people just can't be mollified. Just so you know what could happen—not because we think you're likely to have such troubles—here's what you could expect from a beneficiary who is upset.

Beneficiaries Might Get Upset If ...

- They don't like what they've inherited.
- You are secretive, condescending, or defensive.
- You play favorites among beneficiaries.
- Trust investments don't keep up with inflation.
- You steer trust business to your friends.
- You neglect (or refuse) to keep good records of what you're doing with trust assets or explain why you are making distributions.
- You turn down their requests for trust money.

Request an Accounting

For many unsatisfied or worried beneficiaries, the first step is to ask you for a written accounting that documents how you have invested or spent trust assets. You are required to provide this information, because of your legal duty to keep the beneficiaries reasonably informed about the trust. So if you get a request, comply with it promptly. (See Chapter 11 to learn how to produce proper trust accountings.)

Replace You

Some trust documents give beneficiaries the power to remove a trustee and appoint someone else to take over. For example, surviving spouses generally have the right to remove and replace a trustee at any time, and for any reason, by giving the trustee a certain amount of written notice. Thirty days is typical.

We've also seen trusts that allow a majority of the adult beneficiaries to remove and replace a trustee. In that case, the next named successor will serve as trustee, unless the trust also allows the adult beneficiaries to name a new trustee. Review the trust instrument and see whether it discusses how and when a trustee can be removed. The beneficiaries may need to prove some kind of misconduct (such as bad faith or gross negligence), or they may have the authority to remove you for no reason at all.

Trust Protectors

Every so often, but not that often, we find trusts that name a friend or family member as a "trust protector." This person may have the power to step in and replace the trustee with someone else, either someone named in the trust instrument or chosen by the trust protector. You're not likely to run into a trust protector because they are not common for typical, revocable living trusts. They are used more often when a trust can't be revoked during the settlor's lifetime, such as irrevocable life insurance trusts.

The trust instrument will spell out the trust protector's authority, which typically includes the independent power to:

- remove a trustee if the protector decides the trustee isn't doing a good job for the trust's beneficiaries
- replace the trustee with someone the protector chooses, and
- receive an annual accounting from the trustee.

Ask a Court to Replace You

Beneficiaries can request that a judge remove you because you have committed some bad act, such as gross negligence (such as not paying any attention to trust investments at all) or bad faith (such as theft). If they can prove that you acted in bad faith, you will be removed. All states allow beneficiaries to ask a court for your removal on the grounds that you've breached one of your fiduciary duties. For example, a beneficiary might claim that you haven't treated beneficiaries impartially, failed to disclose important information, or mismanaged trust assets.

Beneficiaries won't be able to get a judge to remove you as trustee simply because they disagree about how to manage trust assets. However, if your relationship with them has become a series of major disagreements, and it's gotten to the point where lack of cooperation is making it difficult to get anything done, that's a possible ground for removal in some states.

In some states that have adopted the Uniform Trust Code (Florida, New Mexico, and North Dakota, for example), a trustee can be removed if all of the qualified beneficiaries request it and the court concludes that removing the trustee best serves the interests of all of the beneficiaries and is consistent with the trust's purposes. States have their own rules about when a court may remove a trustee at the beneficiaries' request. Even the states that have adopted the Uniform Trust Code have implemented it differently, so it's not really "uniform." If you find yourself worried that beneficiaries might ask a court for your removal, get competent legal advice about the rules in your state.

Sue You for Breaching Your Fiduciary Duties

Beneficiaries who aren't reassured by the explanations or accountings you provide may sue you over their losses. For example, an unhappy beneficiary might bring a lawsuit on the grounds that your investment strategy violated your state's investment requirements for trusts. (See Chapter 8 for more on those standards.) Or a disgruntled beneficiary could allege that your accounting is fraudulent.

The lawsuit might have no merit, but you would still need to defend yourself. You could use trust assets to hire a lawyer to defend the lawsuit, but if you lost, you could be personally liable for any losses you caused the trust to suffer.

Heading Off Trouble

The prudent trustee expects the best but plans for the worst. Even if you've done your best to educate the beneficiaries, keep them informed, and be as transparent as you possibly could about transactions with trust assets, it's always possible to get sued. You might be the best trustee in the universe, but that doesn't mean your little brother isn't going to make as much trouble as humanly possible, especially if he's the kid who never got enough of anything, ever. Every trustee in the world is stuck with family dynamics that came into existence long before the trust did.

Again, good communication is probably your best defense against quarrels with beneficiaries. But here are some further steps to take to help head off disputes that you think could turn serious.

> **SEE AN EXPERT**
>
> **If you're concerned about an imminent lawsuit, get a good attorney right away.** The lawyer will help you make sure that your actions are consistent with the trust's directives and your state's laws. A lawyer can also help you document your decision-making process.

Get Beneficiaries' Written Consent Before You Act

To try to prevent challenges from beneficiaries about a specific action you want to take, you can get the beneficiaries to sign a written consent before you go ahead. This won't completely protect you from liability, because a cranky beneficiary could argue that he didn't fully understand what he was agreeing to. Or beneficiaries might argue that they consented to a particular decision, but that you screwed it up in the implementation. Still, it's a good way to put everyone on notice, and it will certainly be useful if you are later threatened with a lawsuit.

The next best thing to getting consent in writing is to take good notes of your oral conversations with beneficiaries. Also keep copies of relevant emails.

> EXAMPLE: Steve, the successor trustee of his late brother's trust, sent out a notice to his siblings and mother, all beneficiaries of the trust, saying that he intended to sell his brother's house. They all agreed with his plan and signed the consent form he included in the letter.

Formally Notify Beneficiaries of What You Intend to Do

In many of the states that have adopted the Uniform Trust Code (and in California), you can engage in certain actions as long as:

- you get the consent of the beneficiaries
- those actions are consistent with the trust's purpose, and
- the actions would be the kind of action that a court would approve.

The idea is that if everyone who is affected by a trustee's action approves it in advance, the court doesn't need to get involved. The beneficiaries' consents are generally called "nonjudicial settlement agreements." Beneficiaries who consent can't later sue you, claiming that the act they consented to was a breach of your fiduciary duty to them or violated the trust's terms. If they object, either they or you can ask the local probate court for a ruling on whether or not you can go ahead with your proposed action. (Executors in probate proceedings have had this ability for years.)

To find out whether your state allows this procedure, see Appendix A. If you think that it might make sense in your circumstances, see an attorney to make sure you follow your state's requirements for giving the notice.

> EXAMPLE: Florence is the successor trustee of the Palatino Family Trust, which she and her late husband created. She lives in Indiana. Her four children are the beneficiaries of the bypass trust that holds assets left by her husband. The trust permits her to use trust principal for her health, education, support, and maintenance. She sends formal notices to her children, stating that she intends to take $100,000 from the trust so that she can move to North Carolina and buy a condo there, and requests their written consent. All of them consent in writing. None of the children can later sue her on the grounds that her use of the money for the move and purchase of the condo violated the terms of the trust and so breached her fiduciary duty to them.

Get Prior Court Approval

If you need to take an action that might upset a beneficiary, or the trust's terms aren't clear and there's a looming disagreement about the proper course of action, you can take the question to the local probate court. You'll ask for a ruling (often called a letter or petition of instruction) stating that the action is permitted by the trust and authorizing you to go ahead. Beneficiaries will be notified of your request and have an opportunity to object to it in court. If the court rules that your action is permitted, you are protected from a later challenge from a beneficiary on the ground that your action was improper under the terms of the trust. Unhappy beneficiaries could appeal the court's ruling, but few do because the appeal process is expensive and time-consuming.

Asking a court for instructions is going to cost time (yours) and money (the trust's). Because you'll probably hire a lawyer to argue on your behalf, a simple petition could cost $2,000 or more and take weeks (or months) depending on the backlog of cases in your probate court. This tactic should only be a last resort, when you're really concerned about a beneficiary's reaction to something or when there's reasonable disagreement about how to understand a trust's terms.

TIP

Consider mediation before you consider court. More and more families are working out their disputes about wills and trusts in mediation, instead of turning them over to a judge. It's a good way to save money, time, and family relationships. In mediation, a neutral third party, the mediator, works with all the parties to help them identify the key issues and come up with their own solution.

To find a trust and estates mediator in your area, try an online directory such as www.mediate.com, contact your local bar association, or search "ADR" (alternative dispute resolution) and your state or county. For a good introduction to mediation and a hands-on guide to how to successfully mediate a dispute, see *Mediate, Don't Litigate*, by Peter Lovenheim and Lisa Guerin (Nolo).

If You Are Also a Beneficiary

It's quite common to be both a trustee and a beneficiary of a trust. The surviving spouse, for example, is almost always the successor trustee and beneficiary of a family trust. Adult children are often the successor trustees of their parents' trusts. It's quite common for one child to be the trustee and all the siblings to be beneficiaries. This can be a difficult position, because as the trustee it's your job to be fair to everyone and never to benefit yourself at another beneficiary's expense. (If you really think you can't work effectively with the whole cast of characters, you should decline the trustee's job; see Chapter 1.)

If you're in this position, be extremely formal about the trust administration. When it comes to record keeping and decision making, pretend you don't know the beneficiaries—treat them like you would strangers, not your siblings or children. That means being sure to:

- keep very good records
- never use trust assets for your own use, and
- if you pay yourself compensation, be prepared to justify what you've charged and what services you provided to the trust.

That isn't really any different from what trustees are always supposed to do, whether or not they're beneficiaries. But trustees who are also beneficiaries can get sloppy, thinking it doesn't matter because trust assets are really "theirs," anyway.

EXAMPLE: Samuel created a trust for the benefit of his wife, Bernadine, and named her as the successor trustee upon his death. Bernadine was to receive all of the income from the trust annually, and if necessary could use trust principal for her health care and support. After Bernadine's death, their three children were to receive the balance of the trust assets.

After Samuel's death, Bernadine took over as sole trustee. She didn't want to tell her children about anything that was going on with the trust funds, because she felt that would be an invasion of her privacy. However, state law required that she, as trustee of an irrevocable trust, provide an annual written accounting to every trust beneficiary—which meant, in her case, her and the three children. The only way around the requirement was to have the beneficiaries agree to give up their right to these accountings—which they didn't want to do.

A few years after Samuel's death, Bernadine became very close to her niece, Linda. In short order, Samuel and Bernadine's kids noticed that Linda started wearing fancy jewelry, and Linda's husband was always doing odd jobs around Bernadine's property. They suspected that Bernadine was tapping into the principal of the trust for unauthorized uses—namely, to make lavish gifts and upgrade the house well beyond what was needed to keep it comfortable.

They asked to see an accounting of the trust covering the period from Samuel's death to the present. They wanted to see whether Bernadine's needs had increased appreciably since Linda entered Bernadine's life. Bernadine felt it was none of their business, but they persisted.

Bernadine had kept all of her bank and brokerage records, so it was easy for her to eventually provide an accounting for the trust and a list of expenses and how she had paid for them with trust principal. Bernadine was able to show that the gifts made to Linda came from her separate funds and that Linda's husband's help was needed to keep the house from deteriorating. The suspicions ceased, and the children learned to appreciate Linda's dedication to their mother.

If You Are Administering an Ongoing Trust

If your trust will last for years, so will your dealings—and challenges—with beneficiaries. Here are a couple of the big ones, both of which are discussed in Chapter 8.

Balancing the interests of different groups of beneficiaries. If there is both an income beneficiary who receives the income from the trust assets for a period of years, and a different ("remainder") beneficiary who will eventually inherit the balance of the trust, you face complicated questions when it comes to investing trust assets. You are going to have to balance your investments so that both kinds of beneficiaries are content with what the trust provides for them. It's not an easy job. That's one big reason to get yourself a competent financial adviser who has experience with trust investments. (See Chapter 7 for tips on how to find one.)

Handling beneficiaries' requests for money. You're going to have to distribute money to the beneficiaries, in some cases by following detailed instructions in the trust instrument and other times at your discretion. You may need to get detailed information from beneficiaries, such as their income tax returns or their college transcripts, before distributing anything to them. No matter what you do, make sure to keep good notes, and use your judgment and common sense—that's why you got the job in the first place.

The First Few Months

Following a death, family members are usually inundated with details and decisions. Almost overnight, they are expected to make decisions about burial or cremation, plan a reception, coordinate arriving relatives, and write an obituary. When is there time to grieve, let alone administer a trust?

Luckily, most trust and estate tasks are not emergencies and can wait a while. You are not expected to get to work the day that grandma dies. But you are expected to administer the trust in a timely fashion. Within a month or so, you should begin to collect information, bills, and documents and to organize a filing system.

You don't need a lawyer to complete most of the tasks outlined in this chapter. Most of them, especially the ones you'll need to do first, are the kind of organizing and logistical jobs that you're probably already familiar with. Some tasks require only a phone call; others may take hours of information-gathering, letters, and follow-up calls. Professional advice will be well worth the money later, when it comes to such things as making good investment decisions, filing tax returns, transferring the ownership of real estate, and funding subtrusts. (See Chapter 7 for more details on how to find the help you'll need.)

If you'll be distributing all the trust property to beneficiaries quickly, you'll probably have done most of your work in about six months. If you are administering an ongoing trust, there will be more work to do, but you'll still have tackled most of the largest tasks.

If you aren't serving as both executor of the estate and trustee of the trust, stay in close touch with the executor during these first few months. You need to know what the executor is doing and why. In many cases, the executor will transfer the estate's assets (assets *not* held in the name of the trust) to the trust, where they become your responsibility. (Chapter 1 discusses the executor's role.)

RESOURCE

Information for executors. For a comprehensive guide to the executor's job, get *The Executor's Guide,* by Mary Randolph (Nolo).

Get Death Certificates

You'll soon discover that you'll need to present a certified copy of the settlor's death certificate to transfer bank and brokerage accounts to the trust, collect life insurance and retirement benefits, and handle debts. Everyone, it seems, requires an official death certificate before they'll deal with you and treat you seriously. This makes sense when you think about it from the perspective of a bank—without conclusive proof, how does the bank know the settlor's really dead? What if she's actually out golfing and you're trying to steal the account? The death certificate protects against fraud.

We usually encourage clients to order eight to ten copies, depending on the number of accounts in the trust. You don't want to have to make another request later, if copies get lost or mangled—it's a hassle.

Usually, for a nominal fee the mortuary helps family members get certified copies of the death certificate. The certificates themselves generally cost $10 to $15 each. Keep track of what you spend—you can be reimbursed later from the trust.

If you don't get certificates through the mortuary, contact the county's vital records office, usually called the county clerk, county registrar, or something similar. You can go in person, send a written request for copies, or—in some places—order directly from the county website. If you have them mailed to you, there will probably be a mailing fee. You'll need to provide the name of the deceased, the date of death, the city in which the person died, and the last known address. You may also need to state why you need the certificate—to head off identity theft, records offices don't want to hand out these certificates, with all their identifying information, to just anyone.

Another option is to use a commercial online service that supplies death certificates from any state, such as www.vitalchek.com. The fee is about $10 per certificate, plus shipping. The service will tell you what information the particular records office requires—it differs from state to state.

**Information You May Need to Provide When
You Order a Death Certificate**

- The deceased person's full name, last known address, and sex
- Month, day, and year of death
- Place of death (city, county, and state)
- Purpose for which you need the copy (explain that you are the trustee)
- Your relationship to the deceased person.

You can also buy copies by mail from your state's agency. Find out how to request vital records—where to order them and how much they cost—in every state by visiting the National Center for Health Statistics portal of the Centers for Disease Control and Prevention at www.cdc.gov/nchs/w2w/index.htm. There may be a discount if you order multiple copies at once.

Find and File the Will

Even when there's a living trust, there's almost always a will, too. If you (or the executor) haven't found the original will, check the settlor's home thoroughly. Estate planning documents are not filed with a court before a death, and they're not usually held at a lawyer's office, although a lawyer who drafts a will for a client may keep a copy. The settlor's will might be in a binder or a large marked envelope in a desk drawer or file cabinet, or stashed in a fire-safe box (in which case we hope someone knows where the key is).

Some people store a will in a bank safe deposit box. If you are a co-owner of the box and have a key, you'll have no trouble getting it. Even if you don't have a key, if you're an immediate family member, the bank will probably give you access to the box to look for the will. They'll have a bank officer present to make sure that's all you take out. If the bank isn't cooperative, you can ask the local probate court for an order allowing you access to the box for the purpose of finding the will.

Do your best to find the original signed documents, not just copies. If you can't, it is possible the settlor destroyed them intentionally, perhaps after signing new documents or simply changing his or her mind about how property should be left. You may need to contact family members and close friends to find the original documents or discover the circumstances behind their disappearance. If you really can't find the original will, you can file the copy with the court. You'll probably also have to submit a signed statement, stating that despite your best efforts you can't locate the original and believe this copy to be the final version of the will.

In most states, the person who possesses an original signed will is responsible for depositing it in the courthouse of the county in which the settlor was a resident. Even if you don't think there will be a probate proceeding, because all or almost all property will pass through the trust, it's important to file the will if you've got it. Later you may discover that a large asset was left out of the trust and need to begin a probate proceeding. In that case, you'll be glad you filed the will, because if you had it in your possession but didn't file it, you could lose your right to serve as executor.

If you think that there are a lot of valuable assets that are not in the trust but should have been, such as real estate or large bank or brokerage accounts, hold off on filing the will until you speak with a lawyer. You might need to begin a probate proceeding or ask the court to transfer the assets into the trust. The lawyer will need the original will to open a probate if that's necessary.

States That Provide for Living Trust Registration			
Alaska	Hawaii	Michigan	Ohio (requires an affidavit to be filed in the county where the trust holds real estate)
Colorado**	Idaho	Missouri*	
Florida*	Kentucky	Nebraska*	

* Not mandatory

** No registration required if all trust property is distributed to the beneficiaries.

Registering the Trust

Some states require that the trustee register the trust with the local probate court. You don't file the trust instrument itself. Instead, you file a trust registration statement with the court that includes the name of the trust, the address, an acknowledgment of the trusteeship, the name of the settlor and the original trustee, and the date of the trust document. There aren't any penalties for not registering, but if the probate court orders you to register the trust, and you refuse, you can be removed as trustee.

Notify the Social Security Administration

In the first few weeks after the death, you or the executor should pick up the phone and notify the Social Security Administration (SSA) of the death by calling 800-772-1213. If the deceased person was receiving monthly Social Security payments, you are required to return any payment that's for the month of death, no matter when the death occurred.

It can be confusing to figure out whether a Social Security deposit needs to be returned. Payments are usually made during the first week of the month for the *prior* month. So, for example, the payment for March arrives in early April. If the settlor received payments for the month of death, the whole amount must be returned, even if death occurred on the very last day of the month.

> EXAMPLE: Stella died on June 30. Her Social Security payment for June is deposited on July 2. That payment and any other that arrives after it must be returned. If Stella had died on July 1, that payment would not be returned, because she was alive during the entire month of June.

If the monthly Social Security benefit was deposited directly to a bank account, request that the bank return any funds received for the month of death or later to Social Security as soon as possible. Be sure not to close the account until you know the money has been returned.

Hardly anyone gets paper Social Security checks anymore, but if the settlor did, do not deposit any checks received for the month of the death or later, and return them to the nearest Social Security office. To find the closest office, check the phone book's federal government listings, call SSA's toll free number, or go to www.ssa.gov. If you mail the check, send it registered mail so that you can get a receipt.

> TIP
>
> **Social Security benefits for the survivor.** A surviving spouse is entitled to a one-time $255 death benefit and might also qualify for survivor's benefits. It is the survivor's responsibility to call or visit the SSA to make a claim.

Notify the State Department of Health

If the settlor received Medicaid (the federal-state program that assists low-income people with medical and nursing home care) and died owning a home, the state department of health and human services may put a lien (legal claim) on the property. This ensures that when the house is sold, the state will get reimbursed for the medical expenses it paid. This is why you have to notify the state health department when there's been a death—it checks its records to see whether there is such a claim to be made. Although you can work directly with the government agency and try to negotiate a reduction in the bill, you may find it easier to work with an attorney familiar with Medicaid reimbursement in your state. It's too late to do much more than pay the bill—the settlor could have done some Medicaid planning earlier, but it's too late for that now.

Identify the Beneficiaries

One of your first jobs is to identify just who the trust beneficiaries are. If you get it wrong and fail to give a beneficiary his or her rightful share of the trust, you will have breached your duty—which could get you sued. So it's important, right at the beginning of the trust administration, to get all the beneficiaries properly identified.

> SEE AN EXPERT
>
> **Don't guess.** If you have any concerns about properly identifying the trust's beneficiaries, get yourself the help of an attorney. Someone familiar with state law and recent cases can help you avoid a major problem down the road.

Gifts to Groups of People

Start by reading the trust instrument and making a list of the people it identifies. A trust may not be perfectly clear about this. If the trust doesn't individually name the beneficiaries, but instead uses a term like "children" or "issue," you might need help understanding what state law does and doesn't include in that term.

Issue. This means lineal descendants. If the settlor has surviving children, they are the settlor's issue. If a settlor's child dies before the settlor, but leaves behind children, those grandchildren are also the settlor's issue.

> **EXAMPLE:** Jason established a living trust, which directs that at his death, the trust assets are to be distributed in equal shares to his "issue." At his death, he is survived by his adult children, Sam, Kate, and Quinn. They each receive a third of the trust's assets, after all of the expenses, taxes, and debts have been paid.

Adopted children. If a trust leaves money to the settlor's children, this includes any children that they have adopted, unless the trust specifically excludes adopted children. This would be an unusual provision.

> **EXAMPLE:** Maxx's trust was to be divided equally among his children. His adopted son Brad is included in that gift.

Stepchildren. Gifts to "children" don't usually include stepchildren, unless those children are mentioned specifically or the trust itself defines children to include stepchildren. (A stepchild who is legally adopted by a stepparent is treated just the same as a biological child, legally.) However, state law differs on the treatment of stepchildren. In California, for example, an adult stepchild may have a claim of inclusion in the term "children" if the stepchild began living with the stepparent as a child, maintained a relationship with that stepparent into adulthood, and would have been adopted except for a barrier to that adoption (such as living parent who refused to consent).

> **EXAMPLE:** Jonas left everything in his trust to "my children." Jonas had two biological sons and also a stepdaughter, Karissa, who had lived with him since the age of three. Jonas, however, was estranged from Karissa, and had no contact with her since she turned 16. She was not a beneficiary of the trust.

Children born outside marriage. If the settlor had a child born outside of marriage, see an attorney to determine whether the child is included in the legal definition of children or not. It depends on state law and the terms of the trust.

> **EXAMPLE:** Jean and George created a living trust. It was, at the death of the second spouse, to be divided into equal shares for each of their three children. Jean died first. After George's death, it turned out that he had fathered a child while in high school. He had never acknowledged the child as his; in fact, no one knew for certain if he'd been aware of her existence. Under the laws of his state, this child was not considered his child for purposes of inheriting trust's assets.

Children born after the trust was made. Most trusts do state that the term "children of the settlor" includes children born after the trust was made. But some explicitly state that only the children alive at the time the trust was signed count.

> **EXAMPLE:** Judy's trust stated that her only living children were Toby and Katherine. At her death, her trust was to be distributed in equal shares to her living children. The trust defined children to include any children of Judy's born after the trust was executed. Two years after she'd completed her trust, she had a son, Vince. All three children shared the trust assets equally after Judy passed away.

Members of a group, like "grandchildren" or "nieces and nephews." Generally, a group like this comprises those members of the group who are alive at the settlor's death. It would not include grandchildren or nieces and nephews born after the settlor's death.

EXAMPLE: Myron's trust left a gift of $100,000, to be divided into equal shares among his grandchildren. When he died, he had five grandchildren. After his death, but before the trust was distributed, his daughter had a baby. The five older grandchildren split the $100,000.

Former spouses. In most states, gifts to a former spouse in a will or trust are automatically revoked by divorce. But that's not always true. Consult a lawyer if you run across this situation.

Have the Beneficiaries Been Changed?

Sometimes settlors want to provide some flexibility in their trust. Rather than just leaving each of his children an equal share, for example, a settlor might want to give his surviving spouse the power to take changed circumstances into account, and give more to a child who has greater financial needs. That way, the child who becomes a wealthy business owner won't necessarily inherit the same amount as another who grows up to be a hardworking teacher who's struggling financially. Or a settlor may want to leave property to charity, but prefer to leave it to the trustee to pick which ones receive trust assets. The settlor might give the trustee an unlimited choice or list a few charities to pick from.

This is called giving someone a "power of appointment." A power of appointment gives the holder of the power the ability to pick (appoint) who will receive trust assets following a certain event. Another way to think about it is that the "power to appoint" really means the "power to disappoint," because it gives someone other than the settlor the power to decide who gets certain trust assets.

There are two kinds of powers of appointment:
- one that can be used during the power-holder's lifetime, called a lifetime power of appointment, or
- one that can be used only at the power-holder's death, called a testamentary power.

If someone holding a power of appointment uses it, it will affect how you distribute trust assets, so you need to know whether your trust grants one and whether or not it's ever used.

Lifetime Powers of Appointment

If the settlor gave someone the power to change the beneficiaries of the trust, and that power could be exercised at any time during the power-holder's lifetime, it's called a lifetime power of appointment.

> EXAMPLE: Catherine is the trustee of her aunt Emily's trust. The trust gives Emily's brother, Laurence, the right to receive the income from the trust for the rest of his life. At Laurence's death, the trust instrument states that the balance of the trust will go to Emily's favorite charity, the local humane society. However, Emily's trust gives Laurence the power to name a different beneficiary, either during his life or at his death. Any changes he makes can take effect immediately or at his death. The trust specifies that Laurence can exercise his power simply by writing a letter to the trustee.
>
> Laurence exercises his power and notifies Catherine that at his death, the remaining trust assets should go to a charity called the Global Poverty Fund. Catherine now needs to treat that organization just like any other trust beneficiary Emily named.

Someone with a lifetime power of appointment can usually act by sending you a letter that specifically refers to the power of appointment. Look carefully at the trust instrument to see what requirements the power-holder must comply with.

If a power-holder does exercise the authority granted in the trust instrument, you'll have new beneficiaries to deal with. Those new beneficiaries will be entitled to trust accountings and all other information you give other beneficiaries.

Testamentary Power of Appointment

If the settlor gave someone the power to change the beneficiaries of the trust, but that power can be exercised only at the power-holder's death, it's called a testamentary power of appointment. You may not be aware whether the power-holder exercised a testamentary power of appointment, because the power-holder does not have to notify you.

EXAMPLE: Naomi is the beneficiary of her husband's trust, which gives her a testamentary power of appointment. The trust instructs Lucinda, the trustee, to distribute as much income or principal to Naomi as is necessary to maintain her lifestyle. At Naomi's death, the balance of the trust is to be split equally between her two daughters, unless Naomi exercises her power of appointment.

After Naomi's death, Lucinda finds that Naomi's will contains a provision exercising the power of appointment. According to the will, the trustee is to distribute 5% of the trust to Naomi's grandson Daniel, and the rest to the two daughters, as before.

The trust instrument will specify what type of document the power-holder must sign to exercise the power of appointment. It could be a will, codicil, or simply a "writing"—a document that refers to the power. You'll have to look through the power-holder's estate planning documents to determine whether the power was exercised and if so, exercised correctly. We have seen many incorrect exercises of a power of appointment—such as when a person uses a letter to the trustee, but the trust says the power can be exercised only through a will. For the most part, those attempts to exercise the power are invalid. If the power-holder correctly exercised the power of appointment, however, the power-holder's instructions supersede those in the settlor's trust.

The trust may have a provision that says a power of appointment will be honored only if the trustee is made aware of it within six months of the settlor's death. If you see a power of appointment in the trust, try to determine quickly whether or not it has been exercised.

Notify Beneficiaries and Heirs

Not so long ago, attorneys told their clients that trusts were private, and that no one could see the details of who inherited and who didn't. In most states, that is no longer the case. Trusts are still much more private than wills, which become public documents once they're filed in the probate court. But in most states, the law requires that certain beneficiaries of the trust, and in some states any legal heir (someone entitled to inherit in the absence of a will), are entitled to see at least the part of the trust that applies to them and get periodic information from the trustee. In many states, beneficiaries have the right under state law to see either a complete copy of the trust, or at least the portion that describes their interest, if they make a request to the trustee.

Don't be afraid of these kinds of disclosure requirements. They can actually help you to administer the trust quickly and with a minimum of bad feelings from the beneficiaries. We can't stress it enough: Poor communication causes an enormous amount of trouble in trust administration. It might start as a simple difference of opinion about how to fix up a house or when to sell it. If people stop talking, before long, beneficiaries get suspicious, trustees get defensive, everyone feels mistrustful, and the whole process gets adversarial. It's such a loss for everyone. The settlor created a trust to *avoid* a costly, time-consuming court proceeding, not to encourage one. (See Chapter 3 for more on how to deal with beneficiaries—it's one of your most important jobs.)

Certain states require you to notify beneficiaries about a trust when it becomes irrevocable—usually at the death of one or both settlors. (Check Appendix A for your state's rule.) States that have adopted the Uniform Trust Code require you to send a notice to "qualified beneficiaries," which means:

- people entitled to receive trust distributions now
- people who would be entitled to receive trust distributions if the current beneficiaries died or became ineligible to receive future trust assets before the trust terminated, and
- those who would be beneficiaries when the trust terminates.

Basically, this means the current beneficiaries and the beneficiaries who will inherit when the current beneficiaries die. For example, if a trust leaves everything to an irrevocable trust for the surviving spouse's lifetime and then everything goes to the adult children, both the spouse and the children must get a notice when the first spouse dies.

Depending on your state's law, you may also be required to notify legal heirs—those people who would inherit from the settlor under state law if there were no will or trust. It doesn't matter whether or not they're trust beneficiaries. Some states allow the settlor to eliminate this notice requirement by putting language to that effect in the trust document, but most states do not. Read the trust document to see whether it waives notice, and then check Appendix A to see whether your state requires notice and whether the beneficiaries have a statutory right to see a copy or an excerpt of the trust.

> EXAMPLE 1: John, a California resident, creates a living trust and leaves the trust property to his two daughters, Diane and Debra. He leaves nothing to his grandson, Gerald, who is the child of John's deceased son, Seth. After John's death, California law requires the trustee of his living trust to send notice to Diane, Debra, and Gerald. Why? Diane and Debra are trust beneficiaries. Gerald gets notice because even though he is not a beneficiary of the trust, he would have been an heir if John had not made a will or trust. (Under state law, he would have received Seth's share of John's estate.)

> EXAMPLE 2: If John had been a Kansas resident, the trustee would be required to send notice to Diane and Debra, but not to Gerald. Under Kansas law, Gerald is not a "qualified beneficiary" because he doesn't ever have a right to trust property.

No state requires you to send beneficiaries a copy of the entire trust before they ask you for it. So you're not under an initial obligation to provide a copy along with notice of the trust's existence, and our advice is to not send a copy with the notice. If the beneficiaries are strangers to you, or you know them all too well and expect one or two to be difficult, consider sending them just the part of the trust that affects their inheritance, if your state permits that. If they demand to see more, then you can send them the whole thing.

> **TIP**
> **Get everyone together.** In addition to sending the required legal notice, you might want to send a friendly letter and gather beneficiaries for an informal meeting, at which you give them an idea of what to expect from the trust administration process. See Chapter 3 for more on this.

A typical state notice law requires you to send a notice within about 60 days after a death. The notice tells the recipients of the settlor's death and the existence of the trust and gives the recipient the opportunity to review the trust instrument. A recipient has a short time (a few months at the most) to file a lawsuit to challenge the trust—for example, on the ground that the settlor lacked the required mental capacity to make a trust or that the settlor was under pressure by someone to make the trust (this kind of lawsuit is often called a "will contest," even if it's about a trust). After that, beneficiaries can't challenge the validity of the trust itself.

Send notice letters by registered mail, so that you have proof that they were delivered. That will also allow you to be certain when the time period has passed for the beneficiaries to formally challenge the trust by initiating a lawsuit. If you hand-deliver the notice, get a receipt from the recipient.

California law gives heirs and beneficiaries 60 days, after they receive a copy of the trust instrument, to file a lawsuit challenging the trust. So if the letter is sent on March 2, then May 1 will be the 60th day after delivery. If no lawsuit is begun by then, the trustee knows that the beneficiaries cannot contest the trust as invalid. The beneficiaries will have the right to challenge the trustee's actions, but not the validity of the trust itself.

The notice requirement is more than just way to limit the ability of unhappy beneficiaries and heirs to contest the trust. It also opens the line of communication between you and the beneficiaries. By complying with your state's notice requirements, you will start a constructive dialog with the beneficiaries so that problems and questions can be discussed before they blow up into a quarrel or a lawsuit. Later, as you prepare accountings and reports for the beneficiaries, the initial contact and information will pay enormous dividends of good will. Your beneficiaries will be more likely to forgive minor mistakes or delays if you routinely apprise them of your progress.

Sample Notice to Beneficiaries

Diane Bennett
123 Main Street
Newtown, CA

Thomas John established the John Family Trust as settlor on September 5, 20xx. Pursuant to California Probate Code Section 16061.7, the trustee of the John Family Trust hereby notifies you of the following:

1. The name, address, and telephone number of the trustee are as follows: Terry Romanov, 1192 Vineyard Way, Grapes, CA 95057. 626-555-9999.

2. The address of the principal place of business of the administration of the trust is as follows: 1192 Vineyard Way, Grapes, CA 95057.

3. You are entitled to receive from the trustee a true and complete copy of the terms of the trust (excluding provisions that applied to the trust before it became irrevocable).

4. **You may not bring an action to contest the trust more than 120 days from the date this notification by the trustee is served upon you or 60 days from the date on which a copy of the terms of the trust is mailed or personally delivered to you during that 120-day period, whichever is later.**

5. If you would like a copy of the terms of the John Family Trust, please complete the form below and send it to the trustee at the address in Paragraph 2, above.

_____   _____

Terry Romanov   Date

To the Trustee of the John Family Trust:

Please send me a true and complete copy of the terms of the John Family Trust. My name and address are:

_____

_____

_____

> ### Special Notice Requirements If a Charity Is a Beneficiary
>
> Some settlors leave at least some trust funds to a favorite charity. If a charity is one of the beneficiaries of your trust, your state may require you to send notice of the existence of the trust to the charity and to that state's secretary of state or whatever agency oversees charitable bequests. To find out whether your state has such a notice requirement, contact your state attorney general's office. If the AG's office is not in charge of overseeing the state's charitable organizations, it will know which agency is. Generally, you'll need to send it a copy of the notice that you sent to the other beneficiaries. You will probably never hear back from the agency.

Inventory Trust Assets

To properly manage trust assets, you have to figure out what the trust owns. Start with the trust instrument, which lists trust assets on the "property schedules" attached to it. That's not enough, however. You also need to find title documents, such as deeds and brokerage statements, which show that the asset was actually transferred to the trustee.

In addition to listing assets on the property schedules, the settlor should have signed documents that state, in essence, "I used to own this asset as an individual, but now I own it as the trustee of my living trust." Each kind of asset requires a different document. For a house, the settlor should have prepared a new deed and recorded it with the county land records office. For cash or investment accounts, the settlor should have filled out and signed transfer forms provided by the brokerages and banks.

Ideally, the settlor completed all of these forms and deeds when the trust document was signed or shortly after. In reality, people often fail to transfer all of their assets into the trust or update the property schedules as their assets change. You may discover that many of the settlor's assets are not in the trust at all, or that the trust's property schedule is lost, missing, or incomplete.

That means you can't rely just on the property schedule to find out what property is held in trust. Some trust assets may not be listed, and some nontrust assets may be erroneously included. Systematically review all of the settlor's paperwork to be sure you haven't overlooked any accounts. Here's how to proceed.

- Go through the settlor's mail and make sure all future mail is sent to you. To do this, change the address online at www.usps. com or submit a change of address postcard (available at any post office) to the post office closest to where the settlor lived. If you're not also the executor of the estate, coordinate with whoever is, so that you don't submit conflicting address change requests.

- If the settlor managed bank and investment accounts online, and you have passwords, you can check account balances online. If you can't log in to see the settlor's accounts, contact the company and ask for access. You'll need to provide proof, of course, of your authority to act on the settlor's behalf—at a minimum, the trust instrument and a certified death certificate.

- Talk to the settlor's accountant, if any, and review any prior income tax returns you can find. Look for records of investment income or dividends, as well as interest or partnership income that will help you make sure you've located all of the settlor's investments.

- Look at property tax bills and homeowners' insurance policies to identify all of the settlor's real estate. Check for "riders" on the homeowners' insurance policy, because that can tip you off to valuable items. A rider is added insurance, above and beyond the basic coverage. For instance, a home may be insured for $400,000 so it could be rebuilt in case of fire. But if there are expensive paintings or musical instruments in the house, the settlor may have added a rider to the basic policy to cover them.

- Go through drawers and shoeboxes to see whether you find anything of value. People have very creative hiding places! We know trustees who've found valuable personal property in freezers, on the backs of inexpensive pictures hanging on the wall, and in the pockets of sport coats.

- Call the Human Resources department of any place the settlor worked, even if the job ended long ago—you don't want to miss any benefits that have accrued. Find out whether or not the settlor was owed any money (wages, commissions, bonuses), owned company stock or stock options, or had other employee benefits (such as deferred compensation or life insurance) with value to the trust beneficiaries. You may find out that these benefits go to named beneficiaries and not to the trust, but it's worth doing some investigation to make sure that you haven't missed any trust asset.

Pension Payments

While you are going through the settlor's mail and bank account records, keep your eye out for any pension or annuity payments that were being received regularly. Ongoing pension payments stop upon the settlor's death unless there's a surviving spouse. Annuities may or may not have a survivorship benefit as well. If someone else is serving as the executor, it's really that person's job to deal with them, but you may be the most likely person to discover the payments.

Check with the settlor's employers, union, and professional organizations to find out whether a surviving spouse or minor child is entitled to any pension benefits. Ask the HR office to review whatever benefits might be available. It's the surviving spouse's responsibility, not yours, to collect any spousal benefit that may be available.

- Veterans benefits aren't trust assets, but at this point you're simply doing your best to ascertain everything the settlor owned or was entitled to. If the settlor was a veteran, survivors can claim any benefits with copies of the veteran's discharge papers, marriage certificate, and other basic information. For more information, contact the U.S. Department of Veterans Affairs at 800-827-1000 or www.va.gov. Many veterans qualify for burial in a national cemetery. Surviving spouses and minor children may qualify for a pension if their annual income is under certain limits. A veteran's spouse (and any children under age 18) may be entitled to payments if the veteran:

- died while in service
- died from a service-related disability, or
- received or was entitled to receive VA compensation for a service-related disability.

As you find assets, it's very helpful to start creating a list of everything. For real estate, write down the address. For financial accounts, put down the name of the company holding the asset, the account number, type of account, and value of the account.

Also record how each one is titled. The easiest way to figure out how an account is titled is look at how the mail is addressed from the bank or brokerage. Some examples of what you're likely to find are below.

Ways Property Can Be Held		
Name on Account	**How Asset Was Owned**	**What Happens After Death**
Jack Jones and Margie Jones, Joint Tenancy	Joint tenancy	Upon the death of one co-owner, the other person is the sole owner of the account.
Jack Jones and Margie Jones, JTWROS	Joint tenancy with right of survivorship	Same as joint tenancy: when one co-owner dies, the other is the sole owner of the account.
Jack Jones and Margie Jones, CommProp	Community property	Available only to married couples and registered domestic partners (where allowed) in community property states. Each spouse can leave half of the community property by will; if there's no will, it goes to the surviving spouse.
Jack Jones and Margie Jones, TTEE Jones 2000 Living Trust	Revocable living trust	When one cotrustee dies, the other will be sole trustee, but other people may be named as trust beneficiaries.
Jack Jones POD Margie Jones	Payable on death— Margie Jones is the P.O.D. beneficiary	At Jack's death, money in the account automatically belongs to Margie.

EXAMPLE: Abigail's father has died, and she is now the trustee of his living trust. Before she can begin to administer the trust, she must identify the assets owned by her father. Here's the list she makes.

Dad's Property

Asset	Type of Asset	Titling of Account	Approximate Value
House at 12 Main Street	Residence	Trustee	$300,000
Wells Fargo Bank Acct. No. xxxxx-692	Checking	Individual	$5,000
Fidelity Investments Acct. No. Yyyy-abc	Brokerage	Trustee	$25,000
IBM Stock	Shares of stock	Joint tenancy with son, Aaron	$250
IBM 401(k) Acct. No. Zzzzzz-123	401(k) plan	Individual, with Abigail and Aaron named as beneficiaries	$150,000

Looking down the list, Abigail sees that as trustee, she is immediately responsible only for the Fidelity account and the house, because those assets are titled in the trust. The IBM stock now belongs entirely to Aaron, and the 401(k) funds will be distributed entirely to Aaron and Abigail, outside of the trust. Abigail will probably ultimately be in charge of the Wells Fargo checking account as well, but first she'll need to figure out how to get the account into the trust, because her father owned it as an individual, not as trustee. (Chapter 5 tells you how to move accounts into a trust.)

Also list the items in the settlor's house. Include the contents of jewelry boxes, a description of pictures hanging on the walls, sets of china, antiques, expensive rugs, and other things that have financial or emotional value to beneficiaries. Note the size and condition of the item, if it's relevant. If you have a hard time describing an item, take a photograph. Photos will also come in handy if you need to distribute the items to beneficiaries who live out of the area. They might want to choose a favorite piece, but have a hard time explaining which of grandma's teddy bears has sentimental value.

If you think something is already missing when you start your inventory, include it on the list and mark it as missing. It may be that someone took the item for safekeeping or will claim to have received it as a gift. You'll have time to figure out a fair distribution of the personal property later.

Protect Trust Property

After you find the trust property, you've got to take good care of it.

Personal Property

Items of personal property, such as furniture, art, and jewelry, don't usually have documents that say who owns them, and so they aren't always formally transferred to the trust the way that real estate and bank and brokerage accounts are. If you're lucky, they will be listed on the property schedule, or you'll find a document called "Assignment of Personal Effects" along with the schedule. It's unusual, but occasionally the will, not the trust, specifies who is to receive personal property. In that case, it's the executor's job to deal with it all. But even if you don't have anything that says these items are trust assets, go ahead and treat them as if they are part of the trust and so your responsibility. Someone has to coordinate where all that stuff goes, and you're the best person for the job.

If some items are especially valuable, you may need to lock them up until it's time to wrap up the trust and turn them over to whoever inherits them. Small items may fit into a safe deposit box, and larger ones can be placed in an offsite storage facility to which you hold the only key. Exercise your judgment on how to secure the personal property, but do not put it at risk. Often, these items are more valuable to family members than real estate or bank accounts.

Real Estate

If you are taking care of a house and don't plan to sell it right away, it may be enough to simply change the locks and maintain property insurance. Let the homeowners' insurance carrier know that you're now in charge—as successor trustee, you'll need to be added to the policy. If you list the property for sale, remove valuable items so that visitors won't pocket loose items during an open house or case the property for a nighttime break-in.

Many trustees find it helpful to have a beneficiary live in the house during the trust administration, because occupied properties are less susceptible to theft. You could charge the beneficiary minimal rent in return for keeping an eye on the property or trade rent for work cleaning up the place. This is almost always a short-term situation, so you probably don't need to go the trouble of having a formal rental agreement with a family member.

If you decide not to sell the property for a while and are contemplating a longer-term tenancy, you should be more formal about it, using a rental agreement and charging the beneficiary-tenant fair market rent. Otherwise you run the risk of breaching your duty to the other trust beneficiaries to make sure that the trust assets generate adequate income or growth.

> **RESOURCE**
>
> **If you need access to well-written and useful legal forms for renting property,** use *Every Landlord's Legal Guide* or *Leases and Rental Agreements*, both by Marcia Stewart, Ralph Warner, and Janet Portman (Nolo).

Can You Give Away Things Now?

Beneficiaries may pressure you to give them money or a keepsake, but it's your duty to say no. Never give out trust money or property to beneficiaries until you're sure that there is plenty of money to pay all debts and expenses. Explain that you're obligated to wait and that it will take at least three to six months to wrap up even a simple trust.

If there's obviously enough money to pay debts and expenses, and a beneficiary is in dire need, you may transfer some money to that person. Be sure to keep detailed records and have the beneficiary sign a receipt. (More on that in Chapter 12.)

You can probably give away a few things early. If the settlor left behind clear, unambiguous instructions about what do with some personal property items—for example, Grandma's lemonade pitcher is supposed to go to her grandson Andy—then go ahead and give that stuff away. It's easier than storing the items. If there are no explicit instructions, or the trust directs the beneficiaries to divide the property as they agree in equal shares, wait until they've discussed the items they want and those they're planning to sell or give to charity. (Chapter 12 offers some ideas about how to fairly—and peacefully—allocate personal property among beneficiaries.)

Get a Taxpayer ID Number for the Trust

You may not remember, but when you opened up your personal bank account, you gave the bank your legal name and Social Security number. The bank used that information for its internal record keeping and to ensure that any interest earned on your account would be reported to you for income tax purposes.

Likewise, when you take over as successor trustee of a living trust, you need to use a separate taxpayer identification number for the trust if it is irrevocable. Do not use your personal Social Security number, or the settlor's, for trust purposes.

There's just one exception: If you're the surviving spouse and you inherit everything in a revocable trust, you will just use your own Social Security number for the trust. All other living trusts will need their own taxpayer ID number. Even if you're going to distribute all of the assets quickly and don't expect to file a tax return for the trust, our advice is to get a number. You will need it to open a bank account in the trust's name and for virtually any other financial transaction in the trust's name.

This number is also called an "employer identification number" (EIN), even though your trust is extremely unlikely to ever have any employees. You can get an EIN on the IRS website, www.irs.gov; search for "EIN Assistant." The online application takes only a few minutes to complete. We'll walk you through the process.

Getting an EIN Online	
Screen	**What to click or type**
Legal Structure	Trusts
Type of Trust	Irrevocable Trust (even though the trust started out as a revocable living trust, now that the settlor has died, it's irrevocable)
Confirm your selection of Irrevocable Trust	Continue
Who is the Responsible Party	Individual
About the Responsible Party	Enter the name and Social Security number of the settlor (called responsible party here).
	If you want to make a Sec. 645 election, check the box. (See below for instructions.)

Making the Section 645 election. You'll need to decide whether or not to check a box that allows you to treat the trust and the settlor's estate as the same for tax purposes, something the IRS calls a Section 645 election. Checking the box means that you can choose your own fiscal year for tax reporting. If the settlor died in May, for example, you could report the trust's income and losses from May through April, instead of January through December (the calendar year). Reporting your trust's taxes with a fiscal, instead of a calendar, year can reduce the number of tax returns you'll have to file before the trust terminates. That's because few people die at the beginning or end of a calendar year, so their trusts will earn income or suffer losses in only part of that first calendar year.

If the trust won't last more than two years—usually because all of the beneficiaries are adults and entitled to receive their shares of the trust as soon as possible—you'll probably want to make the Section 645 election. In addition to minimizing the number of income tax returns you'll have to file, using a fiscal year might result in lower overall income taxes because of when the beneficiaries will report any income that's earned on inherited assets.

> **EXAMPLE:** Carla's mother passed away in May of 2014. Carla decides to use a May through April fiscal year for her mother's trust, so she checks the Section 645 election box on the online EIN application. Her fiscal year ends in April 2015, and then she has three and a half months to file the return. (You get three and a half months to file after a calendar year, too—that's why income tax day is April 15.) She files the trust tax return in July of 2015, reporting the trust's income from May 2014 through April 2015, when all the trust assets were distributed.
>
> If Carla had used a calendar tax year, she would have had to file two returns for the trust. One would have been due in April of 2015 (covering May through December 2014), and another in April of 2016 (covering January through April of 2015).

If the trust will last more than two years, you can't make the Section 645 election, and the trust must use a calendar tax year (January through December).

If you do make the election when you apply for the tax ID number, you cannot change your mind later. So if there's any chance the trust will last more than two years, do not click the 645 election box—and make an appointment with an accountant to discuss your tax strategy.

If you don't make the Section 645 election when you apply for the tax ID number, you can do it later. You must make the election by the original due date of the estate's first fiduciary income tax return, which is about 15 months after the date of death. You'll have plenty of time to talk to your accountant about the election before you file the return.

Getting an EIN Online (continued)	
Screen	**What to click or type**
Who is the Trustee?	Individual
Information about the trustee	Enter your name, and click to indicate that you are the trustee for this trust (not a lawyer or other third party requesting a number on behalf of the trustee).
Trust's Mailing Address	Enter your mailing information.
Name and Location of Trust	Enter the trust's name and confirm your county and state. The date the trust was funded should be the settlor's month of death.
Employees in the next 12 months	No
EIN Confirmation	We recommend that you elect to receive the letter online, so that you can immediately confirm the number and take it to the bank to open trust accounts.
Summary	Confirm your information and request an EIN.

Get Property in Your Name as Trustee

Your next step is to get yourself listed as the successor trustee on each asset that the trust owns. Do it as soon as possible. Your accountant will have a much easier time reporting interest and dividends that come in after the settlor has died if the income is reported under the trust's taxpayer ID number. It also ensures that you will receive all of the mail and information associated with financial accounts. If you keep an account in the settlor's name and rely on the postal service to forward the mail, you may not receive all of the information you need to effectively manage trust investments.

Real Estate

For real estate, you'll file (record) a document with your state or county's vital records office that states that the settlor has died and you are serving as trustee. Attach a certified copy of the death certificate. A sample is below.

Sample Affidavit—Death of Trustee

AFFIDAVIT—DEATH OF TRUSTEE

STATE OF _____)

COUNTY OF _____)

I, NORMA JEAN THOMPSON, of legal age, being first duly sworn, depose and say:

That THOMAS THOMPSON, the decedent mentioned in the attached certified copy of Certificate of Death, is the same person as THOMAS THOMPSON named as one of the parties in the MARCH 25, 20xx Trust Transfer Deed, executed by NORMA JEAN THOMPSON AND THOMAS THOMPSON as GRANTORS to NORMA JEAN THOMPSON AND THOMAS THOMPSON as TRUSTEES of the THOMPSON FAMILY TRUST DATED March 25, 20xx ("Trust Agreement"), recorded in the County of _____ , _____ , covering the property commonly referred to 1867 Pine Street in the City of _____ , County of _____ , State of _____ , more fully described as follows:

LEGAL DESCRIPTION ATTACHED HERETO AND MADE PART OF THIS AFFIDAVIT.

NORMA JEAN THOMPSON is now the sole Trustee of the THOMPSON FAMILY TRUST and has all of the powers, immunities, and discretion given to the original Trustees.

_____ _____

NORMA JEAN THOMPSON, Trustee   Date

[NOTARY]

You might also need to include other county forms to minimize or eliminate taxes, such as property taxes, transfer taxes, or local fees that are associated with the transfer of real estate during trust administration. To find out about additional forms, give the local vital records office a call and ask. You may get transferred to the state or county office that deals specifically with taxes, but that's all right. You want to find out whether any additional property or transfer taxes will be imposed because the settlor has died. In California, for example, a new property tax assessment is done whenever real estate is transferred to a new owner, unless certain exceptions apply.

Financial Accounts

To take over the management of bank and brokerage accounts held in the trust, give a copy of the trust instrument, a certified copy of the death certificate, and the new trust taxpayer ID number (EIN) to the financial institution. If someone asks you for your "letters testamentary," a court-issued document appointing you as the estate's executor, explain that you don't have letters because there is not going to be a probate proceeding for the estate. What they're really asking for is something that establishes your legal authority over the assets. Showing them a copy of the trust document, a death certificate, and your identification should be enough.

> EXAMPLE: Elizabeth Jones is the successor trustee of the Paul Jones Revocable Trust. Following Paul's death, Elizabeth takes a copy of the trust instrument, a death certificate, and the EIN to all of Paul's banks and brokerage companies. The companies may require Elizabeth to complete some company-specific forms, but very soon the accounts will clearly be under Elizabeth's control. Here's what happens:
> - The title of the accounts changes from "Paul Jones, as Trustee of the Paul Jones Revocable Trust" to "Elizabeth Jones, as Trustee of the Paul Jones Revocable Trust."
> - The taxpayer ID number associated with the account changes from Paul's Social Security number to the new EIN Elizabeth got from the IRS.

- The mailing address changes from Paul's address to Elizabeth's.
- The account number may change.
- For checking accounts, Elizabeth gets new checks that show she is authorized to sign.

Review Trust Investments

Most state's laws and most trust instruments require you to invest trust assets prudently. But assuming trust money wasn't stuffed under the settlor's mattress, it's already invested *somewhere*. Do you need to change the investment mix while you're in the initial stages of administering the trust? (Chapter 9 covers investing trust assets over the long term.)

It depends on the trust. If your trust states that you are required to collect the trust assets, pay all of the settlor's debts, and then distribute what remains to the settlor's only adult child, you probably do not need to scrutinize the trust's assets. The trust will not last for very long—just a few months. You will probably hand over everything just as it is to the beneficiary, and not sell assets so that you can distribute cash instead. The beneficiary can then decide whether to sell each stock, piece of real estate, or other investment, or keep it.

If, however, you will be managing some of the trust assets for a year or more under the terms of the trust instrument, you must pay attention to the particular investment mix. You should see a financial adviser soon to reallocate investments based on the needs of the trust beneficiaries, the terms of the trust, and state law.

For example, trust assets might not be diversified. Many trusts are heavily invested in one stock or mutual fund because the settlor didn't want to sell successful investments and pay capital gains tax. But you, as trustee, can sell assets without incurring much, if any, capital gains tax. That's because most trust assets get a fresh tax start following a death, and there won't be a capital gains tax if you sell those assets to diversify the trust portfolio. (We talk more about this in Chapter 10.) What you should know now is that assets that a beneficiary inherits come with a tax basis of the date-of-death value, not what the settlor originally paid for them. This can make a huge difference when the asset is later sold, because capital gain tax is assessed on the difference between the basis and the selling price.

> **EXAMPLE:** At Rachel's death, her trust holds a brokerage account that includes 1,000 shares of Widget Corporation worth $45/share. Rachel bought the stock in 1973 for $1 per share. Her successor trustee, Janice, sells it for $47/share and invests the proceeds in an index mutual fund. The trust will have to pay capital gains tax only on the $2/share gain that occurred from the date of death to the date of sale.

Establish a Record-Keeping System

Are you a naturally organized person? If so, you're destined to thrive as a successor trustee. If not, now is the time to set up a filing and accounting system so that you, too, will be successful.

What you need to keep track of, and how long you need to keep track of it, have everything to do with the kind of trust you're administering. If all you need to do is collect the trust assets, pay the settlor's debts, and distribute what's left to the beneficiaries, you won't need to track income and expenses for very long—probably three to six months, tops. You won't even have to file a trust tax return if the trust doesn't generate more than $600 in income. For a simple trust like that, you may be able to do a good job with chronologically organized bank and brokerage statements, a trust checkbook, and simple notebook.

TIP

Duplicate checks can save you. If you are not good at keeping records, purchase duplicate-style checks. That way you will always have a record of the payee on the account. Always write the purpose of the expense on the memo line of the check.

If you are administering a trust that will exist for more than six months, though, you should buy basic accounting software, such as *Quicken* or *QuickBooks*, to keep track of the movement of money in each trust account. The cost is a perfectly permissible trust-related expense. If you spend a few hours to set up the accounts, you will avoid countless problems at the end of the year.

What about free online accounting programs, such as Mint (www.mint.com)? You can use one, but before you dive in, make sure that you can print out reports showing how the money has been spent for each trust account. Some online programs are organized for instant access, not for printouts.

For most trusts, *Quicken* should be sufficient. It is easy to use it to track various categories of expenses, balance bank accounts, and keep track of multiple investment accounts. If you are administering a trust that has many accounts receivable, or many different customers or businesses, *QuickBooks*, a more full-featured accounting program, might be a better choice. Of course, with a trust like that, there is probably already an accounting system in place that you can simply continue to use.

It is also possible to keep track of all accounts in a spreadsheet. Or you could plan on collecting all account information in a big pile on your bedroom floor, and then give it to your accountant to sort through at the end of the year. But remember, you are ultimately responsible for the trust. You need to have a good understanding of which trust investments are succeeding and which are failing. You are also expected to keep a handle on trust expenses. It's going to be a lot easier for your accountant, and a lot less expensive for you, if you organize the trust's financial information before you take it to your accountant.

If you have an ongoing trust, you'll almost certainly have to prepare an annual financial report, called an accounting, for the beneficiaries. That accounting will detail every asset in the trust portfolio and state its market value at both the beginning and end of the year. It will also note all interest payments and stock dividends throughout the year.

That's another good reason why keeping track of each trust asset and its income and expenses is a good use of your time. You'll need to know the information anyway, and having it at your fingertips will make it easy for you to prepare accountings for the beneficiaries. Now, as you're just beginning your work as trustee, is the perfect time to place the trust on the right track.

TIP

Make a paper trail. Try to avoid using ATMs, cash, or wire transfers, because it is much more difficult to track expenses without paper records like bank statements that detail each check. Always write down the source of any deposits to the bank. Nine months later, when you are preparing the accounting, you might have forgotten about the discovery of a few shares of stock.

Get Assets Appraised

Once you've inventoried trust assets, it is time to get date-of-death values for each and every one of them. This is true for all kinds of trusts, even if the surviving spouse inherits everything. If you're going to sell a car or a house within six months, you can, generally, use the sale value as the date of death value, but otherwise, you'll need an appraisal.

Accurate date-of-death values serve many purposes:

- They tell you the total value of the trust assets, which you will use to determine whether or not the estate will be subject to federal or state estate taxes.
- Beneficiaries need them, because they establish each inherited asset's new tax basis, which will be necessary for capital gains tax purposes down the road.
- They may be necessary to allocate assets between beneficiaries— for example, if you need to split the trust property equally among three siblings, you need to put a value on each one's share.
- For ongoing trusts, they provide a starting point to judge the success or failure of your investment decisions.

Real Estate

You may think you have a good idea of what the settlor's house or other real estate is worth, but a professional appraisal is a must. Hire a licensed, professional appraiser to value real estate held in the trust. Residential appraisals generally cost from $250 to $400.

You cannot simply look at the homes in your neighborhood and estimate the value of the trust's property. Nor can you use a website that provides data from recent sales of comparable properties. Not that it isn't interesting, but if the IRS ever challenges your valuation of the property, it would not accept a value gotten that way. It requires that a qualified appraiser determine the value.

Commercial real estate can be especially difficult to value, but a competent appraiser will look at sales prices of comparable real estate and the rental income of the property to get a good idea of the true value. Commercial appraisals cost more than residential appraisals— they can range from $500 to $5,000. You need to find an appraiser with experience with the type of commercial property you are dealing with.

RELATED TOPIC

For information on how to find a professionally licensed appraiser for residential or commercial real estate, see Chapter 7.

Bank Accounts

To get the date-of-death value of a bank account, look at the bank statement that includes the date of the settlor's death. If there's an entry for each day, there will be a value for the date of death. If the statement doesn't break down the account's value for each day, review the deposits and withdrawals, and any interest that accrued, to determine the account's value at the date of death. You should be able to find all of the information on the statement itself.

EXAMPLE: Mabel died on March 15. In April, her successor trustee, Frederick, received a bank statement for Mabel's checking account, covering the period from March 10 to April 9. The account earned no interest, and the statement shows when each check was drawn on the account. On March 10, the account contained $750. Direct deposits of $100 each were made on March 12 and April 1.

Checks Paid		
Check #	Date Paid	Amount
215	March 11	25.00
216	March 14	300.00
217	March 30	75.00
218	March 13	10.00
219	March 18	35.00
220	April 3	500.00

Frederick calculates that at Mabel's death on March 15, the account contained $515.

Account Activity				
Date	Activity	Withdrawals	Deposits	Balance
March 10				$750.00
March 11	Check 215	($25.00)		725
March 12	direct deposit		$100.00	825
March 13	Check 218	($10.00)		815
March 14	Check 216	($300.00)		515
March 15				$515.00

You'll notice that the checks are not in order. The bank cares about when the check was cashed, not when it was written.

If the account earned interest, but it's paid only once a month, there will be accrued interest from the beginning of the account statement to the date of death. To calculate how much of that monthly interest was earned before the settlor passed away, figure out how many days are in the account statement (probably 30 or 31), then figure out how many

days the settlor lived after the opening day of the statement period.
In our example, Mabel lived five days into the period covered by the
statement, which covered 31 days. The accrued interest is about 5/31 of
the total. Add that to the account total to get a date-of-death value that's
as accurate as you can make it. While this may not be precisely accurate,
because interest is compounded daily (so, the amount of interest earned
each day in a month is not equal), it's accurate enough for valuation
purposes unless the account's enormous. If it is, get the bank to give you
a daily breakdown on the interest earned.

Brokerage Accounts

You probably can't determine the exact date-of-death value of a brokerage account just by looking at the statement. You can, however, use the
statement to determine the exact number of shares of each stock and
mutual fund owned as of the date of death. Many people choose the
"dividend reinvestment" option for their investments, which means
dividends earned aren't paid out in cash but instead are used to buy
more shares of the stock. As a result, every month the number of shares
of stock in the account changes. Check the brokerage statement carefully
to determine when the dividend occurred and was reinvested, and note
the exact number of shares as of the date of death.

> **EXAMPLE:** Jeremy has a brokerage account and receives statements that
> run from the first through the last day of the month. On the 20th of each
> month, he receives a dividend of $.05/share from his shares in Mutual Fund
> A, and that dividend is reinvested to purchase new shares.
>
> On October 1, Jeremy has 500 shares of Mutual Fund A, worth $5/share.
>
> On October 20, those shares produce a $25 dividend (500 shares x $.05),
> with which the brokerage company immediately purchases five more
> shares of Mutual Fund A (five shares at $5/share = $25). Jeremy now has
> 505 shares of Mutual Fund A.
>
> Jeremy's October 31 statement shows that he has 505 shares of
> Mutual Fund A.
>
> On November 20, Mutual Fund A again gives a $.05/share dividend. This
> time, Jeremy gets $25.25 (505 shares x $.05), which goes to buy 5.05 new
> shares of the fund.

If the price of Mutual Fund A shares is static, you will easily be able to find out how much Jeremy's interest in Mutual Fund A is worth at his death. If the price of Mutual Fund A changes day to day, you'll need to do some more work.

If the company handling the account is a full-service brokerage, which offers you a professional adviser who helps you create an investment strategy and advises you what to buy or sell, ask for help. The adviser should be able to print out the date-of-death values for each stock and multiply the value by the number of shares to determine the total value of the account.

If the account is held in a discount brokerage, or the trust holds individual stock certificates, you will need to find out the date-of-death value on your own. You can see whether the company has online historical stock quotes, or go to a basic Web service such as Yahoo! Finance to determine the values. If it's a stock, take the average of the high and low values for the date of death. If it's a mutual fund, use the closing price of the mutual fund—the final price that the fund traded for on that day. You can find this at several websites, such as www.cnn. com/business and www.bloomberg.com. Once you know the stock ticker abbreviation for the fund and the date of death, you can easily get the closing price for that day.

> **EXAMPLE:** Jeremy dies on October 25 owning 505 shares of Mutual Fund A. On that date, Mutual Fund A is worth $4.90/share, so Jeremy's account is worth $2,474.50. If the beneficiary later decides to sell the shares, this is the value (tax basis) from which capital gains will be calculated.

RESOURCE

If the settlor owned a lot of individual stocks and mutual funds, and you want help to get the date-of-death valuations, you can pay $5/stock to Estate Valuation and Pricing Systems, www.evpsys.com. Just provide a list of the stocks and you'll get back a report with the date-of-death values. If you've got a huge pile of stocks to look up, it can be worth the cost.

Life Insurance

If the trust is the beneficiary of a life insurance policy, which is often the case if the beneficiaries are children, you will need to claim it and keep track of its value to the beneficiaries. If someone else is the beneficiary, commonly a surviving spouse or adult children, it is their responsibility to claim the benefits, though they may come to you with questions about what to do. You may also need to know the value of life insurance proceeds because they are included in the settlor's estate for estate tax purposes. (See Chapter 6 for more on claiming life insurance benefits.)

Partnership or LLC Property

The trust might co-own property with someone or be a partner in a partnership or a member of a limited liability company. If so, the appraiser needs to value both the entire co-owned or business asset, and also the trust's share of it.

In certain circumstances, the value of the trust's share may be discounted—that is, a 30% share of an asset might be worth less than 30% of the asset's total value. Values are discounted this way if arrangements between the co-owners reduce the market value of a co-owner's share.

> **EXAMPLE:** Claire's father owned a 20% interest in a shopping center that is owned by a limited partnership. He placed his share of the partnership into his living trust. Claire's appraiser puts the shopping center's worth at $10 million. To value Claire's father's interest, the appraiser takes into account the fact that Claire's father was a minority investor and had no control over management of the shopping center. Because of that, the appraised value of her father's share is going to get a valuation discount and be less than 20% of the total value.

Pay Debts and Creditors' Claims

Beneficiaries don't inherit until a settlor's debts are fully paid. For most trustees, this isn't a huge problem. Most people leave behind relatively small personal debts, like credit card balances and utility bills.

Who Pays?

The settlor's personal debts should be paid with the settlor's personal (nontrust) assets; trust debts should be repaid with trust assets. But if, as in most cases, all of the settlor's assets will ultimately be distributed as directed by the trust, the distinction isn't very important as a practical matter. You're going to pay the debts, and the beneficiaries are going to inherit what's left. Unless the trust says otherwise, debts secured by property, such as mortgages and car loans, are transferred along with the property they are attached to.

If there's not enough money to pay all of the debts, the beneficiaries aren't personally liable to pay them and neither are you, as trustee. Creditors can come after the beneficiaries for the amounts owed, but only up to the amount of the inherited property; creditors can't go after their other assets. Unless the debts are large, though, few creditors go to this trouble and expense. A credit card company is much more likely to write off a $3,000 balance than to sue a beneficiary over it.

Even though you aren't personally liable for the settlor's debts when you're the trustee, you do have a duty to pay those debts *before* you hand out trust property to the beneficiaries. If you don't, and later discover a large unpaid bill, the creditors may go after the beneficiaries to recover what's owed. And if the creditors are successful, it's a pretty sure bet that the beneficiaries will in turn come after you for repayment, saying that you were negligent in not finding out about the claim and settling before you distributed the trust's assets. You can see why it's best to wait to distribute assets until you're sure you've identified and paid all the debts.

Special Rules for the Surviving Spouse

The exception to the general rule is that surviving spouses are often liable for their spouse's debts because these were shared debts. Credit card debt, car loans, and mortgages are often taken on jointly by a married couple. After the death of one, the survivor is still liable. This doesn't necessarily cause any fireworks—if you're the surviving spouse, then what were joint bills, such as utility bills, medical insurance premiums, or credit card bills, become yours alone. You continue to pay them as you did before your spouse died.

If, however, your spouse incurred a debt alone, then your obligation to pay it is determined by state law and by the way the property was owned. (State law also determines whether or not a debt is separate.) You are usually not obligated to use your separate property to pay a spouse's separate debt. Property that you owned as joint tenants or as tenants by the entirety (a method of holding property available to married couples in many states), is also generally protected from a spouse's separate debts, unless you pledged the property as security for that debt.

> **EXAMPLE:** Katie and her husband Cameron hold title to their house as "tenants by the entirety." Katie owns her own business. Cameron is not a co-owner of the business. When Katie dies, she leaves behind two business debts. Because title to the house was held in tenancy by the entirety, Cameron, as surviving spouse, automatically owns the whole thing. Because the business debts were separate debts, incurred by Katie alone, the business creditors can't go after Cameron's separate assets, like the house.

Joint tenancy property may get similar protection from creditors, but it may not. It depends on state law. Generally, the half of the property that belonged to the deceased person must be used to pay that person's debts. In community property states, the community property of both spouses can be used to pay the creditors of the deceased spouse, after that spouse's separate property has been exhausted. But the surviving spouse's separate property is not subject to those creditors' claims.

RESOURCE

Ask first, pay later. If you are a surviving spouse and not sure whether or not you are responsible for a debt left by your spouse, find out before you pay it. One place to go for advice is a nonprofit credit counseling agency. You can find one in your area on the Department of Justice website, www.justice. gov/ust/list-credit-counseling-agencies-approved-pursuant-11-usc-111. Type in the state where you live and you'll get a list of approved credit counseling agencies.

Find the Bills

You've already started collecting the settlor's mail, so you should be familiar with many expenses just from reviewing incoming bills. It's also useful to look through the settlor's house and write down any expense you'd expect to have. You might be able to save the family hundreds of dollars a month if you pay attention and stop unnecessary expenses quickly.

> **EXAMPLE:** Ethan, who was the trustee of his uncle's trust, opened up a bill from the cable company and discovered that his uncle subscribed to premium cable service that cost $130/month. He quickly cancelled the subscription, which was of no use in his uncle's empty house.

Typical Ongoing Expenses
• rent or mortgage
• property taxes
• insurance (homeowners' or renter's, liability)
• utilities: water, gas, garbage, electricity
• cable or satellite TV
• Internet access
• magazines, newspaper, Netflix or other subscriptions
• telephone: land line and cell
• online gaming or research subscriptions

If the settlor received bills online or paid bills automatically through a bank withdrawal or credit card, check all of the credit card and bank statements carefully to look for automatic or repeated withdrawals. Go back a few months—some bills, such as newspapers and other subscriptions, come only quarterly or annually, so if you just check the last month's credit card statement you may not discover the expense. Some expenses simply recur, even though a bill is never sent—for example, some magazine subscriptions automatically renew, and the cost is automatically billed to a credit card, unless you cancel. Even if you're not getting the bills, the trust will still be responsible for paying the expense. So if you think a bill is getting sent electronically, try to get access to the settlor's email. If that is not possible, contact the company and ask for paper statements.

If you have paid some bills out of your own pocket, make a list of the expenses and detail the date of the expense, payee, purpose of the expense, and cost. Attach receipts to the list so that they will be available to any beneficiary who questions your reimbursement. You can reimburse yourself, just as you would pay any other creditor.

Often, beneficiaries end up paying funeral, burial, caregiver, and hospital expenses soon after a death. If any beneficiary paid any bills that should be borne by the trust, such as last funeral expenses or mortgage payments on trust property, help the beneficiary prepare an expense list and write a reimbursement check as soon as the trust has available cash.

Sample Expenses Paid by Beneficiary			
9/12/20xx	Good Samaritan Hospital	Last illness expense— hospital bill	$1,200
9/15/20xx	Family Mortuary	Funeral and burial	$6,000
9/15/20xx	Happy Bloom Florist	Flowers for funeral	$500
9/15/20xx	Yum Yum Catering	Food for reception	$800
		TOTAL	**$8,500**

Which Debts to Pay

Don't be in a rush to pay debts. Except for some of the ongoing expenses discussed above, don't start writing checks until:

- you know how much money you have and
- you're sure you have identified all the bills that need to be paid.

Take your time. You don't want to pay a bunch of creditors only to discover a big unpaid bill that may have higher priority.

Accessing the Settlor's Email and Social Networking Accounts

If the settlor didn't leave behind a list of passwords, it isn't going to be easy to gain access to email or a contact list. Most websites will turn over accounts to next of kin given the right proof, but it will take a while.

Google says that it reviews each situation on a case-by-case basis. Before it will decide whether to disclose the contents of a settlor's email, Google asks for your contact information, driver's license details, and a death certificate.

Once Google is satisfied with this information, it will request either a court order or more proof of your authority to access the account. This is a lengthy process.

Microsoft (outlook.live.com) will give you a CD that contains the settlor's email and contacts, as long as you provide a copy of the death certificate, a copy of your driver's license, and proof of your legal authority to act on the settlor's behalf. You will also need to know approximately when the account was established and last accessed, and what kind of computer you use (to open the CD).

Facebook lets you keep an account open as a "memorialized account" after a death. Facebook will not provide log-in information once an account has been memorialized. It will process special requests for family members, including removing an account, if a person can verify that he or she is an immediate family member or the lawful representative of the settlor's estate. This proof may include the settlor's birth or death certificate, or proof of legal authority. A fill-in form is available in the help section of Facebook, where you can upload your verification details and request that the account be removed.

Some states have enacted or are considering legislation to clarify this murky area, and making digital assets a recognized form of property, and the Uniform Law Commission has created the Fiduciary Access to Digital Assets Act to address this issue. If states start putting rules in effect, expect to see some changes in the policies of service providers.

Once you've got a handle on the amount of money you'll need to pay the bills, take a look at the cash you've got on hand. You may discover that you'll need to sell stock or other assets to get enough money to pay the expected bills.

Real Estate Expenses

Generally, you must continue to pay property-related expenses, including the mortgage, property taxes, and homeowners' insurance. You wouldn't want the property to be foreclosed upon for failure to pay the mortgage, and you should definitely keep insurance to protect the trust in case of a fire or other problems. Keep the water, gas, garbage pickup, and electricity going to keep the property habitable.

If you discover that the settlor's real estate is now worth less than the value of the loans against it, however, consider *not* paying the mortgage. Carol had a client who tried to sell his sister's condominium for more than a year during a declining market, making mortgage payments all the while. All of the cash in the trust went to pay the mortgage. After the cash ran out, the trustee was forced to work with the bank to sell the property for less than the loan value (a "short sale"), leaving the settlor's heirs with no benefit from the trust and the trustee with no cash to pay himself for his hard work.

If the trustee had stopped paying the mortgage earlier, and the bank had begun its foreclosure process sooner, there probably would have been some cash in the estate to distribute to the heirs and trustee. That's because that particular mortgage, under California law, was "nonrecourse," meaning that the lender could recover only against the house. If the foreclosure didn't generate enough funds to pay the debt, the lender couldn't go after other assets in the trust. Whether the lender can only foreclose on the house or also be able to recover from other trust assets depends on state law and whether the mortgage was obtained when the property was purchased or during a refinance.

In any event, mortgage debt is secured by the house; it's not the responsibility of the beneficiaries. If you stop making payments, the lender won't come after you personally. The lender will foreclose on the house and may be limited in its ability to collect against the other assets in the trust.

> **EXAMPLE:** Jose dies owning a condominium with a $300,000 mortgage. A real estate agent tells his successor trustee, Angelina, that the most she'll get for the property is $100,000. She decides to quit making mortgage payments and let the condo go into foreclosure, rather than try to sell it and use the proceeds to pay off the loan. In foreclosure, the bank will sell the condo for as much as it can.

RESOURCE

Talk to a housing counselor for free. If you have questions about whether or not to keep paying a mortgage, discuss your situation with a nonprofit counselor approved by the U.S. Department of Housing and Urban Development. You can find one in your area by going to the HUD website, https://apps.hud.gov/offices/hsg/sfh/hcc/fc.

The Foreclosure Survival Guide, by Stephen Elias (Nolo), also contains very helpful information on how foreclosure works and your options (including short sales, loan modification under new federal programs, and more) when behind on a mortgage.

Credit Card Debt: Low Priority

Credit card bills and similar personal debts are not the responsibility of surviving family members. They should be paid from the trust assets, if there's enough money—but if there isn't, the credit card companies can't come after the survivors personally. In most states, interest stops accruing immediately after a death.

It's definitely worth it to try to reduce the debt by negotiating with the company. We've had great success getting credit card bills cut following a death. Credit card companies know that they run a risk of getting nothing at all because their bills are a very low priority for trustees and family members. If you offer to pay 50% of the outstanding bill within 15 days, the company may be happy to get its partial payment quickly. And if the credit card company accepts a negotiated amount and writes you a letter saying the debt is settled, you've done your job.

Often, after a death, credit card companies sell or assign the debt to collection companies to try to collect a small percentage of the amount due. These collectors, by the way, sometimes neglect to inform heirs that they are not personally liable for this debt. Don't let them talk you into paying the debt with your own money, as if it's some kind of favor to the deceased person.

What to Do If You Fear Big Claims Might Be Coming

In most cases, it's not that difficult for you to determine who the trust's creditors are and what they're owed—you'll pay the bills as they come due. But that can take a while. In most states, creditors have up to a year after a death to ask to be paid. Some government claims, such as bills for underpayment of income tax, can be filed up to three years from the date the last income tax return is filed.

One way around this is to actively solicit claims from potential creditors. It may sound strange, but it can actually protect you. If the settlor was in a profession whose members often get sued (such as doctors, lawyers, and building contractors), consider sending a notice to recent clients or patients notifying them of the settlor's death. The notice may encourage potential claimants to start the ball rolling and contact you or to file a lawsuit. That's no fun, to be sure, but they'll find out about the death anyway, and it's better to get any potential lawsuits started—and settled—sooner rather than later. At least you won't be surprised by a lawsuit on the 364th day after the settlor's death.

If you want even more certainty, check to see whether your state offers a formal creditors' claim process for trusts. (See Appendix A.) Some states now offer trustees a creditors' claims procedure that's similar to the one executors use in probate court proceedings. These procedures are optional for trusts, never mandatory.

In a probate proceeding, the executor must formally notify all of the estate's potential creditors, or at least those the executor knows about or can find out about with reasonable effort. Once they've been notified, creditors have a short time, generally a few months, to present their claims for payment. If they miss the deadline, too bad—they can't submit their claims. The effect is to limit the time that creditors have to make a claim against the estate, so that executors can settle estates knowing that there aren't any unpaid debts lurking. A creditor who doesn't get notice can ask the court for permission to make a late claim; an executor who should have provided notice but didn't can be personally liable for the debt.

SEE AN EXPERT

Talk to a lawyer. Going to the trouble of notifying creditors through a court process is worthwhile only if you are worried about a large claim against the trust, such as a huge medical bill or a malpractice claim against the settlor, and want to cut off claims as soon as possible. If this is an issue for you, see an attorney as soon as you can.

Holding Some Money in Reserve

How do you know when it's safe to go ahead and pay debts and distribute what's left to beneficiaries? If you've looked carefully for bills, paid taxes, and feel confident that there is little likelihood of big future expenses or claims, you're ready. You might, though, want to hold some trust funds in reserve for expenses. (You can read more about this in Chapter 12.)

> EXAMPLE: Lynn was the trustee of her mother's trust. The trust held a savings account with $40,000 in it; a house worth $300,000; and a brokerage account worth $36,000. Her mother's last expenses were straightforward; she had a credit card balance of $1,200; utility bills of $250; medical bills of $5,000; and her funeral expenses were $8,000 altogether. Her mother had been on disability in the last year of her life, so her expected tax bill was low. Lynn sold the house and placed the proceeds of the sale in the brokerage account.

After four months had passed, Lynn had collected all of the trust property, paid debts and taxes, and didn't think any more new bills would come in. She decided to keep $10,000 in reserve and, as the trust document instructed, distribute the rest in equal shares to herself and her three siblings.

If There's Not Enough Money to Go Around

If there's just not enough money to pay off all creditors, you're dealing with what's called an "insolvent trust." You must prioritize the debts, paying off the ones at the top of the list and working your way down until there's no more money. (Although individuals can file for bankruptcy to wipe out debt, trusts cannot.)

Generally, the creditors waiting in line to be paid are the IRS, the state tax collection agency, secured and unsecured lenders, and people who have provided services to the trust, such as lawyers and accountants.

Every state sets its own priorities, but taxes (both federal and state) almost always get paid first. After taxes, your state's priority list will probably look something like this:

- expenses of administration (as in lawyer's fees)
- expenses secured by property, such as mortgages or liens against the property (this assumes you've sold the real estate or other asset to raise cash to pay debts; if the asset itself were going to a beneficiary, the mortgage or lien would go with it)
- funeral and last illness expenses
- family allowances, and
- other debts.

Get a lawyer's help to make sure you've correctly identified all of the debts and are paying them off in the proper order for your state. Sadly, if a trust doesn't have any assets left after the bills are paid, it simply terminates.

Assets That Should Be in the Trust—But Aren't

One of your main jobs as trustee is to find and inventory all the property held in the living trust—bank accounts, brokerage accounts, mutual funds, real estate, and whatever else the settlor transferred to the trust. If you've started going through the settlor's records, you've probably found documents (deeds, bank statements, and so on) that give you a good idea of what assets the settlor held in trust. For example, a bank account might be registered with the bank in the name of "Jane Smithers, trustee of the Jane Smithers Revocable Living Trust."

Unfortunately, it's common for people to forget to transfer some (or even any) of their assets to their living trusts. It's something that they should do after they sign their trust instruments, but it's easy to overlook. So an asset the settlor intended to hold in trust—and maybe even listed on the property schedule attached to the trust instrument—might never have been formally transferred to the trust.

> **EXAMPLE:** Jennifer knows that her father intended to put all of his bank and brokerage accounts into his living trust. He told her that everything was taken care of. But when she checks with the brokerage company after his death, she finds that her father owned the accounts as an individual, not as trustee of his trust. He never got around to formally transferring those accounts to the trust.

When this happens, the settlor's wishes can be frustrated in two ways: The property might have to go through probate, and it might not be ultimately distributed as the settlor intended.

When you come across property that isn't held in the trust, and you think it was *supposed* to be in the trust, what can you do? The good news is that in many instances, there are ways to get the property into the trust.

Trust Assets Not Listed in the Trust Document

You may find assets that are titled in the name of the trust at a bank or brokerage company but are not listed on the property schedule attached to the trust instrument. This can happen when a person opens an account or buys property and takes title as the trustee of a revocable trust but then forgets to update the schedule of assets. This is just a record-keeping mistake and shouldn't be a big problem.

If the account is owned by the trust, then all you have to do is notify the financial institution that you're the successor trustee. It will probably require you to fill out a form stating that you're taking over as the new trustee, and you'll have to attach a copy of the death certificate and a copy of the trust instrument to the form.

What Goes Into the Trust and What Stays Out

Not all assets need to be transferred to the trust. Some, in fact, can't be. Here's how to tell the difference.

Assets That Don't Belong in the Trust

Some assets don't belong in the trust. If the only assets that you find are on this list, you can skip the rest of this chapter; transferring these assets is discussed in Chapter 6.

The main nontrust assets you're likely to run across are:

- **Assets that carry a beneficiary designation, including retirement plan accounts, transfer-on-death securities accounts, and payable-on-death bank accounts.** These assets are transferred to the named beneficiaries outside of the trust or will.

- **Assets that were owned in joint tenancy, tenancy by the entirety, or community property with right of survivorship.** These "survivorship" assets are automatically the property of the surviving co-owner, so they don't need to be transferred to the trust either.
- **Life insurance and annuities proceeds.** These payments come from contracts that the deceased person set up to provide benefits to named beneficiaries. They aren't affected by the deceased person's will or trust.
- **Real estate that passes under a transfer-on-death deed.** These deeds, available in many states, take effect immediately on the death of the property owner. You'll recognize them because they're labeled "transfer on death" and expressly state that they take effect at the death of the property owner.

Assets That *Do* Belong in the Trust

Everything else the settlor owned in his or her individual name, which may include bank accounts, brokerage accounts, and real estate, can go into the trust. Before you start on that task, you need to know what the settlor's will says.

What Does the Will Say?

Your next step is to check the settlor's will, if there is one. If it contains what's called a "pour-over" provision, you're in luck.

If There's a "Pour-Over" Provision

Pour-over wills are created to help trustees deal with precisely the task we're talking about: transferring property into a trust after the settlor's death. A pour-over will directs the executor to transfer all individually owned property to the settlor's living trust. That way, the terms of the trust control who gets what and how the assets are to be managed for the beneficiaries.

If the settlor's will contains a paragraph like this one, you're looking at a pour-over will:

> **Disposition of Residue.** I give the residue of my estate to the trustee then in office of the Randall L. Molina Revocable Trust, to be held and administered by the trustee according to the terms and conditions of that trust including, without limitation, any amendment made to it before my death.

The settlor may decide to leave his grandfather clock to Maria and his model trains to Joey, but the "residue" or "residuary estate"—that is, everything else the person owned that is not specifically left to a beneficiary—is covered by this paragraph. It all goes to the living trust.

If There's No Pour-Over Provision

Not every attorney drafts a pour-over will to accompany a living trust, and not every client signs a pour-over will even if one was drafted. So there may not be a pour-over will in the settlor's packet of estate planning papers. (One of us once worked with a well-educated, wealthy client whose husband had recently died. The couple had met with a lawyer and signed a living trust, but the husband had refused to sign a pour-over will because he was superstitious and thought it would lead to an early demise.)

Unless there is a pour-over will, the nontrust property will be distributed separately from the trust assets. Here's how it works.

- If there's a will, the executor will distribute property according to its terms—which may be different from the terms of the trust.
- If there's no valid will, the nontrust property will be distributed to close relatives according to state law.

EXAMPLE: Hillary's living trust left half of her trust property to two charities and the other half to her three children in equal shares. But when Hillary died, her family discovered that her largest brokerage account had never been transferred to her trust and was not listed on the property schedule. Instead, it was owned in her name as an individual. They could find no will.

As a result, the brokerage account passed to her heirs under state law, her children. The charities received nothing. If Hillary had signed a pour-over will, the brokerage account could have been transferred into the trust and then split among the charities and the children, as she'd wished.

In California, Another Option: *Heggstad* Petitions

If there's no pour-over will, trustees in California have a special tool to use when a settlor neglected to transfer all of the property into a trust. You can ask a court for an order that confirms that the property belongs in the trust. You make this request with what's called a *"Heggstad"* petition. (It's named after a 1993 California Court of Appeals decision, *Estate of Heggstad*.) Basically, you're asking the probate court to let you treat certain assets as trust assets, even though they were never actually transferred to the trust, because the settlor intended them to be in the trust. California lawyers routinely file *Heggstad* petitions requesting courts to declare that all the property on a signed schedule are trust assets.

You'll likely need a list of trust assets, signed by the settlor, that shows the settlor's intent to transfer the listed assets to the trust. This list is often called a Schedule of Trust Assets. Some judges, though, grant requests even without a signed schedule, if they have other evidence of the settlor's intent.

Once the court grants your petition, you can record the court's order with the county recorder if real estate is involved, or give it to a financial institution. Then, as trustee, you'll have control over brokerage or bank accounts.

Going this route takes a few weeks and costs money—about $2,000 for lawyer's fees and $500 for court filing fees. But it costs far less and takes less time than a formal probate procedure. Unfortunately, if you have out-of-state property that should have been transferred to a California trust, but wasn't, you will probably have to file a probate in that other state to transfer that property, even if the property was listed on the schedule of trust assets.

Getting Property Into the Trust

If you've got a pour-over will, the next step is using it to transfer the overlooked assets into the trust. These assets may or may not have to go through probate before they can be transferred to the trust—it depends on the size of the assets and your state's law. Most states allow "small estates" to be transferred without probate, but if the value of the assets is too large, nothing will go to the trust until probate is finished.

Who Is in Charge

As long as the assets are outside of the trust, you are not legally in charge of them—the executor is. (As trustee, you have authority only over trust assets.) If the assets can be transferred outside of a probate proceeding, the executor will transfer them to the trust. If the assets need to go through probate before they can be transferred, the executor will be the one to open the probate and complete the process. Once the trust owns them, you will take over.

Of course, if you're both the executor and the successor trustee—as is common—you'll have both jobs. As far as you're concerned, it doesn't really matter which legal hat you're wearing, but it matters to the courts and to the financial institutions that hold the accounts that you need to transfer.

> EXAMPLE 1: Carl is both the nominated executor of his father's pour-over will and the successor trustee of his father's trust. After his father's death, he finds that one small bank account wasn't transferred to the trust. In his state, a simple sworn statement (affidavit) can be used to transfer small accounts without a probate proceeding. He uses the affidavit to inform the bank that the trust is the beneficiary of the pour-over will, and that he, as trustee of his father's trust, is authorized to collect the estate assets on behalf of the trust. No probate is necessary to get the account into the trust.

EXAMPLE 2: Santiago is the nominated executor of his mother's pour-over will and also the successor trustee of her trust. After her death, he discovers that her house wasn't transferred to the trust. It wasn't listed on the trust's property schedule either, because she bought it after she signed the trust and forgot to update the schedule. Santiago will need to file the will with the local court, get formally appointed as the executor, and begin the probate process. Once the probate is completed (after about six to nine months), the house will be transferred to the trust. The probate will be just as long and expensive as it would have been if his mother had died without a trust.

Will Probate Be Necessary?

Because most people create living trusts to avoid probate, having to go through a probate court proceeding just because the settlor forgot to transfer assets to the trust is unfortunate. Fortunately, many states have made it simple to transfer the assets in small estates without the time and expense of probate. If you can take advantage of these simplified procedures, do. But in the end, if you can't transfer an item to the trust outside of probate, that's not the end of the world.

There are two probate shortcuts, either of which can save you time and money:

- **Claiming property with an affidavit.** No court involvement is required. An affidavit is a short document in which you state, under oath, that the settlor died owning less than a certain amount of property and that you are entitled to certain property under the settlor's will. The affidavit asks the holder of the asset, say a bank, to turn over the asset directly to you, avoiding probate altogether. Most states impose a waiting period (often a month or two) before you can use this procedure.
- **Using a simplified court procedure.** Many states offer a simpler version of probate for small estates. A court may be involved, but not nearly as much as it would be in full-blown probate proceeding. Sometimes you won't even need a lawyer, which will certainly save money.

Probate shortcuts don't usually work for real estate. If the settlor owned real estate individually, not in the trust, in almost all states you're going to have to probate that property before it can be transferred to the trust.

Every state has its own rules; you can find a summary of your state's law in Appendix A. The next step is to contact the court in your county (many have good websites) to see whether it has any special rules and offers forms or helpful information. If you've got real estate in more than one state, you'll have to look at the rules in both states.

What's Probate, Anyway?

Probate is a legal proceeding that begins when a person's will is submitted to the court and ends when the estate is distributed to the beneficiaries named in the will. (If there's no will, the property goes to the heirs as determined by state law.) The purpose of probate is to make sure that the will, if any, is valid, the deceased person's family members are identified and contacted, the estate's property is inventoried and appraised, creditors are notified, and debts are paid.

Typically, property is probated in the state and county where the settlor was domiciled—which is a fancy legal way of saying where the settlor made a permanent home. If the settlor owned real estate in another state, and that property was not held in trust, the real estate will be probated in the county where the property is located, and not where the deceased person lived. Each state has authority (jurisdiction) over its own real estate.

Probate offers a useful way to resolve squabbles within families and to settle disputed creditors' claims. But for most families, where there are no real issues to argue about in front of a judge and no complex financial affairs to resolve, it can cost a lot of money and take a long time without serving any real purpose. If you can avoid it by transferring assets into the trust, you should.

Using an Affidavit

Start by finding out whether or not the state even offers an affidavit option for small estates. If it does, the next things you need to know are:

- the dollar value limit for using it, and
- what type of assets are eligible.

The limit on how big an estate can be varies widely from state to state, and legislatures change the amounts often. For example, in California you can transfer up to $150,000 of personal property with affidavits. In South Carolina, affidavits can be used only if the entire estate is valued at $25,000 or less.

Even if you have a lot of property to transfer, don't despair. States exclude many assets from the total, so you might be surprised at what fits under the legal limit. Many states exclude vehicles or real estate located in another state. Better yet, some states, reasonably enough, don't count property that would avoid probate anyway: joint tenancy property, property with a beneficiary designation (like life insurance and retirement plans), and property in payable-on-death or transfer-on-death accounts. Many states also reduce the value of an asset by any amount owed on it—for example, the market value of a car would be reduced by the amount owned on the loan.

> **EXAMPLE:** Roberta Duvall, an Illinois resident, created a living trust, but did not move all of her assets into her trust before her death. At her death, the successor trustee (who is also her executor) finds the following assets:
> - house worth $250,000, held in the trust
> - brokerage account worth $40,000, not in the trust
> - car worth $22,000 with a loan balance of $10,000, not in the trust
> - IRA worth $25,000, with her mother as the named beneficiary, and
> - checking account with $15,000, not in the trust.
>
> Roberta's successor trustee decides to use the state's affidavit procedure to transfer the assets to the trust without probate. Illinois lets estates worth less than $100,000, not counting real estate, use a small estates affidavit. It also doesn't count property that passes by beneficiary designation, like Roberta's IRA. So Roberta's estate has only $67,000 worth of property that needs to be transferred to the trust through an affidavit.

> The successor trustee uses an affidavit (with a certified copy of the death certificate) to transfer both the brokerage and bank account to the trust, with very little hassle.

If Roberta had lived in Indiana, her successor trustee would not be able to use an affidavit. Indiana allows the use of an affidavit only for estates in which the gross probate estate (property that would otherwise have to go through probate), less liens and encumbrances, is less than $50,000. Indiana would count the $40,000 brokerage account, the car's $12,000 value (minus the loan), and the $15,000 checking account. The house wouldn't be counted because it's held in the trust and wouldn't go through probate.

Most states that offer the affidavit procedure have similar forms. Generally, they require that the claimant:

- Identify the person who has died.
- Explain why you are the right person to receive the assets. With a pour-over will, the trustee is entitled, because the trust is the beneficiary of the will.
- Explain why there doesn't need to be a probate proceeding.
- State that the proper waiting period has passed.
- Identify the property specifically.
- Attach the death certificate.

A sample affidavit for California is shown below. You can probably find a fill-in-the-blanks form for free by checking with your probate court or searching its website. You can also buy forms online. Make sure any form you use meets your state's current requirements—check your state's statute! You'll find a citation in Appendix A, and it's not hard to look statutes up online.

To use an affidavit like this, you would present it to Bank of America, Citibank, and Vanguard along with a certified copy of the death certificate and have the assets in all of the accounts transferred to accounts opened in the name of the living trust. You wouldn't need to attach a copy of the will that shows you are entitled to the assets.

Affidavit for Transfer of Personal Property Without Administration (Prob. Code Section 13101)

STATE OF _____)

) ss

COUNTY OF _____)

I, the undersigned, affirm under penalty of perjury under the laws of the State of California that the following is true and correct:

1. Name of decedent: Richard L. Yee.

2. Date and place of decedent's death: February 22, 20xx.

3. At least 40 days have elapsed since the death of the decedent, as shown in a certified copy of the decedent's death certificate attached to this affidavit.

4. No proceedings are now being conducted or have been conducted in California for administration of the decedent's estate.

5. The gross value of the decedent's real and personal property in California, excluding the property described in Probate Code Section 13050, does not exceed $150,000.

6. The property of the decedent that should be transferred or delivered to the affiant is as follows:

    Bank of America, Account No. 1234-5678

    Citibank, Account No. 4000012345678

    Vanguard Brokerage Account No. 1234-7890

7. The property described in Paragraph 6 above was specifically left to the affiant in the decedent's will.

8. No other person has a right to the interest of the decedent in the described property.

9. The affiant requests that the described property be transferred to the affiant.

Executed on _____ (date), at _____ (city and state).

_____

Amanda Yee, Trustee of the Richard L. Yee Revocable Living Trust

[NOTARY]

Dealing With Stock Certificates

If you have actual stock certificates that you need to transfer into the trust, and their value is below your state's small estate limit, there are a few more steps. Ultimately, you must get those certificates changed so that the trust is the new owner.

The easiest way is to take the certificates to a local brokerage company and ask the brokerage to deposit the stock into an account for the trust. You'll need to provide a small estates affidavit that lists each stock to be transferred. Like any other financial institution that you'll be dealing with, they need to know that you're the proper person to deal with and that the trust is the proper new owner of the stocks. Most discount brokerages are very helpful and more than willing to handle the deposit, especially if you already have funds at the brokerage.

Opening an account means that you'll no longer have the lovely paper stock certificates, but certificates usually have no sentimental value to beneficiaries. Once you turn over the paper certificates, the brokerage will get the stock reissued to the trust. There may be a fee for this, but believe us, it's worth it.

If you want to keep certificates, you'll need to get new ones reissued in the trustee's name. You'll deal with the corporation's transfer agent, the company that the corporation hires to keep track of who owns its stocks and bonds. The transfer agent's name should be listed on the certificates. Send the transfer agent the original stock certificates, a certified death certificate, an affidavit of small estates, an Affidavit of Domicile (a sworn statement that states where the deceased person was a legal resident), and a stock or bond power, which is a document that authorizes the transfer of the shares to the new owner. All of these forms are available from the transfer agent and may be printed on the back of the stock certificate or bond as well. Send everything certified mail. There will be a fee for the reissue of the certificates.

Transferring Vehicles

If the deceased person left vehicles registered with the state motor vehicles department, you'll need to contact the DMV to find out whether it offers forms to transfer vehicles outside of probate. Basically, this is simply the DMV's own version of the affidavit procedure. Instead of supplying your own form, you're filling out theirs, but it's the same idea.

If so, you can use the DMV form to transfer the cars to the trust and then transfer them to the beneficiaries. In the form, you'll identify the deceased person, state that you are the proper person to receive the asset, and say that no probate proceeding is going on.

Using a Summary Probate Proceeding

If no affidavit procedure is available in your state, you still might be able to use a summary probate proceeding to transfer property owned by the settlor into the trust. This is an abbreviated, simpler version of probate that states allow for smaller estates. You'll have to file forms with the probate court, but you won't have to go through a complicated judicial proceeding. In most cases, you'll just be filling out and sending in forms and will not have to appear before a judge at all. To find out whether you can use summary probate, check your state's rule in Appendix A.

Most states require something similar to this: The nominated executor files a document, usually called a petition, with the local probate court requesting the simplified process. The petition describes the assets that need to be transferred—that is, the assets that were not transferred to the trust. The executor will need to submit a copy of the death certificate, the will, and an inventory and appraisal of the settlor's assets. If everything's in order, the court will authorize the transfer of the assets to the trust.

> **EXAMPLE:** If Roberta Duvall (from the earlier example) lived in Oklahoma, which has no affidavit procedure, her trustee could use the summary probate procedure to transfer her assets into her living trust. That procedure is available for estates worth less than $200,000.

Summary probate procedures exist to make it simpler to settle relatively small estates. Whether or not you need help from an attorney familiar with a particular court's rules and procedures depends on what state you're in and whether or not your local probate court offers a helpful website or printed information for do-it-yourselfers.

 RESOURCE

Help with simple probates in California. *How to Probate an Estate in California*, by Julia Nissley (Nolo), has complete instructions on how to handle a summary probate yourself.

Formal Probate Proceedings

The probate shortcuts discussed just above are terrific if you can take advantage of them to move the settlor's property into the trust after death, but they're not available in every case. If you are stuck with too many probate assets to fit within either probate shortcut, the executor has no choice but to open a formal probate proceeding. (Remember, everything that's already in the trust stays out of the probate administration.) If you're not the executor, it's not your job. But if you are, read on.

Opening a formal probate proceeding means that a court will supervise you and ensure that you identify the estate's assets, pay off the estate's creditors, and distribute the property that's left to the people entitled to inherit it.

Unless there's a family fight or messy creditor claims, probate is ordinarily a fairly straightforward process that involves filing forms with the court and following a formal procedure, step-by-step. In the states that have adopted the Uniform Probate Code (UPC), you'll probably be able to finish the entire process without ever setting foot in court. (See Appendix A to see whether your state has adopted the UPC.)

How much probate will cost varies tremendously from state to state. There's a filing fee that you'll have to pay to open the probate to begin with. Generally, this fee runs a few hundred dollars. Each probate court will post its filing fees, either online or in printed materials. In addition to that filing fee, there will be publication fees for notices in a local newspaper, and possibly appraiser fees and attorneys' fees. The executor is also entitled to fees; many family members don't take them, though, because these fees are subject to income tax, while an inheritance is not.

If you hire an attorney to represent you, you'll probably be charged on an hourly basis. But some attorneys charge a flat fee, and in a few states lawyers take a percentage of the estate, ranging from about 1% to 4%, depending on the size of the estate. (Chapter 7 has more about attorneys' fees.)

RESOURCE

Help with simple probates in California. *How to Probate an Estate in California*, by Julia Nissley (Nolo), has complete instructions on how to handle a probate yourself, plus all the California court forms. Even if you don't live in California, you'll find the author's lucid explanations of probate procedures helpful, and it will absolutely give you a useful overview of probate in general.

How long probate will take is hard to predict or generalize, but if you budget six months to a year, you'll probably be about right. Once appointed by the court, an executor can begin to sell assets and pay off the estate's debts. However, the executor typically cannot distribute the bulk of the assets of the estate to the beneficiary (in this case, the trust), until the close of the probate. What makes it hard to predict how long the process will take is the uncertainty of what bumps may lie on the road to completion.

Although every state is different, all probate proceedings follow a similar set of steps to get from the beginning to the end. Here's a very abbreviated overview of how the process works. For this example, we're assuming that you are both trustee and executor.

- **You file a petition** to be named executor in the county where the settlor was living at the time of his death. Most courts provide a fill-in-the-blanks form.

- **You file the original will with the probate court.** If you have already filed it, then you can simply let the court know that. You may have to file sworn statements by people who witnessed the settlor's signing the will, who will attest that the settlor was competent and not under duress at the time.
- **The court schedules a hearing** to give interested parties an opportunity to object to the appointment of the executor named in the will.
- **You send a notice** of the hearing date to all beneficiaries named in the will and heirs under state law. You also publish a notice in a local paper to alert creditors of the settlor's death and the opening of the probate.
- **You are appointed as executor.** If no one objects, the hearing is a formality. You may not even have to appear before the judge. If your request is approved, the court will issue documents that authorize you to act on behalf of the estate. In most places, these are called Letters of Authority or Letters Testamentary. If you don't live in the state where you're conducting the probate, the court may require you to post a bond or appoint someone who is local to accept legal papers on your behalf.
- **Unless the judge says you don't have to, you post a bond.** A bond is a sort of insurance policy, meant to protect the estate in case the executor mismanages assets. Wills commonly waive the bond requirement, but a judge may still require a bond if you live out of state.
- **You send notice to all known creditors.** This lets them know that you have been appointed as executor and that they have a limited time to file a probate creditor's claim.
- **You collect and appraise the property** that is subject to probate. This is usually called an inventory and appraisal. In some states, a "probate referee" is assigned by the court to do the appraisals.
- If the will grants you the authority to act independently (most do) **you can sell estate property** at this point.

- **You pay any creditors who submit a valid claim by the deadline.**
- **You close the estate and end the probate.** This requires a final hearing and sending out a notice to all affected parties. You submit a report to the judge which explains what you've done during the estate administration, including which creditors have been paid, and where the assets should be distributed at the conclusion of the probate. You may also have to file an accounting showing the income the estate received and any losses it incurred during the proceeding. (You should be able to avoid this if you, as executor, will transfer the balance of the estate to yourself, as trustee.)
- **The court grants you permission to distribute the property** to the trust.
- **You file receipts** showing you've distributed the property and ask the court to release you from your job as executor.

If there's real estate, probate proceedings are conducted where the property was located. So that means that if a settlor created a trust in Florida, but owned condos in Alaska and Montana that she never transferred into the trust, there will have to be probate proceedings in both Alaska and Montana to transfer those properties into the trust. The process will result in a court order transferring the property into the living trust. Then the ball will be back in your court—you'll be responsible for taking care of the property and distributing it to the trust beneficiaries.

Life Insurance, Retirement Plans, and Other Assets Outside the Trust

I t might surprise you, but many people die owning large assets that aren't governed by either a trust or a will. That doesn't necessarily mean they were overlooked; in many cases, the owner named someone to inherit them, or knew they would automatically pass to a surviving co-owner.

As the trustee, you're not legally responsible for claiming these assets unless you discover that the trust is a beneficiary. Even if the property doesn't end up in the trust, however, odds are that the beneficiaries will look to you for advice on how to transfer these assets into their names. After all, you got the trustee's job because you are the person the settlor trusted to be financially responsible.

Here are the most common nontrust assets you're likely to deal with:

- Life insurance proceeds
- Retirement plans
- Survivorship property: assets held in joint tenancy, community property with right of survivorship, or tenancy by the entirety
- Transfer-on-death property: bank accounts, brokerage accounts, vehicles, and real estate held in "payable-on-death" or "transfer-on-death" form.

SEE AN EXPERT

See a lawyer if an ex-spouse might inherit. If the deceased settlor's former spouse is named as a beneficiary of any nontrust asset, see a lawyer. In some states, but not all, divorce automatically revokes any beneficiary designations between ex-spouses. Federal law might also figure in, if the settlor's employer provided the policy as part of its employment benefits. The federal Employee Retirement Income Security Act (ERISA) requires that the person named as the beneficiary, even it's an ex-spouse, get the assets, no matter what state law says.

Life Insurance

Life insurance is often a large part of what a settlor leaves behind. Essentially, a life insurance policy is a contract between the policy owner and the insurance company. The owner agrees to pay a monthly or annual premium, and the company agrees to pay a death benefit to the beneficiary if the insured dies during the policy's term, subject to whatever terms and conditions were in the policy.

Finding the Policy and the Company

Your first step is to find out whether or not the settlor had any life insurance policies. This may not be as straightforward as you would imagine. People can often purchase life insurance for minimal cost when they open a new bank or credit card account, take out a mortgage, or travel. They are often covered by free policies at work. They can also buy policies when they leave a job or the military. You'd be surprised by how many life insurance policies are never claimed because families never knew they existed. Some companies assert that as many as 25% of all life insurance policies issued are never claimed.

Here are some good ways to find out whether the settlor had any life policies:

- Ask the settlor's last employer.
- Check pay stubs for automatic salary withdrawals to pay life insurance premiums.
- As you sort through papers, keep an eye out for bills for insurance premiums.
- When inspecting checkbooks, look for payments to companies with life insurance-sounding names—you know, "mutual" this or "national" or "colonial" that. These could be checks for premiums or interest payments on loans taken against a policy balance. (Some policies accrue a cash value that the policyholder can borrow against.)
- Check the settlor's mortgage statements to see if there are any payments for mortgage insurance premiums, which pays the lender if the homeowner can't repay the mortgage loan.

For a fee, you can hire a company to ask hundreds of life insurance companies whether they have records of a policy in the name of the settlor (www.lostlifeins.com) or search a database that contains millions of records on every life insurance policy application submitted for the last 20 years (www.mib.com). As a last resort, contact your state department of insurance to get a list of all the life insurance companies that sell policies in the state where the deceased person lived, and write to them directly to see whether they ever issued a policy to the settlor. This approach is free, but likely to be very time consuming. The American Council of Life Insurers (www.acli.com) has a complete listing of links for each state's department of insurance regulation so that you can get a list of all the insurance companies doing business in your state.

> **SEE AN EXPERT**
> **If there's an irrevocable life insurance trust, see a lawyer.**
> Sometimes life insurance is held in a special kind of trust to avoid the estate tax. If you find a policy owned by a trust, rather than by the deceased person in his or her name, consult an estate planning attorney.

Who Is the Beneficiary?

It is common for a settlor to name a living trust (and not a spouse or children directly) as the beneficiary of an insurance policy. That way, because the money stays in trust, it won't be subject to a probate proceeding when the surviving spouse dies. Or the policyholder might want to make sure that the money is properly managed if the beneficiaries are minors. If the trust is the beneficiary, then you will be responsible for claiming the policy proceeds.

If the trust is not the policy beneficiary, it's not actually your job, as trustee, to file the claim for payment, but you can still be helpful to the policy beneficiaries—usually the surviving spouse or settlor's adult children. As trustee, you are the one most likely to know what insurance policies the settlor owned. After all, you're the one who has been diligently digging through the settlor's personal and financial records.

Most policy owners name both a primary beneficiary and a secondary (contingent) beneficiary. The secondary beneficiary receives the death benefit only if the primary beneficiary does not survive the insured person. It stands to reason that the settlor may have changed beneficiary designations over the years. You may not have their most current designations in your pile of paperwork. So make sure to find out who the insurer has listed as the most current beneficiaries before you do anything else.

Understanding What Kind of Policy You've Got

Life insurance policies vary a great deal. Knowing which kind of policy you have will help you understand whether or not:

- the policy will pay a death benefit
- its death benefit or cash value has been reduced by loans taken against the policy
- its benefits are limited to a specific use.

The customer service department of the insurance company will be able to tell you about the benefits of the policy—but here's a quick rundown of policy types so that you'll know what they're talking about.

Term life insurance covers the insured for a certain period of time, often ten, 15, or 20 years. If the person dies during that term and the policy premiums have been paid, the company will pay the death benefit to the beneficiaries, unless there's been fraud (or, with some policies, if the insured committed suicide). If the insured person died within two years of purchasing the policy, though, the company will do an investigation (called "reunderwriting the policy") to look for any omission or misstatements by the insured before it will agree to pay a death benefit.

If the insured stopped paying premiums on a term life policy, the policy will have lapsed, and there will be no death benefit to claim. When the term ends, the policy terminates, and if the insured person dies later, there's no death benefit to claim unless the insured renewed the policy at the end of the initial term or converted it into a "whole life" policy, discussed below. If the policy terminated before the death, there's no death benefit to claim. Ask the insurance company what the policy's status is.

Whole life insurance covers the insured as long as the premiums are fully paid. Over time, these policies build up a cash value. The insured person can borrow against the cash value (which may reduce the death benefit) or take it out altogether and terminate the policy. If you find a whole life policy, ask these questions:

- Was the policy in force at the time of the insured's death— in other words, was the policy paid up?
- Did the insured ever borrow against it?
- Did the insured cash out the policy?

Universal life insurance is a variation of whole life insurance. It is designed to cover the insured's lifetime. The amount of the death benefit or the amount and frequency of premium payments vary, based on market performance. If the settlor stopped paying on either a universal or a whole life policy at some point, check with the company to see what's available to claim. Normally, insurance companies attempt to contact the owners of permanent policies when premiums go unpaid. If they don't make contact with the owners, they generally use the accumulated cash value that's built up to convert these policies into another kind of policy. The two most common options are a term policy with the same death benefit as the original policy but lasts only as long as the accumulated cash value can be used to pay the premiums, or a permanent policy with a reduced benefit that uses the accumulated cash value to pay the remaining premiums.

Accidental death insurance policies pay benefits only if the insured died in a particular way. If the settlor had such a policy and was current on the premiums, check with the insurance company to see whether the cause of death fits the policy coverage. If so, then you'll be able to claim the benefits.

Mortgage and credit insurance policies pay proceeds that cover only a specific use—paying off a credit card balance or mortgage balance. These policies promise to pay the death benefit directly to the credit card company or mortgage holder. If the settlor had one in effect at the time of death, take advantage of the coverage, but remember the money will go only for the specific purpose named in that policy, not for other expenses.

Filing a Claim for Life Insurance Proceeds

Once you've found evidence that the settlor owned a life insurance policy, contact the company for information on how to claim the death benefit. Call the agent who sold the policy, if you know who it was. If not, contact the company directly. Its customer service department can tell you what you need to send in. All companies require that you fill out their claim form and send in a certified death certificate; some also ask that you mail in the original policy. (Make a copy before you send it off!)

If beneficiaries are claiming the money themselves, you can help by providing a certified copy of the death certificate and helping them fill out the claim forms. Companies vary in how long it takes them to process a claim and in whether or not they begin to pay interest from the date the claim is filed or from the date the claim is approved. Ask how they handle this.

When beneficiaries file a claim form, they may be asked how they want the death benefit paid. Generally, the choices are to take the money out in a lump sum, keep it in an interest-bearing money market account with check-writing privileges, or to have it paid out in a variety of installment plans, some for a specific dollar amount or a percentage of the fund, and some for a specific period of time.

Insurance companies are eager for you to keep the money invested with them and to withdraw it slowly. They encourage you, strongly, to consider not taking the money in a lump sum unless you need it immediately. A typical pitch from one company warns that if you need the funds for ten years or more, "you may need to invest those proceeds in a way that allows them to grow and keep up with your future needs and inflation." We couldn't agree more. The issue is how best to do that—by leaving it for the company to invest or by taking charge yourself.

Although keeping the money in the insurance company's coffers may make sense in certain situations, we don't recommend doing it blindly. A life insurance company may be highly rated (for what it's worth these days), but that doesn't mean that the financial adviser in its affiliated brokerage service carries the same credentials or offers competitive fees.

And it doesn't mean that the company can do a better job managing the insurance money than you or a trusted adviser can.

Do your own research. If you do select a plan that pays out over time, make sure you understand the fees the company charges, the expected rate of return on the investment, and the consequences if returns fall below that target rate. Ask whether or not you can change the way your money's invested, or even take the money out of their plan, if financial conditions change or you just change your mind—often you cannot. We recommend that you run the numbers by a financial adviser you trust before you make any decisions. You may well discover that you can do as well as, or better than, the insurance company by managing a lump-sum payout yourself (with good financial advice) over time.

Especially if the proceeds are trust assets, you need to make sure that the money is adequately diversified and earning competitive returns. A money market account isn't likely to be an adequate trust investment over the long term. (See Chapter 9 for lots about responsible trust investing.)

Pension Plans

Back in the days of black-and-white movies, company pension plans were the norm. The deal was that in return for years of service, businesses guaranteed workers an income in retirement. These plans are around, but there are many fewer of them today. They are called *defined benefit plans* because the benefit is set, usually by the employee's years of service and salary or seniority level.

Payments from a traditional pension plan simply end at the settlor's death, unless the plan provides benefits to the surviving spouse. So if the settlor did not have a surviving spouse, all you'll need to do is notify the company of the death. Many pension plans deposit money directly into a beneficiary's bank account, and if a beneficiary dies midmonth, the plan may require you to return that month's payment. Some plans can do this automatically. Others will require that you send them a check for the overpayment before they'll release any other benefits (such as company-sponsored life insurance) due the settlor's estate or beneficiaries.

If the settlor left a surviving spouse or dependent children, the key question is whether the payments will keep coming. The answer depends on the plan itself and in some cases, on choices the settlor made about how benefits would be paid. The company's human resources department should be able to give you this information and guide you through the process required to receive any benefits that are due.

Traditional IRAs and 401(k) Plans

In the 1970s, when defined benefit pensions began to disappear, *defined contribution plans* replaced them. These are the now ubiquitous Individual Retirement Accounts (IRAs) and employer-sponsored 401(k) plans. For all of these plans, how much is available at retirement depends on what the employee saved during working years. To entice people to save, the government gives an income tax break on the money invested in these accounts, so they're also called *tax-deferred accounts*. Sometimes companies even match contributions so that retirement accounts can grow faster (and they get a nice tax break, too).

People fund these accounts directly from their paychecks with pre-tax money, or make contributions separately and get a tax deduction for them. They may take the money out without penalty after they turn 59½. Everyone is required to start taking out money after turning 70½ (more on that below) and to pay income tax on these distributions at that time.

If there's money left over in those accounts when the plan participant dies, it goes to the beneficiaries that person named. The beneficiaries aren't named in a will or trust, but instead in documents provided by the plan administrator or financial institution.

If you're helping beneficiaries claim retirement plan assets, look at three important questions:

- Who is the beneficiary?
- Had the settlor reached the age of 70½?
- Does the specific plan limit how beneficiaries can handle the money?

Don't despair. It sounds worse in the abstract than it does when you're actually administering an estate. The companies running these plans know the IRS rules and what their own plans permit. They will help you determine exactly what your options are and give you the proper forms to get what you want. As long as you are aware of beneficiaries' options and a few important deadlines, claiming retirement assets doesn't have to turn into a huge headache.

Income Taxes and Retirement Accounts

As a general rule, people who inherit assets don't pay income tax on their inheritance. Inherited retirement plan money is a big exception: A beneficiary who withdraws money from a tax-deferred retirement account after the account owner's death must pay ordinary income tax, not capital gains tax, on the money.

But it's only fair. After all, the money went in before taxes were paid on it (401(k) plans), or the account holder got a tax deduction for contributions (IRAs). The money that didn't go to pay tax stayed in the account, was invested, and earned returns. The whole system is based on the premise that the money will be taxed when it is eventually withdrawn. (This is a slight simplification; if a person funded a 401(k) or IRA with after-tax money or made nondeductible contributions, withdrawals aren't taxed. But that's an unusual situation.)

The slower that money is withdrawn, though, the smaller the tax bite. That's because income tax must be paid on what's withdrawn, but the rest of the account continues to grow (one hopes) tax deferred.

RESOURCE

Further guidance. *IRAs, 401(k)s & Other Retirement Plans: Taking Your Money Out,* by Twila Slesnick and John C. Suttle (Nolo), provides more detailed information and much practical advice about this complicated subject.

The Surviving Spouse

Surviving spouses get the best deal on inherited retirement accounts. They can:

- roll over an inherited 401(k) or IRA into their own IRA account
- keep the plan in the deceased spouse's name, as an "inherited IRA," or
- make an "informal rollover" by contributing to the account or failing to make required withdrawals.

Rollover

Spouses are the only beneficiaries who have the option of rolling over an inherited 401(k) or IRA and turning it into their own IRA account. Rolling over an account has several major advantages.

- Spouses can wait until they are 70½ before they are required to start taking out money (and paying income tax on it).
- They can name their own beneficiaries for the money.
- They are able to draw the money out more slowly over their lifetime than other beneficiaries can.
- If the plan requires that retirement money be distributed in a lump sum, as some do, putting the money into their own IRA lets it be withdrawn slowly over the spouse's lifetime.

Because of these advantages, most surviving spouses roll over retirement accounts into their own IRAs. There's no deadline for a spouse to roll over inherited retirement money.

Inherited IRA

Another option is to keep a plan in the deceased spouse's name and maintain the account as what's called an inherited IRA. A surviving spouse who is younger than 59½ and needs the money immediately might want to do this. That's because he or she could withdraw money from the inherited IRA without paying an early withdrawal penalty of 10% on top of the income tax that is always due. Rolling the money over into his or her own IRA, and then taking out money before reaching age 59½, would trigger an early withdrawal penalty.

If, however, the deceased spouse had already turned 70½ and was required to make minimum withdrawals, the situation changes. The surviving spouse must begin to take money out by December 31 of the year after the death. If the deceased spouse died before turning 70½, the survivor can wait to begin withdrawing money until the year that spouse would have turned 70½, or the year after the death, whichever is later.

> **EXAMPLE:** Sheila is the beneficiary of her husband, Ryan's, IRA. Ryan was 62 when he died and had not begun to take distributions from his IRA. Sheila is 50 years old. She can either roll Ryan's account into her own IRA or keep it in Ryan's name as an inherited IRA.
>
> If she keeps it in Ryan's name, she will need to start taking money out in nine years, when Ryan would have been 70½. She could also withdraw money without penalty before she turns 59½. In contrast, the rollover option would allow her to delay those distributions for 12 more years, until she turns 70½. Because she doesn't need to withdraw any money right now, she decides to roll the account over.

Informal Rollover

Finally, there's what's called an "informal rollover" option for IRAs (but not for 401(k) accounts). These are accounts that are automatically converted into a surviving spouse's name because the surviving spouse either:

- fails to make a required minimum withdrawal for the year of death, or
- makes additional contributions to the IRA.

If the deceased spouse was already older than 70½ and so required to make minimum withdrawals, the surviving spouse must make the required minimum withdrawal for the year of death. If it isn't made, the account becomes the surviving spouse's rollover IRA. If the survivor makes any additional contributions to the account, the IRS will treat the IRA as the surviving spouse's own as well.

Our advice: Avoid the informal route. If the surviving spouse wants to roll over an account, it's cleaner to just fill out the forms and do it actively rather than passively. That way you'll have an accurate record of when the account was created and what its value was at that time.

General Rules for Nonspouse Beneficiaries

Only surviving spouses can roll inherited retirement accounts into their own names and can wait until the year after they turn 70½ to begin withdrawing money. Everyone else must begin drawing out the money by the end of the year after the plan owner's death (or sooner, if the settlor was older than 70½) and must keep the account as an inherited IRA—not under their own name. These rules are complex, but the plan administrator (the company that holds the account) should be able to help you. When you know who the beneficiaries are and how old the settlor was, you can figure out what to do and when to do it.

Most beneficiaries have three options when it comes to withdrawing money they inherit. They can take it out:

- immediately
- by the fifth year after the death, or
- over the beneficiary's own life expectancy.

A beneficiary's freedom to choose among these options depends on two things: the specific plan's rules and IRS rules.

Some plans may limit beneficiaries' options. Some, for example, require beneficiaries to withdraw the entire amount within five years—they don't want beneficiaries to remain invested with the plan over the long term.

Under IRS rules, only "designated beneficiaries" can take advantage of the last option, often called "stretch-out planning," which is the most desirable for tax reasons. Only individuals and certain qualified trusts are designated beneficiaries. (Simple living trusts generally do qualify—see below.) Charities, corporations, and nonqualifying trusts don't have the option of stretch-out planning. If they're named as beneficiaries the money has to come out either right away or within five years, depending on the specific plan's rules.

For designated beneficiaries, the advantages of stretch-out planning can be huge. It lets a beneficiary spread out minimum withdrawals over the beneficiary's statistically expected life expectancy, a number that the IRS helpfully supplies. (You can get the life expectancy tables, as well as a worksheet to help you determine your minimum required distribution, from IRS Publication 590, *Individual Retirement Arrangements*, at www.irs.gov.) Any competent financial planner can help you work through the numbers, too, and for many of us that's a more realistic way to figure out what to do. Understanding stretch-out planning isn't beyond anyone with normal intelligence, but it's a lot easier to understand when you work with someone who deals with it all of the time. The big point to keep in mind is that taking money out slowly over time lets the beneficiaries avoid a big income tax hit (remember, retirement plan distributions are taxed as ordinary income) and get the benefit of tax-deferred growth as long as possible.

> **EXAMPLE:** Jaime dies at the age of 72 with an IRA worth $300,000. His son Mark, who is the named beneficiary, is only 40 years old. Mark can take out the $300,000 immediately, but if those funds were added to his annual income, which is $75,000 after deductions, he would owe about $107,000 in federal income tax (not to mention state or local taxes) on an income of $375,000. Part of that income, the amount over $190,150, would be taxed at 33%.
>
> Instead, Mark can elect to take the funds out over his lifetime. If he uses his life expectancy, he will be required to take out only about $7,000 from the IRA in the first year. If he takes just the minimum required, he'll owe about $16,000 total in federal tax on his $82,000 adjusted gross income. None of his income will be taxed at more than the 25% rate.

Beneficiaries who elect to take the funds out over their lifetimes can always change their minds and withdraw more. The IRS requires only that they take out at least a minimum distribution that's calculated as a fraction of the entire account. They can always take out more—there are no early withdrawal penalties on inherited IRAs.

There's one more wrinkle. If the plan owner died after reaching age 70½, the beneficiaries must make the withdrawal that the owner would have made in the year of death, unless it was already made. You can find out whether the required minimum withdrawal was made by checking with the plan administrator. After that, if the plan allows it, the beneficiary can begin to withdraw the money based on his or her own life expectancy.

To determine the minimum required withdrawal amount, beneficiaries can use the IRS life expectancy tables. First, they find the number that corresponds to their age in the first year of distribution. Then they divide the amount of money in the account by that number. The next year they reduce that number by one and again divide the account value by it. Honestly, though, you really don't need to go to all of this trouble. The plan administrator will calculate your required minimum distribution for you. You can even set it up so that taxes are automatically withheld.

> **EXAMPLE:** Penny, who is 65, is the beneficiary of her sister Jane's IRA. Jane was 73 when she died. In the first year, Penny must withdraw the amount of money that Jane was required to withdraw. The next year, she uses the IRS table to look up her own life expectancy, which is 21 years. Her required minimum distribution in year two is the amount of money in the account divided by 21. Her required minimum distribution in year three is the amount of money in the account divided by 20.

More Than One Beneficiary

If the settlor named more than one beneficiary—for example, three adult children—stretch-out planning becomes more complicated. The IRS requires that the oldest beneficiary's life expectancy be used. As a result, if one child is significantly older than the rest, the younger ones will have to withdraw their money more quickly than they would if they could use their own life expectancy. Fortunately, there's a fix: Divide the account into separate accounts, one for each child, so that each can use his or her own life expectancy to determine the withdrawal requirements. This can be done by December 31 of the year following the settlor's death, as long as the plan allows it.

> **EXAMPLE:** Guillermo leaves his IRA equally to his four children, the oldest of whom is 20 years older than the youngest. He dies in 2016. Before December 31 of 2017, the children ask the plan administrator to split the account equally into four separate inherited IRAs. The youngest daughter, Cathy, who is 20, can now withdraw her share over her statistical life

expectancy, 63 years. In year one, she must withdraw at least 1/63 of her plan balance. Her brother Diego, who is 40, must withdraw at least 1/43 of his plan balance in that year.

Charitable Beneficiaries

It's a great idea to leave money to a charity from a retirement account because the charity doesn't have to pay income taxes on that withdrawal. But leaving part of a retirement account can cause trouble for the other beneficiaries if they want to use stretch-out planning. Luckily, the trouble is easy to fix.

The complications arise because if the settlor named a charity as a beneficiary of a retirement plan along with other individuals, none of the beneficiaries is considered a "designated beneficiary." As a result, all of them have to withdraw their shares of the money by the fifth anniversary of the owner's death.

The executor can solve this problem by notifying the plan administrator that beneficiaries want the charity to receive its share of the account by September 30th of the year after the settlor's death. Although you can't add new beneficiaries after the plan owner dies, you can remove them, by paying them their share, before this date. The remaining designated beneficiaries can then use stretch-out planning. Charities generally don't care about stretch-out planning, because unlike individuals, they don't pay income tax on money that's left to them from a tax-deferred retirement account.

> **EXAMPLE:** Russell designates the nonprofit Doctors Without Borders and his son, Dewayne, as the beneficiaries of his IRA. Dewayne is the executor of his father's estate and successor trustee of his father's trust. After Russell passes away, Dewayne wants to maximize his ability to grow the IRA tax-free over his expected lifetime and minimize the tax he'll have to pay on the withdrawals.
>
> Dewayne, as executor, notifies the plan administrator that it should distribute one half of the account directly to Doctors Without Borders by September 30 of the year after Russell's death. Then, as the only remaining

beneficiary, Dewayne can use his statistical life expectancy to calculate his minimum required withdrawals. Because Doctors Without Borders isn't subject to income tax, it's happy to receive the money in a lump sum and invest the funds with its usual investment company.

If a Trust Is the Beneficiary

If the settlor named the living trust as the beneficiary of the retirement plan, trust beneficiaries may be able to use their life expectancies to stretch out withdrawals, just as if they'd been named directly as beneficiaries of the plan. If the trust qualifies as a designated beneficiary under IRS rules, the beneficiaries will not have to withdraw all of the money within five years.

Family living trusts generally do qualify as designated beneficiaries. What's required is that:

- The trust is valid under state law.
- The trust becomes irrevocable at the death of the retirement plan participant.
- The beneficiaries can be identified. That means that the trust clearly states who will inherit the trust's assets after the death of the settlor. Usually, these are the settlor's children.
- The trustee provides the trust instrument and any other requested documents (usually a list of the beneficiaries and any amendments that have been made to the trust) to the plan administrator within a certain time after the death.

If the trust meets these requirements, then your job as trustee will be to take over the account and manage it for the benefit of the beneficiaries. This is done by having the settlor's IRA rolled over into what's called an "inherited IRA." The plan administrator will want to see a copy of the trust instrument in order to get this done. You will have to begin minimum withdrawals by December 31 of the year following the settlor's death, as long as the settlor was under 70½ at death. If the settlor was older than 70½ and was already receiving required minimum distributions, then you'll have to withdraw their required minimum distribution for the year of death. After that, you must begin taking out an annual minimum distribution. If there's more than one beneficiary, you will have to use the age of the oldest one to determine the minimum required distributions. Unfortunately, you can't split up the account into separate accounts to avoid this. Our advice is to consult an estate planning attorney who has experience with retirement assets to determine how best to withdraw assets and manage them for the beneficiaries. They will need to review the trust instrument to see what powers you, as trustee, have over these distributions.

If for some reason the trust does not qualify as a designated beneficiary, then the assets must all be distributed to the trust in five years.

No Beneficiary or the Estate Is Named

It's unusual, but sometimes no beneficiary was named on a retirement plan. In that case, plan funds may go to the estate or to the surviving spouse, if there is one, depending on what the plan's rules say. If it goes to the estate, the funds will be distributed as part of a probate proceeding. And because there was no designated beneficiary (estates don't qualify) the five-year rule will be triggered if the plan owner died before reaching 70½. If the plan owner died after age 70½, the beneficiaries will be able to withdraw the money using the plan owner's life expectancy.

Roth Plans

The latest addition to the world of retirement savings are Roth accounts, named after the senator who invented them. Just when we were all getting used to the idea of traditional 401(k) and IRA accounts—saving for our retirement during out highest earning years and paying the income tax on the money later, when we didn't earn as much—along comes a plan that flips this whole idea upside down. With a Roth 401(k) or a Roth IRA, you make your contributions with money that's already been taxed. When you withdraw money (as long as you have had the account for at least five years), it's not taxed. That can mean years of tax-free growth.

Unlike traditional retirement accounts, the owner of a Roth plan does not need to start making required minimum distributions after age 70½. You can leave as much money as you want in a Roth account, and at your death it goes to your beneficiaries. (They, however, may be subject to minimum withdrawal rules, as discussed below.) That makes it possible to accumulate a significant amount in these accounts to leave to one's family.

The Surviving Spouse

A surviving spouse who inherits a Roth IRA or 401(k) can elect to treat it as his or her own Roth IRA, just as with a traditional IRA, by rolling it over into his or her own Roth IRA. The surviving spouse can then make contributions to it, and there are no required withdrawals. The surviving spouse can also designate new beneficiaries.

Nonspouse Beneficiaries

Nonspouse beneficiaries do not get to treat an inherited Roth IRA as if it were their own. They don't have to pay income tax on the withdrawals, as long as the account was open for at least five years, but they can't contribute to an inherited Roth IRA or combine it with any Roth IRAs that they've established themselves. They have to either withdraw all of the money within five years or stretch out the payments over their life expectancy (if the plan permits this) starting by December 31 of the year following the owner's death. Failure to take these required minimum distributions results in a whopping 50% penalty of what should have been distributed.

EXAMPLE: Lacy inherited her father's Roth IRA, which had a balance of $120,000. By December 31 of the following year, she began to withdraw the money, calculating the minimum amounts based on her statistical life expectancy. She decided that, because there would be no tax on the withdrawals, she would withdraw all the money over five years to pay for her daughter's college expenses.

Survivorship Property

If the settlor owned nontrust property with someone else, chances are the surviving co-owner now legally owns the entire property. The surviving owner automatically inherits the deceased owner's share if the property was held in one of these ways:

- joint tenancy
- community property with right of survivorship, or
- tenancy by the entirety.

Community property and tenancy by the entirety are available only in certain states, and only to married couples or registered domestic partners.

The property passes to the surviving owners, regardless of what a will or a trust says, because of the way it is held. In legal terms, this is called the "right of survivorship." In practical terms, the surviving owner automatically owns the property. Real estate, bank accounts, cars, and investments can be owned in this way. These are not trust assets, but as trustee, beneficiaries may consult with you about how to deal with them.

No probate proceeding is needed to make this change in ownership. The new owner will, however, need to complete some paperwork to get the property retitled in the survivor's name. This is called clearing title to the property. The process is different depending on whether the property was held in joint tenancy, tenancy by the entirety, or community property with right of survivorship. The next sections look at what kinds of paperwork are required for different kinds of assets.

Bank and Brokerage Accounts

Look for statements that list two or more owners for an account. Usually there will be an abbreviation after the last name:

- JT for joint tenancy
- CPWROS for community property with right of survivorship
- TBE for tenancy by the entirety (also called tenancy by the entireties).

The surviving owner should go to the bank with a certified copy of the settlor's death certificate to retitle the account. Even before the name on the account is changed, however, the surviving co-owner can still use the money in the account.

Brokerage institutions usually have forms for surviving co-owners to fill out in addition to providing a certified copy of the death certificate. Most of the big ones have websites that allow you to download the proper forms. First, search "forms" to get to the right area of the website. Then look for one that's used to update the registration of an account after the death of an account owner. These forms are commonly called "Estate Conversion Form," "Change of Ownership Form," or something similar.

Many of these forms require something called a "signature guarantee." This is a special stamp that only banks and some brokers have access to. It is supposed to protect against forgeries on important financial documents. A notary stamp won't do. If your form requires a signature guarantee, take it to your local bank or credit union along with your identification and ask them to guarantee your signature. Don't sign it before you get there; the bank officer must see you sign.

Stock or Bond Certificates

If you have to deal with actual stock certificates, rather than stock held electronically in a brokerage account, it's more difficult to change the name of the surviving joint owners or transfer-on-death beneficiaries.

The easy way is to open a brokerage account and deliver the stock certificates to the company that you've opened the account with. They hold the stock for you. The hard way is to return the physical certificate and have it reissued in the surviving owner's name or the name of the beneficiary.

Corporations have what are called "transfer agents" who keep track of the people and entities that own their stock. Most transfer agents are banks or brokerage companies, but some companies are their own transfer agents. The transfer agent's name should be listed on the stock or bond certificates themselves. Many brokerage companies will open up an account and assist in the transfer of the certificates of publicly traded certificates into the surviving co-owner's name, sometimes for a fee and sometimes for free.

If the stock isn't publicly traded, you'll have to go to the transfer agent or company directly. If you want to transfer the certificates yourself, send the transfer agent the original certificates, a certified death certificate, and these two documents:

- **Affidavit of Domicile,** a sworn statement that states where the deceased person was a legal resident. The transfer agent should be able to provide this. It needs to be notarized.
- **Stock or bond power,** a document that authorizes the transfer of the shares to the new owner. It is available from the transfer agent and may be printed on the back of the stock certificate or bond as well. It requires a signature guarantee.

EXAMPLE: Deborah's husband passed away, leaving behind a shoebox full of stock certificates that he'd purchased in both their names, as joint tenants. They were all for well-known publicly traded companies. She wanted to keep the stock certificates, so she contacted the transfer agent for each company, sent in the forms that each required, and received new certificates issued in her name alone. She could have instead opened up a new brokerage account and deposited the stock certificates with the brokerage house.

Real Estate

There's nothing more local than real estate, and every state and county has its own rules for how to transfer legal ownership of land within its borders. Generally, though, the requirements are similar. The surviving owner needs to file a document that confirms the death of the other owner, such as a certified death certificate, and something that establishes that the surviving owner is now the sole legal owner of the property. These documents are filed (recorded) not with a court but with the county land records office, which in most places is called the county recorder, registrar of deeds, or something similar.

Most of the time, the surviving owner will file a statement that sets out the facts and explains why he or she is the surviving owner. If the statement's notarized, it's called an Affidavit of Death of Joint Tenant (or something similar); if it's a statement under penalty of perjury (but not notarized) it may be called a declaration. It usually must contain:

- The legal description of the property. You can find this on the property deed.
- A description of how the property was owned—for example, "as joint tenants." This is also on the original deed.
- Information that identifies the previous deed (a unique identifying number and the date it was recorded).
- The name and date of death of the deceased owner. Often you'll be required to attach a certified copy of the death certificate.
- The name of the new owner.

If you're not sure what to include or how to get this done, ask a local title company, the local county recorder or registrar of deeds office responsible for recording deeds, or an estate planning attorney in your area. Make sure to ask whether there are any other forms that you'll need to file at the same time, such as property tax information. For example, in some states, like California, a new property tax is assessed when there's been a change in the ownership of land. So anyone filing a deed that transfers ownership has to fill out a form detailing who the new owner is and whether or not the new owner is exempted from such a reassessment. These rules vary from state to state. Before you record a deed that changes the legal ownership of a property, either consult with an estate planning attorney or, at a minimum, call your local county clerk or assessor's office and ask them if there are going to be any new taxes assessed after such a change.

Payable-on-Death Property

Owners of bank accounts, brokerage accounts, and U.S. savings bonds can designate beneficiaries for them on forms provided by the issuer or financial institution. The settlor could have set up these "POD" designations easily, either when opening up an account or later. You will see the words "Totten Trust," "FBO," or "POD" on bank statements or "TOD" on brokerage statements. At the death of the account owner, the assets in those accounts are transferred by the bank or brokerage company to the named beneficiary. No probate is necessary, and these assets are not trust assets either. (If the settlor had transferred the accounts into the trust, that would have cancelled the payable-on-death designation.)

All a beneficiary has to do to claim POD accounts is to notify the bank or brokerage company that the account holder has died, supply a certified copy of the death certificate, and provide proper identification. The company will transfer the assets into the new owner's name.

You may very well encounter disgruntled beneficiaries who can't believe that the settlor left his four children an equal share of the trust assets, but left an entire checking account to only one of them. It happens. And it's completely legal. A payable-on-death designation controls what happens to the account, regardless of what the trust says.

> EXAMPLE: The assets in Ruth's living trust were to be split equally among her three children. After her death, her oldest son, Tim, discovered that he was the payable-on-death beneficiary of her checking account, which had a balance of $24,000. The trust assets equaled $300,000. Each of the three children received $100,000. The checking account money went to Tim alone.

U.S. savings bonds with a payable-on-death designation are automatically transferred to the beneficiary when the original owner dies. The beneficiary can hold onto the bond, redeem it by taking it to a bank or other financial institution that pays savings bonds, or get it reissued in their name alone or with another person. To get the bond reissued, the new owner needs to complete Form 4000, *Request to Reissue United States Savings Bonds*, which is available at www.treasurydirect.gov or at a bank.

Cars and Other Vehicles

If the settlor had a car, truck, or boat, you may be able to transfer it without probate easily. You may discover, especially if you're the surviving spouse, that you owned a vehicle in joint tenancy with the settlor—which means that upon the settlor's death, you are the legal owner, and there's no need for probate. The vehicle may be registered to "Jane Quinon and Dale Quinon as Joint Tenants," or, it may say "Jane Quinon or Dale Quinon"—which, in some states, (such as California and Connecticut), means that same thing. You will also be able to transfer it easily if the vehicle was owned in another way with right of survivorship, such as tenancy by the entirety or community property with right of survivorship.

States vary in exactly how title is changed to the surviving co-owner, but generally you'll need to give the state motor vehicles department a copy of the death certificate (check with your state to see if this copy must be a certified one), the vehicle's title slip, and its registration card. If you can't find the title slip, you can request a copy from the state motor vehicles department. Your state probably also has a transfer form and may require proof of insurance and proof that the car can pass a smog test.

If your state has a transfer-on-death registration law, you may find that the vehicle has a POD beneficiary. That means that, like a bank account with a payable-on-death registration form, the vehicle is transferred to the named beneficiary directly. If so, the state motor vehicles department will have a form that you can fill out to transfer ownership to the named beneficiary, outside of probate. There may be a small fee for the transfer, but it's not likely to be a big hassle.

States That Permit Transfer-on-Death Vehicle Registration			
Arizona	Connecticut	Kansas	Nevada
Arkansas	Delaware	Maryland	Ohio
California	Illinois	Missouri	Vermont
Colorado	Indiana	Nebraska	Virginia

Finally, your state department of motor vehicles may have a form that you can use when there's not going to be a probate proceeding (in your case, because all the big assets are passing to the beneficiaries through a trust). In that case, there might be a simple form that you can fill out, affirming that there will be no probate and requesting that the vehicle be transferred to the executor of the will—who can then transfer it to the appropriate beneficiary or sell it.

Usually you'll be asked to submit an application for a new certificate of ownership, the old certificate, and a certified death certificate. Some states also require that the vehicle pass a smog test.

If you're not sure whether or not a vehicle is registered in joint tenancy or in transfer-on-death form, take a look at your state's department of motor vehicles website. It should explain how joint tenancy is established in your state for vehicles and whether or not TOD registration is available. It should also provide the forms you'd need to transfer a vehicle outside of probate even if there's no surviving joint tenant or no transfer-on-death registration on file.

TIP

For a link to your state's motor vehicle agency, check the State of Nevada's Department of Motor Vehicles handy map with links to all 50 state DMV sites, at www.dmvnv.com/50_state_dmv_list.html.

Transfer-on-Death Deeds

Many states permit transfer-on-death deeds (also called beneficiary deeds), which are simple deeds that allow owners to leave real estate to named beneficiaries without probate. If you are dealing with a transfer-on-death deed, it will say that directly on the deed. Look for language that says something like "Jonathan Steiner, a single man, transfers on death the following property …."

To clear title to transfer-on-death real estate, the new owner will have to file (record) something in the county's registrar of deeds or county recorder's office. The documents required vary from state to state, but you'll most likely have to record an affidavit (sworn statement) or declaration stating why you're the new owner, describe the property, provide a reference number for the original deed, and attach a certified copy of the death certificate.

Check with the local land records office before you file anything, to find out exactly what you need.

States That Permit Transfer-on-Death Deeds			
Alaska	Hawaii	Nebraska	South Dakota
Arizona	Illinois	Nevada	Texas
Arkansas	Indiana	New Mexico	Virginia
California	Kansas	North Dakota	Washington
Colorado	Minnesota	Ohio	West Virginia
District of Columbia	Missouri	Oklahoma	Wisconsin
	Montana	Oregon	Wyoming
Florida*			

* Enhanced life estate deed permitted.

Getting Help When You Need It

Feeling overwhelmed? If so, that's normal. Being a trustee *is* a lot of work, and sometimes you might feel like heading for the hills. But don't. Help is on the way. You're allowed to, and even encouraged to, hire help to make some of your tasks less daunting.

Start by figuring out what you need to get done and who is best equipped to help you. If you're in charge of a trust that will last for years, you need a different team of advisers from someone wrapping up a simple trust in just a few months.

Regardless of whom you hire or what you hire them for, always keep in mind that you, not they, are legally responsible for what happens to the trust assets. You must always stay actively involved in the trust's administration. If you delegate tasks to others, you must be well informed about what they are doing and why. If you're not paying attention and the trust suffers losses as a result, you could be personally liable.

> **EXAMPLE 1:** Davis was the successor trustee of his Aunt Janet's trust. The trust was for the benefit of Davis' four nieces, who were all minors when Janet died. Davis sold his aunt's house and put the proceeds, along with her other assets, into some mutual funds, on the advice of his friend Dale. Ten years later, when the trust was to end, the beneficiaries were horrified to discover that the trust had diminished in value during a time of rising stock values.
>
> Davis, it turned out, had never even opened the account statements from the brokerage company, let alone rebalanced the portfolio over time. And Dale, it turned out, had no financial or investment expertise. Davis was negligent both in following Dale's advice and in not bothering to pay attention to the trust portfolio's performance over the years. He also failed to communicate with the beneficiaries—they didn't know what was going on all that time. The beneficiaries sued him for breach of fiduciary duty and won; he was personally liable to them for their losses.
>
> **EXAMPLE 2:** Charlotte was the successor trustee of her father's trust. She interviewed five certified financial planners, all of whom had been recommended to her by her local bank's trust officer, had more than ten years of experience, and had advised trustees before. She hired one and together they developed a trust investment statement, which specified the returns the trust would aim for and the kinds of investments it would

make. She met with the adviser every six months to monitor the trust's performance in light of the goals. When it was necessary to change the investments, she worked with the adviser to find appropriate ones.

EXAMPLE 3: Judith liked being the successor trustee of her sister's trust. She was a careful investor and enjoyed keeping track of the trust's assets, which were invested in mutual funds. She hired an accountant to help her with the trust's annual accounting and tax return. They met each quarter to go over the trust's income and expenses, and the accountant helped Judith set up a system to accurately track both. Each year they had a meeting to go over the trust's tax returns and the Schedule K-1 statements that they issued to each of the trust's beneficiaries. Judith never signed a return until she was certain it was correct.

Working With Advisers: Keys to Success

- Before you hire anyone, evaluate their relevant experience and credentials.
- Find out what's a reasonable fee for the work the expert is doing.
- Don't be shy about firing someone if you're not happy with the results or your working relationship.
- Keep notes on important decisions and why you made them and the advice you got from the adviser, just in case an unhappy beneficiary later challenges you over the consequences of a decision.

Virtually all trust instruments authorize trustees to hire experts and use trust funds to do so. If the trust instrument doesn't say anything about hiring experts, your authority to get help comes from state law. In many states, state law authorizes you to hire experts for jobs that are complex or difficult if it's "prudent" to do so. In some states, such as California, you have a duty not to hire experts for tasks that you can do yourself. But in practice, no matter where you live, if hiring an expert is justifiable given the trust's purpose, and you legitimately need help getting it done, you can go ahead.

You can deduct the fees paid to these experts if they are incurred because of the trust administration (such as fees from attorneys, appraisers, or accountants) on either the trust's income tax return (IRS Form 1041) or, if there is one, the estate tax return (IRS Form 706). You cannot deduct costs for general financial advice from a financial adviser, but you can deduct the cost of advice that's specific to coming up with an investment strategy for a trust. Nondeductible expenses that are legitimate trust expenses can still be paid for with trust money. And even if your trust doesn't need to file a trust tax return (because it didn't earn more than $600 in gross income or *any* taxable income), you should definitely speak with a tax adviser about whether it makes sense to file one anyway. In some circumstances, available deductions may flow through to the trust beneficiaries, who can use them on their personal returns.

Now let's look at the major tasks you might need help with.

Experts You Might Need		
• Accountant	• Enrolled agent	• Financial adviser
• Appraiser	• Estate organizer	• Lawyer
• Contractor	• Estate liquidator	• Tax preparer

Real Estate Maintenance

If you're in charge of a house, you may need to repair it, paint it, or maintain landscaping. You'll certainly have to keep up routine maintenance. If you don't watch *This Old House* for fun and don't have a clue how to turn on automatic sprinklers or alarm systems, you may need to hire some help right away.

For regular house and yard work, you can hire gardeners and contractors. Of course, make sure to check their references and comparison shop to ensure you're not paying too much. Receipts are a must as well. When work is being done, make sure that the house is secured properly and that you adequately supervise the workers so that nothing is damaged or stolen. Don't, for example, give out house keys to people you don't know or invite workers in to do work when there's no one else there. (See Chapter 4 for more on how to secure and protect trust property.)

Organizing Personal Property

One of your first trustee jobs is likely to be sorting through a lifetime's worth of the settlor's things. Following the instructions in the trust instrument, you'll have to decide what to keep for beneficiaries or let them take what they want. (See Chapter 12 for suggestions on how to make this process run smoothly.) You'll likely be left with everyday items of no particular sentimental or monetary value, like furniture, pots and pans, clothes, and books. If sorting through that stuff and then donating it or hauling it away is an overwhelming task, you can hire help.

Estate Organizers

Some trustees we know have hired day laborers to help them haul away years worth of recyclables or thousands of books. Others have brought in professional cleaners to rid a house of accumulated grime. Still others have hired professional estate organizers, who can help:
- gather important papers
- monitor incoming mail
- set up a good filing system
- inventory and organize the settlor's possessions
- get professional appraisals of valuable property, and
- coordinate the sale of property.

Estate organizers are often professional organizers who have developed an expertise in working on estates. Most of them charge by the hour. Their fees can range from $50/hour to over $100—it depends where you live and exactly what services they'll be providing. They can serve as your central point of contact for other service providers, bringing in haulers, cleaners, painters, or others as needed. If you are an out-of-town trustee or are unable to spend the time it takes to get the home cleaned up and get the settlor's possessions organized, this can be an invaluable service.

To find someone in your area, search online for "estate organizers" or check the National Association of Productivity and Organizing Professionals website, www.napo.net, which has a directory of professional organizers that you can search by zip code.

Estate Liquidators

You can have your own garage sale or auction items on eBay, but if you want a professional to do it for you, look for an estate liquidator. Different liquidators work in different ways, but usually they either offer to buy the entire estate for a fee and simply take it away and resell it themselves, or they conduct an estate sale for you in return for a commission, usually 25% to 35% of the total sales.

If you hire liquidators to conduct a sale, you'll need to know how they plan to organize, set up, price, advertise, and conduct the sale. Here are a few other things you should ask:

- Are they bonded? This protects you in case they damage something or don't pay you the money from the sale.
- Can they provide you with local references?
- Can they give you an estimate of the estate's total value?
- What will happen to the items that don't sell? Will they donate them to charity or recycle them? Can you select the charities?

Legal Advice

Most trustees need some legal advice before they begin administering a trust—remember, if you breach your trustee duties, you can be personally liable for the trust's losses. The trust is paying for your appointment with a lawyer, so do yourself a favor and make one.

You may not need ongoing legal advice if the trust you are administering is a simple one. But it's prudent to make sure, before you start, that you understand what your duties are and that you have a clear understanding of what the trust requires you to do. It's also helpful for many trustees to get an overview of the whole process from beginning to end. Like many of life's journeys, if you know where you're going, you'll know what matters along the way. For example, knowing you're going to have to give the beneficiaries an annual accounting makes it obvious why you need to keep good records, right from the start. Knowing whether or not you'll have to file a trust tax return, and if so when, helps you to focus on the trust's income and expenses in a whole new, attentive way.

Even if you're a do-it-yourself type, it's worth finding a lawyer you trust at the beginning of a trust administration. In our experience, nearly all trustees run into something that they have questions about, be it a disgruntled beneficiary, a real estate agent who has never sold trust property before, or an argument over what the trust instrument means. Get a lawyer in your corner before these issues come up. Most attorneys work on an hourly basis for trust administrations, so you'll just pay as you go and get their assistance only when you need it, to answer questions as they come up

If you decide to turn over as much work as you can to a lawyer, how much will it cost? Of course, every trust is different and it's difficult to generalize, but a relatively simple trust can usually be administered in five to 20 hours of an attorney's time. So at $300/hour, the trust will spend somewhere between $1,500 and $6,000.

Finding a Lawyer

How can you find a qualified trust administration attorney whom you feel comfortable working with? Referrals from friends, family, accountants, and financial advisers are the best places to start. From there, you might ask neighbors or members of your church who they've worked with and liked.

Be sure that you get names of attorneys who concentrate on estate planning. A lawyer who did a great job on your friend's divorce may not know a thing about trusts.

Online Lawyer Directories

There is an abundance of websites that list lawyers. Generally, lawyers pay for listings, so the lists are not entirely comprehensive or unbiased. We recommend that you use them as tools to get started. They can help you find some practitioners in your area, and you can follow up with a face-to-face meeting.

Here are two directories that differentiate themselves from the pack:

- The Martindale directory, www.martindale.com, features well-established local attorneys, quite often those in the larger law firms. They have a peer-rating system, which is a great way to get a sense of what the other lawyers in that practice area think of a given lawyer.
- Nolo has its own lawyer directory, www.nolo.com/lawyers. It offers in-depth profiles of attorneys, including the usual education, background, and practice areas, but also providing insight into the attorney's personality and philosophy. Nolo has confirmed that every attorney advertiser has a valid license and is in good standing with the state bar association where the attorney practices.

After you've got a few names that look promising, take a look at their websites; they may give you more information and insight into the lawyers. Many terrific lawyers (usually older ones) don't have websites, though. Don't hold it against them.

When you're ready to move ahead, give each person on your short list a call. Try to speak directly to the lawyer and ask some initial questions. If you can't, that could be an indication that they'll be hard to reach. If you can, ask these questions:

- Do you offer a free initial meeting or do you charge for your time?

- What percentage of your practice is estate planning in general, and of that, what percentage is trust administration?
- Can you provide references for your trust administration services? (Not all attorneys have a list of references, because clients must give their approval before their names can be used. But it's worth asking. If you get some names, contact the former clients and ask them whether or not they were satisfied with the work that the lawyer did for them. If so, why? If not, why? Also, make sure to find out what kind of work they did; it might not be similar to what you need. Find out whether the lawyer was responsive to their questions and returned phone calls and emails promptly. Find out if the bill was in line with what they were expecting and whether any necessary follow-up got done.)
- How do you charge for trust administration—hourly, flat fee, or some other way?
- What's your hourly rate? If some of your work will be done by paralegals, what's that rate? (Don't expect to pay less than $200/hour—in many areas of the country that would be a bargain. Attorneys charge $300 to $800 an hour where we practice.)
- What's your preferred way of working with a trustee? (Some like monthly meetings; others prefer to communicate over the phone or through email after the initial few meetings.)
- How long does it take to settle a relatively simple trust—one that quickly distributes all assets to adult beneficiaries?
- Do you prepare trust accountings or tax returns? (It's not a bad thing if they don't, but it's a drawback if you prefer one-stop shopping.)

There's no way to sugarcoat it—there are lawyers out there who overcharge people for trust administration by taking advantage of their grief and unfamiliarity with the process. There's nothing we hate more than getting a phone call from a recent widow or widower who has been ripped off by a trust administration attorney. It won't happen to you because you're reading this book!

Don't Pay a Percentage Fee

Whatever you do, don't agree to pay a lawyer on a percentage basis for trust administration services. Please. Instead, insist that you be charged on an hourly basis for all services or, possibly, a flat fee that's based on that attorney's best guess of the scope of the project. Either way, the lawyer needs to be able to justify the bill.

A percentage fee is often many times more than an hourly bill would be. You can do the math: If someone quotes you a percentage fee, divide the amount of the fee by $200 (an hourly rate that's on the low side) to get a rough sense of how many hours the lawyer would have to work before charging you that much. For example, an attorney charging 1% to settle a trust worth $1 million would collect $10,000. That works out to 50 hours of lawyer time—which is absurd for a straightforward trust.

Unscrupulous attorneys will tell you that a percentage fee, often 1% of the trust's value, is reasonable given that probate fees can run to two or three times that amount. But people create trusts to *avoid* the expense and delay of probate. It's irrelevant how much probate costs—what's important is how much time it's going to take an attorney to help you settle the trust. Period.

Get an Engagement Letter in Writing

Before you agree to work with a trust administration attorney, get the lawyer to write you a detailed engagement letter. This letter should specify:

- **The hourly fee.** This differs regionally, but will probably be $200 to $800 per hour. It should also specify the hourly fees of anyone else in the office who may do some of the work, such as paralegals or other administrative staff.
- **The flat fee.** If the attorney offers a flat fee, the letter should spell out exactly what the fee includes.
- **Services to be provided.** These are normally counseling you on a trustee's duties and responsibilities, retitling real estate, transferring brokerage and bank accounts, communicating with beneficiaries, and other trust administration services as required.

- **Services not provided.** Some trust attorneys prepare income and estate tax returns, some do not. Some help you prepare trustee accountings, some do not. Just make sure that you know which pieces of the process they will not take on.
- **How you'll be billed.** Find out whether you'll need to pay a retainer to get started and then whether you'll be billed monthly, at the end of the process, or in some other way. Most attorneys ask for a retainer before they get started. It would be reasonable to require that you pay for a few hours up front. This money should be placed in the attorney's trust fund, and withdrawn by the attorney as the work is done.
- **Other costs.** You should know whether or not to expect bills for expenses such as filing fees, postage, appraisals, or any other third-party services.
- **An estimate of the total fee.** It is difficult to know for certain how much trust administration will cost when it is billed hourly because often you're not sure at the beginning what's likely to come up during the process. But it's important to get at least an estimate before you jump in.

Remember, You're in Charge

You can always fire your lawyer. Don't let yourself be intimidated because you don't know the ins and outs of trust administration. You do know (because you're reading this book) what your trustee job entails, and you deserve to work with someone who makes that easier, not harder.

If your questions aren't being answered thoughtfully, if your phone calls aren't returned promptly, if things aren't getting done, or your billing statements aren't specific and accurate, find yourself a better lawyer. You are entitled to get your client files back if you do go to another attorney, although your original attorney will make and keep a copy.

> EXAMPLE: When Marlene's husband unexpectedly passed away, she met with a trust administration attorney who agreed to represent her for a flat 1% of the value of the trust assets. He required a $5,000 advance on

this fee, which would have been $30,000 in total. After two months, the attorney hadn't done anything on the administration.

Marlene called another trust administration attorney to see whether that fee was reasonable. When she was told that it was about ten times more than it should be, based on that attorney's estimate of the time required to administer her simple trust, she was aghast. She fired the first attorney and asked for her file back. He told her that he would keep the $5,000 advance although he'd done virtually no work on the case. She reported him to the state bar association, which contacted him and asked for a detailed accounting of the work that he'd done on the case. He then returned $3,000 of the retainer.

RESOURCE

For helpful articles about working with lawyers, see www.nolo .com/legal-encyclopedia/lawyers-lawfirms/tips.html.

Appraisals

If your trust holds real estate, you will almost certainly need to get that property appraised to establish its value. There are many reasons for doing so. One is to establish a new basis for capital gains tax or to complete an estate tax return. (More on both subjects in Chapter 10.) Another is to accurately determine an asset's value so that trust assets can be split among multiple beneficiaries as the trust directs.

There's one exception to this general rule: If a property is going to be sold quickly after the settlor's death you can skip the appraisal; in that case, the sales value will be its value for tax purposes or distributions. By "quickly," we mean within just a few months. Getting an appraisal may still make sense even then, because it will help you price the property properly.

Finding a Qualified Appraiser

The IRS requires that any appraisal relied upon for tax purposes be prepared by a qualified appraiser. You can't rely on online sites, you can't use the sales prices of comparables in your neighborhood, you can't rely on Aunt Mildred who was an appraiser before she retired 20 years ago, and you can't do it yourself.

A qualified appraiser must:

- have earned an appraisal designation from a recognized professional appraisers organization for demonstrated competency in valuing the type of property being appraised, or meet certain education and experience requirements, which differ state to state.

The appraiser must also:

- regularly prepare appraisals for pay
- have experience in appraising the specific type of property being appraised, and
- not have been prohibited from practicing before the IRS for three years before the date of the appraisal.

What this means in real life is that you must hire a professional appraiser who is licensed by the state. The appraiser must know the type of property you're having appraised, know the local market, and have access to data that will make a comparison to similar properties accurate and meaningful. If you need a house appraised, you can't hire an appraiser whose experience has been evaluating farmland, and for commercial property you don't want a residential specialist.

The industry's governing standards are set by the Appraisal Foundation (www.appraisalfoundation.org), which publishes the *Uniform Standards of Professional Appraisal Practice* (USPAP). Your appraiser's work should comply with the current USPAP standards.

Most trust administration attorneys know good local appraisers, because this is part of nearly every trust administration. Local real estate agents, too, can be a great source of referrals; they often work with appraisers when they buy or sell properties. Another good source is the website for the Appraisal Institute, www.appraisalinstitute.org.

Types of Appraisals

The most common kind of appraisal is known as a "walk-through."
The appraiser walks through the property and the neighborhood, then
completes a detailed document called a Uniform Residential Appraisal
Report. This report includes an evaluation of the neighborhood, details
about the property, a comparison to at least three similar properties,
improvements made to the property, issues that may reduce its value
such as noise or poor access, its estimated sales time, and its estimated
market value. The cost for a typical walk-through appraisal is $350 to
$600. Appraisals of commercial properties cost more, usually $500 to
$5,000, depending upon the size and location.

With a less expensive "drive-by" appraisal, the appraiser doesn't enter
the property but instead relies on a survey of the neighborhood and
comparable properties nearby. This isn't the kind of appraisal you want.
Better to spend more money up front to establish a defensible value in
case you or a beneficiary gets audited by the IRS when the property is
sold many years later.

Taxes

There are at least two, and possibly three, federal tax returns that you
(most likely) will be responsible for filing after the settlor's death, plus
state returns as well. (See Chapter 10.) For most trustees, it's worth it to
get professional, experienced help on these returns, even if you file your
own income tax returns every year.

The first reason to get professional help is that you've got a lot of
other trust-related tasks to complete, and tax preparation lends itself
to outsourcing. A better reason is that you're going to be liable for any
mistakes in these filings to both the IRS and the beneficiaries. You don't
want to take the chance that you'll file the returns, pay the tax due,
distribute the rest of the trust assets, and then face an audit, and possibly
back taxes and penalties, two years later. Spend what it costs to get the
returns done correctly the first time.

There are two primary kinds of tax professionals: enrolled agents and certified public accountants:

- **Enrolled agents (EAs)** are licensed by the federal government to represent taxpayers before the IRS for audits, collections, and appeals. They have to pass an exam or work for the IRS for at least five years to get that designation; there are no other educational requirements. They specialize in tax matters exclusively.

- **Certified public accountants (CPAs)** are licensed by each state. They have an undergraduate degree, usually in accounting, finance, or management, and have passed a test that covers business law, auditing, and accounting.

Experience is more important than the label. What you really need to know is whether or not the person you're talking to has experience in preparing fiduciary, as opposed to personal, income tax returns. All EAs and many CPAs regularly prepare personal income tax returns, but you'll also need help with fiduciary income tax returns for the trust (Form 1041) and possibly an estate tax return (Form 706). (Chapter 10 explains these returns and when to file them.) Ask how many such returns the person has filed in the last five years. Don't just ask whether the person can complete one—the person might be happy to do it, but that's not the same as having experience. Try to work with someone who has done at least five to ten trust income tax or estate tax returns.

The typical cost of preparing a trust tax return is from $500 to $1,000. Preparing an estate tax return, which is very complicated, can cost anywhere from $3,000 to $8,000. Make sure to get an estimate before the work gets started.

Investing

If you're managing an ongoing trust, you'll almost certainly need professional investment advice. You want to find someone who can give you unbiased, knowledgeable advice on how best to invest the trust assets.

Finding the right financial adviser can be slightly trickier than finding the right tax professional. That's because virtually anyone can call themselves a financial planner, financial consultant, investment consultant, or wealth manager—the field is not as heavily regulated as many others, like insurance, tax preparation, or even appraising. Some financial advisers are really just salespeople with fancy titles, pushing proprietary products on which they earn high commissions.

So how can you find the good advisers and avoid the bad? Three steps:

1. Take the time to understand what professional credentials are available to planners and require that yours have one of them.
2. Get at least three referrals from trusted friends or other advisers.
3. Visit the planners who meet your criteria and ask them lots of questions.

Check Credentials

Although there's no state or federal licensing process for financial planners, several private bodies offer credentials to help identify competent planners. We recommend working with someone who has at least one of the following three credentials or is close to completing the requirements.

Certified financial planner (CFP). The best known credential for financial planners is the CFP. This credential is granted by the nonprofit Certified Financial Planner Board of Standards. To get a CFP, a planner has to have at least a bachelor's degree in any discipline from an accredited college or university. Then the person must pass a comprehensive and difficult exam, have three years of full-time relevant personal financial planning experience, and complete an application that requires disclosure of involvement in any criminal, civil, governmental, or agency proceeding or inquiry. Finally, applicants agree to adhere to a code of ethics and practice standards and to take continuing education courses.

Personal financial specialist (PFS). A certified public accountant who becomes a certified financial planner is called a personal financial specialist. To get that designation, a CPA must be a member of the

American Institute of Certified Public Accountants (which binds members to a code of ethical standards), have 3,000 hours of financial planning business experience, pass a comprehensive exam, and take continuing education courses.

Chartered financial consultant (ChFC). This title is usually held by life insurance agents and others in the financial industry. To get the designation, a candidate must have three years' experience in some aspect of the financial industry and pass an exam that covers income tax, insurance, investments, and estate planning. This credential does not require a college degree and has no code of ethics associated directly with it. In our opinion it isn't as strong a credential as the CFP or the PFS, but it's certainly a sign of commitment to the field of financial planning.

Finally, you may find financial advisers who don't hold any of the above credentials but do have a Master's in Business Administration (MBA). If they have good references and are members of the major professional associations discussed below, the MBA certainly qualifies them as financially literate. Ask why they don't have a CFP credential and listen closely to the answer. Someone who is studying for the exam has a really good reason for not having a CFP. But if the person just doesn't do enough financial planning to make the credential worthwhile, you should reconsider your choice.

Look for Membership in Professional Associations

It's always a good idea to make sure that your adviser is a member of one of the major financial planner organizations. It's a sign that they are in good standing within their own professional community and some assurance that they're up to date on current law and economic conditions. We recommend that you check the National Association of Personal Financial Advisors (www.napfa.org) and the Financial Planning Association (www.fpanet.org). Both sites have directories of planners in your area and helpful articles on how to find a planner who suits your needs.

Check State and Federal Websites

Don't work with an adviser who isn't listed with either the federal Securities and Exchange Commission (SEC) or your state's security licensing authority. It's an indication that they aren't properly licensed.

Some advisers who give advice about buying securities, called investment advisers, have to submit certain information to the SEC. Most financial planners are investment advisers, because they do provide advice concerning the purchase of securities. Not all investment advisers, though, are financial planners—they may not offer advice on all aspects of your financial situation, including retirement, income taxation, and estate planning.

Any person who manages assets of $100 million or more has to file a document (Form ADV) annually with the SEC. The form has two parts. Part One has information about an investment adviser's education, business, and any disciplinary history. You can look up this information at the SEC's public disclosure website, www.sec.gov; under "Education," select "Check Your Investment Professional." Part Two details an investment adviser's fees, services, and investment strategies. Advisers must give you this information if you ask for it.

Investment advisers who manage less than $100 million in assets must disclose similar information to their home state's agency that regulates investments in securities. You can find out which state agency or department regulates securities in your state at the North American Securities Administrators Association's website at www.nasaa.org. Click on "Contact Your Regulator."

Compensation

It helps to know how your financial planner is making money before you begin to work together. Will your adviser make money because of which stocks you buy, or will you pay for advice by the hour or the year? Financial planners are compensated in one of three ways: fee-only, commission, or a combination of the two. Honest, competent planners work under each model. In truth, the method of compensation matters less than the quality of the advice and services you're getting. Our point is simply to encourage you to understand how your adviser's business is structured before you sign up.

Fee-only. Fee-only planners charge just for their advice. Some charge by the hour, commonly at a rate of $75 to $250/hour. Some charge by the service they provide—for example, they might create a financial plan, outlining trust investments, for a fee of $500 to $1,500. Some charge an annual fee based on the size of the assets they'll be managing for you, usually 0.75% to 2%, depending on the size of the account. Because they don't benefit from any of the investments you ultimately make, fee-only planners argue that they provide the most unbiased opinions about what you should do and the widest possible choice of financial options. This is certainly possible, but what really matters is whether their advice suits your needs and they have expertise in advising trustees.

Commission. Planners who work on commission make their money from the investments that you make following their advice. You don't write them a check; instead, you give them money to buy, say, a mutual fund, and they receive a commission from the mutual fund's owners. Ultimately, these commissions are built into the cost of the products, so you do end up paying for their advice, just not directly. Ethical commission-based advisers feel that this compensation model can serve clients well, especially those who don't have a lot of assets. (Many fee-based planners have account minimums; few commission-based planners do.) Further, they argue that unless they are investing your assets well, you'll simply take your business elsewhere, so that the incentives for both of you are consistent. Unethical commission-based planners act less like planners and more like salespeople, trying to steer clients toward the investments that bring them the biggest commissions.

Hybrid: fees and compensation. Some planners, often called fee-based planners, combine both models. They offer advice for a fee that is either offset by the commissions they earn or provide some services for a fee, such as the creation of a written financial plan, along with some that generate a commission for them, such as the purchase of specific mutual funds or life insurance products.

Ask Questions

After you've gotten several referrals and investigated credentials and professional associations, it's time to make an appointment, to see what you think in person. Most advisers do offer a free initial consultation. When you go, here are some questions to ask:

- What experience do you have in managing ongoing trusts?
- What qualifications do you have that are specifically relevant to trust investments, as opposed to individual investments?
- What's your specific investment policy? (You're looking for someone who understands that trusts must have diversified, balanced portfolios, not someone who likes high-risk investing.)
- Are you familiar with the Prudent Investor Act? (You want to find an adviser who doesn't mumble, "Let me get back to you on that." Anyone who has worked with trustees before will know the law well.)
- How are you compensated for your services?
- How can I be sure that you're giving me objective investment advice?
- Will you give me a written engagement letter detailing the services that you will provide and their cost to the trust?
- Can you give me references—clients who have had similar assets and similar objectives?
- Can you provide a cost estimate for your services in the first year of trust administration and after?
- Have you ever been formally disciplined by any regulatory agency?

If the planner is dismissive of your concerns, unable to answer your questions clearly, or unwilling to commit to a written description of the services that will be provided, steer clear.

Trust Accountings

You may not need help with creating a trust accounting—a document showing how you've managed trust assets—for the beneficiaries. (See Chapter 11 for information on how they're done and what they contain.) They don't need to be complex, just accurate. You might decide to have an expert prepare one for you the first year, and then take it from there if you're administering an ongoing trust.

If you'd like help, ask the accountant who's doing the trust's tax return or the trust administration attorney you're working with whether they prepare accountings and if so, how much they would charge to create one. It's difficult to predict an average cost, because every trust is different. Just ask the hourly rate (many lawyers have experienced paralegals prepare accountings, so it's cheaper than if they did it themselves) and how long they think preparing your trust's accounting would take.

Managing Ongoing Trusts

Most trusts end shortly after the settlor has died. But some—for example, a trust for young children—go on for years. If you're in charge, you may have a big job in front of you.

You'll have lots of decisions to make. How should you invest trust money? What can you spend trust income or principal for? If the trust owns a business, should you try to keep it running? How do you report trust income to the IRS?

Here, first we explain how to set up your particular kind of ongoing trust, so you can get organized for the long haul. Each trust has different set-up tasks because each has a distinct structure, depending on what the settlor was trying to accomplish. Then we cover the big issues you'll face as you manage the trust over the years: primarily, how to invest and distribute trust assets.

The human side of things is also very important, of course. The terms of a trust always reflect the settlor's judgments about what that trust's beneficiaries need or are capable of. Beneficiaries might not like the restrictions that the settlor put on their inheritance or understand your role in managing and distributing trust assets. That's why we devote an entire chapter (Chapter 3) to how to deal with beneficiaries.

It's easy to get lost in the financial details and forget the people who are behind the numbers. Try not to. If you become secretive or defensive about what you're doing, you could turn what might have been a cooperative relationship into an acrimonious one.

One good way to help keep that from happening is to get expert help. You can and should get experts—attorneys, financial planners, accountants, and others—to help you with allocating assets to subtrusts, investing trust assets, creating the trust's accountings, and filing trust tax returns. Getting objective and well-informed professional advice will help you be able to justify your decisions and free up your time so that you can be attentive to the beneficiaries and keep them informed about what's going on with trust assets. But even with a team of advisers, you're still the conductor of the orchestra. Each of those experts reports to you, and the more you understand about what you're asking them to do, the better you'll be about holding them accountable and making sure that they're working for you and not the other way around. (See Chapter 7 for more on working with experts.)

Kinds of Ongoing Trusts

Before getting started, you need to determine what kind of ongoing trust you're administering.

Ongoing Trusts	
If...	**You've got a...**
You are the surviving spouse, and your deceased spouse had a separate trust that left money to you in trust	Single Trust
You are the surviving spouse, and the family trust assets are to be held for your benefit in a revocable living trust	Simple Couple's Trust
You are the surviving spouse, and the family trust now divides into two trusts: the bypass (credit shelter) trust and survivor's trust	AB Trust
You are the surviving spouse, and the family trust now divides into three trusts: the bypass (credit shelter) trust, marital or QTIP trust, and survivor's trust	QTIP Trust or ABC Trust
The trust is for children or young adults	Children's Trust
The trust is for an adult or child with a disability who receives public benefits	Special Needs Trust

So far, as you identified and collected trust assets, you've been adding them to the living trust created by the settlor. Let's call that the family trust. You'll see from the table above that when the settlor dies, a trust often splits into several parts, called "subtrusts."

A subtrust holds some or all of what the family trust held before the settlor's death. If the family trust says that certain assets are to be held in trust for the surviving spouse or others, identifies beneficiaries, and sets out rules for how the money is to be distributed, it creates a subtrust. Subtrusts have different names depending on whom they benefit—for example, a subtrust may be called a "Trust for Children," or it might be called the "Survivor's Trust." The name doesn't really matter. If the trust you're administering puts certain assets aside, in trust, for the benefit of a particular person or group of people, you've got a subtrust.

Subtrusts have different purposes. Some are designed to save on estate tax after the surviving spouse dies. Others are created to manage property for children until they are mature enough to handle their own money. Others are created because the settlor wanted to provide for both a surviving spouse and children from a previous marriage. Some subtrusts provide supplemental benefits for a person with a disability, without jeopardizing essential government benefits.

If you're in charge of multiple subtrusts, get expert help to decide which trust assets will go into which subtrust. Then you'll change the legal ownership of assets from the family trust to the new subtrusts. Once that's done, you'll manage and invest the assets and follow the trust's instructions about distributing the money to beneficiaries.

Much of the rest of your ongoing trust administration job is going to be financial: paying taxes, distributing assets to the beneficiaries, and properly accounting for trust activity (Chapters 10 and 11). At some point—when the assets have all been spent, or the beneficiaries reach a certain age—you'll terminate the trust.

Trusts for Surviving Spouses

If you're the surviving spouse now in sole charge of a trust, you might be wondering whether you'll have to change the way you manage your assets or whether or not your adult children have any legal claim on the trust during their lifetimes. Relax. Even the most complex form of couple's trust is designed to provide for the surviving spouse's needs first.

If you and your spouse made a living trust together, you're probably going to be the trustee now, if the trust was intended to continue after the death of the first spouse. Typically, you will also be the sole beneficiary of the ongoing trust during your lifetime.

If you and your spouse made separate trusts, but each of you left assets for the benefit of the other (commonly done in states that do not have community property rules), the arrangement is essentially the same. You are likely to be the sole beneficiary and trustee of an ongoing trust for your lifetime. This trust could be a revocable living trust, in which case it's exactly the same as the simple couple's trust. Or it could be an irrevocable trust, in which case you should read the discussion of AB trusts below. It doesn't really matter whether you and your spouse started with one trust or two; what we care about now is what you're administering after the death of your spouse.

Simple Couple's Trust

A simple couple's trust leaves all the trust's assets for the benefit of the surviving spouse in a fully revocable trust. So, as the surviving spouse, you have complete control over trust assets. You can even revoke the trust if you choose. The trust exists only to spare your family the expense and delay of probate court proceedings after your death. It doesn't have any effect on either income tax or estate tax.

Because you can revoke the trust at any time, it's not a separate taxpayer to the IRS. If trust assets earn income, you report it under your own Social Security number, just as you did while your spouse was alive. You do *not* need to get a separate taxpayer ID number for the trust. If your late spouse's Social Security number was used to report the trust's income, you'll need to update the records of the banks and brokerage accounts so that your Social Security number is used from now on.

Read the trust document carefully to see whether it says that:

- the family trust will continue to exist for the benefit of the surviving spouse, or
- all trust assets are to be held in trust, to be known as the "survivor's trust," for the benefit of the surviving spouse.

It doesn't really make any day-to-day difference for you—you'll still have complete control over trust assets, and you'll still have the power to revoke the trust. But it does make a difference in how you hold title to the trust assets. If a new survivor's trust is created, you either need to retitle trust assets in the name of the survivor's trust, or amend the trust to say that all assets held in the name of the family trust are to be treated as assets of the survivor's trust. If the old trust continues, you won't need to retitle anything.

If your trust says the family trust will continue to exist for the benefit of the surviving spouse, you will need to notify each bank and brokerage account in writing of your spouse's death. Some institutions will accept a written letter, and others have forms that must be completed. It is important that the institution recognize that you will act as the sole trustee and that your Social Security number will be used to report trust income.

We suggest you call the toll free number of each institution before finalizing your letter. If the institution requires certain forms, they should be able to email you the appropriate paperwork or direct you to the relevant pages on their website.

> **EXAMPLE:** After Norah's husband, Nick, died, the family trust was to continue for her benefit. She sent their banks and brokerage accounts the following letter:

To Whom It May Concern:

On May 15, 20xx, my husband, Nicholas Strumland, passed away. I have enclosed a certified copy of his death certificate. He and I were the settlors and trustees of the Strumland Family Trust, dated January 1, 20xx. Account Number _____ is held in the name of this trust.

I am now the sole trustee of that trust. Please report all income from the trust account to my Social Security number, xxx-xx-xxxx.

Sincerely yours,

Norah Strumland

Norah Strumland

If your trust says that all trust assets are to be held in a survivor's trust for the benefit of the surviving spouse, and uses a new name for the new trust, you'll need to fill out change of ownership forms with your banks and brokerages. If the trust holds real estate, you must prepare and record a new deed, showing you as owner, with the county land records office.

> **EXAMPLE 1:** John and Leslie's trust specified that when one of them died, the trust's assets were to be held by the "Survivor's Trust: Bartoski Family Trust" for the benefit of the surviving spouse. When Leslie died, John had

to change the legal ownership of the bank and brokerage accounts and the house from the Bartoski Family Trust to the Survivor's Trust: Bartoski Family Trust.

The bank asked him to bring the trust and a certified copy of the death certificate to the bank to change the legal owner of the bank accounts to the Survivor's Trust. He had to send in a change of title form to the brokerage account, along with a copy of the trust and a death certificate. He had to record a deed to transfer the house from the Bartoski Family Trust to the Survivor's Trust: Bartoski Family Trust. All of the survivor's trust assets use his Social Security number as their tax identification number. John's Social Security number was the number the couple had used before Leslie died, so he didn't have to change that.

EXAMPLE 2: Julian and Glenda created a simple trust, called the Gallagher Family Trust, to hold their assets. When Glenda died, the trust continued as a trust for the benefit of Julian for his lifetime. He continued to report his income and expenses under his own Social Security number, which was the number that the family trust had used.

It's also important to notify your homeowners' insurance company that you are now serving as trustee and should be listed as the insured. A sample letter is below.

To Whom It May Concern:

My home, located at 65 Elm Drive, Pleasantville, OH, is covered by homeowners' insurance policy number 123456-999888. The home is owned by the Strumland Family Trust. On May 15, 20xx, my husband, Nicholas Strumland, passed away.

I am now the sole trustee of that trust. Please change your records to show that I, as trustee of the Strumland Family Trust, am now the insured under the policy.

Sincerely yours,

Norah Strumland
Norah Strumland

Simple Couple's Trust Checklist

☐ Find out whether the trust requires a new name, and if it does, change official records to show that assets are held by the new survivor's trust.

☐ Instruct financial institutions to report income from trust assets under your Social Security number, if they don't already.

☐ Notify your homeowners' insurance company and make sure that you're listed as the trustee for each policy that insures trust real estate.

Disclaiming Some of What You Inherit

If you discover that if you add the property your spouse left you to your own assets, your taxable estate is now larger than what can pass free of the estate tax—$11.18 million for deaths in 2018—get advice from an attorney or CPA. You have nine months after your spouse's death to do some tax planning and disclaim some of your inheritance. This is a way of formally saying "no thanks" to the money. If you disclaim a portion (or all) of your inheritance, the disclaimed property will go to whomever the trust says should inherit if you had died before your spouse. (You can't control who gets the assets.)

A disclaimer is useful if you think that you may have an estate that will be subject to estate tax, or if you want to give some assets to the next-in-line beneficiaries (your children, perhaps) before your death. If you think you may want to disclaim, you need to do so within the nine-month period and follow other tax rules, so get expert advice right away.

AB Trust

An AB trust is most commonly used by couples who want to make sure that their assets will eventually go to their children, not to anyone else, if the surviving spouse remarries. It can also be used to minimize the estate tax that is assessed at the death of the surviving spouse.

Deciding How to Split the Trust

In an AB trust, the surviving spouse is almost always the trustee. You will need to divide the trust's assets into two ongoing subtrusts:

- the bypass trust (sometimes called the exemption trust, credit shelter trust, or B trust), which holds the assets of the first spouse to die, usually up to the amount that's excluded from estate tax in the year of death, and
- the survivor's trust, which holds the surviving spouse's assets.

Both are usually for the exclusive benefit of the surviving spouse, although some bypass trusts also benefit minor children.

The survivor's trust is revocable. You can revoke or amend it at any time, and you have complete control over the trust assets. You can spend trust money on whatever you want to spend it on.

The bypass trust, however, is irrevocable; you can't terminate or amend it. Its purpose is to hold assets for the benefit of the surviving spouse in a way that doesn't make these assets part of the surviving spouse's estate at death. (The trust assets "bypass" the surviving spouse's estate—hence the name.) The bypass trust allows the surviving spouse to *use* the trust assets without *owning* them. As the surviving spouse, you can use the money only for certain purposes, and you can't change the beneficiaries who will receive the assets after your death (with limited exceptions). Depending on how your trust is drafted, you may need to prove the assets in the survivor's trust are all gone before dipping into the bypass trust. In return for all these restrictions on the use of the bypass trust, the first spouse to die will rest assured knowing that his inheritance is secure, and there could be a huge estate tax benefit if the couple is extremely wealthy.

How an AB Trust Saves on Estate Tax

The tax savings from an AB trust come at the death of the surviving spouse. When the surviving spouse dies, the money in a bypass trust isn't subject to estate tax, because that trust is not owned by the surviving spouse. Only the assets the surviving spouse owned are subject to estate tax at his or her death.

For families that have taxable estates (most don't), this can result in huge tax savings. To understand why, you have to know two things about our complicated federal estate tax laws. The first is that you can leave an unlimited amount of property to your spouse free of estate tax (as long as your spouse is a U.S. citizen). The second is that every person gets to exclude a certain amount of money from estate tax. Since 2012, married couples can share their estate tax exemptions; this is called "portability" of the exemption. (See Chapter 10 for more on the federal estate tax and portability.)

If a surviving spouse doesn't use portability, each person can use only his or her exempt amount and there's a potential (though unlikely) tax trap when the second spouse dies. Say a woman dies leaving all of her assets to her husband, as she would using a simple couple's trust or if all of their assets were held in joint tenancy. As long as her husband is a U.S. citizen, there won't be any estate tax at the woman's death, regardless of whether she is a pauper or an internet billionaire. But when the husband dies years later, the IRS will consider all of the assets owned by the husband. That means the husband's estate could be taxed on his money and his wife's money, too—if, and it's a big "if" these days, the husband dies with a taxable estate. Keep in mind that in 2018, the husband's estate would have to be over $11.18 million to be subject to estate taxes.

If the wife had put her money into an AB trust for her husband's benefit instead, he would have had lifetime use of that money for specified purposes, and no estate tax would be due on it at his death. Only the husband's assets would be subject to estate tax, and only if they were worth more than the estate tax exclusion amount in the year of the husband's death. The estate tax exclusion amount has risen more than tenfold in the last 15 years and is scheduled to remain high until at least 2025. Many couples made AB trusts before the federal estate tax exemption became so high. So, at the death of the first spouse, they must divide up the assets into subtrusts, even though the couple doesn't have a taxable estate under current exemption levels.

When it comes to allocating assets between the two subtrusts, get expert help, probably from a trust administration attorney. There are a lot of issues to consider when splitting the assets: capital gains tax, estate tax, and sometimes even income tax. It's not something you should do on your own.

One important thing to discuss with your expert adviser is the best way to deal with your home. If possible, it's usually best to place the entire residence in the survivor's trust. Here's why:

- **Refinancing.** It makes it possible for you to refinance the property in the future. If the bypass trust owns your house, you probably won't be able to use it as collateral for a loan because banks don't generally make loans on property that is owned by irrevocable trusts. This is especially important if you think you might get a reverse mortgage in the future.

- **Capital gains tax.** You will be able to exclude $250,000 of capital gains from taxation if you later sell the house, provided you used it as your principal residence for at least two of the five years before the sale. If the bypass trust owns your home, you can't take that $250,000 exclusion because trusts don't have principal residences.

- **Inheritors' tax basis.** If your children inherit the home after your death, its value at that time will become their tax basis in the property—which means that if they sell it right away they'll owe no capital gains tax, even if the house has increased greatly in value since you and your spouse first purchased the property. If the bypass trust owned your home, your children's tax basis would be the value it had when it was placed into the trust (the value of the property at the death of the first spouse to die), not what it was worth at your death. (See Chapter 10 for a discussion of tax basis.)

Putting your residence in your revocable survivor's trust is problematic, however, if there aren't enough other assets in the family trust to go in the bypass trust. One option is to put a partial interest in your house, say half, into the bypass trust and the other half into the survivor's trust. To avoid splitting the interest like this, clever lawyers can do fancy things with loans between trusts. It's definitely a discussion you need to have before making any allocations to subtrusts.

Before you can start allocating assets, you need to determine the value of each trust asset at your spouse's death. (Chapter 4 explains how.) You will plug these values into a spreadsheet, listing each asset, its date-of-death value, and how it was owned. The reason you're listing how an asset was owned is that often you'll have to transfer assets into the trust before you do the subtrust allocation. (See Chapter 5 for information on how to do this.)

Then, you and the attorney will work out an allocation of the assets to each subtrust. It's difficult to generalize about the proper way to do this. First, it depends on how the trust is written. The most common kind of bypass trust says that the size of the bypass trust cannot exceed the estate tax exclusion amount. (This is called a "formula" clause.) In other words, the trustee is supposed to put as much of the deceased spouse's property into the bypass trust assets as can pass free of estate tax. For deaths in 2018, that amount is $11.18 million, which in most families is more than enough to hold all of the deceased spouse's property. If the deceased spouse left assets worth more than that, the rest of the deceased spouse's property will be distributed to the survivor's trust.

> EXAMPLE: Harris is the successor trustee of the AB trust he created with his wife. The trust contains $4 million in total assets, owned equally by Harris and his late wife. Here's one way the trust's assets could be allocated.

Trust Assets Worksheet

Asset	How Owned	Date-of-Death Value	Bypass Trust	Survivor's Trust
House	Trust	$ 700,000	$ 350,000	$ 350,000
Rental Property	Trust	800,000	400,000	400,000
Brokerage Account	Trust	2,500,000	1,250,000	1,250,000
Total		$ 4 million	$ 2 million	$ 2 million

> If he divided up the assets like this, Harris would need his tenants to write two rent checks each month, one to each trust. And having half of his house in each trust would make it hard for him to refinance the property.

Here's another way it could be done.

	Trust Assets Worksheet			
Asset	How Owned	Date-of-Death Value	Bypass Trust	Survivor's Trust
House	Trust	$ 700,000		$ 700,000
Rental Property	Trust	800,000	$ 800,000	
Brokerage Account	Trust	2,500,000	1,200,000	1,300,000
Total		$ 4 million	$ 2 million	$ 2 million

If Harris divides up the assets this way, the rental property will be easier to administer. Tenants will write just one check, to the bypass trust. He'll be able to refinance his house because it will be entirely owned by the revocable survivor's trust. If he sells the house, he'll be able to deduct the first $250,000 from capital gains tax because he (or his revocable trust, which is the same thing for tax purposes) owns the house. Harris decides to use this allocation.

Transferring the Assets

Once you and your attorney or CPA agree on the proper allocation of the trust's assets into the bypass and survivor's trust, you have to actually transfer these assets. This is called funding the subtrusts. (Some attorneys don't formally change the legal ownership of assets from the family trust and instead use an internal ledger to record the subtrust's ownership, but we don't recommend it.)

For real estate, there's one extra step. Before you transfer your property into either subtrust, you'll need to file (record) an affidavit (a sworn statement) stating that your spouse has died and that you are now the sole trustee of the trust. This takes your spouse off of the title, so that you can then transfer the property from the family trust into a subtrust.

Formally transferring the assets creates a paper trail that you will need later. You'll be able to identify the date when the assets were transferred, and you'll have a documented value for them on this date as well. You'll also be on firm ground should the IRS ever challenge the exclusion of the bypass trust assets from the surviving spouse's taxable estate. While that happens only rarely, it's worth remembering that the whole reason the bypass trust assets can be kept out of the surviving spouse's taxable estate is that they are kept separate from the assets that the surviving spouse owns. So the more separation, the better. Finally, formal transfer of each asset will make it easier for you to track each subtrust's income and distributions, which you'll need to file tax returns each year.

You may be requesting and filling out the paperwork summarized below yourself, or your attorney may be organizing it and simply asking you to come in and sign the documents. The table below shows what you'll probably need to provide to transfer the most common kinds of assets.

> **EXAMPLE:** Trudy and her husband Jackson created an AB trust before he died. That trust held a home, rental property, and brokerage account. They each had a $1 million life insurance policy that named the trust as a beneficiary.
>
> After Jackson died on July 1, Trudy requested that her broker provide the value of her portfolio as of Jackson's date of death. The estate value is an average of the high and low trading price for each stock on July 1, and brokers have software to calculate it. She gave the broker's report, called an "EVP" (Estate Valuation and Pricing) report, to her lawyer. She had the home and rental apartment appraised. She claimed the life insurance policy proceeds and put the $1 million into a bank account that she opened in the name of the family trust. Ultimately, it will be split between the bypass and survivor's trusts.
>
> She worked with the attorney to allocate the rental property, $500,000 of the life insurance money, and half of the brokerage account into the bypass trust. The home, the other $500,000 in life insurance proceeds, and the other half of the brokerage account were allocated to the survivor's trust. She sent change of title forms to the brokerage company and bank to create the accounts owned by the bypass and survivor's trusts. The lawyer recorded an affidavit and deeds with the county land records office. The affidavit established that Trudy was the sole trustee of the family trust, and the deeds transferred the rental property to the bypass trust and the house to the survivor's trust.

Transferring Assets Into Subtrusts		
Kind of asset	**What to do**	**What the institution might require**
Bank Account	Go to the bank and fill out new paperwork, listing the new subtrust as legal owner and you as trustee.	Copy of the trust, your identification, tax ID number for the subtrust, death certificate, list of the successor trustees who will take over after your death
Brokerage Account	Fill out the brokerage company's change of title form, listing the new subtrust as the legal owner and yourself as trustee.	Copy of the trust, identification of the successor trustees, tax ID number, and death certificate, medallion guarantee (a stamp only a brokerage company or bank officer can provide)
Stock Certificates	Send them to the company's transfer agent and have them reissued in the name of the subtrust or, if the company is public, open a brokerage account for the shares.	Death certificate; tax ID number; Affidavit of Domicile; stock power
Privately Held Company	Have an attorney review the trust and business's governing documents to see whether or not the business can be transferred into a subtrust.	Depends on the business's structure, whether the surviving owners agree with the transfer, and whether or not shareholders or partners must consent
Real Estate	Record (1) sworn statement that the settlor has died and that you're the sole surviving trustee and (2) deed transferring property from the family trust to the proper subtrust.	Death certificate and property description, attached to the sworn statement

Trudy got the bypass trust its own tax identification number from the IRS. (See Chapter 4 for step-by-step instructions.) Income from assets in her revocable survivor's trust will be reported under her own Social Security number.

AB Trust Checklist

☐ Read the trust document to see how it directs you to allocate assets to subtrusts.

☐ Get a date-of-death value for the trust's assets.

☐ Allocate assets to the bypass trust and the survivor's trust.

☐ Get a tax ID number for the bypass trust. Use your Social Security number to report income from the survivor's trust.

☐ Change the title of brokerage accounts, bank accounts, and other financial assets to either the bypass trust or the survivor's trust by filing out the proper forms from the financial institutions.

☐ For real estate, record, with county land records office, (1) affidavit that states you are now sole trustee of the family trust and (2) deed that transfers the property to the proper subtrust.

☐ Notify homeowners' insurance company that insured property is now in a subtrust and that you, as trustee, should be the named insured.

QTIP Trust

A QTIP trust is a variation on the AB trust. (QTIP is an abbreviation for "Qualified Terminable Interest Property.") But instead of splitting into two ongoing subtrusts at the first death (as an AB trust does), the family trust splits into three. Sometimes this is called an "ABC" or a "marital" trust. You're going to have this structure only if you and your spouse had so much money that a bypass trust couldn't hold the deceased spouse's half of your assets and you wanted to make sure that the deceased spouse's beneficiaries would receive all of the deceased spouse's assets following the survivor's death (instead of some assets going to the survivor's beneficiaries). This is a common goal of very wealthy couples who have children from previous marriages or are concerned about the possible effect of remarriage after the first spouse's death.

The three subtrusts created when the first spouse dies are:

- the bypass trust, which holds the assets of the first spouse to die, up to the current estate tax exclusion amount
- the QTIP trust, which holds the assets that belonged to the first spouse to die that exceeded the estate tax exclusion amount, and
- the survivor's trust, which holds the assets owned by the surviving spouse.

The survivor's trust is revocable. You can revoke or amend it at any time, and you can spend trust money on whatever you want.

The bypass trust is irrevocable; you can't revoke or amend it. Its purpose is to hold assets for your benefit in a way that doesn't make these assets part of your taxable estate at death. It lets you *use* the trust assets without *owning* them for tax purposes. As the surviving spouse, you can use the money only for certain purposes, and you can't change the beneficiaries who will receive the assets after your death (with limited exceptions). Depending on how your trust is drafted, you may need to prove the assets in the survivor's trust are all gone before dipping into the bypass trust. In return for all these restrictions on the use of the bypass trust, the first spouse to die will rest assured knowing that his inheritance is secure, and there could be a huge estate tax benefit if the couple is extremely wealthy.

The QTIP trust is also irrevocable. It holds the deceased spouse's assets that did not fit into the bypass trust. If the deceased spouse's assets aren't larger than the applicable federal estate tax exclusion, the QTIP trust may not need to be created.

If you are the surviving spouse and are administering a QTIP trust, you should also have a trust administration lawyer review the trust to see if it provides you with any flexibility to use the portability election (discussed in more detail in Chapter 10) and fund the QTIP trust instead of the bypass trust.

Some trusts drafted after 2013 provide the surviving spouse with options in trust funding that earlier trusts did not (because before 2013 there was no use for it). Basically, after the first death, these new provisions allow the surviving spouse to consider whether the survivor's estate will likely be subject to estate taxes, given the value of the couple's assets (trust, retirement, insurance, and other assets outside the trust) and the current federal estate tax exclusion. If it isn't likely that the total value will exceed the estate tax exclusion at the survivor's death, then the trust instrument may allow the survivor to choose to fund the QTIP trust instead of the bypass trust with the decedent's assets. Keep in mind that a purpose of the bypass trust is to bypass estate taxes, but if that isn't a concern, and if the bypass trust was established primarily to ensure that the trust assets will be distributed to the first spouse's children after the surviving spouse's death, then we consider other tax implications of trust funding. By funding the QTIP trust instead of the bypass trust, you will be able to save the first spouse to die's children from paying capital gains taxes on the sale of appreciated assets after your death. Assets held in the QTIP trust will count toward your taxable estate but will also get what's called a "stepped-up" basis on all those assets. This means that the deceased spouse's children will inherit those assets at your date-of-death value, reducing or eliminating capital gains taxes when those children sell those assets after your death.

> EXAMPLE 1: Sebastian's wife, Zoe, died in 2016. Her assets totaled $2 million. After consulting with his CPA and attorney, Sebastian decided to fund the QTIP trust with Zoe's $2 million, not the bypass trust. He was advised to do so because, with a total estate of $4 million, Sebastian wasn't going to have a taxable estate at his death, and it would be helpful to his children to inherit all of those assets at the higher basis at Sebastian's death.

> EXAMPLE 2: Anna's husband, Cliff, left an estate worth $12 million. At his death in 2018, the federal estate tax exclusion was $11.18 million. Anna funded the bypass trust with $11.18 million of his assets and the QTIP trust with the remaining $820,000.

EXAMPLE 3: Richard's wife Sarah owned $5 million in assets at her death. That year, the federal estate tax exclusion was $11.18 million. Richard funded the bypass trust with $5 million. He didn't create the QTIP trust because he could avoid estate tax by putting all of the assets in the bypass trust and because that type of funding was not specifically authorized in his trust document. His attorney advised Richard that they could go to court and ask the judge for authorization to fund the QTIP trust instead of the bypass trust, but it wasn't worth the cost.

Deciding How to Split the Trust

As trustee, it's your job to value the trust's assets, appraise the real estate, and then allocate the assets among the three subtrusts. You'll definitely need expert help—your choices will have significant tax and other consequences. See the discussion of allocation in "AB Trust," above.

The QTIP Subtrust

The assets in the QTIP trust are held for the benefit of the surviving spouse for life and then go (either in trust or outright) to the final beneficiaries, usually the deceased spouse's children. It's not up to you —as the surviving spouse, you cannot revoke this trust or change its beneficiaries (with limited exceptions).

Under federal law, the surviving spouse must annually receive all of the income generated from the trust. But, some QTIP trusts say that the surviving spouse can't receive any trust principal until the assets of the survivor's trust have been used up; review your trust to see whether that's true in your case.

The purpose of the QTIP trust is to make sure that the deceased spouse controls where his or her money ultimately goes. The surviving spouse can use the money, but if there's any left, it goes to the bene-ficiaries named by the deceased spouse, and the surviving spouse can't change that except in limited circumstances. Unlike assets in the bypass trust, the assets in a QTIP trust will be subject to the estate tax in the surviving spouse's estate. But the tax due, if any, won't be due until that second death. If the surviving spouse spends all of the assets, that's fine by the IRS (although the final beneficiaries will be disappointed).

EXAMPLE: Caroline and Henry had both been married before. Caroline had a son, Doug, from her first marriage; Henry had twin girls, Sienna and Hayden, from his first marriage. After Henry died, his $15 million in assets was allocated this way:

- $11.18 million in the bypass trust
- $3.82 million in the QTIP trust.

Caroline's assets were placed in the survivor's trust. Caroline lived for another seven years. When she died, her survivor's trust had $1 million in assets. This was distributed to her son, Doug. The QTIP trust had $5 million in it. It was included in Caroline's taxable estate, but no estate tax was due because in that year, the estate tax exclusion amount was $11.35 million. The $5 million, along with the now $14 million left in the bypass trust, was divided equally between Henry's children, Sienna and Hayden.

Noncitizen Spouses: Special Rules

A QTIP trust is available only if the surviving spouse is a U.S. citizen. That's because you can avoid estate tax on large gifts to surviving spouses (gifts over the applicable exclusion amount) only if the spouse is a citizen. The IRS is concerned that a noncitizen might go back to his or her home country, where the IRS won't have the authority to collect estate tax at the survivor's death.

So if you are not a U.S. citizen, *and* your spouse left more than what could pass free of the estate tax (which excludes nearly all of us), you need to do additional tax planning. You can establish what's called a qualified domestic trust (QDOT) and get most of the tax deferral that U.S. citizens can get. If you are in this situation you will already be filing an estate tax return (IRS Form 706) with the IRS, and you should discuss this with your estate planning attorney and accountant. In a nutshell, you'll have to find a U.S. citizen or institution who will act as your cotrustee and limit the amount of principal that you can take from the trust. It's a lot more paperwork, but it will help you avoid a big estate tax bill coming due nine months after your spouse's death.

Both the bypass trust and the QTIP trust are irrevocable. They must be to accomplish certain tax objectives. As a result, each needs its own tax identification number, and you must file an annual trust tax return for each one. (Chapter 4 explains how to get a tax ID number from the IRS.)

QTIP Trust Checklist

☐ Read the trust instrument to see how it directs you to allocate assets among the bypass, QTIP, and survivor's subtrusts.

☐ Get a date-of-death value for the trust's assets.

☐ Get tax ID numbers for the bypass trust and the QTIP trust. Use your Social Security number to report income from the survivor's trust.

☐ With expert help, allocate assets among the bypass, QTIP, and survivor's subtrust.

☐ Change the title of brokerage accounts, bank accounts, and other financial assets to either the bypass trust, the QTIP trust, or the survivor's trust by filling out the proper forms from the financial institutions.

☐ For real estate, record, with county land records office, (1) affidavit that states you are now sole trustee of the family trust and (2) deed that transfers the property to the proper subtrust.

☐ Notify homeowners' insurance company that insured property is now in a subtrust and that you, as trustee, should be the named insured.

Trusts for Children

Many parents of young children leave money to them in a trust until they are relatively mature adults. The trust will hold all of the family trust's assets (and also life insurance proceeds and retirement accounts, if the trust was named as the beneficiary of those accounts) for the benefit of children until they reach 25, 30, or whatever age their parents felt was reasonable for the children to invest and manage the money on their own.

The family trust may require you to establish a separate trust for each child or to combine the assets in a "sprinkling" or "pot" trust that pools the money for all the children. If your trust requires the creation of separate trusts or a sprinkling trust, see a lawyer to make sure that you're doing it properly. Basically, you're going to be setting up a new trust or trusts for the benefit of the children. Because a trust for children is irrevocable, you'll need to get a tax identification number for each separate trust or one for the pot trust. (Instructions are in Chapter 4.)

Once you've got the taxpayer ID number, you will transfer the assets from the family trust to the new children's trust or trusts. If you will be splitting the family trust into separate subtrusts for multiple children, it is especially important to get real estate appraised and determine current values for all bank and brokerage accounts to be sure the trust assets are allocated as the trust directs. For example, if you are supposed to split assets equally among three subtrusts, you can't do it without knowing what the assets are worth. (See the discussion of valuing assets in Chapter 4.)

If you are administering a trust established by a single person, the children's trust or trusts will probably be created immediately after the settlor's death. If a married couple created the trust, it is possible that some of the assets used to fund the children's trust or trusts came from the bypass trust and the rest from the survivor's trust. You will need to reappraise the assets in both the bypass trust and the survivor's trust after the survivor's death to ascertain the value of the trusts and to determine how to divide the assets among the children's subtrusts.

> **EXAMPLE:** Judith is the trustee of her brother's living trust. The trust directed her to create a sprinkling trust for her brother's three children, all of whom were under age 18 at his death. The trust held a house, a bank account, and a brokerage account. Her brother also had a $1 million life insurance policy that named the trust as the beneficiary.

Taking over as trustee, Judith went to the IRS website and got a tax identification number for the children's trust. She had the house appraised and determined the date-of-death value of the bank and brokerage accounts. She claimed the life insurance policy proceeds and put the money into a bank account that she opened in the name of the children's trust, using the trust's tax ID number.

She sent change of title forms to the brokerage company and bank to create the accounts owned by the children's trust. The lawyer filed an affidavit and deed with the county land office, first to establish that Judith was the successor trustee of the family trust and then to transfer the house to the children's trust.

As trustee of a child's trust, you'll have lots of decisions to make over the years about both investment and, especially, distributions. In other words, what should you spend the finite trust funds on? See "Who Gets Trust Money and When?" below.

Children's Trust Checklist

☐ Read the trust document to see whether the trust assets should be split into separate shares or held in one sprinkling trust.

☐ Get a date-of-death value for the trust's assets.

☐ Get a tax ID number for the children's trust (or for each child's trust, if there is more than one).

☐ Change the title of brokerage accounts, bank accounts, and other financial assets to either the bypass trust or the survivor's trust by filling out the proper forms from the financial institutions.

☐ For real estate, record, with county land records office, (1) affidavit that states you are now sole trustee of the family trust and (2) deed that transfers the property to the proper subtrust.

☐ If the children's trust holds real estate, notify the homeowners' insurance company that the property is now in a subtrust and that you, as trustee, should be the named insured.

Special Needs Trusts

A settlor who wants to provide for a child with a disability who receives or is eligible for government benefits may establish what's called a special needs (or supplemental needs) trust. Special needs trusts are carefully constructed. They provide money that supplements, but does not replace, government services that are available for the disabled.

When such a trust is created, the beneficiary's "designated payee" (the person who receives the beneficiary's benefit checks), must disclose the existence of the trust to the agencies that pay for the beneficiary's care, including the Social Security Administration and state department of health services. In some circumstances, the agencies may request a copy of the trust as well. Like other irrevocable trusts, a special needs trust needs its own taxpayer ID number (see Chapter 4) and must file an annual trust tax return.

If you are setting up a special needs trust for the benefit of someone with a disability, get expert advice right away. As long as you carefully follow the trust's requirements (and as long as that trust was properly drafted), you will be able to provide for the beneficiary without jeopardizing public benefits, but you'll definitely want to get to know an expert who can help you as needed.

A person 18 or older with a disability who has less than about $2,000 in the bank (this figure is adjusted every year for inflation) is eligible to receive Supplemental Security Income (SSI) from the federal government, along with Medicaid (known by other names in some states) from the state. Those benefits are substantial. They provide money for the person's food, clothing, shelter, and most medical coverage, including nursing home care. For someone who can't, because of a disability, get a job that provides health insurance, Medicaid can be absolutely essential. But a person who receives even a small inheritance (unless it's held in a special needs trust) will be kicked out of these government programs until the funds have all been spent, because the money makes them ineligible.

Although the government typically pays for most food, clothing, shelter, and medical needs, it doesn't pay anything to help a person enjoy life. That's where special needs trusts can make a huge difference.

For example, the trust could pay for special therapy and equipment or travel, sporting equipment, movie or theater tickets, a TV, or dental or other medical care that is not covered by Medicaid.

Commonly, a special needs trust provides that you, the trustee, can pay only for expenses that are supplemental to what government programs provide. The payments cannot be in a form that could be easily converted to cash or be used to provide for the beneficiary's basic needs that should be covered by government benefits; if you pay for food or housing, the beneficiary's monthly SSI checks will be reduced dollar-for-dollar up to a maximum of amount set annually by the federal government.

> **EXAMPLE:** Naomi is the trustee of a special needs trust for the benefit of her cousin, Mathilda, who is severely autistic and lives in San Francisco. Mathilda's favorite sports team is the Los Angeles Dodgers. Every year, Naomi pays for Mathilda to go to all of the games in which the Dodgers come to San Francisco to play the Giants. As a special treat, Naomi takes Mathilda to Los Angeles to see the Dodgers in a playoff game. Naomi can buy Mathilda a nonrefundable plane ticket, because that cannot be converted to cash for basic needs. She can also buy Mathilda some souvenirs at the game. But Naomi cannot pay for a hotel room for the trip, because that is technically shelter, and the payment could reduce Mathilda's SSI for the month. Instead, Naomi and Mathilda spend the night with family friends who live near the Dodgers' ballpark.

The rules for what you can spend trust money on are complex. But all people with special needs trusts confront the same issues, so one good source of information is likely to be a family support group, if there's one in your area. Another, if you can afford it, is to consult with a lawyer who specializes in working with special needs trusts. Another still may be to consult your county agency, called a Regional Center, that assists people with developmental disabilities, about its guidelines for proper use of special needs trust funds. The agency may have its own guidelines for what are permissible and disallowed expenses, and it may advise you of when the government is willing to look the other way (especially on travel expenses, because most tickets can be resold or returned, and one night of hotel is hardly "shelter").

It is sad, but we've encountered trustees who make no distributions from a special needs trust because they are so worried that the government will come after them for a mistaken expenditure. Don't be that overcautious—the trust won't fulfill its purpose if the money is never used for the beneficiary. Just do the best that you can to stay within the rules. If you make an ineligible payment, and the government decides to reduce the beneficiary's monthly check, you might decide that the enhancement to the beneficiary's life was worth it.

Special Needs Trust Checklist

☐ Get expert help to establish and administer the trust.

☐ Get a tax ID number for the trust.

☐ Transfer the specified assets to accounts in the name of the special needs trust.

☐ Notify the Social Security Administration and the state department of health services of the existence of the trust

---

RESOURCE

Special Needs Trusts, **by Kevin Urbatsch and Michele Fuller (Nolo),** does a great job of explaining what you can and can't use trust assets for. It also provides clear, concise explanations of the government's requirements for special needs trusts. The website of the National Alliance on Mental Illness, www.nami. org, is very helpful, with good information on special needs estate planning.

Who Gets Trust Money and When?

Every trust identifies its beneficiaries. Sometimes one beneficiary, such as the surviving spouse, receives money for life, and other beneficiaries, such as children, receive what's left of the trust assets after that. If that's the case, the surviving spouse is the primary beneficiary—the one who receives trust assets first. The children are the "remainder" beneficiaries, who receive trust assets only after the primary beneficiary dies.

It's also common to distinguish between income beneficiaries and those who are entitled to receive trust assets (principal). Often the surviving spouse receives the income generated by trust assets. (Income includes interest earned on trust investments, cash dividends, and rents.) Other beneficiaries may receive principal either now or at some point in the future.

Trusts set out standards for you, as trustee, to follow when you make distributions of principal and income. They may be broad, general standards—for example, directing you to use trust principal for the surviving spouse's "comfort, welfare, and happiness." Or they may be quite specific, such as limiting you to use trust principal only to pay for a beneficiary's education at an accredited four-year college or university.

A well-drafted trust clearly states who is entitled to money, when they are entitled to it, under what circumstances, and what it can be used for. As trustee, it's your job to follow those rules as best you can. Here are examples of the standards that we see most often.

Trust Accounting Vocabulary

- **Principal.** Assets that the trust owns.
- **Income.** Rent, profits, dividends, or royalties earned on principal.
- **Distribution.** Payment by the trustee from the trust to a beneficiary.

Simple Couple's Trust: Distributions for "Comfort, Welfare, and Happiness"

If you are the surviving spouse and have a survivor's trust, the most common distribution standard is that all trust income is to be distributed to you annually and that the principal is available for your "comfort, welfare, and happiness." This is a lawyerly way of saying that there are no legal restrictions on your use of the money. You are free to use it, give it away, invest it, or spend it as you wish.

EXAMPLE: Julian and Rebecca created a simple couple's trust. The trust stated that after one spouse died, all of the trust assets were to be held for the survivor's benefit and could be used for the survivor's welfare, comfort, and happiness. After Rebecca's death, Julian simply went on using the trust assets as he had before.

Bypass or Children's Trust: Distributions for "Health, Education, Maintenance, and Support"

Trusts almost always direct that income from a bypass trust is to be used for the benefit of the surviving spouse, and sometimes for minor children. The principal, however, typically can be used only for a beneficiary's "health, education, maintenance, and support." We tell our clients that this means that the money can be used for anything a beneficiary *needs*, but not everything a beneficiary *wants*.

Bypass Trusts

The distinction between what a beneficiary wants and needs gets to the primary tax purpose of a couple's bypass trust. (That's the irrevocable trust created when one spouse dies after setting up an AB or QTIP trust.) That trust is created to keep the assets in it from being taxed in the surviving spouse's taxable estate at death. To get that tax benefit, the spouse can use the money but cannot own it—which means the spouse can't have unfettered control over it.

If the surviving spouse did own the trust assets, the assets would be included in his or her estate for estate tax purposes. That's why estate planners don't allow unrestricted use for things like "comfort and happiness." Instead, they require that the spouse use the money only for "health, education, maintenance, and support."

Over the years, the IRS and the courts have interpreted this standard to mean that the trustee can pay out of principal whatever the surviving spouse needs to maintain the standard of living the couple had before the first spouse's death. What's important about the standard is that, at least theoretically, a third party, like a judge, could figure out whether or not you were spending it in the way you had before your spouse's death. They could look at what you spent then and what you spend now and compare the two.

When might this ever happen? It's unlikely, but an unhappy remainder beneficiary could sue you for breach of your fiduciary duty for improperly distributing trust principal to yourself (which would reduce the beneficiary's eventual inheritance). Keep in mind that your spouse's primary purpose for creating the bypass trust may not have been tax-driven, but instead could have been to ensure that his or her assets would be preserved for the spouse's children and the principal would be available only for those needs which are not covered by your own assets and income. Or the IRS could contend that assets in the bypass trust should be taxed in the surviving spouse's estate, on the grounds that you (the surviving spouse) treated the bypass trust as your personal piggy bank and didn't limit your withdrawals to health, education, maintenance, and support. That's unlikely, too. But you still want to understand why that standard is stated in the trust and why you must follow it.

From a practical perspective, you will first use the money in your survivor's trust, which *is* available for your unrestricted use. This makes tax sense, because this money will be subject to the estate tax at your death if you don't use it up. Normally, you would take money out of the bypass trust only when you truly need it for your health, education, maintenance, or support—things that you really need, not just want. After all, bypass trust money will pass tax free to children or others if you don't spend it.

> **EXAMPLE:** Harlin and Judy created an AB trust. After Harlin died, Judy worked with her attorney to divide the assets into a bypass trust and a survivor's trust. She continued to live just as she had before Harlin's death. She took annual vacations to exotic locales, maintained the house, and bought annual subscriptions to the theater and symphony. Her survivor's trust had sufficient assets to pay for it all, and she regularly received income from the bypass trust as required by the trust instrument. She didn't need to withdraw any principal from the bypass trust until the house needed a major plumbing repair.

Children's Trusts

Ongoing trusts for children typically use the "health, education, maintenance, and support" distribution standard as well. That's because it gives the trustee the discretion to decide whether a beneficiary's request is reasonable in light of the trust's purpose and the settlor's intention to provide for a young beneficiary's needs. If a trustee and a beneficiary don't agree as to whether a particular item is a "need" or a "want," it's the trustee's call.

> **EXAMPLE:** Fred is 18 years old and the primary beneficiary of a trust created by his grandmother, Georgia. Georgia's trust authorizes the trustee to make distributions of trust principal for Fred's health, education, maintenance, and support. Fred lives with his parents in a modest suburban home and just graduated from the local public high school, like most of the kids in his neighborhood. It would be appropriate for the trustee to buy Fred a sensible car so that he can attend community college and get to his part-time job. It would not be appropriate for the trustee to buy him a cherry red Mercedes.

Taking Other Resources Into Account

An important part of trust distribution rules is whether or not, when making distribution decisions, you are supposed to take into consideration a beneficiary's other sources of income. If you must consider other sources of income, and the beneficiary appears to have basic needs covered, you aren't required to make distributions.

> **EXAMPLE 1:** Peter, a college student, is the beneficiary of a child's trust. The trustee is to use trust principal for his health, education, maintenance, and support, taking into consideration his other sources of income. Peter's parents left him a 529 college savings plan that completely covers his tuition at a state college. His grandparents currently pay his rent and food expenses. He works part time at the college bookstore. Janice, his aunt and the trustee of his trust, does not distribute principal to him for the fall semester.

> **EXAMPLE 2:** Jonah is the trustee of a trust established by his father for his four nephews and nieces. The trust is to be used for their education and

medical expenses not covered by insurance. As trustee, Jonah is supposed to take into account all other resources available to the beneficiaries.

One beneficiary, Wilson, requests $25,000 for tuition at a local culinary school after he graduates from high school. Jonah asks Wilson for a list of his other assets and researches tuition at five local culinary programs. Jonah decides that the tuition is reasonable compared to the other schools and documents this in a file that he keeps on trust distributions. He also keeps the spreadsheet that Wilson created, along with supporting account statements, that shows that Wilson has a savings account with $2,500 in it and a part-time job at a restaurant. Because Wilson does not have any other resources to pay for tuition, Jonah pays it directly to the school's business office, just to make sure that the money is used for tuition and not for anything else.

If you are directed not to take these other sources of income into account, though, the fact that a beneficiary is already financially stable shouldn't affect your distributions to them.

EXAMPLE: Joan is the beneficiary of a trust established by her parents. The trust's terms direct the trustee to distribute trust principal for Joan's main-tenance and support if "the trust's income is insufficient for this purpose." The trust does not require the trustee to consider other sources of income for Joan; in fact, it makes that inquiry irrelevant. If the trust's income doesn't cover Joan's basic needs (for things like food and rent in New York City, where she lives), the trustee must distribute trust principal to cover these expenses. The trustee should still get Joan to document her basic needs.

Sprinkling Trust: You Decide Who Gets What

The trust you're administering may provide that the assets are to be held for multiple primary beneficiaries—and that you decide how much each one gets. This type of trust, known as a "sprinkling trust," or a "pot trust," is most commonly used in a trust for the benefit of minor children, often until one of them begins or finishes college. At the designated milestone, the sprinkling trust is split into separate subtrusts for each beneficiary. Until the split, a sprinkling trust can be extremely challenging to administer. You have a lot of decisions to make.

EXAMPLE: Charlie is the trustee of a trust created by his aunt and uncle for the benefit of their five children (Charlie's cousins). The oldest cousin is 28 years old, and the youngest is 15. The trust directs Charlie to hold the assets in one trust for all of the cousins until the youngest turns 23.

Charlie is to use as much of the net income and principal of the trust as he deems necessary for the beneficiaries' health care, education, support, and maintenance. He has authority to spend more on some cousins than others, if he decides that it's appropriate in light of the size of the trust and the needs (current and future) of each of the cousins. Payments to each cousin come out of the trust as a whole; there are no fixed shares for each of them.

How does Charlie decide how much to spend on each beneficiary? He will have to look at the circumstances, including the value of the trust and each beneficiary's needs. If Charlie had discussed these priorities with his aunt and uncle, that would have been helpful, of course. But if he didn't, he's just going to have to do his best. The oldest cousin is done with college and able to support himself. The younger ones have college in the near future and will need help paying for tuition, housing, books, and other living expenses.

Charlie knows that his aunt and uncle paid for the older cousins' education, so he is inclined to do the same for the younger beneficiaries. If there is less than $200,000 in the trust, he may find himself pinching pennies, or encouraging the younger cousins to attend public universities, because the cost of private school could deplete the entire trust. If any child has special educational needs or cannot live without assistance, he may decide that those expenses are a higher priority.

It's tough to keep everybody happy. This is a familiar dilemma for any parent. Families primarily take care of what each child needs, without limiting one child's share to a fixed percentage of the family's resources. If a child gets sick or needs special care, the family does its best to provide assistance, even if that means that other children get less.

Trustees sometimes face a difficult juggling act. They have to be fair to all beneficiaries and also do their best to carry out the trust's purpose—often to provide for each beneficiary's health, education, maintenance, and support—as best they can. But if one beneficiary needs more than another, it may well mean that everyone won't receive an equal amount of trust principal. But as anyone old enough to read knows, fair doesn't always mean equal. That's why the settlor put you in charge, to make the tough choices. (See Chapter 2 for more on fiduciary duties.)

The settlor could have divided the trust into separate shares, so that each beneficiary would get an equal share of the money. Instead, the settlor chose to combine the assets in a larger trust to account for unforeseeable circumstances. It is up to you, as trustee, to exercise reasonable judgment to care for the beloved beneficiaries.

Mandatory Distributions at Particular Times

Some trusts instruct the trustee to give a beneficiary a certain amount of principal at a certain time. Here are some of the most common scenarios.

Achieving Milestones

Your job is simple if the trust directs you to give money at a certain time. Usually, it's when the beneficiary reaches a certain age or achieves a certain goal, such as college graduation. If the beneficiary reaches that age or goal, you must make the required distribution of principal. You don't have a choice, even if you suspect that the beneficiary will squander the funds.

> EXAMPLE: Dora's trust provides that her son, Mario, will receive all of the income from the trust annually. At age 25 or at college graduation, whichever occurs sooner, Mario will receive half of the balance of the trust.
>
> At age 22, Mario has just graduated from college. He doesn't have a job, is living with his girlfriend and her family, and hasn't visited his grandmother in three years. Can the trustee withhold the funds and make Mario wait until age 25? No. The trust instrument requires the trustee to distribute half of the trust funds to Mario at college graduation. This is not a discretionary distribution, determined by Mario's actual needs; it's mandatory.

Fixed Regular Distributions: Annuities

Sometimes a settlor wants to give a beneficiary more than just the income that trust assets generate, but doesn't want to give the trustee the authority (and the pressure) to decide on amounts. The settlor may instead decide to give a beneficiary a fixed amount every month or year.

> EXAMPLE: John has two children and an elderly mother, Mildred. He wants to make sure that his children get the bulk of his property, but he also is concerned about taking care of his mother if she survives him. Currently, he gives her a little something each month. John decides to leave most of his assets in trust to his children, but sets aside $40,000 in a separate trust for Mildred's benefit.
>
> It's more trouble to set up a separate trust, but he doesn't want to make his children and his mother beneficiaries of one trust, because that could end up making them compete against each other for the funds. It could also give the trustee impossible decisions to make—if his mother became ill, how would the trustee decide between paying medical expenses and paying for a child's college education?
>
> Following John's death, every month, the trustee is to transfer $500 to Mildred's bank account so that she can spend it as she wishes. It doesn't matter whether the money comes from earned interest or principal; the payments are fixed. The money should last almost seven years; given Mildred's age, it is unlikely the trust will be depleted by her death. Following Mildred's death, whatever's left in her trust will go to John's children in trust.
>
> The purchasing power of the $500 payments will decline over time, but given Mildred's advanced age, John is not concerned about inflation. It's possible that Mildred may have unanticipated needs that the payments won't cover and the trustee can't accommodate. But John knows that his siblings could help with emergencies. He just wants to make sure that the trustee doesn't have to deal with her day-to-day concerns about being short of funds.

Fixed Percentage Payments: Unitrusts

A settlor who is concerned about inflation and wants to strike a balance between the primary beneficiaries and the remainder beneficiaries may decide to give a primary beneficiary a fixed percentage of the value of the trust, calculated annually. This is called a "unitrust" amount.

The amount the beneficiary receives changes every year, but the percentage does not. If the assets in the trust appreciate, the payment grows as well. If the assets lose value, trust payments decline.

> **EXAMPLE:** Gabriel creates a unitrust that will benefit his friend Sasha for the rest of her life. After her death, what's left will be distributed to his favorite charity. Each year, Sasha will get 4% of the value of the trust as of January 1.
>
> Every year, on January 1, the trustee will calculate the value of all of the assets in the trust, using the market value of the securities on that date or the appraised value of real estate. The trustee will then pay Sasha 4% of that value, either from income or principal. If the assets grow in value (or more than 4% income is earned by the trust), the trust will be worth more the next year, and Sasha will receive a larger payment. If trust investments do not have a good year, Sasha will get less the next year.

Typically, if the settlor chose the unitrust option, you don't have any discretion when it comes to payments. You do not get to spend principal if the beneficiary has extraordinary, unexpected needs. The beneficiary simply gets the unitrust amount, regardless of need, at any given time.

Incentive Trust: Payments When Beneficiaries Earn Them

Some parents or grandparents worry that a beneficiary who inherits a lot of money (also known as a "trust fund baby" or "trustfundista") may be unmotivated to work. One way to attack this problem is to create what's called an incentive trust, which gives beneficiaries money only if they're doing something productive with their lives. It's typically a feature of trusts for the very wealthy (who, unlike most of us, have enough money to threaten their children's moral standards), but some middle-class parents do provide incentives for children.

Typically, an incentive trust directs the trustee to distribute income or principal to the beneficiary only in amounts that match what the beneficiary earns. A beneficiary who spends a year sitting on the couch watching TV and playing video games won't get any trust money that year. A beneficiary who earns money as a firefighter, teacher, or independent film producer will get matching funds, usually dollar for dollar, from the trust.

If you are the trustee of an incentive trust, you'll probably have another way to give the beneficiary money as well. It's common for these trusts to allow discretionary payments to a beneficiary who is productive but doesn't earn money. For example, a beneficiary might choose to stay home and raise a family, care for an elderly relative, or work as a volunteer. If you think those activities are worthwhile, you usually have the discretion to make payments to the beneficiary. You might give someone a distribution equivalent to the salary they would earn in a similar job, or provide enough money for living expenses; it would depend on what the trust says and what the beneficiary needs.

A variation of the incentive trust is a trust that requires the beneficiary to beat a drug, alcohol, or other addiction before receiving trust funds. We have drafted trusts that require a beneficiary to spend a certain period of time in an inpatient treatment center, complete an AA program, or stay out of jail to inherit from the trust. Just like the earnings-matching incentive trust, though, the beneficiary has to be motivated to act. The financial incentive may be just enough to give the beneficiary the proverbial kick in the pants that the settlor was not able to give before.

It takes a lot of communication between beneficiaries and trustees to make incentive trusts work smoothly. As trustee, you may need to review the beneficiary's income tax returns, check up with employers, confirm AA attendance, or take other similar steps before you can make distributions. Keep in mind that any settlor who chose to create an incentive trust had concerns about the beneficiary's motivation. If the beneficiary falls off the wagon or goes back to bad habits, it is not your fault. Sometimes money is not enough.

Investing Trust Assets

A big part of your job as trustee of an ongoing trust is to manage the trust's investments. There is no standard mix of investments that's right for every trust—it depends on the goals of the trust. To determine the kind of investments you can and should make, look to the terms of the trust itself and state law.

The trust. If the trust gives you specific directions on investing, you are bound to follow them. For example, a trust might forbid you from investing in a certain industry, such as diamond mining, or require that a certain percentage of the trust's assets be invested in no-load mutual funds or certificates of deposit.

State law. Most trusts don't have specific investment instructions, but state statutes set out trust investment standards. Every state has laws that require you to exercise reasonable care, skill, and caution in managing the trust's assets.

Common law. Trustees also have duties under "common law"—a set of customs and practices that have been developed and enforced by courts over many, many years. You have a duty to make trust assets productive, which means that they generate income or increase in value. You also have a duty to get rid of unproductive assets, such as houses that sit empty or investment accounts earning minimal interest.

The Duty to Invest Prudently

Almost all states have adopted a set of standards for how trustees should make investment decisions, generally called the Prudent Investor Rule. The particulars come from either a law called the Uniform Prudent Investors Act (adopted by many states) or states' own laws. These standards are a set of best practices for modern trust investment.

Under the prudent investor rule, trustees are judged by the performance of the trust's portfolio as a whole, rather than on the performance of each individual asset. You are required to use what's called modern portfolio theory, which emphasizes diversification. It's the "don't put all your eggs in one basket" theory of investing. Instead of holding one kind of asset (say stocks) or one narrow asset class (say only large blue-chip companies), the theory says that investing in many different kinds of assets and many different sectors of the economy is the best way to balance out the risks inherent in investment. By owning assets that act differently from one another (stocks may go up when bonds go down), the overall portfolio won't be so volatile.

Managing risk against the trust's desired return is your central consideration. Your job as trustee is not just to preserve the trust's value (making sure that its assets don't decrease in value), but to maintain its value in the face of inflation.

Old Law: The "Prudent Man" Rule

The old rule, known as the "Prudent Man (or Person) Rule," evaluated a trustee with respect to each individual trust investment. If one investment lost value, a trustee could be held accountable for the loss, even if the rest of the portfolio had grown. The only defense was to prove that the choice of that particular investment had been prudent. All trust investments had to generate income—trustees couldn't buy stocks that didn't, even if those stocks were growing like wildfire. (In the 1980s, for example, you couldn't have bought Microsoft stock because it didn't pay dividends.) The trustee had no duty to grow the trust's principal and only limited power to delegate investment responsibilities to professional advisers.

In practice, much to the frustration of professional money managers, this standard meant that trustees would invest only in safe investments, because there was no way to balance riskier, high-growth investments with stodgier, fixed-income ones. So trust assets were often invested in things like long-term bonds instead of stocks, even ones with great growth potential. In inflationary times, this made it hard for trusts to generate returns that could keep up. They couldn't even invest in mutual funds, because that was considered an improper delegation of investment authority to the fund's managers.

Permissible Investments

These prudent investor standards read more like government nutritional guidelines than like fabulous recipes. It's easy to say you need to balance proteins, fats, and carbohydrates in each meal, but difficult to do well in practice. It's the same with money. It's one thing to read that you must prudently balance a portfolio, but where on earth do you start?

You can invest in any kind of asset that plays an appropriate role in the risk and return objectives of the trust as a whole. That means that both high-growth stocks and fixed-income securities like bonds are just fine, as long as together they add up to a prudent investment.

You are not limited to investing in only traditional assets, such as stocks, bonds, mutual funds, and certificates of deposit. Esoteric derivatives, options, or second deeds of trust are permissible—if you understand the investments and how the risks correspond with expected return. But your job is to be prudent, not adventurous. If a promoter promises 30% annual growth and only a 5% chance of the investment failing after five years, you may take the risk for a small part of the trust portfolio—though it's hard to imagine why you would. Do not get suckered into an investment that sounds too good to be true.

To determine whether or not an investment is prudent, it's not just enough to understand how it is structured and has performed. You also need to take a broad view of all the trust's investments. Ask these questions regularly and reevaluate trust investments as the answers change:

- What's the current and expected inflation rate?
- Is the economy expanding or is it in a recession?
- Where can you get the best return for trust investments?
- How old are the beneficiaries, and what are their anticipated needs?
- If the trust directs me to take into consideration the beneficiaries' other resources, what are they?
- Is a particular asset essential to the purposes of the trust or special to one or more of the beneficiaries?
- What are the tax consequences of different investment strategies?

The trust might require you to keep a certain asset or even state that you do not have to diversify trust investments. But even if the trust gives you some relief from the basic standards of prudent investments, we strongly suggest that you stick to those standards as closely as you can. You are unlikely to be faulted by a beneficiary for diversifying to account for changes in the economy. And no beneficiary will want you to keep a security that is past its prime simply because 15 years ago the settlor said not to sell it—though you would need to inform the beneficiaries of the intended sale, explain why you thought it was prudent, and get their consent before the sale.

> **EXAMPLE:** Herbert worked at the world's leading automobile manufacturer for 25 years. In his trust, he wrote that the trustee could not sell the trust's shares of the company for any reason, because the company was a good investment and had taken care of him and his family. He specified that the stock should be distributed in equal shares to the beneficiaries when each one attained age 40.
>
> Ten years after Herbert's death, the company stock declined dramatically. Although the trust specified otherwise, the trustee decided he had to sell the stock and sent a letter to the beneficiaries, notifying them of his plan. The beneficiaries were happy that the trustee was paying attention to the stock's decline and gave their written consent to the sale. The trustee sold the stock immediately after he heard from all of the beneficiaries.

Getting Help From Investment Experts

You can hire qualified advisers and give them authority to make investment decisions, as long as you select the advisers carefully, clearly establish the scope and terms of what you're delegating to them, and periodically review their performance. (Chapter 7 explains this in detail.)

If you find a competent adviser who understands your state's investment guidelines and makes reasonable investments based on good information, you'll have done the prudent thing. Even if the portfolio doesn't grow as fast as one beneficiary might like or produce enough income to please another, you'll be able to justify what you've done as rational and responsible—in a word, prudent.

But you cannot rely on any adviser completely, even a stellar one who has done a fabulous job for other clients. You need to have a reasonable method for selecting investments and must oversee the work of the adviser. We recommend that you meet with the adviser twice a year to review the investment mix. If you don't understand the costs and expected return of any investment, either educate yourself about it or get out of the investment completely.

It's a good idea to work with your adviser to generate a written investment policy. The policy should describe the trust's assets, investment objectives, and the strategy for achieving those goals. The policy will give you something specific to review on a regular basis with the adviser and objective ways to measure whether or not the trust's portfolio is meeting your investment goals. You can, and will, revise it over time, but it's important to get your initial strategy in writing.

A written plan is a great tool for explaining to the beneficiaries what you're doing, and it protects you against charges of acting rashly or of not having a plan at all. A good way to communicate your strategy is to create a summary and share it with the beneficiaries.

The Beneficiaries' Needs

You can and should take the beneficiaries' circumstances into account when making investment decisions. For instance, if young beneficiaries live in a great school district and it makes sense for them to stay in the settlor's home for a few more years, even if that's not the best possible investment from a financial point of view, you don't have to sell the house if other trust assets can cover the beneficiaries' daily needs. Or if the family's vacation home means a lot to the beneficiaries, you don't have to sell it to raise cash, even if the property earns no rent, incurs substantial annual maintenance costs, and is unlikely to appreciate over time, as long as other trust assets provide the necessary income and principal to meet the beneficiaries' needs.

Trust Investment Strategy: Garcia Family Trust

Background. The Garcia Family Trust was created on May 18, 20xx by Ralph and Adela Garcia. Upon Ralph's death, the assets were held in trust for the benefit of Adela, who died ten years later. The successor trustee is Raul Garcia.

Trust directions. The trust states that after Adela's death, each child (Raul Garcia, Louisa Garcia Ramirez, Angel Garcia, and Julie Garcia) shall receive an equal share upon reaching the age of 26. While the assets are held in trust, they are to be distributed at the discretion of the trustee for the health, education, maintenance, and support of the trust beneficiaries. The trust states that the trust assets are to be invested using the Uniform Prudent Investor Act, which requires that the trustee diversify investments, exercise reasonable judgment in picking investments, and balance risk with potential return.

Trust assets. The trust assets are a house, cash, and marketable securities currently worth a total of $1,825,000.

Immediate distributions to beneficiaries. Raul Garcia is 30, and Louisa Garcia Ramirez is 28, which means each of them is entitled to receive their shares of the trust assets outright. Angel Garcia and Julie Garcia are both 21, so the trustee will invest their shares until they reach 26.

Specific investment goals. The trustee will sell the Garcia house and invest the cash from the sale into marketable securities. The principal is expected to appreciate 5% on an average annual basis. There will be no margin or short-sale transactions, and the portfolio will be invested in index mutual funds to minimize risk. The trustee will select an investment manager to manage the trust assets in light of these objectives. The trustee will monitor the performance of the funds at least quarterly and provide updates to the beneficiaries every quarter as well.

Once you understand what the trust directs you to do, your adviser can help you find investments that meet your objectives. For example, if a beneficiary is 17 and about to attend college, you must make investments that are liquid, so that cash will be available for tuition and books. If an income beneficiary is 80 and needs a steady stream of income, you should consider investing more heavily in bonds and other fixed-income securities.

If you're administering a unitrust—a trust that pays beneficiaries a fixed percentage of the trust's value every year—then you can simply invest for the best total return. It doesn't matter whether the investments earn ordinary income or grow with the economy, because the beneficiary is going to receive a set percentage regardless of how it's earned by the trust.

Balancing the Needs of Current and Future Beneficiaries

One thing that makes investing difficult is when some beneficiaries are entitled to receive the income the trust generates, while others are entitled to receive the principal. You have to be fair to everyone (even if the trust says you can favor one beneficiary's needs over another's). That means your trust investments have to achieve a balance between assets that produce income (rents, dividends, and interest) with those that produce growth (stocks that increase in value but don't pay much or anything in dividends). If you are the trustee and also a beneficiary, which is common, you really have to be careful, because you are forbidden to do anything that benefits yourself at the expense of other trust beneficiaries.

> **EXAMPLE 1:** Joann is the trustee of a trust created by her father, Todd. Joann's stepmother, Tandy, is the primary beneficiary and is entitled to all the income generated by trust assets. Joann and her two brothers are the remainder beneficiaries, who get nothing now but will inherit all of the trust after their stepmother dies.

Obviously, it would be in Joann's own interest to invest for growth, so that she and her brothers will have more to inherit after Tandy dies. However, Joann must be fair to all of them. She must invest in a diversified portfolio that provides both enough income for Tandy's needs and a reasonable amount of overall growth that will ultimately benefit her and her brothers.

EXAMPLE 2: Wilma is both trustee and primary beneficiary of a trust established by her late wife, Charlotte. The trust provides that Wilma is entitled to all of the income from the trust in quarterly or more frequent installments. It also states that if Wilma believes the income is insufficient, she is entitled to instruct the trustee to invest in income-producing assets, even if it limits the growth of the trust.

That means that Wilma can, if she wants to, invest trust assets solely in income-producing investments such as certificates of deposit and government bonds. If the assets in the trust don't grow over time, they will decline in purchasing power due to inflation, but Wilma will not violate her duties as trustee because the trust authorizes her to concentrate on producing income.

Handling Real Estate

You are supposed to evaluate real estate just as you would any other trust investment. Does it fit into the total trust portfolio? Is the risk-to-reward ratio within the guidelines of your investment strategy? If it's not producing income, will other trust investments provide the beneficiaries with adequate income? Does the property carry with it significant management costs, or risks from economic trends or government regulations? How much will it cost to keep it? Could you sell it for a reasonable price? These are all reasonable questions. But real estate—especially the family residence—is not just like other trust investments.

The Family Home

Many trusts own one important piece of real estate: the settlor's home, which to beneficiaries is usually more than just another investment. What to do with the house is an emotional issue as well as a financial one.

Many trusts explicitly allow the trustee to keep the settlor's home if it would be in the best interests of a beneficiary. That means that you can keep the home, even if it's not a prudent financial move, because a beneficiary needs to live there and that's in keeping with the settlor's purpose in establishing the trust. Even in the absence of such language, the prudent investor rule lets you take into account the special emotional attachment that the beneficiaries have to the home and keep it—as long as other trust assets generate enough income and principal growth to take care of their needs.

> **EXAMPLE:** Ned's trust permitted the trustee to keep his home in the trust if that were in the best interest of his young children. When Ned died, his children were in middle and high school. The house was in a terrific school district. The trustee discussed whether or not to sell the home with the children and their guardian, and together they decided it would be best to let the children to live there and finish high school. So the house was kept in trust for a few more years, while the trustee paid for property taxes and maintenance. When the youngest child started college, the trustee sold the house. She put some of the money in short-term investments so that there was money to pay for college and some in longer-term investments.

Of course it's not always simple to hang on to the settlor's home while being fair to all of the beneficiaries, which is another of your trustee duties. If one sibling wants to keep the settlor's home and live there, but three others want to sell it and invest in other assets, what are you to do? If the one who wants to stay in the home can't afford to buy out the others, or the others aren't interested in making the house into a rental property and charging their sibling fair market rent, fairness requires that the house be sold and the proceeds reinvested in more productive assets.

Commercial Real Estate and Rental Property

If your trust holds commercial real estate, you'll have to decide whether to sell or keep the property in your investment portfolio, as part of your overall investment strategy. Even if you do decide to sell it, it's your job to keep it clean, repaired, and rented until it's sold. (See Chapter 4.) If tenants don't pay rent on time, it's your duty to get them out and get the property rented to someone more reliable.

Evaluate risks. Get the property appraised and inspected so that you know of any liabilities it might subject the trust to—environmental risks such as asbestos, toxic waste, or looming large repair jobs, like plumbing fixes or a new roof. Also review any loans on the property, any leases with existing tenants, and any agreements with service providers such as contractors, building managers, gardeners, or cleaning crews. You want to make sure that you understand the terms of these contracts and obligations. You don't want to be surprised by a balloon payment due on a loan or be stuck in a contract that's way above market rates. If this feels outside of your area of expertise, get some help from a real estate lawyer, professional building manager, or other expert.

Get insurance. Make sure the property has sufficient insurance to cover the risks you've identified. The trust needs to be protected from losses from fire or natural disasters, and also from liability for accidents or injuries that might happen on the premises. Make sure that you're a "named insured," as trustee of the trust, on the insurance policies.

Let the beneficiaries know what you intend to do, either in a face-to-face meeting or by letter. If you want to sell the property and think beneficiaries might object, notify them formally of your intent to sell and give them a limited period of time in which to object. (See Chapter 3 for detail on this process.) Keep beneficiaries informed about offers you receive, price changes, and any contracts you sign with a real estate agent.

EXAMPLE 1: Marjorie and Thomas lived in their family home for 40 years. After Thomas died, Marjorie stayed in the home, which was in their simple couple's trust. After Marjorie's death, the trust assets went into a special needs trust for her son, Henry. Because Henry lived in an assisted living facility, the trustee sold the home to provide the cash needed for Henry's supplemental needs and diversify the trust's portfolio.

EXAMPLE 2: Thorton owned a four-unit apartment building in an older part of town. The property was held in the AB trust he created with his wife, Sally. After he died, the rental was allocated to the bypass trust. Working with her accountant, Sally, as successor trustee, decided to sell the building, which had appreciated a lot but didn't generate much rental income, and reinvest the proceeds for a higher rate of return over the long run. She exchanged it for another apartment building in a better section of town that generated more income. Because of the way the sale was structured, she was able to defer the capital gains tax that would otherwise have been due on the transaction.

Should You Form an LLC or a Corporation?

If you decide to keep real estate as an investment, consider whether it would be prudent to change the way the trust owns it. It might make sense to create a business entity, such as a limited liability company or a corporation, transfer the property to that entity, and have the trust own the entity. Creating a separate business entity protects other trust assets (cash, stocks, bonds, and any other real estate) from liability. If someone were injured at the building, the trust wouldn't be directly liable for the loss. The company would be liable, but only to the extent of its own assets, which might not be anything but the property itself.

RESOURCE

More for landlords. *Every Landlord's Legal Guide*, by Marcia Stewart, Janet Portman, and Ralph Warner (Nolo), covers everything you need to know if you're responsible for rental property. There's also lots of good free information in the Landlords & Tenants section of www.nolo.com.

What to Do With Business Assets

If there's a business in the trust, you may find yourself in the property management business, the owner of a family business, a member of a partnership or other business entity, or a shareholder in a private corporation. If so, get yourself competent help—owning a business is not a do-it-yourself trustee moment. You'll have a lot of decisions to make, and you're going to need help reviewing leases, corporate bylaws, and partnership agreements. You may also have to deal with other shareholders, partners, tenants, or customers who have their own concerns and interests.

First, check to make sure that the trust instrument authorizes you to manage the business. Usually, this is part of the laundry list of powers that trusts give to trustees. If you don't see language like that, you can continue to operate it for a reasonable period of time, until you sell it, but you'll need to get court authority to manage it long-term.

But do you want to run it? Businesses tend to be the hardest trust assets to manage. Not only that, but if the trust owns a piece of a sole proprietorship (solo business) or a general partnership, you will be personally liable for the business debts if trust assets aren't sufficient to cover them and you caused the debts. If the trust owns a corporation or LLC, you must carefully observe all the legal formalities to make sure that you or the trust aren't liable for the business's debts. If that's not enough to keep you awake at night, we don't know what is.

Some businesses, like dental practices or law offices, require that the owner be professionally licensed. If you don't have those credentials, you'll need to sell the practice to someone who does.

Also consider the issue of management skill. A business without competent management isn't likely to remain profitable for long. The settlor may have been great at running the business—but that doesn't mean that you are. The business may not generate enough cash to allow you to hire a good manager. If the settlor had partners, or other shareholders, they may be unwilling to work with you. There may be agreements in place that forbid them to work with you.

Trust Issues With Common Business Entities	
General Partnership	The trust may need specific authority, granted by the partnership agreement, to participate in the partnership. Partners may have the right to reject a trust. Partners have unlimited liability for partnership's debts. Often partners have an agreement that lets surviving partners buy out a deceased partner's interest.
Limited Partnership or Limited Liability Company	The trust would have limited liability and no management control. You should decide if the investment itself is a prudent one for the trust to hold; it may be hard to sell. Often the partners have some sort of agreement in place that lets surviving partners buy out the deceased partner's interest.
Closely Held Corporation	Family-held corporations are often placed in trusts. The trust's liability is limited to the equity of the corporation. If the stock isn't producing either dividends or growth, you may have to sell it and diversify the trust's portfolio. The trust may, however, let you hold the stock.
S Corporation	S corporation shareholders are taxed as if they were partners. The corporation itself pays no corporate taxes. You must sell the trust's shares within two years unless the trust qualifies as an S corporation shareholder. If you want to keep the stock longer, have an attorney review the trust to see whether the trust qualifies.

And then there are family members. They may be the other managers in a family-run business and not want you to take management power away from them. They may also be trust beneficiaries, which means that they may have an interest in having the company pay out income at the expense of long-term growth. Any management decisions that you make as trustee must balance the beneficiaries' needs against what the business needs.

It all adds up to a complicated set of issues. If you think the trust is going to continue to operate the business, rather than sell it, have the business evaluated to see whether it's a prudent investment choice. Take a look at the projected cash flows, projected expenses, and projected income over the next several years. Consider the tax consequences of continued operation versus a sale.

Get yourself good advisers, such as business lawyers, brokers, or consultants, who can help you figure out whether the trust should simply sell its interest to the other partners or shareholders or continue to operate it. As with any investment decision you'll make on the trust's behalf, keep records of what you base your decision on, any analyses you have done on the business, and any data that you collect on projected income and expenses.

RESOURCE

If you do decide to sell the business, take a look at *The Complete Guide to Selling a Business*, by Fred S. Steingold (Nolo). It covers how to find the right buyer, analyze tax issues, and limit your liability. It includes sales agreements, promissory notes, and consulting agreements and more.

Dealing With Taxes

axes are going to be on your to-do list as trustee—there's just no way to avoid them. Living trusts cut probate costs, but they have no effect on tax liability. The good news is that only very large estates have long and complex tax returns to file. Many trusts, including ones that are left to surviving spouses as revocable trusts, and those that are quickly distributed to beneficiaries, won't have to file a trust tax return at all. If you do run into a complicated tax matter, expert help is available—and you can use the trust's assets to pay for it.

Even after people die, their assets (bank accounts, rental properties, investments, and the like) can continue to earn income or generate losses. So that the IRS doesn't lose a penny of taxable income, it has devised a method that captures any income that's earned from the moment a person dies until the property is transferred to the people who inherit it, when it becomes the new owners' responsibility. During that in-between time, when assets are in a trust or estate (after the owner's death but before they are transferred to inheritors) you're responsible for seeing that the trust or estate pays any tax that's due.

There's Always a Taxpayer

Think of it like a relay race, where someone is always carrying the baton around the track. There are three main players.

The personal representative (that's the IRS term) of the deceased person must file a personal income tax return for the year in which the settlor died (January 1 until the date of death). The person responsible for distributing the settlor's property is also responsible for filing the return; when the bulk of the assets are held in a living trust, it's generally the trustee. (The executor could do it, but if the money to pay the taxes will come from the trust, the trustee usually deals with the taxes.)

The trustee is responsible for reporting income earned and paying the taxes on it during the period from the date of death to the date that the property is distributed.

The beneficiaries ultimately file their own returns to report any income that they earn on the property that they inherit.

Neat, isn't it? Someone is always on the hook to pay income tax on the property, from January 1 of the year of death until it gets into the hands of those who inherit it.

> **EXAMPLE:** Sofia is the successor trustee of her brother Rafael's living trust. He dies on March 15, 2018. She distributes all of the trust assets to the beneficiary, Rafael's son Jorge, by December 31 of that year. On April 15, 2019, she files a Form 1040 individual tax return for her brother, covering his income from January 1, 2018 until his death on March 15, 2018. She also files Form 1041, *Income Tax Return for Estates and Trusts*, to report the trust's income from March 15, 2018 to December 31, 2018. Once Jorge owns the trust assets, he is responsible for paying tax on any income they produce.

Careful: You Could Be Personally Liable

The money to pay taxes comes out of the deceased person's assets, not your personal assets, unless you are the surviving spouse and are personally liable for the taxes due.

But if you fail to file the tax returns required for the trust or don't pay the tax due for the trust, or fail to adequately investigate and determine how much tax the trust owes, and distribute the trust's assets even though you know that you haven't paid all the tax due, you could be personally liable for the trust tax bill, plus the penalties and interest that result from your failure to file on time. Your liability is limited to the amount that would have been available to pay the tax, plus penalties and interest. In other words, you're on the hook for what the trust should have paid before the assets were distributed. When it comes to deciding who gets paid first, taxes take precedence over just about all other debts of the trust. Pay them first.

That means that before you distribute any money to trust beneficiaries, make absolutely sure there's enough money left in the trust to pay the taxes. If you distribute the trust assets and then find out you've got a big tax bill to pay, the IRS could go after you for up to the amount you distributed. It could also go after the beneficiaries who received property that wasn't rightly theirs (because it should have gone to the IRS), up to the amount they received.

> **EXAMPLE:** Delia is the successor trustee of her sister Sally's trust. Sally's adult daughter, Imogene, inherits all the trust property. Delia distributes Sally's house and bank accounts to Imogene—and months later, discovers that income tax is due for Sally's last year. There aren't any assets left in the trust. Imogene should pay that bill promptly to avoid having penalties and interest tacked on.

If you forget to file a trust tax return and then file it late, you are personally liable for the taxes, interest, and penalties that resulted from your error. Interest is calculated on what you owe, at a rate set by the IRS every three months. Lately, this rate has been about 4% per year. Two different penalties may be imposed:

- For failure to file a return, you are charged 5% of the tax due for each month the return is late, up to a maximum of 25% of the total.
- For failure to pay the tax, you are assessed a 0.5% penalty for each month the tax isn't paid, and there's no maximum.

If your tax preparer files the return late, even without your knowledge, interest and penalties will accrue. You could sue the tax preparer, but it's still your ultimate responsibility to get the return filed on time.

Tax Returns You May Have to File

There are three possible federal returns that might need to be filed after a death, but very few trustees have to deal with all three. (All of them are discussed in more detail later in the chapter.)

Possible Federal Tax Returns		
Kind of Return	**Required If**	**Due Date**
Final income tax return Form 1040	The deceased person earned more than a minimal amount of income in the year of death.	April 15 of the year following death
Trust income tax return Form 1041	The trust receives more than a minimal amount of income, or any taxable income.	April 15 of the year following death*
Estate tax return Form 706	The person died with more than the amount excluded from estate tax or the surviving spouse files a return solely to request "portability"—the right to use the deceased spouse's unused exemption amount. Only large estates file.	Nine months after death

* The trust can choose a different tax reporting year. See "What Reporting Year Should You Use?" below.

Final Federal Individual Income Tax Return

First, there's an individual tax return for the person who died, Form 1040, that covers the period from January 1 of the year the person died to the date of death. Unless someone died on January 1 or had very minimal income, you'll need to file this one. It is due by April 15 of the year after the death.

Federal Trust Income Tax Return

If the trust earns more than $600 of gross income, or any taxable income, you must file Form 1041, for the period from the date of the settlor's death until the end of that same taxable year. This return is usually due on April 15 of the year following the settlor's death, though you can choose a different reporting period (which we'll discuss below). Trusts that are ongoing, or that take longer to distribute than the period between the settlor's death and the end of that taxable year, will file a trust tax return for each taxable year in which the trust earns more than $600 of gross income, or any taxable income, until the trust is fully distributed.

You will **not** have to file a federal or a state tax return for your trust if:

- you distribute the trust assets quickly or the assets don't generate at least $600 in gross income, and no taxable income, or
- you are the surviving spouse and inherited your spouse's assets through a trust that leaves everything to you in a revocable living trust. You will report income or loss from those assets on your individual tax return.

Federal Estate Tax Return

Finally, for the wealthy, there's a federal estate tax return, Form 706, that is due nine months after the date of death (although the IRS will give you a six-month extension if you ask). For deaths in 2018, only estates with more than $11.18 million in taxable assets were required to file this return. That was less than 2,000 estates in the U.S. Some estates may choose to file an estate tax return even if it's not required, to take advantage of the "portability" provision available to married couples, which lets spouses share their federal estate tax exemptions. (See "The Federal Estate Tax Return," below.)

State Tax Returns

States require their own tax returns. If your state has a state income tax, you'll need to file a state income tax return for the deceased person's last year. You may also need to file a state income tax return for the trust, if it continues after the settlor's death.

Some states also have their own inheritance tax or estate tax. If there's a state estate tax, it is paid from the estate of the deceased person, before assets are distributed. (If your state has an inheritance tax, it is paid by those who inherit the property, not the estate; see "Beneficiaries and Taxes," below.)

Some states, in an effort to gain revenue, are instituting state estate taxes for the first time. Currently, about half of the states impose estate tax (which falls on the estate), inheritance tax (which falls on the beneficiaries), or both. (See "State Estate Tax," below.)

Possible State Tax Returns		
Kind of Return	**Required If**	**Due Date**
Final state income tax return	The deceased person earned more than a minimal amount of income in the year of death.	April 15 of the year following death
State trust income tax return	The trust receives more than a minimal amount of income.	Depends on state law
State estate tax return	The state has its own estate tax (most don't) and the estate is large enough—the amount varies from about $1 million to the amount of the federal estate tax exemption.	Depends on state law
State inheritance tax return	State imposes it (most don't).	Depends on state law

Beneficiaries and Taxes

As trustee, you aren't responsible for helping beneficiaries with tax matters—but of course, they may come to you for advice. Here are some basics they need to know.

Income Tax

Many people don't know that property they inherit isn't subject to income tax—so you might get to deliver this happy news.

The basic rule is that inherited property is not treated as taxable income. Someone who inherits property, however, must pay tax on any income that inherited property earns. That tax is due when the beneficiaries file their own individual Form 1040 returns.

EXAMPLE 1: Marla inherits a brokerage account worth $55,000 from her mother's trust. When she files her personal tax return on April 15 of the next year, the $55,000 she inherited is not taxable income. In the next year, she earns $1,000 in income from that account. She must, however, report and pay income tax on the $1,000 of income.

EXAMPLE 2: Michael, 23, is the beneficiary of his mother's trust, which contains a brokerage account worth $55,000. The trust directs the trustee to keep the account in trust until Michael turns 35, but to distribute all income that the account earns to Michael every year. Michael must pay income tax on that money.

The big exception to the basic rule is that people who inherit money from a tax-deferred retirement plan, such as a traditional IRA or 401(k), must pay income tax on the money as they withdraw it. (See Chapter 6 for more on this.)

Inheritance Tax

A few states levy a tax, called an inheritance tax, on people who inherit property. It's different from an estate tax.

The tax rate depends on the inheritor's family relationship with the deceased person. Spouses are always exempt from inheritance tax. Other persons pay a rate that depends on how closely they were related to the deceased person. In Pennsylvania, for example, there's a 4.5% tax on money left to one's lineal descendants (children, grandchildren, and so on), a 12% tax on money left to siblings, and a 15% tax on money left to more distant relatives. Inheritance tax is imposed by the deceased person's state, regardless of where the new owner lives.

EXAMPLE: Irving, who lives in California, inherits $100,000 worth of stock from his brother William, who was a Pennsylvania resident. A year later, Irving is surprised to receive an inheritance tax bill from Pennsylvania for $12,000 (12% of the value of the stock). Because his brother was a Pennsylvania resident, the stock is subject to Pennsylvania's inheritance tax.

States With Inheritance Tax			
State	**Max Tax Rate**	**State**	**Max Tax Rate**
Iowa	15%	Nebraska	18%
Kentucky	16%	New Jersey	16%
Maryland	10%	Pennsylvania	15%

Capital Gains Tax

When someone sells property they've inherited, they might—or might not—owe capital gains tax. It all comes down to the concept of "tax basis."

Every piece of property has a tax basis. Generally, it's the amount the owner paid for the property. When someone dies, though, the new owner's tax basis in the inherited property is its value at the former owner's death. (If the estate was large enough to file an estate tax return, the tax basis may be a different value; see "The Federal Estate Tax Return," below.) Because property generally goes up in value when it's held for long periods, the new basis is called a "stepped-up basis." It can save inheritors a bundle on taxes when inherited property is later sold.

A beneficiary who sells an inherited asset will owe long-term capital gains tax, currently at 15%, for single filers with taxable income of up to $425,800 ($479,000 for married couples filing jointly) and 20% for people above that threshold. That's why the higher the basis, the lower the tax.

> **EXAMPLE:** Carla buys a house for $100,000, so her tax basis is that amount. At her death ten years later, she leaves the house to her daughter Jennifer. The house is appraised at $200,000 as of Carla's death, so Jennifer gets a $200,000 stepped-up basis. Jennifer keeps the house as her vacation home.
>
> Five years later, Jennifer sells the house for $250,000. She will owe capital gains tax on the $50,000 difference between her basis and the sales price. In other words, she pays tax only on the gain in value from the date she inherited the property until the date she sold it.

Married couples in community property states (see Chapter 4 for a list) who own their property as community property get an even better break. The value of the whole property is stepped up, not just the half the surviving spouse inherits.

> EXAMPLE: Sumiya's husband, Ralph, passed away. They lived in California, a community property state and owned a home together as community property that they'd purchased in 1963 for $25,000. They placed the home into a living trust. When Ralph died, the property was appraised at $900,000. Because they owned the house as community property, Sumiya gets a stepped-up basis in it equal to $900,000. If she sells the house a year after Ralph's death for $900,000, she will owe no capital gains tax at all. To the IRS, it's as if she bought the house for $900,000 (its value when Ralph died) and then sold it for the same amount.

A surviving spouse who owned property as a joint tenant with the deceased spouse, and put that property into a trust, will get a stepped-up basis on half the value of the property. The other half, which already belongs to the surviving spouse, will still have its original tax basis (half of what they paid for it originally).

Property That Doesn't Get a New Tax Basis

Tax-deferred retirement plans, like 401(k)s and IRAs, go to beneficiaries without a new stepped-up tax basis. These plans let people save for retirement during their peak earning years and withdraw the money later, when they aren't earning so much. The withdrawals are taxed at whatever their income tax rate is at that later time.

People who inherit the assets in these plans are required to begin withdrawing the money by the end of the year after the original owner died, and they must pay income tax on the withdrawals. (Chapter 6 explains how withdrawals work and what options the beneficiaries have with respect to taking them quickly or slowly.)

People who inherit Roth IRAs and Roth 401(k)s must begin withdrawing the money in those accounts by the end of the year after the original owner's death, but no tax is due on these withdrawals because the owner was taxed on the money before it was deposited into these plans.

Missing Returns

If you can't find copies of old tax returns, it may be that they're just lost. But it's fairly common to discover that a deceased person forgot to file tax returns in previous years. There are lots of reasons that taxes get overlooked as people get older. Ill health might have made it difficult. Some people think that if their only income is Social Security payments, they don't need to file income tax returns. (This is not always true; it depends on the recipient's total income and marital status.)

If you're not sure whether or not returns were filed, or you just need a copy of a return that you know was filed, you can get help from the IRS. For returns filed during the previous three years, you can request:

- a free tax return transcript, which is a summary of an income tax return as it was filed
- a free tax account transcript, which shows later modifications to the original filed return, or
- a complete copy of a return, for a fee of $50.

You'll have to send the IRS a copy of the trust showing that you were named the successor trustee and certified copy of the settlor's death certificate. The transcript is the best place to start. It includes most line items contained on the return as it was originally filed. If you need a statement of the settlor's tax account which shows changes the settlor or the IRS made after the original return was filed, request a "tax account transcript." Both transcripts are generally available for the current and past three years and are provided free of charge, in about 30 days.

Getting Information on Old Returns From the IRS			
Information	Form to Submit	Cost	How Long
Tax return transcript or tax account transcript	IRS Form 4506-T, *Request for Transcript of Tax Return*	Free	10-30 days
Complete copy of a return	IRS Form 4506, *Request for Copy of Tax Return*	$50 each	60 days

You can make your requests online, through the mail, over the phone (800-908-9946), or in person at an IRS office. You can get the form you need to make these requests on the IRS website, www.irs.gov, or order a transcript at www.irs.gov with the "Get Transcript" tool.

If some tax returns never got filed, it's your job to file them on behalf of the deceased person and pay any tax due before you distribute trust assets. If you don't, you run the risk that you'll settle the trust, distribute the assets, and then get a surprise tax bill from the IRS. If the assets have been completely distributed by then, the IRS could go after you or (more likely) go after the beneficiaries for the back taxes. If they go after the beneficiaries, you can be sure that the beneficiaries will be mad at you, because by that time penalties and interest will probably have been added to the bill.

Do your best to make sure there are no such nasty surprises lurking. Ideally, you should try to find the last ten years of the settlor's filed tax returns—that way you can be sure you're not missing any. There's no time limit—that's right, no time limit—on the IRS's ability to collect unpaid taxes. If a return was never filed, theoretically the IRS could come after the beneficiaries (and you) years later. As a practical matter, the IRS tends to pursue missing returns within a year and a half after they were due, but why take a chance?

When you actually file a return, though, the IRS has only three years to assess additional tax or sue to recover the tax due. That's one reason that it's so important to get returns filed, even if you're not sure that you've got all the relevant information. You can always file an amended return if you discover some income later.

You can also ask the IRS to review the settlor's records and let you know about any taxes due by filing Form 4810, *Request for Prompt Assessment*. Once you make that request, the IRS must review the file and get back to you within nine months with a report of any taxes due. Filing this request does put the settlor on the IRS's radar, but at the same time it limits its ability to go after back taxes to 18 months from the date you file this request.

> **SEE AN EXPERT**
>
> **Don't try this yourself.** If the deceased person failed to file income tax returns, get professional help to file the missing returns.

The Final Personal Income Tax Return: Form 1040

You'll need to file a final income tax return for a deceased person for the year of death if the person earned more than a minimal amount of income. This return is exactly the same as the 1040 anyone files, except that you're supposed to write "Deceased" and the date of death across the top of it. If you are filing the return electronically, you'll enter the date of death, and the word "deceased" and the date of death should appear prominently at the top of the form. If you are the surviving spouse, you can still file this final return as married, filing jointly.

For the 2017 tax year, the filing thresholds were:

- Single person: gross income of more than $10,400
- Persons 65 or older, or blind: $11,950
- Married couple filing jointly: $20,800, plus $1,250 for each spouse over 65 or blind.

State income limits vary, but generally, if a federal return is required, so is a state return.

Even if a return is not required, it is often a good idea to file one anyway, to make sure that if there's a refund due, you'll get it. If you file Form 56, telling the IRS that you're the trustee, this refund should go to you. (We discuss Form 56 below, in "Letting the IRS Know You're in Charge.") If you didn't file that form, you will need to request a check from the IRS. It may require you to provide proof of your authority to act for the deceased person—such as a statement under oath that there's no probate proceeding and that the trust is the beneficiary of the will.

> **EXAMPLE:** Margaret, an unmarried editor, earned a gross income of $5,000 in the year of her death. Because this is less than the threshold amount, her personal representative does not have to file a 1040 return for her. He files one anyway, just in case Margaret was due any tax refund.

If a person died before filing returns for the previous year, you're going to have to file those, too.

> **EXAMPLE:** Shawna died in March 2018, before filing her 2017 income tax return. Her brother Alexander, her trustee, had to file two income tax returns for her. In April 2018, he filed one for calendar year 2017. In April 2019, he filed her final income tax return, covering January to March 2018.

Tracking Down Income

Because gross income includes more than just someone's salary, you might have to do some detective work to figure out what money came in during the last year of life. To get an accurate number, look at all sources of income from property, such as rents, interest, and dividends, as well as pensions, retirement distributions, profits from businesses, and royalties.

If you can find the person who prepared the deceased person's tax returns in prior years, you'll most likely be able to quickly gather the necessary information, or at least know where to look. If you can't, you're going to have to go through the mail and the files, to try and identify all the income that you will need to report on the final return. Look especially for the Form 1099 that banks and other financial institutions mail to taxpayers each January to report income, interest, and dividends they earned.

> **EXAMPLE:** Soriya is the successor trustee of her father's trust. During 2018, he worked until March 14; he died on June 18 of that year. Soriya has a W-2 statement from his employer showing his wages for that period. Her father's other sources of income were:
> - An account at a brokerage firm. Soriya gets the statements for the account for January through June of 2018 and records the income earned on it. She also keeps an eye out for the 1099 forms that he received in January 2018 to report income, interest, and dividends.
> - An apartment building. The rent collected for January through June is taxable income.
> - An income-bearing savings account. Soriya will need to get the bank statements issued January through July, and on that July

statement, she'll need to calculate the interest earned until June 18 to report as personal income; the rest of that month's interest goes on the trust's return.

Once you find the sources of income, you need to determine how much income to report on the final personal income tax return, and how much to report on either the trust's tax return or a beneficiary's tax return. (Remember, there's always a taxpayer.) To do this, you'll need to figure out how much income the settlor earned from the beginning of the tax year to the date of death.

> **EXAMPLE:** All of the income earned *after* Soriya's father's death—the interest on his brokerage account and savings account, as well as the rent his tenants paid from June through December of 2018—will be reported on the trust's income tax return (Form 1041). That return is due April 15, 2019. Soriya needs to file a return for the trust for 2018 because she doesn't distribute all the trust's assets to her three siblings by December 2018, and the trust earns more than $600 of gross income during this time.

If the deceased person was self-employed, you'll probably also need to pay federal self-employment tax, which is reported on Schedule SE of Form 1040, in addition to regular income tax. For deaths in 2018, self-employment tax is due if the deceased person earned more than $400.

Special Rules for Surviving Spouses

There are a few tax breaks for surviving spouses. First, you can file jointly for the last tax return (unless you remarry during that year).

Second, if you have a dependent child you may qualify for a special tax rate for two years after your spouse's death. The "qualifying widow or widower status" will lower your tax bill, because it means you are taxed at the rate that normally applies to married couples.

To qualify, you must:
- Have been entitled to file a joint return with your spouse for the year your spouse died. It doesn't matter whether or not you actually did file jointly.
- Not have remarried.

- Have a child or stepchild for whom you claim an exemption and who lived in your home all year except for temporary absences.
- Have paid more than half the cost of keeping up a home for the tax year, such as mortgage, rent, upkeep, property taxes, and utilities.

RESOURCE

For more detailed information, see IRS Publication 17, *Your Federal Income Tax*. For any federal tax forms, call the IRS at 800-TAX FORM (800-829-3676) or go to www.irs.gov and order or download them.

Logistics

You must file the final 1040 for a deceased person when it would have been filed if the person were still alive. Usually, that's April 15 of the year following the death.

If you are the surviving spouse and file a joint return, sign it yourself and add "filing as surviving spouse." If you are filing as the trustee, sign the last return yourself and write "filing as the Personal Representative for the Estate of _____ , Deceased."

The Trust's Income Tax Return: Form 1041

After the settlor's death, the next taxpayer steps up to report the income earned by the trust's assets. Think of that relay race again—the person holding the baton (the assets) has to report income and pay tax that's due. If the trust that's holding the deceased person's assets stays in existence a while and has gross income of more than $600, or any taxable income, you must file a return for the trust itself.

The trust income tax return is Form 1041, *U.S. Income Tax Return for Estates and Trusts*. It is called a "fiduciary" return because you aren't reporting personal income, but rather are reporting as the person in charge of the deceased person's assets. Form 1041 is similar in many ways to an individual Form 1040, but it's not exactly the same—there are certain things that trusts can deduct that people cannot. If you need to file a trust income tax return, get help from a tax expert. (Chapter 7 discusses different kinds of experts who can help you with taxes.)

You'll file an annual trust tax return, usually on April 15 of the following year (more on that below) every year until the trust ends. When you distribute the last of the trust assets to the beneficiaries and close down the trust, you'll file a final tax return for the trust. (See Chapter 12 for a discussion of the final return.)

If you are the surviving spouse and are in charge of a bypass trust, (an ongoing irrevocable trust that holds assets for your benefit), you'll definitely want to get expert help to create that trust and file tax returns for it. After the first few years, when you're used to the process, you might consider going it alone. (See Chapter 8 for more detail on how to set up the bypass trust.)

For the first two years of trust administration. you aren't required to file quarterly estimated tax returns. After that, if the trust is ongoing, you must begin to pay estimated taxes if you expect that the trust will earn more than $1,000 in a year.

Do You Need to File?

Not every trustee needs to file a Form 1041 income tax return. If you've got a simple trust and distribute the assets quickly, you probably won't have to file a trust tax return.

Only trusts that earn more than $600 of gross income, or *any* taxable income, in a year need to file a trust tax return. To calculate the trust's taxable income, start with its gross income and then deduct the costs of administering the trust and any tax you paid on trust real estate.

> **EXAMPLE:** Quinn is the successor trustee of her father's trust. The trust left everything in equal shares to Quinn and her brother Zack. The trust assets consisted of a house, a savings account with $10,000, and a checking account with $15,000. The trust was completely distributed to the beneficiaries four months after the settlor's death. In those four months,

the savings account earned $100 in interest, and Quinn spent $1,000 on attorney's fees. Quinn does not have to file a trust tax return because the trust earned less than $600 in gross income ($100) and had no taxable income (because of the fees paid to the attorney).

Second, only irrevocable trusts—trusts that cannot be revoked— become separate taxpayers. If you are the surviving spouse and inherited your deceased spouse's assets in a revocable simple couple's trust, you don't need to file a separate return for the trust. Any income from trust assets will simply be reported on your 1040 return as personal income.

> **EXAMPLE:** Doris and Stanley created a living trust that left everything in trust to the surviving spouse. The surviving spouse had the power to revoke this trust at any time. After Stanley died, Doris did not need to file a trust tax return and continued to report all income and expenses on her personal tax return.

What Reporting Year Should You Use?

Almost all of us report and track our personal income on a calendar year basis, from January through December. The forms that our employers and financial institutions send out in January (W-2s and 1099s) track our income in this way, too.

People, however, hardly ever die at a time that makes this reporting simple, because it takes some time to pay the trust's debts and distribute the assets. So even for a simple trust that ends after the settlor's death, you may need two trust returns: one for the calendar year of the settlor's death and one for the year after, when you finish distributing the assets to the beneficiaries.

> **EXAMPLE:** Phillip is the successor trustee of his sister's living trust. She died in October of 2018. He files an income tax return for the trust in April of 2019 to report the trust's income from October 2018 through December 2018. By the end of October 2019, he distributes all the trust assets and closes down the trust. In April of 2020, he files another return for the trust to report its 2019 income (from January through October).

You may be able to avoid having to file two trust returns, however. If the trust you are administering will last for two years or less, you can elect instead to use the 12-month period that begins on the date of death. That's called a fiscal year. If you do that, the return is due by the fourth month of the next fiscal year.

If you want to use a fiscal year that starts at the date of death, you need to let the IRS know. The easiest place to do this is when you're applying for a taxpayer ID number (EIN, discussed below) for the trust. You can check a box (called the Section 645 Election) when you apply for the number, which tells the IRS you want to treat the trust like an estate for tax purposes. That's because estates report their income from the date of death through the following 12 months. If you forget to check the box, you can still make this election when you file the trust's income tax return by including IRS Form 8855, *Election to Treat a Qualified Revocable Trust as Part of an Estate.*

> **EXAMPLE:** Phillip decides to use an October through September fiscal year for his sister's trust. He elects to treat the trust as an estate when he checks the Section 645 election box on the online EIN application. In January of 2020, he files a trust tax return to report the trust's income from October 2018 (when she passed away) through September 2019 (when the trust assets were all distributed to the beneficiaries).

There can be income tax advantages to choosing a fiscal, rather than a calendar, year for your trust's tax reporting. It can let you delay reporting income. That might help trust beneficiaries with their tax returns in the next (calendar) year, because it will postpone when they have to report and pay tax on that income. It can also help reduce the trust's tax obligations, because the strategic use of a noncalendar year may make it possible to report trust income at the same time you report a large tax expense (like your trustee's compensation) to offset that income. It's also simpler and less expensive to file one, rather than two, trust returns.

Because all financial institutions and employers use a calendar year to report income, though, using a different accounting period can make it harder to allocate income and expenses to the trust. Discuss the options with a tax expert early in the trust administration process, before you request a taxpayer ID number for the trust. Once you decide to use a fiscal year, you can't change your mind.

Getting a Taxpayer ID Number for the Trust

Before you can file a trust tax return, you need a taxpayer ID number for the trust. You can't report trust income under the deceased person's Social Security number. You need a new number that's just for the trust, called an Employer Identification Number (EIN). It's easy to get online. (Chapter 4 has step-by-step instructions.)

Once you've gotten the trust's EIN, you'll file trust returns using it, and financial institutions will report earned income using it. With its own taxpayer ID number, the trust becomes a brand-new taxpayer. This new taxpayer exists only until all of its assets are transferred to the beneficiaries, who then become the responsible taxpayers.

Letting the Right People Know

Once you've gotten a taxpayer ID number for the trust, promptly notify each institution holding trust assets that it should report income under this new number and not the settlor's Social Security number. They may have started keeping separate records as soon as you notified them of the death—they know that whenever there's a death, they need a new tax ID number to report the asset's income. (See Chapter 4 for how to notify institutions that you're taking over.)

At the end of the tax year, you should get a Form 1099 from each institution, showing the trust's income. If you're lucky you'll also get a separate Form 1099 that shows the deceased person's income from the beginning of the year until the date of death. That will really help you sort out where to report what income—on the settlor's personal return or the trust's return.

EXAMPLE: Haleigh notified the bank, the brokerage firm, and the mutual fund company that her mother had passed away on April 30. The following January she got two 1099s from each institution. The first showed the income that her mother earned from January 1 until her death on April 30. Haleigh will report this income on her mother's last personal income tax return, due on April 15. The second 1099 showed the income that the trust earned from May 1 to December 31 of the year. Haleigh will report that income on the trust's income tax return for that year.

Letting the IRS Know You're in Charge

If you're going to be filing tax returns for the trust, you have to let the IRS know that you're in charge. You do this by filing IRS Form 56, *Notice Concerning Fiduciary Relationship*. It's pretty straightforward. The form simply tells the IRS that it should send all tax-related information concerning the settlor to you. You can't file it until you get a taxpayer ID number (EIN) for the trust. (Trusts that don't generate sufficient income before they're distributed or that remain revocable won't need to file this form because you won't be filing trust tax returns.)

Send the form to the IRS office where you will be filing the deceased person's income tax return—the office where the settlor filed returns. If you can't find the address from previous tax returns, the easiest way to find it is to go to the IRS website and type "local office" into the search box. That will take you to a page where you can find your local office, www.irs.gov/uac/Contact-Your-Local-IRS-Office-1. You can also contact the IRS at 800-829-1040.

When you terminate the trust by distributing all of the assets or if you later resign as trustee, you'll use this form again to notify the IRS that you're no longer in charge or that the property has been distributed.

If you are the trustee, and a different person is the executor of the will, just one of you should send in this form. Obviously, you need to coordinate with each other to make sure that there's only one cook in the kitchen. The IRS wants to know who is responsible for the deceased person's assets—that's the fiduciary whom the IRS calls the Responsible Party. That's going to be the trustee, if the trust is where the assets are.

Filling in Form 56

- Part I. Identification: Enter the deceased person's name, Social Security number, and last address. Then enter your name and address.
- Section A. Authority: Check the box (d) that says you are acting as the trustee under a trust.
- Section B. Nature of Liability and Tax Notices: On line 3, check "Income." On line 4, check "1040" and on line 5 enter "all years subject to audit 20____ to 20____" ending in the year of the settlor's death and going back five years (just to be on the safe side). Check the box in line 6. Leave the other lines blank.
- Part II. Leave blank.
- Part III. Signature: Sign your name on the "Fiduciary's signature" line as Trustee and enter the date.

How Distributions to Beneficiaries Affect Trust Taxes

If your trust will exist only for a few months and then end when you distribute all its assets, income distributions to beneficiaries aren't going to be an issue for you. But if you're administering an ongoing trust— for young beneficiaries, for example—and distribute trust income (as distinguished from trust principal) to the beneficiaries at some point, it will affect the annual trust income tax return.

It has to do with what kinds of expenses trusts can deduct from the gross income on their tax return. Trust deductions are similar in many ways to those allowed to individuals. But there are a few unique trust deductions, including:

- the first $600 in income
- a standard deduction, depending on the terms of the trust. If the terms of the trust require you to pay out all income each year, you've got what the IRS calls a "simple trust," which gets a standard deduction of $300. Most trusts do not require this and are called "complex trusts"; they have a $100 standard deduction.

- expenses of administering the estate—fees for lawyers and accountants, for example
- losses on the sale of a trust asset, and
- trust income (for example, interest on a bank account) that is paid out to beneficiaries.

The most important deduction may be the deduction for trust income that is paid out to beneficiaries. Trusts can accumulate income, in which case the trustee will report and pay tax on it. Or trustees can use the trust like a pipeline and pay trust income—up to a certain limit—out to beneficiaries, who then report it on their personal income tax returns. (We're talking about income that the trust assets earn—not the trust assets themselves. When beneficiaries inherit trust assets, they don't pay income tax on them. But for new income, there's always a taxpayer.)

As trustee, you might distribute trust income to beneficiaries both because the trust document directs you to do so and because there's a tax advantage. Trust tax rates are higher than individual income tax rates. Trusts pay the top income tax rate, currently 37%, on any income over $12,500. Individuals don't get to that rate until they earn more than $500,000! So for all but the wealthiest, a beneficiary will be taxed at a lower rate than a trust will—there's a built-in incentive not to accumulate income in the trust.

In addition, a 3.8% tax is now imposed on certain investment income. This new tax affects trusts because it is imposed on the lesser of undistributed net investment income or gross income over a certain threshold ($12,300 in 2018). This threshold is lower for trusts than it is for individuals, whose modified adjusted gross income has to exceed $200,000 for a single taxpayer ($250,000 for a married person filing jointly) before this additional tax is imposed.

If you give a beneficiary trust income, you must also provide, at year's end, a document called a Schedule K-1, which shows the amount of trust income the beneficiary received. Your accountant can prepare the schedules. The beneficiaries will then report this income and attach the K-1 to their personal income tax returns. You, on the trust tax return, will deduct the income you distributed.

EXAMPLE: Jamie is the trustee of the Meuller Family Trust. The trust requires that all income be distributed annually to Ramona, the trust beneficiary. During the year, the trust assets earn $12,000 in bank interest and $2,000 in stock dividends, all of which Jamie pays out to Ramona. At the end of the year, Jamie sends a Schedule K-1 to Ramona showing the $14,000 distribution. Ramona is responsible for reporting that income on her personal income tax return by April 15 of the following year.

On the trust's income tax return (Form 1041), Jamie reports the interest and dividends earned by the trust. He also claims deductions for the accountant, attorney, and trustee fees necessary to administer the trust and for the amount of income paid out to Ramona. As a result of these deductions, the trust has no taxable income and owes no income tax.

The Federal Estate Tax Return

You won't need to file an estate tax return, IRS Form 706, unless the deceased person's gross estate is more than a certain amount, called the applicable exclusion amount. This amount is indexed for inflation, so it changes each year. Here are the most recent numbers:

- For deaths in 2015: $5.43 million
- For deaths in 2016: $5.45 million
- For deaths in 2017: $5.49 million
- For deaths in 2018: $11.18 million.

In 2018, Congress voted to temporarily double the estate tax exemption for persons dying between 2018 and 2025. In 2026, the exemption will drop down to around $6 million ($5 million indexed for inflation) unless the larger exemption is made permanent.

Given that you don't need to deal with estate tax unless the deceased person left many millions of dollars, it's obvious that you should get help from a qualified tax expert—an experienced attorney or CPA. Don't assume that your trusted tax preparer is qualified to do this return. Don't hire anyone who hasn't prepared a least half a dozen tax returns in the last five years.

Generally, accountants and estate planning attorneys charge $2,000 to $5,000 to prepare this long and complicated return, which gives you some idea of the time it takes to do it right. The trust will pay for their time and effort. It's help well worth paying for.

Do You Need to File?

A person's gross estate includes the fair market value of all of the assets owned at death, wherever they're located. This includes life insurance proceeds, retirement accounts, annuities, personal property, real estate, investment accounts, and bank accounts. It doesn't matter whether the property is held in a trust, passes under the terms of a will, or is subject to a beneficiary designation—it's all counted for estate tax purposes.

> **EXAMPLE:** At his death, Brian, an unmarried man, owns an unmortgaged home worth $340,000, a brokerage account worth $1.5 million, a checking account with $25,000, a savings account with $40,000, and a 401(k) plan worth $500,000. That gives him a gross estate of $2,405,000. Because that's less than the exclusion from the estate tax in the year of his death, no federal estate tax return needs to be filed for Brian's estate.

It's possible that you might need to file an estate tax return even though it's clear that no tax is due. One reason for this would be because your gross estate is over the applicable exclusion amount but is reduced by a series of deductions to arrive at the taxable estate. The taxable estate is the amount that will be subject to the estate tax. For example, there are deductions for assets left to charity and a deduction for all property left to one's spouse.

> **EXAMPLE:** When Veronica dies in 2016, she and her husband own a home worth $3.2 million, a rental property worth $3.4 million, a brokerage account worth $2 million, an IRA worth $900,000, and a life insurance policy that paid $1.5 million upon her death. She lived in a community property state, so her share of each asset was one-half of the total value. That puts her gross estate at $5.5 million, just over the $5.45 million exclusion amount in 2016. So her trustee must file a federal estate tax return within nine months of her death.

Veronica, however, left $500,000 to the nonprofit charity Society for the Protection of Animals and everything else to her husband. The trustee will file the estate tax return, but no tax will be due because Veronica used both the charitable and marital deductions to reduce her taxable estate to zero.

Another reason to file an estate tax return after the death of a spouse, even if no tax is due, is to make use of "portability," which is the surviving spouse's right to use the deceased spouse's unused exclusion later, when the surviving spouse dies. (For more on this, see "Filing to Preserve Portability of Your Spouse's Exclusion Amount," below.)

> EXAMPLE: When Shirley died in 2016, her estate totaled $2.45 million, which she left to her two adult children. Her husband, Russell, filed an estate tax return for Shirley, even though she didn't have a taxable estate. Russell filed the return so that after his death, his estate would be able request portability and use Shirley's unused $3 million of estate tax exemption. There's a box to check on the estate tax return to request this. If Russell remarries, and his second wife dies before him, he'll lose this additional $3 million exemption.

If you must file a return, it's due nine months after the date of death, although you can get a six-month extension from the IRS for the asking. You must still pay any tax due by the original nine-month deadline, so you'll have to send in your best estimate at that point.

Putting a Value on Assets

It's not always easy to figure out whether someone's gross estate is above or below the estate tax threshold, especially when real estate values are changing (up or down) quickly. As discussed in Chapter 4, you'll probably need to get valuable assets appraised by a qualified professional.

The only other way to find the value is to sell the property soon after the death. After all, what's a better indicator of an asset's market value than what someone freely pays for it? If you sell property within just a few months of death, you can use that value when you're preparing an estate tax return.

On the estate tax return, you have a choice: You can use either the value of an asset at the date of the settlor's death OR its value six months later (or when it was actually sold), which is called the alternate valuation date. The choice of an alternate valuation date is available only if the resulting tax would be less, and it's optional. Because it can be used only to reduce the estate tax, you cannot pick the alternate valuation date if all of the assets will be distributed for the benefit of the surviving spouse or if the date-of-death value is less than the applicable exclusion amount. You have to select one date or the other for all assets; you can't pick and choose.

Make this decision carefully, because it will affect both the estate tax that may be due now and the capital gains tax that will be due later, when the beneficiary eventually sells the asset. A lower value now may mean lower estate tax now, but higher capital gains tax later.

The value you pick will be the new owner's tax basis. The lower the tax basis, the higher the capital gains tax will be when the new owner eventually sells the asset. (Tax basis is discussed above, in "Beneficiaries and Taxes.") But a lower tax basis may mean lower estate tax, too, and the estate tax rate is higher than the capital gains tax rate. That's where a tax expert's judgment can help you decide which valuation date to use.

> EXAMPLE 1: Rose is the successor trustee of her aunt Ruby's trust. Ruby owned a home, a rental property, and stocks. At her death in 2016, these assets were worth $5.6 million. Six months later, after a drop in both real estate prices and the stock market, her assets are worth $4.1 million.
>
> By choosing the alternate valuation date, Ruby's estate will not have to pay any federal estate tax, because the value of Ruby's assets on the date six months after Ruby's death is less than the estate tax exclusion amount ($5.45 million) in effect at her death. Rose, however, will have to file an estate tax return, because the value of the gross estate at the date of death was greater than $5.45 million. Rose recognizes that the election to use the alternate valuation date may make the beneficiaries pay more capital gains tax someday when they sell the appreciated assets, but the immediate tax savings make that trade-off worth it.

If Ruby's estate had been worth $5.6 million at her death and fallen to $3.9 million six months later, and Rose takes her time selling the assets, the calculation would be different. If Rose chose to use the date-of-death value, the estate would owe estate tax of $20,000 (40% of $50,000—assuming that the taxable estate, after fees, was $5.5 million). But if the assets climbed back in value to their date-of-death values by the time they were ultimately sold, the beneficiaries would save $255,000 in federal capital gains tax (on the gain of $1.5 million at a 15% long-term capital gains tax rate) plus state taxes.

EXAMPLE 2: At his death, Frank leaves a large estate, including a house that's worth $1.5 million. Six months later, it's appraised at just $1 million. Picking the value at the alternate valuation date ($1 million) reduces the estate tax due now but also gives Frank's son Jason, who inherits the house, a lower tax basis.

If property values go back up and Jason sells the house for $1.2 million, he'll owe tax on his $200,000 of gain. Had the date-of-death value of $1.5 million been chosen, he wouldn't owe any capital gains tax (and could in fact claim a loss).

Filing to Preserve Portability of Your Spouse's Exclusion Amount

At the end of 2012 (well, actually in January of 2013), Congress passed an estate tax law that made permanent a provision called portability, which allows the surviving spouse to use any of the federal estate tax exemption that was not used by the first spouse to die. In order to use portability, though, the surviving spouse must file an estate tax return for the deceased spouse even if it isn't legally required—that is, even if the first spouse to die didn't have a taxable estate.

For example, if the wife died in 2016, with an estate of $1.5 million, her husband could decide to file an estate tax return for her estate. That would let him request that the $3,950,000 of his wife's federal estate tax exemption that she didn't use be available to his estate at his death. (The estate tax exemption for deaths in 2016 was $5.45 million; subtracting $1.5 million leaves $3,950,000.)

Filing that return will probably cost the husband about $3,000 (the preparer's fee). For him, it's worth filing the return, because he owns several pieces of valuable real estate that he would like to pass on to his children free of estate tax. He expects the real estate to go up in value, and the extra $3.95 million in exemption will help shelter the appreciation from estate tax.

State Estate Tax

Most states used to collect part of the estate taxes paid to the federal government; they didn't have their own separate estate tax system. But that system, called a pick-up tax, has been phased out, so many states (listed below) have instituted their own estate tax.

States With Estate Taxes		
State	**2018 Exempt Amount**	**Maximum Tax Rate**
Connecticut	$2.6 million	12%
District of Columbia*	$11.18 million	16%
Hawaii	$5.49 million	16%
Illinois	$4 million	16%
Maine	$5.6 million	12%
Maryland	$4 million	16%
Massachusetts	$1 million	16%
Minnesota	$2.4 million	16%
New York	$5.25 million	16%
Oregon	$1 million	16%
Rhode Island	$1.538 million	16%
Vermont	$2.75 million	16%
Washington	$2.193 million	20%

* The district estate tax is tied to the federal estate tax.

Property in More Than One State

If a deceased person's trust owned property in more than one state, the trust may owe some kind of estate tax in more than one state as well. The state where the deceased person lived can tax all of his or her personal property and real estate in that state. If the deceased person owned property in another state, that state can tax it. If you're not sure where someone really lived, look to see where they registered to vote, paid state income tax, and had a driver's license. If the answer's still not clear, see a lawyer.

Other Taxes You Need to Be Aware Of

Sigh. It can feel sort of endless, these taxes. Here are a few other taxes that you need to know about.

Real Estate

If the trust holds real estate, you may need to pay property tax during the trust administration.

Business

If the trust owns a small business, you will have to pay all the taxes that the business is required to file, including payroll taxes and estimated quarterly taxes. The deceased business owner probably had a bookkeeper or outside accountant to help with this. If not, find one pronto. And we mean pronto. The IRS deals harshly with those who don't pay payroll taxes. They can assess penalties of up to 100% of the taxes due and even shut down a business for failure to pay them.

Trust Accountings

We've mentioned accountings often throughout this book; now is the time to get to the nitty-gritty details. Fortunately, there's nothing very complicated.

An accounting is a report of all of the money that flows into and out of a trust during a certain period of time. It lists all of the trust assets at the beginning of the period and the end. It shows how the asset mix changed during the period of the accounting—for example, you might have sold real estate and bought a CD with the proceeds.

An accounting is intended to give beneficiaries a clear picture of what you're doing with their money. It follows that it should be very easy to read; you shouldn't have to be a lawyer or an accountant to understand how trust assets have been managed.

Depending on the size and complexity of your trust, an accounting may take some work, but we can guarantee you'll feel extremely satisfied when the document is complete. And beneficiaries will have a lot less to complain about if they are well-informed about what you've done.

How Often Must You Prepare Accountings?

Many states require trustees to prepare annual financial reports, unless the beneficiaries voluntarily give up (waive) their right to an accounting. (See Appendix A to determine whether your state requires annual accountings.) Even if your state does not require an annual accounting, we advise you to do it anyway, as part of fulfilling your duty to keep the beneficiaries reasonably informed about the trust.

Typically, annual accountings are sufficient for most trusts. Beneficiaries may ask for more frequent accountings if they are genuinely concerned that you are not properly spending or investing trust funds. Requests for accountings must be reasonable—a beneficiary cannot constantly request reports when there's no good reason. If a beneficiary hears that you're tooling around in a Ferrari (instead of the five-year-old Toyota that you used to drive), it might be reasonable for the beneficiary to take a look at the books more than once a year.

Why would a beneficiary ever waive the right to a formal accounting? Although beneficiaries always legally have the right to see all of the changes in the trust assets, they might not feel that the cost and time involved to prepare the accounting are warranted if the trust will be entirely distributed soon after the settlor's death. Ordinarily, you'd be preparing a final accounting even then, but in the case of a quickly settled trust, the beneficiaries may decide that the distribution is enough of a record of what the trust owned and where it went.

Beneficiaries might also waive their right to see the information in a prescribed format if instead, you give them copies of all of the bank and brokerage statements and explain the purpose of each outgoing payment. Beneficiaries are not stuck with the waiver forever. If circumstances change, the beneficiary is always entitled to end the waiver and begin receiving accountings.

If the beneficiaries are willing to waive their rights to an accounting, you'd best get their consent in writing. Below is an example form you could use.

Anderson Revocable Trust—Waiver of Accounting

I, Sophia Anderson, a beneficiary of the Anderson Revocable Trust, hereby waive my right to a formal accounting by the trustee for the actions taken by the trustee from January 1, 20xx to December 31, 20xx.

Sophia Anderson
_____   _____
Sophia Anderson   Date

Who Should Prepare Accountings?

You don't have to be a lawyer or accountant to prepare a basic accounting for beneficiaries. Although you can use formal accounting software, such as *QuickBooks*, many trustees find it just as easy to work with a basic spreadsheet program such as Microsoft *Excel*. If you include all of the financial information for the accounting period and double-check your work, it won't make any difference which program you use to crunch the numbers.

Many states do not require a particular format for trust accountings, as long as beneficiaries get all of the information they need. In fact, the states that have adopted a set of laws called the Uniform Trust Code call accountings "reports" to emphasize that there is no required style. Regardless of the requirements in your state, which you can find out by either asking the trust administration attorney that you're working with or checking your state's probate code, aim for clarity and detail, so the beneficiaries can understand what you've done with their money.

If you do decide to hire a professional to handle the work for you, make sure that the person has experience with trust or estate accountings. You do not want someone who's only prepared income tax returns. If your accounting is uncomplicated, you may be able to hire a bookkeeper, rather than a certified public accountant. Bookkeepers keep track of businesses' profits and expenses, and many can easily translate that experience to trust accountings. They usually charge about a third of an accountant's hourly rate. (For more about getting expert help with accountings, see Chapter 7.)

SEE AN EXPERT

Get help if you're sued. If a beneficiary sues you or threatens to do so and challenges your spending or the accuracy of your report, you will need to present an accounting that precisely follows the format required by state law, if there is one. Hire an attorney to prepare the accounting and defend you in court.

A Typical Simple Trust Accounting

The idea of preparing an accounting may seem onerous, but if you have kept all your trust bank account statements and made notations about the purpose of each expense, you shouldn't have any problem getting an annual accounting together in a couple of hours. (That's why we urge you to establish a good record-keeping system—see Chapter 4.)

Accountings contain several standard categories of information (listed below). Put each one on a separate schedule, on a separate page. If you use accounting software, the software will print out the schedules separately and categorize the information. If you use a spreadsheet program, we suggest you put each category on a separate page (or "sheet," in Microsoft *Excel* parlance), so that you can easily organize the information. If you put everything on the same page, you run the risk of confusing categories, your columns will be aligned strangely, and it will be difficult for you to print descriptive headers and footers.

We provide some sample sections in this chapter. Your accounting may be much more complicated. For one thing, we have not separated out the receipts and expenses by income and principal. If you have one beneficiary who is entitled to receive income and another beneficiary who gets principal during the term of your trust, we suggest you hire a skilled accountant to sort it out.

Elements of an Accounting

- Opening balance
- Inflows
- Outflows
- Change in type of asset
- Ending balance, and
- Summary of account.

Opening Balance

It is very important to start with an accurate opening balance for the trust. For the first accounting, use the balance from when you began to act as trustee. In the following years, you will use the closing balance from the prior year as the opening balance.

List all of the trust assets as of the date you began to act as trustee and put down account numbers and the value of each asset. If an asset is hard or expensive to reappraise, such as real estate, you can usually use the appraised value at the settlor's death or the cost to acquire the property (if after the settlor's death). That's called the carrying value. Adjust the carrying value and get a new appraisal only if a beneficiary expresses concern about the value or when it's time to distribute the asset.

> **EXAMPLE:** Herman is the trustee of an ongoing trust with assets worth approximately $750,000. Herman became trustee on January 1 after his sister, who was trustee after the settlor, became ill, and now he is responsible for preparing an accounting for his first year on the job. His sister had obtained an appraisal for the settlor's home very soon after the settlor's death. Herman prepares his first accounting early the next year, and lists in the Opening Balance the value of the trust bank account and mutual fund as of January 1, the opening date of the accounting. To avoid additional expense, he will not get another appraisal for the real estate, but will just use its carrying value (the value at the settlor's death) for the real estate. The opening balance schedule is shown below.

Opening Balance	
Asset Description	**Value as of January 1**
124 Main Street (personal residence)	$ 400,000 (carrying value)
Bank savings account	50,000
Mutual fund	300,000
Total Assets	$ 750,000

Inflows

An inflow, also known as a receipt, occurs when assets are added to the trust. The most common inflows are property added to the trust and income or dividends received by the trust.

Each type of inflow requires a special schedule in the trust accounting, which is then organized by the dates assets were received. Don't merely summarize the income over the year, even if all of it came from just one account. The beneficiaries might think you have something to hide if you do not lay out each income entry separately.

EXAMPLE: On February 15, Herman discovers some additional assets that belonged to the trust and should have been included in the opening balance: a $3,000 checking account and 15 shares of stock with a market value of $100/share. He lists them on a separate schedule, as shown below.

Additional Property Received		
Date	**Asset**	**Value**
February 15, 20xx	Bank checking account	$ 3,000
February 15, 20xx	15 shares of XYZ stock	1,500
Total Assets Added During Accounting Period		**$ 4,500**

During the year Herman is administering this trust, it earns between $700 and $800 each month in interest. The mutual fund also distributes a dividend of $250 each quarter. On a separate schedule, Herman lists all that income, as shown below.

Interest and Dividends Received		
Date	**Asset**	**Value**
January 2, 20xx	Savings account interest	$ 750
February 2, 20xx	Savings account interest	700
March 2, 20xx	Savings account interest	725
March 15, 20xx	Mutual fund dividend	250
April 2, 20xx	Savings account interest	710
May 2, 20xx	Savings account interest	735
June 2, 20xx	Savings account interest	790
June 15, 20xx	Mutual fund dividend	250
July 2, 20xx	Savings account interest	705
August 2, 20xx	Savings account interest	745
September 2, 20xx	Savings account interest	775
September 15, 20xx	Mutual fund dividend	250
October 2, 20xx	Savings account interest	750
November 2, 20xx	Savings account interest	780
December 2, 20xx	Savings account interest	715
December 15, 20xx	Mutual fund dividend	250
Total Income During Accounting Period		**$9,880**

If the information is difficult to present, or if your trust receives income and dividends from many different sources, you may report each source of income on separate subschedules—for example, one for the savings account interest and another for the mutual fund dividends. Then total the subschedules at the bottom of the page. This will help beneficiaries of ongoing trusts understand the productivity of each asset.

Other less common types of inflows include gains from selling trust property and net income from a trade or business. If an ongoing business is a trust asset, you will need to add a schedule to your accounting. The beneficiaries do not want to see a detailed report for the business, just the end result—the net income to the trust.

EXAMPLE: On March 5, Herman sells the trust real estate for $430,000. After expenses, the trust receives $402,000. Herman reports the sale on a separate schedule, shown below.

	Gains on Sales of Property			
Date	Asset Description	Net Profit	Carrying Value	Gain
March 5, 20xx	124 Main Street	$402,000	$400,000	$2,000
	Total Gain During Accounting Period			$2,000

Outflows

The two most common types of outflows are payments of trust expenses and distributions to beneficiaries. List these outflows on separate schedules, chronologically, so that it will be very easy for the beneficiaries to understand what's gone out of the trust.

EXAMPLE: During the accounting period, Herman pays for some of the utilities for 124 Main Street because the property is listed for sale, and the water and electricity need to be on for potential buyers. Herman also has accountant and attorney expenses, which he pays for with trust funds.

Payments of Trust Expenses

Date	Check #	Payee	Purpose	Amount
January 10, 20xx	101	Gas and Electric Co.	Utilities	$ 25
January 11, 20xx	102	Water Co.	Utilities	15
February 10, 20xx	103	Gas and Electric Co.	Utilities	25
February 11, 20xx	104	Water Co.	Utilities	15
March 10, 20xx	108	Gas and Electric Co.	Utilities	25
March 11, 20xx	109	Water Co.	Utilities	15
April 25, 20xx	110	John F. Jones, CPA	Tax Prep.	500
September 17, 20xx	113	Margaret Grey, Esq.	Consult	350
December 20, 20xx	114	Herman Manzoni	Trustee	3,200
		Total Disbursements		**$ 4,170**

If you compensate yourself for serving as trustee, include that information as well. Remember: Every payment must show up for the accounting to accurately reflect your management of the trust. Include the amount and date of the payment, and then separately explain how you calculated your fee.

EXAMPLE: Herman is claiming $3,200 in trustee's fees. He should detail both his work as the trustee and his method for calculating his compensation.

Unacceptable Statement

Trustee's Fee—January 1 to December 31—64 hours @ $50/hr.

More Detailed and Acceptable Statement

> Trustee's Fee—January 1 to December 31—$50/hr.
>
> 4 hours: Review settlor's estate planning documents, transfer accounts to Herman as successor trustee, consult prior trustee about trustee duties.
>
> 4 hours: Consult attorneys and accountants about trustee duties, income tax issues.
>
> 5 hours: Prepare house for sale by coordinating cleaning service, gardener, hauler, and transporting personal property to beneficiaries.
>
> 37 hours: Work on sale of house with real estate agent and title company.
>
> 14 hours: Telephone and in-person conferences with beneficiaries about their issues with the trust and prior trustee.

It's best to detail each and every interaction with a beneficiary, prior trustee, attorney, accountant, real estate agent, and so on, by date, so that it is easy to calculate total hours spent and the purpose of the time spent.

Herman's trust states that the trustee is to distribute $5,000 to each of the settlor's grandchildren within six months of the settlor's death. Herman made those distributions in late February. In August, one of the settlor's children asked Herman if she could get some of her inheritance early (a preliminary distribution) because she wanted to remodel her kitchen. Because Herman was expecting a tax audit, he wasn't ready to distribute the entire trust, but he determined that preliminary distributions to both of the settlor's children would not break the bank. Herman met with his attorney to review the accounting and discuss the potential liabilities, and then distributed $100,000 to each of the settlor's two children in early September. On a separate schedule, Herman reports the distributions, as shown below.

Distributions to Beneficiaries

Date	Check #	Beneficiary	Amount
February 28, 20xx	105	Mark Goldstein	$ 5,000
February 28, 20xx	106	Margie Goldstein	5,000
February 28, 20xx	107	Ronald Fine	5,000
September 5, 20xx	111	Mildred Goldstein	100,000
September 5, 20xx	112	Jonathan Fine	100,000
Total distributions to beneficiaries			**$ 215,000**

Add other schedules to the accounting, if it's necessary. In our example of Herman selling the house, if the proceeds from the sale of the house were $375,000 instead of $402,000, there would have been a loss of $25,000, which would be reported on a schedule called "Losses on Sales of Property." The value of the trust would be less than it was before the house was sold at a loss. Another common outflow schedule is "Net Loss From a Trade or Business," which occurs if a business owned by the trust is in debt, and trust funds must be used to keep it operating.

Change in the Type of Asset

You should always prepare a schedule showing any account that has changed names and what you bought and sold within the trust. This schedule is simply to add clarity for the beneficiaries. If the beneficiaries see that at the beginning of the year there is a house, and at the end of the year a large brokerage account but no house, they will probably assume that you sold the house and moved the funds into a brokerage account. But it's always better to spell it out.

Change of Assets During Accounting Period

Asset in Trust at Settlor's Death	Description	Transferred To:	Value on Transfer
123 Main Street Anytown, MI	Settlor's residence	Sold and proceeds deposited in bank savings account	$402,000
Total change of assets			$402,000

Ending Balance

Finally, prepare a schedule showing the assets in the trust at the end of the year or when you close the trust. This list will look a lot like the "opening balance" schedule from the beginning of the year.

EXAMPLE: Herman prepares a schedule showing the trust's ending balance for the year.

Ending Balance

Asset Description	Value (as of December 31)
Bank savings account	$ 242,710
Mutual fund	300,000
Bank checking account	3,000
15 shares of XYZ stock	1,500
Total Assets	$ 547,210

Summary of Account

When you organize the accounting for the beneficiaries, the first page should be the account summary: a one-page statement of the positive and negative cash flow for the trust, and a table of contents for the rest of the accounting. But before you can prepare it, you'll need to complete your other schedules. Below is a sample summary, using the figures from Herman's trust.

The total charges have to be equal to the total credits. (Isn't it nice how Herman's accounting balances?) If the accounting is off, even by a nickel, you need to figure out what's wrong. Check all of your figures.

Summary of Account	
Charges	
Property on Hand at Beginning of Account	$ 750,000
Additional Property Received	4,500
Interest and Dividends Receipts	9,880
Gains on Sale	2,000
Total charges	**$ 766,380**
Credits	
Payment of Trust Expenses	4,170
Distributions to Beneficiaries	215,000
Property Remaining on Hand at End of Period	547,210
Total credits	**$ 766,380**

Who Gets a Copy?

A trust is a private relationship between the settlor, trustee, and beneficiaries. You do not need to file an accounting in the local courthouse. But you do need to provide a copy to the current beneficiaries (people entitled to income or principal), and to the trust protector, if any. Some states (discussed below) also require you to send accountings to the people who would inherit if the current beneficiaries died or become ineligible to receive distributions before the termination of the trust.

Remote potential trust beneficiaries are not automatically entitled to receive a copy of the accounting. If your trust lists beneficiaries who will inherit only in the unlikely event that both the current and the alternate (also called secondary or contingent) beneficiaries die before the trust is scheduled to end, don't bother to send them a copy.

Most states that have adopted the Uniform Trust Code allow current and secondary beneficiaries to automatically receive an accounting (which the UTC calls a report). Remote potential beneficiaries may *request* an accounting, and in that case you must send a copy to them as well.

> **EXAMPLE:** Frank is the trustee of a trust established by his sister, Pearl. The trust provides that Pearl's children, Diane and Charlie, are the beneficiaries of the trust, entitled to receive distributions of income and principal as needed. When both of the beneficiaries reach age 30, the trust assets will be split equally between Diane and Charlie, and the trust will terminate. The trust also states that if either beneficiary is deceased, their share will go to their children. If they leave no children, the trust will be distributed entirely to the surviving beneficiary. Only if none of Pearl's descendants survive will the trust be distributed to Pearl's friend Mabel.
>
> When Frank prepares his accounting, Diane and Charlie are both alive. He will need to send a copy of the accounting to Diane and Charlie, and any of Diane or Charlie's children who are over age 18. Unless she requests a copy, Frank does not have to send a copy to Mabel.

If a minor child is a current beneficiary, do not send the child an accounting directly. If the child has a court-ordered guardian or conservator, which is highly unlikely, send the accounting to them. Otherwise, send the notice to the child's parent or to the person the trust instrument specifically authorizes to receive accountings and notice on behalf of a child.

Delivering the Accounting to Beneficiaries

You should complete your accounting within eight weeks after the end of your accounting year. This should give you enough time to collect end-of-year statements and consult with your advisers, if needed.

Send the accounting by certified mail, return receipt requested. Keep the receipts to show that every eligible beneficiary received a copy of the accounting and the delivery date. In many states, beneficiaries have a limited period of time, after receiving an accounting, to file a lawsuit against you in the local court for breach of trust.

> **EXAMPLE:** California law states that a settlor may limit the time for a beneficiary to send a written objection of the accounting to the trustee. The deadline may not be shorter than 180 days from the delivery of the accounting. A beneficiary who has sent a written objection to the trustee has three years to sue the trustee for breach of trust.

If your state or trust has a deadline for lawsuits, you don't hear a peep from the beneficiaries, and the accounting accurately reflects the transactions within the trust, the beneficiaries cannot successfully sue you later on for prudent investment choices or distributions you made during the period of the accounting. (They may, however, still be able to sue you if they feel the salary you took as trustee was excessive or if you intentionally made terrible investments.) This provision can limit your liability, and many trustees are hesitant to distribute all of the funds to the beneficiaries until the deadline for complaints has passed.

If the settlor included a provision in your trust that limits the time period for the beneficiaries to file a lawsuit about the accounting, and such a limit is permissible under your state's laws, include a letter that explains the time frame. (A sample is shown below.)

If you are concerned that beneficiaries might sue you, speak with a trust administration attorney or an accountant to find out how long a beneficiary has to sue in your state. In most states, there's a deadline of a few months to a few years. Some states do not impose any deadline. If your state does not, we recommend that you hire an attorney to prepare an accounting using your state's required accounting format, and ask the local probate court to approve it. Only then can you breathe a sigh of relief and know for sure that a prior decision cannot lead to a lawsuit. (See Chapter 12 for a discussion about how to protect yourself when you're ready to terminate the trust.)

Letter to Beneficiaries

John Smith, Trustee
Jones Living Trust
123 Main Street
Galesburg, MO 69552

November 18, 20xx

Suzie Jones
456 Tunnel Road
Galesburg, MO 69552

Re: Accounting of the Jones Living Trust

Dear Ms. Jones:

Enclosed is a copy of the Accounting for the Jones Living Trust from January 1, 20xx to December 31, 20xx. Please review it carefully and let me know if you have any concerns.

Please note the following:

1. You are entitled to petition the court to obtain a court review of the account and of the acts of the trustee.

2. Under state law and the terms of this trust, you have 180 days to object to the accounting. Any objection you make must be in writing. It must be delivered to the trustee within the period stated above and must state your objection clearly. Your failure to deliver a written objection will permanently prevent you from later asserting this objection against the trustee.

Very truly yours,

John Smith

John Smith, Trustee

Terminating the Trust

All good things must come to an end, including trust administration. Your trust may last for three months, a few years, or a lifetime, but eventually it will be your job to officially close the trust.

When Does the Trust End?

To determine when the trust is to end, read your trust instrument very carefully.

If it says that a beneficiary is to receive a share "outright and free of trust," it's your job to distribute that share as soon as possible. In fact, if all of your beneficiaries are to receive their shares outright, you may be ready to think about closing the trust less than six months after you set it up.

Some trusts, however, last for decades, and end only at a certain date or when certain events occur. Once your trust has reached the milestone set forth in the trust instrument, you have an obligation to terminate the trust as soon as possible.

> **EXAMPLE 1:** Mira creates a trust for her son, Ethan. During the term of the trust, he will get all of the income from the trust assets. Ten years after Mira's death, Ethan is to receive the balance of the trust property. On that date, the trustee should terminate Mira's trust and give Ethan the remaining trust funds.

> **EXAMPLE 2:** Connor creates a trust to benefit his twin sons, Colin and Logan. At age 25, the brothers receive half of the trust assets, and at age 30, they get the rest. On Colin and Logan's 30th birthday, the trustee terminates the trust and splits the remaining trust funds between them.

> **EXAMPLE 3:** Luanne creates a special needs trust for her daughter, Maria, who has a disability that makes it unlikely that she will ever become self-sufficient. This trust will last for Maria's lifetime. After Maria's death, the trustee will transfer the remaining funds to Maria's sister, Jane, and terminate the trust.

EXAMPLE 4: Sofia creates a trust for her grandchildren and, worrying that they won't be responsible with money, specifies that they shouldn't receive their shares until they turn 40. But by the time the grandchildren are in their mid-30s, the trust assets have been almost entirely spent on legitimate expenses such as college, graduate school, house down payments, and so on. With just a few thousand dollars left in the trust, the grandchildren all agree that the trust should be terminated. State law allows the trustee to end the trust in these circumstances.

How to Distribute Trust Assets

When it's time to wrap up the trust, how should you distribute the remaining assets?

If you're settling a simple trust, which states that a certain beneficiary is to receive a specific asset such as a car or shares of stock, transfer it to the beneficiary as soon as possible. In fact, in most states, if you are supposed to distribute assets outright and you take more than a year to do it, the beneficiary is entitled to receive the asset plus interest on the money during the delay.

Beneficiaries Who Are Minors

If you are distributing assets to minors, but not to an ongoing trust for their benefit, review the trust instrument to see whether or not it has a paragraph (usually hidden in with the powers of the trustee) that gives you the power to give the minor's money to a custodial account, with that child's parent as custodian. That will avoid a court-ordered guardianship over the child's property, which would end when that child turns 18 and would probably require the guardian to submit annual accountings to the court.

Here's an example of such a paragraph:

> **Payments to Legally Incapacitated Persons**. If at any time any trust beneficiary is a minor, or it appears to the trustee that any trust beneficiary is incapacitated, incompetent, or for any other reason not able to receive payments or make intelligent or responsible use of the payments, then the trustee, in lieu of making direct payments to the trust beneficiary, may make payments to the beneficiary's conservator or guardian; to the beneficiary's custodian under the Uniform Gifts to Minors Act or Uniform Transfers to Minors Act of any state; to one or more suitable persons as the trustee deems proper, such as a relative of or a person residing with the beneficiary, to be used for the beneficiary's benefit; to any other person, firm, or agency for services rendered or to be rendered for the beneficiary's assistance or benefit; or to accounts in the beneficiary's name with financial institutions. If there is no custodian then serving or nominated to serve by the settlor for a beneficiary, the personal representative or trustee, as the case may be, shall designate the custodian. The receipt of payments by any of the foregoing shall constitute a sufficient acquittance of the trustee for all purposes.

If your trust has a paragraph granting you the authority to give a minor's property to their parent as a custodian under the Uniform Transfers to Minors Act (UTMA), which has been adopted in every state but South Carolina, you're in luck. The minor's parent will be able to open up a custodial bank or brokerage account, for the benefit of the minor, and you can distribute the money to that account.

If the trust doesn't have such language, you have two options. If the amount of the gift is less than a few thousand dollars, you can give the money to that minor's parent on the minor's behalf.

If the gift is for more than a few thousand dollars, and the trust makes no provision for managing that money in a trust for the minor and provides you with no flexibility to distribute it to a custodial account, you may need to set up a guardianship in your local probate court before you can distribute the money to that beneficiary. Usually the court will appoint someone to serve as the property guardian for that money until the beneficiary is 18. The guardian must regularly report to the court on how the minor's assets have been managed and spent. If you need to create a probate guardianship, get advice from a lawyer familiar with your state's probate code. There may be an alternative to a formal guardianship proceeding. In many states (like California), the probate court has power to appoint a custodian under the UTMA. The court may also be able to direct that the funds be placed in a blocked account at a bank. An adult has limited authority over the account and may withdraw funds only with court approval.

Beneficiaries Who Have a Disability

If you are directed to make a distribution to someone who has a disability, and your trust does *not* have a special needs trust provision for that person's share, get expert legal advice before you distribute any money. Improperly distributing such money could cause a beneficiary to lose disability benefits until the money is spent. There may be ways to either create a special needs trust to hold that person's inheritance without causing a loss of benefits for a period of time, or to reform the original trust document to add a special needs trust provision. (Chapter 8 discusses special needs trusts.)

Assets the Settlor No Longer Owned

Sometimes specific assets mentioned in the trust instrument are no longer in the trust at the settlor's death. The settlor might have already given the item to the beneficiary; or the settlor may have sold it or given it to someone else.

It can be tricky to determine what to do in this situation. Generally, if a trust makes a specific gift—for example, it says to give the settlor's blue 1967 Mustang to a specific beneficiary, but that car was sold long before the settlor died, the beneficiary gets nothing. In legal terms, this is called "ademption."

But if the settlor left his nephew "500 shares of stock in Company X," and then sold the stock, it's possible that the nephew might be entitled to the money received for the sale, even though the shares themselves are no longer part of the trust. The difference can turn on a consideration of what the settlor actually intended to give: a specific thing or just money. If you find yourself in this situation, get expert help from an experienced local lawyer.

Divvying Up Assets

If the trust simply says that a percentage of the trust assets is to go to one person and another percentage to someone else, take a hard look at the assets in the trust. First, you will need to value the assets as of the date you intend to distribute them. The date-of-death values you got earlier may not be good enough, depending on the kinds of assets. You'll definitely need to revalue the stocks and mutual funds, and you might need to reappraise the real estate if the market has been in flux since the settlor's death. (See Chapter 4 for information on valuing assets.)

In most circumstances, you won't distribute part of each and every asset to the beneficiaries (known as a "pro rata" distribution), because beneficiaries probably won't want to co-own inherited property with someone else. Instead, typically, trust documents empower trustees to divvy up property on the basis of its value (a "non-pro-rata" distribution). In other words, you can pick which assets go to one beneficiary and which go to another, as long as the total value of each share matches the percentage set out in the trust instrument.

> **EXAMPLE:** Marvin's trust left the assets in equal shares to his two children, Barbara and Debbie. The trust owned a home, worth $320,000, a brokerage account worth $220,000, a savings account with $50,000, and stock in a public company worth $50,000. Sheila, the trustee, after discussing this with the children, distributed the house to Debbie, and the brokerage account, savings account, and stock to Barbara. Each received trust assets worth $320,000.

Even if you have the authority to make a non-pro-rata distribution, we strongly recommend that you speak with the beneficiaries before you go ahead. Beneficiaries may have strong preferences about which assets they receive as part of their shares. A beneficiary who has been living in a rental property owned by the settlor, for example, may prefer to receive the property as a part of the inheritance. But if the property has no significance to any of the beneficiaries, none of them has experience managing rental property, or they live out of state, they may request that you sell the property and distribute the proceeds equally.

Likewise, some assets in a trust have built-in income tax liabilities. Savings bonds are an example. It may not be fair for you to distribute savings bonds to one beneficiary and mutual funds to the other, because the beneficiary with the bonds will be hit with income tax as soon as the bonds are sold. In that case, if the bonds cannot be neatly divided, you should sell them, pay the tax from trust funds, and give the proceeds to the beneficiaries.

Ultimately, however, the decision rests with you. If you're uncomfortable making non-pro-rata distributions, you may find it easier to distribute the specific gifts as required by the trust instrument, and then sell the rest of the trust assets and distribute the cash. There may be capital gains taxes to pay as a result of these sales, depending upon the difference in the asset's value from date of death to date of sale. (See the discussion on capital gains in Chapter 10.)

Personal Property

Most trusts are intentionally vague about how to distribute tangible personal property, such as automobiles, furniture, jewelry, and heirlooms. It's common for the trust to simply leave personal property to the surviving spouse or, if there's no surviving spouse, to the kids. But we've seen trusts that invite all family members over to pick out objects of sentimental value and direct the trustee to sell what's left and donate the proceeds to charity. Others instruct the trustee to sell items to family members for half their market value and distribute the proceeds to the beneficiaries.

If the trust simply says that the assets are to be distributed in equal shares to the settlor's children, "as they shall agree, or as the trustee, in the trustee's sole discretion, shall determine if the children cannot agree," it's up to you to make some decisions. Determining who gets what can be dicey. Many items that are not especially valuable do have emotional significance, and a distribution perceived as unfair could cause problems at family dinners for years to come.

Here are two ways to distribute personal items in a way that will placate most beneficiaries.

Family Photos

Happily, in a digital age, there's no need to fight over photographs. If more than one beneficiary wants the settlor's photographs, offer to take them to a photo store that will scan them and either replicate them on high-quality paper or put them on CD or DVD. The cost should be borne equally by the beneficiaries who want the photos, regardless of who gets the originals and who the copies.

Suggestion 1: Let Beneficiaries Make Lists

One way to move toward a fair distribution is to ask the beneficiaries to write down all of the items that they want. If one beneficiary's list is especially short, encourage that person to take another look over the settlor's possessions. The beneficiary might honestly want only a few mementos—or might just not want to be seen as greedy.

Look through the lists and distribute the items that do not show up on more than one. Then review what's left. Talk to the beneficiaries who are interested in the same item and ask them what they want you to do. Maybe they'll be willing to trade with each other. Maybe they think certain items belong together in a set. You won't know until you ask. If the beneficiaries can't agree how to share them, try Suggestion 2.

Suggestion 2: Hold a "Draft"

Another way to divvy up items is to get family members together for a "draft." In other words, let everyone take turns picking items.

First, talk to the beneficiaries and set up the guidelines ahead of time, so that nobody thinks that the deck is stacked. Also, ask whether some items should be kept together in a single lot or whether some items are so valuable that they are worth two picks in the draft.

Next, write down numbers on slips of paper for the number of beneficiaries who will be picking personal items (if there are four, make four slips, numbered 1 through 4) and throw them into a bowl. Ask each beneficiary to pull out a number, which will determine the order for selecting the settlor's personal items.

Let each beneficiary start picking items. After each beneficiary gets a turn, start again with Beneficiary 1. You're done when all of the settlor's items have been selected or the beneficiaries have received everything they want.

> EXAMPLE: Shari is the trustee of a trust for the benefit of three friends, Louis, Hercules, and Patrick. They decide to divide the settlor's personal property by using a draft. First, they agree that the settlor's car is worth two draft picks and the diamond ring is worth three. They also agree that certain items must be kept together: electronics in a given room and furniture that was purchased as a set. Here are the picks in the first five rounds.

Round	Hercules (#1)	Louis (#2)	Patrick (#3)
1	China cabinet	Antique silver	Diamond ring (= three picks)
2	China	TV and DVD (one lot)	(pass)
3	Car (= two picks)	Oriental rug	(pass)
4	(pass)	Pinball game	Wall hanging
5	Dining room set (table and chairs)	Living room couches	Candlesticks

Although not every beneficiary got every item he wanted, they are all satisfied with the result, because the rules were fair.

Early Withdrawal Penalties

If the settlor held a certificate of deposit (CD) at a bank or credit union, there is probably an early withdrawal penalty if the CD is cashed out before it matures. The penalty can be very high. Depending on the bank, it can range from three months worth of interest, to all of the interest earned within the CD during its term. Some banks even dip into principal.

Some banks, however, allow an executor or trustee to withdraw the funds penalty-free if an account owner dies. But the account must be closed soon after the death, and the CD cannot have rolled over into a new CD following the death.

See how much time is left in the CD term and discuss the penalties with the bank before you decide what to do. If the penalty is too steep, let the beneficiaries know what you're doing and keep the account open until the end of the CD term.

What About the Leftovers?

If some items are not claimed, you'll need to dispose of them yourself. Given that all of the good stuff was probably taken by the beneficiaries, what's left isn't likely to be valuable. Consider hiring an estate liquidator who will sell it all for a percentage of the revenue. (See Chapter 7.)

If the beneficiaries want leftovers to go to charity, but a charitable gift isn't mentioned in the trust itself, technically the gift isn't from the trust. It's a gift from the beneficiaries to the charity, and the beneficiaries should share the charitable income tax deduction. You'll need separate receipts for each beneficiary who is claimed as a donor.

Moving Personal Property for the Beneficiary

Many trusts direct the trustee to pay all packing and shipping charges and consider them costs of administration. In that case, transportation costs should not come out of any one beneficiary's share. If the trust doesn't mention it, deduct the cost of shipping from the share of the beneficiary who's getting that item.

> **EXAMPLE:** When they chose among the settlor's personal items, Louis and Hercules picked large, heavy things, but Patrick's choices were small. If the trust states that packing and shipping charges are costs of administration, the expense will be borne equally by all three trust beneficiaries, even if Hercules ships his car and furniture to Greece but Patrick fits all of his items in his pickup truck.

Cash

The easiest asset to distribute is cash in a bank account or credit union. You can simply write a check to the beneficiary. Money in certificates of deposit (CDs) and money market accounts can also be transferred to the trust checking account to be distributed.

Real Estate

Now that you are ready to terminate the trust, you'll need to prepare a new deed transferring the property from you, as trustee, to the beneficiary. This deed may be called a grant, quitclaim, or warranty deed, depending on your state. (It's never, however, called a trust deed—that's another animal completely.) After you prepare the deed and get your signature notarized, you'll file (record) it in the county where the property is located.

If you've been working with a trust administration attorney, he or she will probably prepare the deeds and record it for you in the proper county. You can also ask a title company to prepare and record the deed for you for a flat fee. You're most likely to get help from a title company if you've already done business, such as a house sale or a refinance, with it. Depending on where you live, they may not offer this service—some states consider it the unauthorized practice of law.

> **EXAMPLE:** Toby is the trustee of a trust that holds real estate. The title to the property is in his name as trustee of the trust. To transfer the property to his niece, Betty, the beneficiary of the trust, he signs a new deed and records it at the county land records office. Below is a sample deed Toby could use.

Recording requested by:
Toby Drummond
Mail to and mail tax statements to:
Betty Luwinski
456 Lilac Lane
Pleasant Village, New Jersey
Parcel Number: xxxxxxxx

SPACE ABOVE THIS LINE FOR RECORDER'S USE

Grant Deed

The undersigned Grantor declares under penalty of perjury that the following is true and correct: DOCUMENTARY TRANSFER TAX IS $0. There is no consideration for this transfer. Not a sale. This is a transfer to the beneficiary of a trust pursuant to the terms of the trust instrument.

GRANTOR: Toby Drummond, as Trustee of the Solomon Settlor Revocable Trust, dated June 14, 20xx, hereby **GRANTS to:** Betty Luwinski, a married woman, as her sole and separate property, the following described real property in the Town of Pleasant Village, County of McMann, State of New Jersey :

[insert legal description]

Commonly known as 456 Lilac Lane, Pleasant Village, New Jersey

_____   _____
Toby Drummond   Date

State of _____)
) ss.
County of _____)

[notary acknowledgment form]

_____   SEAL
Signature of Notary

Every state has its own laws about the information deeds must contain, as well as its own rules about how to execute and record them. All states require that your signature on the deed be notarized; some also require witnesses to the signature. All states require the transferor to explain whether the transfer is a gift or sale, because the type of transfer will affect transfer taxes. You may also have to explain the relationship between the settlor and the beneficiary on the deed to avoid or minimize property taxes.

In California, for example, if a parent transfers a home to his or her children, the children are allowed to keep paying the property taxes that the parent paid, which under California law are almost certain to be much less than the property taxes would be for a new owner. Although the parent-child relationship is not identified on the deed itself, it is stated on a form called the *Preliminary Change of Ownership Report* (PCOR), which is filed with each deed, and is also described on a separate form called a *Claim for Reassessment Exclusion (Prop. 58)*, available from the county assessor's office. States differ, of course, on what they require you to report when recording a deed that transfers ownership. Just make sure that you know what yours requires before you record the deed that transfers property from the trust.

To determine how to transfer the property, first speak with the land records office in the county in which the property is located to learn the filing procedure, and whether they require any additional forms to be filed with the deed. Make sure to find out how much it will cost to file the deed, too. It costs more if the deed is more than one page long, for example. The cost of filing, though, could be anywhere from $20 to $100. Many county offices have helpful websites that explain how to file documents. If the website does not explain the proper procedure or provide you with any county-specific forms that must be filed with the deed, simply call the county land office and ask the best way to get your deed filed and how to get any county-specific forms. In our experience, these offices (in our state, the county assessor's office) are well-staffed and happy to help you figure these things out. (That's how they collect property taxes, after all.)

> ### If the Beneficiary Is Married
>
> If the trust says to give real estate to Mary Jane and she is married, she may ask you to transfer the property to herself and her husband as joint owners. Don't do it. Follow the trust's instructions and transfer the property to Mary Jane alone. She can always add her husband as a co-owner. Your legal responsibility is to transfer the property only to Mary Jane, following the settlor's wishes. It could be very important later in a property dispute or divorce.

Unless the trust explicitly directs otherwise, real estate will go to the new owner subject to all liens and encumbrances such as mortgages and property taxes. If there is a mortgage on the property, we suggest that you and the beneficiary talk to the lender to see whether the beneficiary can assume it. If the lender is not interested, work with a reputable lender who will help the beneficiary refinance to a new mortgage at the same time the property is transferred. The title company selected by the lender will handle all of the paperwork. The lender will agree to lend to the beneficiary only if the beneficiary has an adequate credit history and ability to repay the loan.

If the trust does direct you to transfer real estate free and clear of all encumbrances, you'll need to pay those debts before you turn over the property to the beneficiary.

> **EXAMPLE:** Roberto is the trustee of a trust that instructs him to transfer the settlor's home to Jaime free of any liens or encumbrances. Roberto must use other trust assets to pay off the mortgage and pay that year's property tax before the home can be transferred to Jaime.

Securities

How to transfer securities, such as stocks or mutual funds, depends on how the trust holds these assets.

Securities in a Brokerage Account

Most commonly, securities are held in a brokerage account. If you have a financial adviser at that company, or someone who is assigned to the account, call and ask about making the transfer. If you don't have an individual person to call, call customer service and ask to be directed to the estates department, where there are people who are trained to help you with transferring accounts and rolling over inherited IRAs. Most likely, the beneficiary will need to open a separate individual account with the brokerage company. Then you, as trustee, will authorize the transfer of the securities to the new account.

If the beneficiary wants the funds transferred directly from the trust to a different brokerage company, you will have to determine whether the new brokerage company is allowed to manage the particular securities. Some mutual funds are proprietary, meaning they can exist only within a particular brokerage company. In that case, you'll have to sell those funds and distribute the proceeds to the beneficiary, to be invested as the beneficiary prefers.

Paper Stock Certificates

If the trust owns securities and actually has paper stock certificates, or the securities were bought directly from a mutual fund company (such as Vanguard or Fidelity), work with the company's transfer agent. Start by checking the website or calling the toll-free number for the transfer agent that administers that company's stock or mutual fund to learn how to transfer securities after a death. They'll undoubtedly ask for a copy of the trust instrument, proof of your authority to act as the successor trustee (usually, the settlor's death certificate), a letter of instruction (which is a form that they'll supply authorizing them to transfer the stock), a stock power or endorsed stock certificate, and an Affidavit of Domicile (there's a sample below).

If the transfer agent doesn't have a letter of instruction for you, you can write your own. Here's an example:

Letter of Instruction to Brokerage

Tessa Trustee
123 Main Street
Anytown, DE

Massive Transfer Agent
456 Center Lane
New York, NY

RE: Letter of Instruction
100 Shares of Big Corporation, held in the name of the
Cho Revocable Trust

Dear Sir or Madam,

I am the successor trustee of the Cho Revocable Trust. Enclosed for your reference is a copy of the Cho Revocable Trust and a certified copy of Sarah Cho's death certificate. You'll note that Section 4.1 of the trust states that in the event of Ms. Cho's death, I am to serve as the successor trustee.

The Cho Revocable Trust was the owner of 100 shares of Big Corporation. Please reissue those shares to Benjamin Cho, one of the beneficiaries of the trust. Benjamin's address is 55 Elm Street, Philadelphia, PA.

Enclosed are the endorsed stock certificates and an Affidavit of Domicile for Ms. Cho. Also enclosed is a check for $_____ as payment for services.

Thank you very much for your attention to this matter. If you have any questions or concerns, please do not hesitate to contact me.

Sincerely,

Tessa Trustee

Tessa Trustee

cc. Benjamin Cho

The transfer agent will also require you to sign your name either on the back of the original stock certificate itself or on a separate transfer document created by the brokerage company, called a "stock or bond power." Either way, your signature must be witnessed by a person who is able to affix a "medallion guarantee" to the document. Most banks and brokerage companies provide this service; a notary public cannot. You will not be able to transfer the securities without the guarantee from the financial institution. So call ahead and make sure that the person who is able to provide this service is available when you're ready to transfer the securities to the beneficiaries. The financial institution may charge a nominal fee for this service.

Typically, an Affidavit of Domicile is provided by a bank or other financial institution. The affidavit is a document in which you assert where the settlor resided, affirm that the settlor filed income taxes in that state, and promise that the settlor has no remaining outstanding debts. You must get your signature notarized. The institutions will not transfer or close the settlor's account without such an affidavit. You may find that the fill-in-the-blanks form provided by the institution is written for the executor of an estate, rather than a trustee. Just modify the form as needed, as in the sample below.

Filing the Final Fiduciary Income Tax Return

You must file a final trust income tax return with the IRS (Form 1041) and your state if the trust earns more than $600 worth of gross income or any taxable income. The return is typically due on April 15 of the year following the end of the year the income was earned (or 3½ months after the close of the trust's year, if the trust is reporting income on a fiscal year). You can file it earlier if you are ready to distribute the entire trust.

This fiduciary return is called a "final" return, and the tax preparer will check off a box on the first page to notify the IRS that the trust has (or is about to be) terminated. If the trust terminates just a few months after the settlor's death, but earns enough income to require a fiduciary income tax return, the tax return may be a "first and final" return— meaning it's both the first and the last return to be filed for the trust.

Affidavit of Domicile

NOTE: This affidavit must be filled in and signed before a notary.

State of _____)

) ss.

County of _____)

I, _Omna Morgan_ , being duly sworn, depose(s) and say(s) that I reside at _123 Mockingbird Lane, Sunnyvale, CA 97887_ , and acting as ~~the Surviving Tenant, Executor, or Administrator of the Estate of~~ _Trustee of the Ronald Morgan Revocable Trust, which was established by Ronald Morgan_ , Deceased, who died in the State of _California_ on _October 14, 20xx_ ; that at the time of his /her death the domicile (legal residence) was at _123 Mockingbird Lane, Sunnyvale, CA 94086_ ~~: (if the decedent resided in another State within 3 years prior to his or her death, indicate the name of the State where he or she previously resided)~~; that all debts of and taxes and claims against the decedent's Estate have been paid or provided for; that this affidavit is made for purposes of securing the transfer or delivery of property owned by the decedent at the time of his/her death to a purchaser or the person or persons legally entitled thereto under the laws of decedent's domicile; and that any apparent inequality in distribution has been satisfied or provided for out of other assets of the Estate.

_____

Omna Morgan, Affiant

[notary jurat form]

[SEAL]

[Signature of Notary]

You do not need to wait until you have distributed all of the money from the trust to file the final income tax return. A trust does not pay income tax unless its gross annual income is greater than $600, or it earned any taxable income, so a small amount of interest income won't require you to file another return. If you're concerned that there might be more debts and expenses to pay, you may choose to distribute most of the money and file the final return, but leave a small reserve in trust to pay those liabilities (see below). That small amount in reserve should not necessitate filing an additional tax return.

> **EXAMPLE:** In December 2016, Steve, the trustee of his uncle Larry's trust, distributes Larry's home and stock accounts to the beneficiaries of the trust. He keeps $5,000 in reserve in a checking account at a credit union, which earns interest at a rate of 0.75% annually. He files the trust's final tax return, for 2016, in April 2017. In June 2017, Steve is ready to distribute the balance of the trust. Because the checking account earned less than $20 in interest during 2017, Steve was not required to file a fiduciary income tax for 2017.

You may find that the income tax liabilities are somewhat different in the final tax return than in previous years. That's because the net income and deductions flow through to the beneficiaries in the final year. For instance, in most states, if you sell trust real estate or securities for a profit, the capital gain is considered an increase in principal, and the trust pays capital gains tax. But in the final year, the capital gains are reported in a Schedule K-1, and the trust beneficiaries pay them. Similarly, certain deductions are usually allowed only at the trust level, but are distributed to the beneficiaries in the final tax year so that the beneficiaries can take advantage of them on their personal income tax returns.

> **EXAMPLE:** Edward is the trustee of a trust that is about to terminate. He sells an apartment building for a loss of $50,000. By April 15 of the next calendar year, Edward will file the final fiduciary income tax return for the trust. Because the trust had no other income or loss during the year, the entire $50,000 loss will flow through to the beneficiaries on their Schedules K-1. They will be able to use that loss to offset any capital gains (but not ordinary income) they have from their own investments.

Keeping Some Trust Money in Reserve

Before you transfer all of the trust assets to the beneficiaries, consider holding back a reserve. A reserve is a small amount of funds that you keep in the trust to pay for any expenses that could show up later, such as bills from an accountant, attorney, or the IRS. (If you already know about an upcoming expense, pay it before you distribute assets to the beneficiaries.)

If you don't hold back enough money, the beneficiaries are legally liable for the trust expenses, but it will probably be very difficult for you to collect from them. Especially if you are one of the beneficiaries, you could easily be left holding the bag.

You don't want too big a reserve, because the beneficiaries could complain that you are stalling the distribution of the trust assets—possibly to generate higher fees for yourself—in violation of the trust instrument. Also, if you keep a lot of income-generating assets, the trust will owe income tax the next year, and you'll have to file another return and pay the tax (and a tax preparer). So hold back only a little more than you think you will need. A good way to arrive at a number is to estimate what the trust might owe and then round up to the next $1,000.

> **EXAMPLE:** Shoshanah is the trustee of a trust that her father set up for her and her siblings. She's already sold the house, filed her father's final income tax return, and figured out how much is left in the trust. She thinks it's possible her attorney could have about two hours' more worth of work (at $250/hour), expects the accountant to charge $400 to prepare the trust's income tax return, and expects the tax bill to be around $750. That adds up to $1,650; she decides to hold back a reserve of $2,000, just to be absolutely sure.

Keep the reserve funds in a basic FDIC-insured checking account until you're ready to pay the bills and distribute what's left. Once you're confident that all trust expenses have been paid, you have an obligation to distribute the remaining money to the beneficiaries.

Of course, this leads to the next question: how long do you hold the reserve? We suggest that you hang on to it through the next tax cycle—usually just a little after April 15 of the following year, unless you've decided to report taxes using a fiscal year. That way, you can make sure that there are no outstanding tax liabilities or preparer expenses. However, if you think that the IRS might audit the settlor's previously filed returns (the IRS can do that, even after someone dies) or the trust returns, consider holding the reserve until the end of the three-year audit period. Talk to your tax preparer for an honest assessment. Some red flags to look out for are:

- the settlor had a sole proprietorship
- there was unreported income from rental properties or other "under the table" income
- the settlor filed large charitable deductions, or
- the settlor owned assets that probably earned dividends, but the dividends weren't reported in prior income tax returns.

In that case, because beneficiaries are usually eager to receive their money as soon as possible, let them know in writing that you will be holding back a significant reserve for three years to protect the trust in case of audit. (See "Heading Off Trouble" in Chapter 3.)

Receipts From Beneficiaries

It is very important to obtain signed receipts from the beneficiaries, showing that you have given them everything they are entitled to receive from the trust. We've seen situations where beneficiaries (usually ones who have been in and out of jail) have claimed that they never received their inheritances, years after the funds were distributed to them. Showing those beneficiaries the receipts they signed ends the matter.

Get the receipts at the same time you distribute the funds to the beneficiaries. Try to handle the disbursements in person, if at all possible. It's easy to do if you bring a check to the beneficiary's house.

If the transfer has to go through a governmental agency or financial institution (for example, you need to record a deed or retitle a security in the name of the beneficiary), try to get the agency or institution to send the completed documents to you. That way, you can take the documents to the beneficiary and get a receipt. If the documents are sent directly to the beneficiary, you'll need to follow up by finding out when they were received and then get a receipt. If you must make the transfer by mail or private delivery service, require a signature showing the package was delivered. In the package, include the receipt and a stamped envelope addressed to you, so that it will be extremely easy for the beneficiary to sign the receipt and put it back in the mailbox. Also, if you send a check, be sure to get a copy of the cancelled check from the bank, showing that the beneficiary endorsed it. You can never be too careful.

If you're holding some funds in reserve, get a receipt for whatever amount you do distribute. The receipt can state that the beneficiary may be entitled to some or all of the remaining funds, after all expenses have been paid.

Anderson Revocable Trust
Receipt of Distribution

I, Sophia Anderson, a beneficiary of the Anderson Revocable Trust, acknowledge receipt of $25,000 from John Anderson, Trustee.

I acknowledge that this amount constitutes the bulk of the funds that I am entitled to receive from the Anderson Revocable Trust. I will receive additional funds only if the small reserve, retained by the trustee for any additional expenses, is not depleted during the trust administration.

_____   _____
Sophia Anderson   Date

Should You Ask Beneficiaries to Sign Releases?

If you're at all worried that a beneficiary might sue you, you can ask the beneficiary to sign a release of all possible claims against you as trustee. In most instances, trustees find it difficult to get releases from all beneficiaries. They are most likely to sign a release if they see an accurate accounting and are convinced that you made investments and distributions in their best interest.

If the beneficiary doesn't want to sign a release, you still must distribute the inheritance to the beneficiary. A release isn't the only way to protect yourself from lawsuits—both giving a solid final accounting and holding back an appropriate reserve will help.

In many states, if your trust includes a short time limitation to complain about an accounting, beneficiaries are prohibited from suing you after the deadline passes. Try to make the final distribution soon after an annual accounting to avoid the need for *another* accounting to show what's happened in the intervening months.

> **EXAMPLE:** Deborah is the trustee of her parents' trust. On March 1, she sends all of the beneficiaries an accounting, showing her actions as trustee from January 1 to December 31 of the previous year. The trust states that if Deborah sends an accurate accounting to the beneficiaries, the beneficiaries have only 180 days to complain about her actions. Deborah does not hear from any of the beneficiaries about the investments or disbursements made during the previous year, and waits until September 1 (180 days after the accounting) to distribute the bulk of the funds to the beneficiaries. She has already prepaid the accountant's bill for next year's final fiduciary income tax return, so her reserve is small.
>
> All of the beneficiaries sign receipts, but Deborah does not ask them to sign releases. She knows that they have no claim against her for her actions in the previous year because the 180-day period has expired. Although the beneficiaries could sue her for actions she took during the current year, the amount remaining in the trust is small, and it's sitting in a basic checking account. It is very unlikely the beneficiaries would have anything substantial to complain about.

SEE AN EXPERT

If you're worried about lawsuits, get legal advice. If your trust does not give beneficiaries just a short time to challenge a trust accounting, you may want to seek court approval for your actions as trustee to protect yourself from a beneficiary's lawsuit for breach of trust. Consult an attorney.

Final Correspondence With the Beneficiaries

When you have paid all of the expenses and are ready to close the last bank account, it's time to distribute what's left of the reserve. We suggest you write a letter to the beneficiaries, telling them how you spent (or saved) the reserve, and include their final check, if any. If your state, or the trust, requires you to provide an annual accounting, it also requires an accounting at the termination of the trust. But whether or not it's required, you should do it. It's just a good idea. However, if the reserve was small and the transactions uncomplicated, a detailed list of bills paid should be enough to satisfy the requirement. You can include it with your letter.

Telling the IRS You're No Longer Trustee

Finally, once you've distributed the reserve to the beneficiaries, take a few moments to fill out and file IRS Form 56, *Notice Concerning Fiduciary Relationship*. (Like all IRS forms, it's available at www.irs.gov.) This notifies the Internal Revenue Service that you have ended your service as trustee of the trust. It's a good way to tell the IRS that the trust has in fact been terminated (as discussed above, a "final" fiduciary income tax return does not necessarily mean that there are no assets in the trust—just that its annual income is less than what's required for filing) and legally relieves you of any future tax-related responsibilities.

If you are a trust beneficiary as well as trustee, or if you are the easiest person for the IRS to contact, the IRS might contact you if it has any questions or concerns about the unaudited fiduciary income tax returns. But responsibility for payment of underpaid taxes will rest on the trust beneficiaries.

Final Letter to Beneficiaries

John Smith, Trustee
Jones Living Trust
123 Main Street
Parkside, MT 59800

December 9, 20xx

Suzie Jones
Annabeth Jones-Collins
Marcus Jones

Re: Termination of the Jones Living Trust

Dear Suzie, Annabeth, and Marcus,

As you know, on September 1, I distributed to each of you most of your interests in the Jones Living Trust. Thank you for promptly returning your receipts, which I have in my trust file.

By now, you should have received your Schedule K-1, showing amounts received from the trust, from the trust accountant. Please be sure to report the appropriate amount of income from the trust on your income tax returns. You will also note that the trust had some deductions that could not be fully used on the trust income tax return. You may report those deductions on your returns as well, which may reduce your income tax. The accountant who prepared the K-1s will have divided up both the income and the deductions, so you'll know what your shares of both are.

You may recall that I held back a small reserve to pay the final income tax, preparation of the return, and other small expenses. I am now confident that all of the known trust expenses have been paid, and am distributing 1/3 of the remaining reserve to each of you. Please sign the enclosed receipt, acknowledging your receipt of the reserve, and return it to me. On the following page is a detailed list of the bills I paid since the last annual accounting.

Final Letter to Beneficiaries (continued)

Although I have paid all of the settlor's known expenses and the expenses associated with the trust, it is always possible—however unlikely—that the IRS or the state tax authorities will request additional information associated with the trust's filed income tax returns. The accountant assures me that all taxes have been paid. However, if for any reason a tax authority were to audit or challenge a return, the three of you would be jointly responsible for the underpaid taxes, because you received the settlor's assets.

It has been a pleasure to work with you.

Sincerely,

John Smith

JOHN SMITH, Trustee

Bills Paid Since Last Accounting Period:

    Emma Gleeson, CPA: $500 for preparation of final tax return

    IRS: $750, taxes

    Crandell and Ratchett, Attorneys: $500, trust administration

Glossary

For more plain-English definitions, see the free online legal dictionary at www.nolo.com.

Administrator. The person appointed by a probate court to serve on behalf of the estate, if there is no executor named in a will who is available to serve.

Affidavit. A written sworn statement of fact.

Basis. See Tax basis.

Beneficiary. A person or entity that is legally entitled to receive gifts under a legal document such as a will or trust.

Codicil. A separate legal document that alters or amends a signed and properly witnessed will.

Community property. A form of owning property that's available for married couples only (or registered domestic partners) in nine states. Community property is owned equally by both spouses.

Corpus. See Principal.

Disclaimer. The right to refuse to accept property left by will or trust, letting it pass to the next beneficiary in line. Disclaimers are often used to minimize estate and gift tax.

Distribution. A payment of trust principal or income to a beneficiary by a trustee.

Durable power of attorney. A document that appoints someone to act on behalf of the person who created it (called the "principal") and that remains effective even if the principal becomes incapacitated. The person authorized to act (called the "attorney in fact" or agent) can make health care decisions and/or handle financial matters for the principal, depending on the authority granted in the document.

Estate. All property left behind at death. The estate can be measured in different ways depending on whether the concern is taxes (the taxable estate), probate (the probate estate), or net worth (the net estate).

Estate tax. A federal tax on the assets belonging to a person at death (whether the assets are held in a trust, in a retirement account, or other form). There is no estate tax on assets that are transferred to a U.S. citizen spouse or tax-exempt charity, and everyone can leave a large amount of assets free from federal estate tax. Some states have their own estate or inheritance tax.

Executor. The person named in a will who manages the estate, deals with the probate court, collects assets, pays debts, and distributes property according to the terms of the will. Called a "personal representative" in some states. If a person dies without a valid will, the court appoints someone, who is usually called an "administrator," to fill this role.

Fiduciary. A person who is responsible for someone else's assets, such as an executor or trustee. A fiduciary is required by law to always act in the best interest of the beneficiaries.

Grantor. A person who puts property into a trust. Also called a "settlor" or "trustor."

Income. Rent, profits, dividends, or royalties earned on principal.

Inheritance tax. A tax, imposed in some states, on people who inherit assets. Also see Estate tax.

Inter vivos trust. See Living trust.

Intestate. Dying without a will. Compare Testate.

Irrevocable trust. A trust that cannot be altered or revoked. A living trust becomes irrevocable when the settlor dies. Some trusts are irrevocable when created, such as trusts to hold life insurance and charitable remainder trusts.

Issue. Lineal descendants, including children, grandchildren, and great-grandchildren, for example.

Joint tenancy. A method of holding title to property. If an asset is held in joint tenancy with someone else, and one co-owner dies, the survivor will own the entire asset. A joint tenancy asset is not transferred through a will or trust.

Letters testamentary. A document issued by a probate court, giving the executor authority to take control of assets and act on behalf of the deceased person's estate.

Life insurance. A contract between an insurance company and policy owner, in which the company agrees to pay a beneficiary a certain sum of money at the covered person's death.

Living trust. A revocable trust that is created by a living settlor and benefits other beneficiaries after the settlor's death. The settlor can change or revoke the trust at any time during the settlor's life. It is usually created to avoid probate. Also called an inter vivos trust.

Living will. A directive to physicians regarding the level of end-of-life medical care you want if you are unable to communicate your wishes.

Minor. Someone under the age of 18. Minors can't enter into legal contracts or own more than a few thousand dollars without adult supervision.

Personal property. What you own that's not land or buildings attached to land, such as cars, bank accounts, and jewelry.

Personal representative. The person named in a will to take care of the property of the person who has died. If there's a probate, this person is named as the executor.

Portability. A provision of the estate tax that allows the personal representative of the deceased spouse to make an election on the estate tax return to use the deceased spouse's unused exclusion ("DSUE") amount, which increases the surviving spouse's estate tax exclusion.

Pour-over will. A will that provides that property be transferred to an existing trust and distributed under the trust's terms.

Principal. 1. The assets held in a trust. Sometimes called "corpus," the Latin term. 2. The person who creates a power of attorney.

Probate. A court proceeding after death. It involves (1) authentication of a will, if any, (2) confirmation of an executor or appointment of an administrator, (3) oversight of the payment of taxes and debts, (4) identification of heirs, (5) distribution of property, and (6) appointment of guardian for the person and property of minor children.

QTIP trust. Short for "qualified terminable interest property trust," this is a trust that makes the settlor's surviving spouse the lifetime beneficiary of income generated by trust assets. This type of trust protects principal for ultimate beneficiaries. No estate tax is assessed on the trust property until the surviving spouse dies. This is used most frequently to ensure that the settlor's children will receive the trust principal in the event the surviving spouse remarries.

Real property. Land or buildings permanently attached to land.

Remainder beneficiary. Beneficiary who receives trust assets only after the life beneficiary dies.

Revocable living trust. See Living trust.

Settlor. A person who establishes a trust, also called a grantor or trustor.

Successor trustee. A person or institution that becomes the trustee after the original trustee dies, resigns, or is removed. The successor trustee has the same rights and responsibilities as the original trustee.

Tax basis. The purchase price of an asset plus any improvements. This is used when the asset is later sold, to determine whether there's been a capital gain or loss on that asset for tax purposes.

Tenancy by the entirety. A form of owning property that's only available for married couples. It is similar to joint tenancy because the surviving spouse has a right of survivorship—meaning they own the entire property by operation of law.

Testate. Dying with a valid will.

Testator. A person who makes a will.

Trust. A legal agreement or declaration under which a person or institution (the trustee) controls property given to the trust by a person (the settlor or grantor) for the benefit of a person or institution (the beneficiary).

Trustee. The person or institution that manages a trust and makes decisions about investments and discretionary trust distributions.

Uniform Trust Code. A set of mostly uniform state laws that governs the creation and administration of trusts. It has been adopted, with some modifications, in many states.

State Information

Here are summaries of state rules that you may be interested in as you settle a trust. When you look up information for your state, please keep in mind two important considerations:

- **These are only summaries of state laws.** Citations to the statutes are included so that you can look them up and read the law itself. It may contain details that are critical in your situation.

- **Laws change.** Before you rely on any statute listed here, make sure it hasn't changed since this book was printed. To take just one example, states might have increased the limit on what they consider a "small estate" eligible for probate shortcuts.

This book does not cover Louisiana law.

Alabama

Topic	State Rule
Creditor's claims procedure for trusts	Yes. Ala. Code § 19-3B-505
Uniform Trust Code	Yes
Nonjudicial settlement procedure	Yes. Ala. Code § 19-3B-111
Do beneficiaries have statutory right to see trust?	Yes. Ala. Code § 19-3B-813
State inheritance tax	No
State estate tax	No
State taxing authority website	revenue.alabama.gov
Community property	No
Affidavit procedure for small estates	No
Summary probate for small estates	Yes. Available to surviving spouse, or to other inheritors if there is no real estate. Estate's value cannot exceed $25,000 (adjusted annually for inflation). Ala. Code §§ 43-2-690 and following
Uniform Probate Code	No
Trustee must send notice after change of trustee	Yes. Ala. Code § 19-3B-813
Trustee must send notice after grantor dies	Yes. Ala. Code § 19-3B-813
Trust registration	No
Uniform Prudent Investor Act	Ala. Code §§ 19-38-901 and following
Statutory requirement for annual accounting to beneficiaries	Yes. Ala. Code § 19-3B-813

Alaska

Topic	State Rule
Creditor's claims procedure for trusts	Yes. If the personal representative of the settlor's estate doesn't do it, the trustee can. Alaska Stat. §§ 13.36.368 and following
Uniform Trust Code	No
Nonjudicial settlement procedure	No
Do beneficiaries have statutory right to see trust?	No. Trustee has duty to provide current beneficiaries with terms of the trust relevant to their interest. Alaska Stat. § 13.36.080
State inheritance tax	No
State estate tax	No
State taxing authority website	dor.alaska.gov
Community property	Yes, if married couples sign an agreement making their property community property. Alaska Stat. §§ 34.77.030, 34.77.090
Affidavit procedure for small estates	Entire estate, less liens and encumbrances, consists only of vehicles with a total value up to $100,000 and personal property (other than vehicles) worth up to $50,000; 30-day waiting period. Alaska Stat. § 13.16.680
Summary probate for small estates	Value of entire estate, less liens and encumbrances, does not exceed homestead allowance, exempt property, family allowance, costs and expenses of administration, funeral expenses, and medical and hospital expenses of the last illness. Alaska Stat. §§ 13.16.690, 695
Uniform Probate Code	Yes
Trustee must send notice after change of trustee	Yes. Alaska Stat. § 13.36.080
Trustee must send notice after grantor dies	No
Trust registration	Yes. Alaska Stat. §§ 13.36.005 and following
Uniform Prudent Investor Act	Alaska Stat. §§ 13.36.225 and following
Statutory requirement for annual accounting to beneficiaries	Yes. Alaska Stat. § 13.36.080

Arizona

Topic	State Rule
Creditor's claims procedure for trusts	No
Uniform Trust Code	Yes. Ariz. Rev. Stat. Ann. § 14-10101
Nonjudicial settlement procedure	Yes. Ariz. Rev. Stat. Ann. § 14-10111
Do beneficiaries have statutory right to see trust?	No. Trustee has duty to give qualified beneficiaries copy of the portions of the trust that are necessary to describe a beneficiary's interest. Ariz. Rev. Stat. Ann. § 14-10813
State inheritance tax	No
State estate tax	No
State taxing authority website	azdor.gov
Community property	Yes
Affidavit procedure for small estates	1. Value of all personal property in estate, less liens and encumbrances, is $75,000 or less. 30-day waiting period. Ariz. Rev. Stat. Ann. § 14-3971.B 2. Value of all Arizona real property in the estate, less liens and encumbrances, is $100,000 or less at the date of death, and all debts and taxes have been paid. Six-month waiting period. Ariz. Rev. Stat. Ann. § 14-3971.E
Summary probate for small estates	Value of entire estate, less liens and encumbrances, does not exceed allowance in lieu of homestead, exempt property, family allowance, costs of administration, funeral expenses, and expenses of the last illness. Six-month waiting period. Ariz. Rev. Stat. Ann. §§ 14-3973, 3974
Uniform Probate Code	Yes
Trustee must send notice after change of trustee	Yes. Ariz. Rev. Stat. Ann. § 14-10813
Trustee must send notice after grantor dies	Yes. Ariz. Rev. Stat. Ann. § 14-10813
Trust registration	No
Uniform Prudent Investor Act	Ariz. Rev. Stat. Ann. §§ 14-10901 and following
Statutory requirement for annual accounting to beneficiaries	Yes. Ariz. Rev. Stat. Ann. § 14-10813

Arkansas

Topic	State Rule
Creditor's claims procedure for trusts	No
Uniform Trust Code	Yes. Ark. Code Ann. §§ 28-73-101 and following
Nonjudicial settlement procedure	Yes. Ark. Code Ann. § 28-73-111
Do beneficiaries have statutory right to see trust?	Yes. Qualified beneficiaries have right to see copy of trust upon request. Ark. Code Ann. § 28-73-813
State inheritance tax	No
State estate tax	No
State taxing authority website	dfa.arkansas.gov
Community property	No
Affidavit procedure for small estates	Yes. Value, less encumbrances, of all property owned by decedent, excluding the homestead of and the statutory allowances for the benefit of a spouse or minor children, if any, does not exceed $100,000. 45-day waiting period. Ark. Code Ann. § 28-41-101
Summary probate for small estates	Personal property does not exceed that to which the surviving spouse, if any, or minor children, if any, are by law entitled free of debt, as dower or curtesy and statutory allowances. Probate court can order entire estate to surviving spouse and/or minor children. Ark. Code Ann. § 28-41-103
Uniform Probate Code	No
Trustee must send notice after change of trustee	Yes. Ark. Code Ann. § 28-73-813
Trustee must send notice after grantor dies	Yes. Ark. Code Ann. § 28-73-813
Trust registration	No
Uniform Prudent Investor Act	Ark. Code Ann. §§ 28-73-901 and following
Statutory requirement for annual accounting to beneficiaries	Yes. Ark. Code Ann. § 28-73-813

California

Topic	State Rule
Creditor's claims procedure for trusts	Yes. Cal. Prob. Code §§ 19000 and following
Uniform Trust Code	No
Nonjudicial settlement procedure	Yes. Cal. Prob. Code §§ 16500 and following
Do beneficiaries have statutory right to see trust?	Yes. Beneficiaries and heirs have right to see trust. Cal. Prob. Code § 16061.7
State inheritance tax	No
State estate tax	No
State taxing authority website	ftb.ca.gov
Community property	Yes
Affidavit procedure for small estates	1. For personal property in estates up to $150,000 in value, as calculated using exclusions listed in "summary probate" section, below; 40-day waiting period. Cal. Prob. Code §§ 13050, 13100, and following 2. For real estate up to $50,000 in value. Six-month waiting period. Cal. Prob. Code §§ 13200 to 13208
Summary probate procedure for small estates	Value up to $150,000. Excluded from calculating value: real estate outside California; joint tenancy property; property that goes outright to a surviving spouse; life insurance, death benefits, and other assets not subject to probate that pass to named beneficiaries; multiple-party and payable-on-death accounts; any registered manufactured or mobile home; any numbered vessel; registered motor vehicles; salary up to $15,000; amounts due decedent for services in the armed forces; property held in trust, including a living trust. Cal. Prob. Code §§ 13150 and following
Uniform Probate Code	No
Trustee must send notice after change of trustee	Only if trust is irrevocable. Cal. Prob. Code § 16061.7
Trustee must send notice after grantor dies	Yes. Must notify trust beneficiaries and deceased person's heirs (people who would inherit under state law in the absence of a will or trust). Cal. Prob. Code §§ 16060.5-16061.8
Trust registration	No
Uniform Prudent Investor Act	Cal. Prob. Code §§ 16045 and following
Statutory requirement for annual accounting to beneficiaries	Yes. Cal. Prob. Code § 16062

Colorado

Topic	State Rule
Creditor's claims procedure for trusts	No
Uniform Trust Code	No
Nonjudicial settlement procedure	No
Do beneficiaries have statutory right to see trust?	No. Current beneficiaries have right to copy of terms of the trust which describe or affect their interest and with relevant information about the assets of the trust. Col. Rev. Stat. Ann. § 15-16-303
State inheritance tax	No
State estate tax	No
State taxing authority website	colorado.gov/revenueonline
Community property	No
Affidavit procedure for small estates	Estates where fair market value of property that is subject to disposition by will or state intestate succession law, less liens and encumbrances, is $60,000 (adjusted annually for inflation) or less. (This excludes joint tenancy property, property in a living trust, payable-on-death bank accounts, and other kinds of property that don't pass under a will.) Ten-day waiting period. Col. Rev. Stat. Ann. § 15-12-1201
Summary probate for small estates	Value of entire estate, less liens and encumbrances, does not exceed the value of personal property held by the decedent as fiduciary or trustee, exempt property allowance, family allowance, costs of administration, funeral expenses, and medical expenses of last illness. Colo. Rev. Stat. § 15-12-1203
Uniform Probate Code	Yes
Trustee must send notice after change of trustee	Yes, if there is also a duty to register the trust. Colo. Rev. Stat. §§ 15-16-101 and 15-16-303
Trustee must send notice after grantor dies	Yes. Colo. Rev. Stat. §§ 15-16-101 and 15-16-303
Trust registration	Yes, for irrevocable trusts, unless all assets are distributable outright to beneficiaries. Colo. Rev. Stat. §§ 15-16-101 and following
Uniform Prudent Investor Act	Colo. Rev. Stat. §§ 15-1.1-101 and following
Statutory requirement for annual accounting to beneficiaries	Yes. Col. Rev. Stat. Ann. § 15-16-303

Connecticut

Topic	State Rule
Creditor's claims procedure for trusts	No
Uniform Trust Code	No
Nonjudicial settlement procedure	No
Do beneficiaries have statutory right to see trust?	No
State inheritance tax	No
State estate tax	Yes, for estates of more than $2 million. Conn. Gen. Stat. Ann. § 12-391
State taxing authority website	https://portal.ct.gov/drs
Community property	No
Affidavit procedure for small estates	No
Summary probate for small estates	No real estate (except real estate held in survivorship form), estate not exceeding $40,000 in value. Conn. Gen. Stat. § 45a-273
Uniform Probate Code	No
Trustee must send notice after change of trustee	No
Trustee must send notice after grantor dies	No
Trust registration	No
Uniform Prudent Investor Act	Conn. Gen. Stat. Ann. § 45a-541
Statutory requirement for annual accounting to beneficiaries	No

Delaware

Topic	State Rule
Creditor's claims procedure for trusts	No
Uniform Trust Code	No
Nonjudicial settlement procedure	Yes. Del. Code Ann. tit. 12, § 3338
Do beneficiaries have statutory right to see trust?	No
State inheritance tax	No
State estate tax	Yes, for estates with a value exceeding the amount of the federal estate tax exemption. Del. Code Ann. tit. 30, §§ 1501 and following
State taxing authority website	revenue.delaware.gov
Community property	No
Affidavit procedure for small estates	Estates without solely owned Delaware real estate and a value of no more than $30,000. (Jointly owned property, and death benefits that pass outside of probate, such as insurance or pension proceeds, are not counted toward the $30,000 limit.) 30-day waiting period. Available only to spouse, certain relatives, or funeral director. Del. Code Ann. tit. 12, § 2306
Summary probate for small estates	No
Uniform Probate Code	No
Trustee must send notice after change of trustee	No
Trustee must send notice after grantor dies	No
Trust registration	No
Uniform Prudent Investor Act	Substantially similar law: Del. Code Ann. tit. 12 § 3302
Statutory requirement for annual accounting to beneficiaries	No

District of Columbia

Topic	State Rule
Creditor's claims procedure for trusts	Yes. D.C. Code Ann. § 19-1305.5
Uniform Trust Code	Yes. D.C. Code Ann. §§ 19-1301.01 and following
Nonjudicial settlement procedure	Yes. D.C. Code Ann. § 19-1301.11
Do beneficiaries have statutory right to see trust?	Yes. Trustee must provide copy of the trust upon request to qualified beneficiaries. D.C. Code Ann. § 19-1308.13
State inheritance tax	No
State estate tax	Yes, for estates of more than $1 million. D.C. Code Ann. §§ 47-3701 and following
State taxing authority website	otr.cfo.dc.gov
Community property	No
Affidavit procedure for small estates	Deceased person owned nothing but one or two motor vehicles. D.C. Code Ann. § 20-357
Summary probate for small estates	Property subject to administration in D.C. has value of $40,000 or less. D.C. Code Ann. §§ 20-351 and following
Uniform Probate Code	No
Trustee must send notice after change of trustee	Yes. D.C. Code Ann. § 19-1308.13
Trustee must send notice after grantor dies	Yes. D.C. Code Ann. § 19-1308.13
Trust registration	No
Uniform Prudent Investor Act	D.C. Code Ann. § 19-1309.01
Statutory requirement for annual accounting to beneficiaries	Yes. D.C. Code Ann. § 19-1308.13

Florida

Topic	State Rule
Creditor's claims procedure for trusts	No
Uniform Trust Code	Yes. Fla. Stat. Ann. §§ 736 and following
Nonjudicial settlement procedure	Yes. Fla. Stat. Ann. § 736.0111
Do beneficiaries have statutory right to see trust?	Yes. Trustee must provide copy of the trust upon request to qualified beneficiaries. Fla. Stat. Ann. § 736.0813
State inheritance tax	No
State estate tax	No
State taxing authority website	floridarevenue.com
Community property	No
Affidavit procedure for small estates	No
Summary probate for small estates	1. No real estate, and all property is exempt from creditors' claims except amounts needed to pay funeral and two months' last illness expenses. Upon letter to court, court will authorize transfer of property to people entitled to it. Fla. Stat. Ann. § 735.301 2. Value of entire estate subject to administration in Florida, less the value of property that is exempt from creditors' claims, doesn't exceed $75,000, OR decedent has been dead more than two years. Petition must be filed with court. Fla. Stat. Ann. §§ 735.201 and following
Uniform Probate Code	Substantially similar law. Fla. Stat. Ann. §§ 735.005 and following
Trustee must send notice after change of trustee	Yes. Fla. Stat. Ann. § 736.0813
Trustee must send notice after grantor dies	Yes. Fla. Stat. Ann. § 736.0813
Trust registration	No. Trustee must file notice of trust. Fla. Stat. Ann. § 736.05055
Uniform Prudent Investor Act	Substantially similar law: Fla. Stat. Ann. §§ 518.11 and following
Statutory requirement for annual accounting to beneficiaries	Yes. Fla. Stat. Ann. § 736.0813

Georgia

Topic	State Rule
Creditor's claims procedure for trusts	No
Uniform Trust Code	No
Nonjudicial settlement procedure	No
Do beneficiaries have statutory right to see trust?	No. Trustee must provide any beneficiary with the terms of the trust that describe or affect the beneficiary's interest. Ga. Code Ann. § 53-12-243
State inheritance tax	No
State estate tax	No
State taxing authority website	dor.georgia.gov
Community property	No
Affidavit procedure for small estates	Yes. Ga. Code Ann. § 7.1-239. There is no will and less than $10,000 is in a financial institution. Can be claimed by spouse, then children, then parents. If not claimed within 90 days, money can be used to pay funeral and last illness expenses directly to creditors.
Summary probate for small estates	There is no will, estate owes no debts (or creditors have consented), and all heirs have amicably agreed on how to divide the property. Ga. Code Ann. §§ 53-2-40 and following
Uniform Probate Code	No
Trustee must send notice after change of trustee	Only if trust is irrevocable. Ga. Code Ann. § 53-12-242
Trustee must send notice after grantor dies	Yes. Ga. Code Ann. § 53-12-242
Trust registration	No
Uniform Prudent Investor Act	No
Statutory requirement for annual accounting to beneficiaries	Yes. Ga. Code Ann. § 53-12-243

Hawaii

Topic	State Rule
Creditor's claims procedure for trusts	Yes. Haw. Rev. Stat. § 560:3-801
Uniform Trust Code	No
Nonjudicial settlement procedure	No
Do beneficiaries have statutory right to see trust?	No. Trustee must provide current beneficiary with the terms of the trust that describe or affect the beneficiary's interest. Haw. Rev. Stat. § 560:7-303
State inheritance tax	No
State estate tax	Yes, for estates with a value exceeding the amount of the federal estate tax exemption. Haw. Rev. Stat. § 236E-6
State taxing authority website	tax.hawaii.gov
Community property	No
Affidavit procedure for small estates	Value of property deceased person owned in Hawaii is $100,000 or less. Can transfer motor vehicles this way regardless of value of estate. Haw. Rev. Stat. §§ 560:3-1201 and following
Summary probate for small estates	Value of all property deceased person owned in Hawaii doesn't exceed $100,000. Haw. Rev. Stat. §§ 560:3-1205 and following
Uniform Probate Code	Yes
Trustee must send notice after change of trustee	Yes. Haw. Rev. Stat. § 560:7-303
Trustee must send notice after grantor dies	No
Trust registration	Yes. Haw. Rev. Stat. §§ 560:7-101 and following
Uniform Prudent Investor Act	Haw. Rev. Stat. §§ 554C-1 and following
Statutory requirement for annual accounting to beneficiaries	Yes. Haw. Rev. Stat. § 560:7-303

Idaho

Topic	State Rule
Creditor's claims procedure for trusts	No
Uniform Trust Code	No
Nonjudicial settlement procedure	Yes, Idaho Code §§ 15-8-301 and following
Do beneficiaries have statutory right to see trust?	No. Trustee must provide current beneficiaries with the terms of the trust that describe or affect the beneficiary's interest. Idaho Code § 15-7-303
State inheritance tax	No
State estate tax	No
State taxing authority website	tax.idaho.gov
Community property	Yes
Affidavit procedure for small estates	Fair market value of property subject to probate, wherever located, less liens and encumbrances, is $100,000 or less. 30-day waiting period. Idaho Code §§ 15-3-1201 and following
Summary probate for small estates	1. Value of all property deceased person owned, less liens and encumbrances, doesn't exceed the homestead allowance, exempt property, family allowance, costs of administration, funeral expenses, and medical expenses of the last illness. Idaho Code §§ 15-3-1203 and following 2. A surviving spouse who inherits everything can file petition with court, which will issue a decree to that effect. Idaho Code § 15-3-1205
Uniform Probate Code	Yes
Trustee must send notice after change of trustee	Yes. Idaho Code § 15-7-303
Trustee must send notice after grantor dies	No
Trust registration	Yes. Idaho Code §§ 15-7-101 and following
Uniform Prudent Investor Act	Idaho Code §§ 68-501 and following
Statutory requirement for annual accounting to beneficiaries	Yes. Idaho Code § 15-7-303

Illinois

Topic	State Rule
Creditor's claims procedure for trusts	No
Uniform Trust Code	No
Nonjudicial settlement procedure	Yes, 760 Ill. Comp. Stat. § 5/16.1
Do beneficiaries have statutory right to see trust?	No
State inheritance tax	No
State estate tax	Yes, for estates of more than $4 million. 35 Ill. Comp. Stat. § 405/2
State taxing authority website	www2.illinois.gov/rev
Community property	No
Affidavit procedure for small estates	Gross value of all deceased person's property that passes under a will or by state law, excluding real estate, is $100,000 or less. 755 Ill. Comp. Stat. § 5/25-1
Summary probate for small estates	Gross value of property subject to probate in Illinois does not exceed $100,000. All heirs and beneficiaries must consent in writing. 755 Ill. Comp. Stat. § 5/9-8
Uniform Probate Code	No
Trustee must send notice after change of trustee	No
Trustee must send notice after grantor dies	No
Trust registration	No
Uniform Prudent Investor Act	Substantially similar law: 760 Ill. Comp. Stat. §§ 5/5, 5/5.1
Statutory requirement for annual accounting to beneficiaries	Yes. 760 Ill. Comp. Stat. § 5/11

Indiana

Topic	State Rule
Creditor's claims procedure for trusts	No
Uniform Trust Code	No
Nonjudicial settlement procedure	No
Do beneficiaries have statutory right to see trust?	Yes. Ind. Code Ann. § 30-4-3-6
State inheritance tax	No
State estate tax	No
State taxing authority website	in.gov/dor
Community property	No
Affidavit procedure for small estates	Value of gross probate estate, less liens and encumbrances, does not exceed $50,000. 45-day waiting period. Ind. Code § 29-1-8-1
Summary probate for small estates	Value of property subject to probate does not exceed $50,000. Ind. Code Ann. §§ 29-1-8-3 and following
Uniform Probate Code	No
Trustee must send notice after change of trustee	No
Trustee must send notice after grantor dies	No
Trust registration	No
Uniform Prudent Investor Act	Ind. Code Ann. § 30-4-3.5
Statutory requirement for annual accounting to beneficiaries	Yes. Ind. Code Ann. § 30-4-5-12

Iowa

Topic	State Rule
Creditor's claims procedure for trusts	Yes. Iowa Code § 633A.3109
Uniform Trust Code	No
Nonjudicial settlement procedure	Yes. Iowa Code § 633A.6308
Do beneficiaries have statutory right to see trust?	Yes. Qualified beneficiaries can request a copy. Iowa Code § 633A.4213
State inheritance tax	Yes. Iowa Code § 450.10
State estate tax	No
State taxing authority website	tax.iowa.gov
Community property	No
Affidavit procedure for small estates	No real estate (or real estate passes to spouse as joint tenant) and gross value of the deceased person's personal property is $25,000 or less. 40-day waiting period. Iowa Code § 633.356
Summary probate for small estates	Gross value of property subject to probate does not exceed $100,000. Iowa Code § 635.1
Uniform Probate Code	No
Trustee must send notice after change of trustee	No
Trustee must send notice after grantor dies	Yes. Iowa Code §§ 633A.3110 and 633.237
Trust registration	No
Uniform Prudent Investor Act	Iowa Code §§ 633.4301 and following
Statutory requirement for annual accounting to beneficiaries	Yes. Iowa Code Ann. § 633A.4213

Kansas

Topic	State Rule
Creditor's claims procedure for trusts	Yes. Kan. Stat. Ann. § 58a-818
Uniform Trust Code	Yes. Kan. Stat. Ann. §§ 58a and following
Nonjudicial settlement procedure	Yes. Kan. Stat. Ann. § 58a-111
Do beneficiaries have statutory right to see trust?	Yes. Qualified beneficiaries have right to request a copy of the portions of the trust instrument that relate to their interest or a copy of the trust instrument if specifically so requested. Kan. Stat. Ann. § 58a -813
State inheritance tax	No
State estate tax	No
State taxing authority website	ksrevenue.org
Community property	No
Affidavit procedure for small estates	Value of total assets subject to probate is $40,000 or less. Kan. Stat. Ann. § 59-1507b
Summary probate for small estates	Simplified estate procedure available if court approves it, based on size of estate, wishes of heirs, and other factors. Kan. Stat. Ann. §§ 59-3202 and following
Uniform Probate Code	No
Trustee must send notice after change of trustee	Yes. Kan. Stat. Ann. § 58a-813
Trustee must send notice after grantor dies	Yes. Must notify qualified trust beneficiaries. Kan. Stat. Ann. § 58a-813
Trust registration	No
Uniform Prudent Investor Act	Kan. Stat. Ann. §§ 58-24a01 and following
Statutory requirement for annual accounting to beneficiaries	Yes. Kan. Stat. Ann. § 58a-813

Kentucky

Topic	State Rule
Creditor's claims procedure for trusts	No
Uniform Trust Code	Yes. Ky. Rev. Stat. Ann. § 386B
Nonjudicial settlement procedure	Yes. Ky. Rev. Stat. Ann. § 386B.1-090
Do beneficiaries have statutory right to see trust?	Yes. A qualified beneficiary may request a copy of the trust. Ky. Rev. Stat. Ann. § 386B.8-130
State inheritance tax	Yes. Ky. Rev. Stat. Ann. § 140.010
State estate tax	No
State taxing authority website	revenue.ky.gov
Community property	No
Affidavit procedure for small estates	No
Summary probate for small estates	No will leaves personal property, and there is a surviving spouse and value of property subject to probate is $15,000 or less, or if there is no surviving spouse and someone else has paid at least $15,000 in preferred claims. Ky. Rev. Stat. Ann. §§ 391.030, 395.455
Uniform Probate Code	No
Trustee must send notice after change of trustee	Yes. Ky. Rev. Stat. Ann. § 386B.8-130
Trustee must send notice after grantor dies	Yes. Ky. Rev. Stat. Ann. § 386B.8-130
Trust registration	Yes. Ky. Rev. Stat. Ann. § 386B.2-050
Uniform Prudent Investor Act	Ky. Rev. Stat. Ann. § 386B.9-010
Statutory requirement for annual accounting to beneficiaries	Ky. Rev. Stat. Ann. § 386B.9-130

Maine

Topic	State Rule
Creditor's claims procedure for trusts	No
Uniform Trust Code	Yes. Me. Rev. Stat. Ann. tit. 18-B
Nonjudicial settlement procedure	Yes. Me. Rev. Stat. Ann. tit. 18-B, § 111
Do beneficiaries have statutory right to see trust?	Yes. Qualified beneficiaries have right to copy of the trust upon request. Me. Rev. Stat. Ann. tit. 18-B, § 813
State inheritance tax	No
State estate tax	Yes, for estates with a value exceeding the amount of the federal estate tax exemption. Me. Rev. Stat. Ann. tit. 36, §§ 4062 and following
State taxing authority website	www.maine.gov/revenue
Community property	No
Affidavit procedure for small estates	Value of entire estate, wherever located, less liens and encumbrances, does not exceed $20,000. 30-day waiting period. Me. Rev. Stat. Ann. tit.18-A, §§ 3-1201, 1202
Summary probate for small estates	Value of entire estate, less liens and encumbrances, does not exceed homestead allowance, exempt property, family allowance, costs of administration, reasonable funeral expenses, and reasonable medical expenses of the last illness. Me. Rev. Stat. Ann. tit.18-A, § 3-1203
Uniform Probate Code	Yes
Trustee must send notice after change of trustee	Yes. Me. Rev. Stat. Ann. tit. 18-B, § 813
Trustee must send notice after grantor dies	Yes. Me. Rev. Stat. Ann. tit. 18-B, § 813
Trust registration	No
Uniform Prudent Investor Act	Me. Rev. Stat. Ann. tit. 18-B, §§ 901 and following
Statutory requirement for annual accounting to beneficiaries	Yes. Me. Rev. Stat. Ann. tit. 18-B, § 813

Maryland

Topic	State Rule
Creditor's claims procedure for trusts	Yes. Md. Code Ann. [Est. & Trusts] § 14.5-508
Uniform Trust Code	Yes. Md. Code Ann. [Est. & Trusts] § 14.5
Nonjudicial settlement procedure	No
Do beneficiaries have statutory right to see trust?	Yes. A qualified beneficiary may request a copy of the trust. Md. Code Ann. [Est. & Trusts] § 14.5-813
State inheritance tax	Yes. Md. Code Ann. [Tax-Gen.] §§ 7-201 and following
State estate tax	Yes, for gross estates over $2 million in 2016, $3 million in 2017, $4 million in 2018, and the amount of the federal estate tax exemption in 2019. Md. Code Ann. [Tax-Gen.] §§ 7-301 and following
State taxing authority website	comp.state.md.us
Community property	No
Affidavit procedure for small estates	No
Summary probate for small estates	Property subject to probate in Maryland has a value of $50,000 or less, or if surviving spouse is the only beneficiary, $100,000 or less. Md. Code Ann. [Est. & Trusts] §§ 5-601 and following
Uniform Probate Code	No
Trustee must send notice after change of trustee	Yes. Md. Code Ann. [Est. & Trusts] § 14.5-813
Trustee must send notice after grantor dies	Yes. Md. Code Ann. [Est. & Trusts] § 14.5-813
Trust registration	No
Uniform Prudent Investor Act	Substantially similar law: Md. Code Ann. [Est. & Trusts] § 15-114.
Statutory requirement for annual accounting to beneficiaries	Yes. Md. Code Ann. [Est. & Trusts] § 14.5-813

Massachusetts

Topic	State Rule
Creditor's claims procedure for trusts	No
Uniform Trust Code	Yes. Mass. Gen. Laws ch. 203E
Nonjudicial settlement procedure	Yes. Mass. Gen. Laws ch. 203E § 111
Do beneficiaries have statutory right to see trust?	No. Trustee must keep qualified beneficiaries reasonably informed. Mass. Gen. Laws Ann. ch. 203E-813
State inheritance tax	No
State estate tax	Yes, for estates of more than $1 million. Mass. Gen. Laws ch. 65C, §§ 1 and following
State taxing authority website	mass.gov/dor
Community property	No
Affidavit procedure for small estates	No
Summary probate for small estates	1. Estate contains no real estate and is worth no more than $25,000 plus value of vehicle. Interested person files will (if any), inventory of assets, and list of heirs with court, and offers to serve as voluntary personal representative. Mass. Gen. Laws ch. 190B, §§ 3-1201, 1202 2. Value of entire estate, less liens and encumbrances, does not exceed exempt property, family allowance, costs of administration, funeral expenses, and expenses of the last illness. Personal representative may immediately disburse estate and file closing statement. Mass. Gen. Laws ch. 190B, §§ 3-1203, 1204
Uniform Probate Code	Yes, in part
Trustee must send notice after change of trustee	Yes. Mass. Gen. Laws ch. 203E § 813
Trustee must send notice after grantor dies	No
Trust registration	No
Uniform Prudent Investor Act	Mass. Gen. Laws ch. 203C, §§ 1 and following
Statutory requirement for annual accounting to beneficiaries	Yes. Mass. Gen. Laws ch. 203E § 813

Michigan

Topic	State Rule
Creditor's claims procedure for trusts	Yes. Mich. Comp. Laws § 700.7608
Uniform Trust Code	Yes. Mich. Comp. Laws §§ 700.7101 and following
Nonjudicial settlement procedure	Yes. Mich. Comp. Laws § 700.7111
Do beneficiaries have statutory right to see trust?	No. Trustee must provide qualified beneficiaries with a copy of the trust's terms that describe or affect the beneficiary's interest upon request. Mich. Comp. Laws § 700.7814
State inheritance tax	No
State estate tax	No
State taxing authority website	michigan.gov/treasury
Community property	No
Affidavit procedure for small estates	Estate does not include real estate, and value of the entire estate, less liens and encumbrances, doesn't exceed $15,000. 28-day waiting period. Mich. Comp. Laws § 700.3983
Summary probate for small estates	1. Value of gross estate, after payment of funeral and burial costs, is $15,000 or less. Court can order property turned over to surviving spouse or heirs. Mich. Comp. Laws § 700.3982 2. Value of entire estate, less liens and encumbrances, does not exceed homestead allowance, family allowance, exempt property, costs of administration, and reasonable expenses of last illness and funeral. Mich. Comp. Laws § 700.3987
Uniform Probate Code	Yes
Trustee must send notice after change of trustee	Yes. Mich. Comp. Laws § 700.7814
Trustee must send notice after grantor dies	Yes. Mich. Comp. Laws § 700.7814
Trust registration	Yes. Mich. Comp. Laws § 700.7209
Uniform Prudent Investor Act	Mich. Comp. Laws § 700.1501
Statutory requirement for annual accounting to beneficiaries	Yes. Mich. Comp. Laws § 700.7814

Minnesota

Topic	State Rule
Creditor's claims procedure for trusts	No
Uniform Trust Code	Yes. Minn. Stat. Ann. Chapt. 501C
Nonjudicial settlement procedure	Yes. Minn. Stat. Ann. § 501C.0111
Do beneficiaries have statutory right to see trust?	No
State inheritance tax	No
State estate tax	Yes, for estates over $1.6 million in 2016, over $1.8 million in 2017, and over $2 million in 2018 and thereafter. There is an additional exemption for certain farm and business property, so that the total tax-exempt amount can be up to $5 million. Minn. Stat. Ann. §§ 291.005 and following
State taxing authority website	revenue.state.mn.us
Community property	No
Affidavit procedure for small estates	$50,000 limit for entire probate estate, wherever located, including any contents of a safe deposit box, less liens and encumbrances. 30-day waiting period. Minn. Stat. § 524.3-1201
Summary probate for small estates	If court determines that no property is subject to creditors' claims (because it is exempt from claims or must be set aside for the spouse and children), can order estate closed without further proceedings. Minn. Stat. Ann. § 524.3-1203
Uniform Probate Code	Yes
Trustee must send notice after change of trustee	No
Trustee must send notice after grantor dies	No. Permissible under Minn. Stat. Ann. § 501C.0605
Trust registration	No
Uniform Prudent Investor Act	Minn. Stat. Ann. § 501C.0901
Statutory requirement for annual accounting to beneficiaries	No. Settler can provide that trustee not send accountings. Minn. Stat. Ann. § 501C.0813

Mississippi

Topic	State Rule
Creditor's claims procedure for trusts	No
Uniform Trust Code	Yes. Miss. Code Ann. §§ 91-8-101 and following
Nonjudicial settlement procedure	Yes. Miss. Code Ann. § 91-8-111
Do beneficiaries have statutory right to see trust?	No; trustee may provide abstract of the trust instead. Miss. Code Ann. § 91-8-813 Settlor can waive the requirement of sending a copy or abstract of the trust. Miss. Code Ann. § 91-8-105
State inheritance tax	No
State estate tax	No
State taxing authority website	dor.ms.gov
Community property	No
Affidavit procedure for small estates	For bank accounts only, up to $12,500, if there is no will. Person claiming money must sign bond guaranteeing to pay any lawful debts of the deceased to the extent of the withdrawal. Miss. Code Ann. § 81-14-383
Summary probate for small estates	Value of estate is $500 or less. Miss. Code Ann. § 91-7-147
Uniform Probate Code	No
Trustee must send notice after change of trustee	Yes. Miss. Code Ann. § 91-8-813 (unless waived under § 91-8-105)
Trustee must send notice after grantor dies	No
Trust registration	No
Uniform Prudent Investor Act	Miss. Code Ann. §§ 901-9-601 and following
Statutory requirement for annual accounting to beneficiaries	No

Missouri

Topic	State Rule
Creditor's claims procedure for trusts	Yes. Mo. Rev. Stat. § 456.5-505
Uniform Trust Code	Yes. Mo. Rev. Stat. §§ 456.1-101 and following
Nonjudicial settlement procedure	Yes. Mo. Rev. Stat. § 456.1-111
Do beneficiaries have statutory right to see trust?	Yes, qualified beneficiaries can request a copy. Mo. Rev. Stat. § 456.8-813
State inheritance tax	No
State estate tax	No
State taxing authority website	dor.mo.gov
Community property	No
Affidavit procedure for small estates	No
Summary probate for small estates	Value of entire estate, less liens and encumbrances, is $40,000 or less. Mo. Rev. Stat. § 473.097
Uniform Probate Code	No
Trustee must send notice after change of trustee	Yes. Mo. Rev. Stat. § 456.8-813
Trustee must send notice after grantor dies	Yes. Mo. Rev. Stat. § 456.8-813
Trust registration	Yes. Mo. Rev. Stat. §§ 456.027 and following
Uniform Prudent Investor Act	Mo. Rev. Stat. §§ 469.900 and following
Statutory requirement for annual accounting to beneficiaries	Yes. Mo. Rev. Stat. § 456.8-813

Montana

Topic	State Rule
Creditor's claims procedure for trusts	No
Uniform Trust Code	Yes. Mont. Code Ann. §§ 72-38-101 and following
Nonjudicial settlement procedure	Yes. Mont. Code Ann. § 72-38-111
Do beneficiaries have statutory right to see trust?	No. If beneficiary requests it, trustee must provide portions of the trust that describe beneficiary's interest. Mont. Code Ann. § 72-38-813
State inheritance tax	No
State estate tax	No
State taxing authority website	mt.revenue.gov
Community property	No
Affidavit procedure for small estates	Value of entire estate, wherever located, less liens and encumbrances, is $50,000 or less. 30-day waiting period. Mont. Code Ann. § 72-3-1101
Summary probate for small estates	Value of entire estate, less liens and encumbrances, doesn't exceed homestead allowance, exempt property, family allowance, costs of administration, funeral expenses, and medical expenses of the last illness. Mont. Code Ann. § 72-3-1103
Uniform Probate Code	Yes
Trustee must send notice after change of trustee	Yes. Mont. Code Ann. § 72-38-813
Trustee must send notice after grantor dies	Yes. Mont. Code Ann. § 72-38-813
Trust registration	No
Uniform Prudent Investor Act	Mont. Code Ann. §§ 72-38-901 and following
Statutory requirement for annual accounting to beneficiaries	Yes. Mont. Code Ann. § 72-38-813

Nebraska

Topic	State Rule
Creditor's claims procedure for trusts	No
Uniform Trust Code	Yes. Neb. Rev. Stat. §§ 30-3801 and following
Nonjudicial settlement procedure	Yes. Neb. Rev. Stat. § 30-3811
Do beneficiaries have statutory right to see trust?	Yes, qualified beneficiaries can request a copy. Neb. Rev. Stat. § 30-3878
State inheritance tax	Yes. Neb. Rev. Stat. §§ 77-2001 and following
State estate tax	No
State taxing authority website	revenue.nebraska.gov
Community property	No
Affidavit procedure for small estates	**Personal property.** Value of all personal property in estate, wherever located, less liens and encumbrances, is $50,000 or less. 30-day waiting period. Neb. Rev. Stat. § 30-24,125 **Real estate.** Value of all real estate in state is $50,000 or less. 30-day waiting period. Neb. Rev. Stat. § 30-24,129
Summary probate for small estates	Value of entire estate, less liens and encumbrances, doesn't exceed homestead allowance, exempt property, family allowance, costs of administration, funeral expenses, and medical expenses of the last illness. Neb. Rev. Stat. § 30-24,127
Uniform Probate Code	Yes
Trustee must send notice after change of trustee	Yes. Neb. Rev. Stat. § 30-3878
Trustee must send notice after grantor dies	Yes. Neb. Rev. Stat. § 30-3878
Trust registration	Yes. Neb. Rev. Stat. §§ 30-3816 and following
Uniform Prudent Investor Act	Neb. Rev. Stat. §§ 30-3883 and following
Statutory requirement for annual accounting to beneficiaries	Yes. Neb. Rev. Stat. § 30-3878

Nevada

Topic	State Rule
Creditor's claims procedure for trusts	Yes. Nev. Rev. Stat. Ann. § 164.025
Uniform Trust Code	No
Nonjudicial settlement procedure	No
Do beneficiaries have statutory right to see trust?	No
State inheritance tax	No
State estate tax	No
State taxing authority website	tax.nv.gov
Community property	Yes
Affidavit procedure for small estates	Gross value of property in Nevada doesn't exceed $100,000, and no Nevada real estate (if spouse); or $25,000 (if anyone else). 40-day waiting period. Nev. Rev. Stat. Ann. § 146.080
Summary probate for small estates	1. Gross value of estate doesn't exceed $300,000, if court approves. Nev. Rev. Stat. Ann. §§ 145.020 and following
	2. Gross value of estate, less encumbrances, doesn't exceed $100,000. Court can set aside all property for surviving spouse or minor children, or if there are neither, to pay debts. Nev. Rev. Stat. Ann. § 146.070
Uniform Probate Code	No
Trustee must send notice after change of trustee	No
Trustee must send notice after grantor dies	Not required, but doing so limits the time a beneficiary has to contest the trust's validity. Nev. Rev. Stat. Ann. § 164.021
Trust registration	No
Uniform Prudent Investor Act	Nev. Rev. Stat. Ann. §§ 164.705 and following
Statutory requirement for annual accounting to beneficiaries	Yes. Nev. Rev. Stat. Ann. § 165.1214

New Hampshire

Topic	State Rule
Creditor's claims procedure for trusts	No
Uniform Trust Code	Yes. N.H. Rev. Stat. Ann. §§ 564-B and following
Nonjudicial settlement procedure	Yes. N.H. Rev. Stat. Ann. § 564-B:1-111
Do beneficiaries have statutory right to see trust?	Yes. Trustee must furnish a copy of trust to a qualified beneficiary who is over the age of 21. N.H. Rev. Stat. Ann. § 564-B:8-813
State inheritance tax	No
State estate tax	No
State taxing authority website	revenue.nh.gov
Community property	No
Affidavit procedure for small estates	No
Summary probate for small estates	If there is a will naming the surviving spouse or, if no spouse, an only child, or if no spouse or child, a parent, as sole beneficiary, and that spouse or child or parent is appointed administrator; or if there's no will and the surviving spouse or, if no spouse, an only child, or if no spouse or child, a parent is the sole heir and is appointed administrator. Administrator's filing (between six months and a year after the death) and probate court's approval are all that are required. N.H. Rev. Stat. Ann. § 553:32
Uniform Probate Code	No
Trustee must send notice after change of trustee	Yes. N.H. Rev. Stat. Ann. § 564-B:8-813
Trustee must send notice after grantor dies	Yes. N.H. Rev. Stat. Ann. § 564-B:8-813
Trust registration	No
Uniform Prudent Investor Act	N.H. Rev. Stat. Ann. §§ 564-B:9-901 and following
Statutory requirement for annual accounting to beneficiaries	Yes. N.H. Rev. Stat. Ann. § 564-B:8-813

New Jersey

Topic	State Rule
Creditor's claims procedure for trusts	No
Uniform Trust Code	Yes. N.J. Stat. Ann. §§ 3B:13-1 and following
Nonjudicial settlement procedure	Yes. N.J. Stat. Ann. §§ 3B:31-11 and following
Do beneficiaries have statutory right to see trust?	Yes. N.J. Stat. Ann. § 3B:31-67
State inheritance tax	Yes. N.J. Stat. Ann. §§ 54:33-1 and following
State estate tax	No. Repealed effective Jan. 1, 2018. N.J. Stat. Ann. § 54:38-1.a(4)
State taxing authority website	www.state.nj.us/treasury/taxation
Community property	No
Affidavit procedure for small estates	No
Summary probate for small estates	Two procedures, available only if there is no valid will: If value of all property doesn't exceed $50,000, surviving spouse or domestic partner is entitled to all of it without probate. N.J. Stat. Ann. § 3B:10-3 If value of all property doesn't exceed $20,000 and there is no surviving spouse or domestic partner, one heir, with the written consent of the others, can file affidavit with the court and receive all the assets. N.J. Stat. Ann. § 3B:10-4
Uniform Probate Code	Yes. N.J. Stat. Ann. §§ 3B:1-1 and following
Trustee must send notice after change of trustee	No
Trustee must send notice after grantor dies	No
Trust registration	No
Uniform Prudent Investor Act	N.J. Stat. Ann. § 3B:20-11.1
Statutory requirement for annual accounting to beneficiaries	No

New Mexico

Topic	State Rule
Creditor's claims procedure for trusts	No
Uniform Trust Code	Yes. N.M. Stat. Ann. §§ 46A-1-101 and following
Nonjudicial settlement procedure	Yes. N.M. Stat. Ann. § 46A-1-111
Do beneficiaries have statutory right to see trust?	Yes, qualified beneficiary can request copy. N.M. Stat. Ann. § 46A-8-813
State inheritance tax	No
State estate tax	No
State taxing authority website	www.tax.newmexico.gov
Community property	Yes
Affidavit procedure for small estates	**For real estate:** If married couple owns principal residence, valued for property tax purposes at $500,000 or less, as community property, surviving spouse may file affidavit with county clerk if no other assets require probate. Six-month waiting period. N.M. Stat. Ann. § 45-3-1205 **For other property:** Value of entire estate, wherever located, less liens and encumbrances, is $50,000 or less. 30-day waiting period. N.M. Stat. Ann. § 45-3-1201
Summary probate for small estates	Value of entire estate, less liens and encumbrances, doesn't exceed personal property allowance, family allowance, costs of administration, funeral expenses, and medical expenses of the last illness. N.M. Stat. Ann. § 45-3-1203
Uniform Probate Code	Yes
Trustee must send notice after change of trustee	Yes. N.M. Stat. Ann. § 46A-8-813
Trustee must send notice after grantor dies	Must notify qualified trust beneficiaries after taking over as trustee. N.M. Stat. Ann. § 46A-8-813
Trust registration	No
Uniform Prudent Investor Act	N.M. Stat. Ann. §§ 45-7-601 and following
Statutory requirement for annual accounting to beneficiaries	Yes. N.M. Stat. Ann. § 46A-8-813

New York

Topic	State Rule
Creditor's claims procedure for trusts	No
Uniform Trust Code	No
Nonjudicial settlement procedure	No
Do beneficiaries have statutory right to see trust?	No
State inheritance tax	No
State estate tax	Yes, for estates with a value of more than the federal estate tax exemption at that time without taking into consideration the doubling of the exemption in the Tax Cuts and Jobs Act of 2017. N.Y. Tax L. § 952.
State taxing authority website	www.tax.ny.gov
Community property	No
Affidavit procedure for small estates	No
Summary probate for small estates	Property, excluding real estate and amounts that must be set aside for surviving family members, has a gross value of $30,000 or less. N.Y. Surr. Ct. Proc. Act § 1301 and following
Uniform Probate Code	No
Trustee must send notice after change of trustee	No
Trustee must send notice after grantor dies	No
Trust registration	No
Uniform Prudent Investor Act	Substantially similar law: N.Y. Est. Powers & Trusts Law § 11-2.3
Statutory requirement for annual accounting to beneficiaries	Yes. N.Y. Surr. Ct. Proc. Act § 2309(t)

North Carolina

Topic	State Rule
Creditor's claims procedure for trusts	No
Uniform Trust Code	Yes. N.C. Gen. Stat. §§ 36C-1-101 and following
Nonjudicial settlement procedure	Yes. N.C. Gen. Stat. § 36C-1-111
Do beneficiaries have statutory right to see trust?	Yes. Trustee must provide a qualified beneficiary with a copy of the trust. N.C. Gen. Stat. § 36C -8-813
State inheritance tax	No
State estate tax	No
State taxing authority website	ncdor.gov
Community property	No
Affidavit procedure for small estates	Value of personal property, less liens and encumbrances, is $20,000 or less ($30,000, not counting spousal allowance, if the surviving spouse is the sole heir). N.C. Gen. Stat. §§ 28A-25-1 and following
Summary probate for small estates	If surviving spouse inherits everything. N.C. Gen. Stat. §§ 28A-28-1 and following
Uniform Probate Code	No
Trustee must send notice after change of trustee	No
Trustee must send notice after grantor dies	No
Trust registration	No
Uniform Prudent Investor Act	N.C. Gen. Stat. §§ 36C-9-901 and following
Statutory requirement for annual accounting to beneficiaries	Yes. N.C. Gen. Stat. § 36C-8-813

North Dakota

Topic	State Rule
Creditor's claims procedure for trusts	No
Uniform Trust Code	Yes. N.D. Cent. Code §§ 59-09-01 and following
Nonjudicial settlement procedure	Yes. N.D. Cent. Code § 59-09-11
Do beneficiaries have statutory right to see trust?	No. Trustee must give a qualified beneficiary a copy of the portion of the trust that relates to the beneficiary's interest. N.D. Cent. Code § 59-16-13
State inheritance tax	No
State estate tax	No
State taxing authority website	www.nd.gov/tax
Community property	No
Affidavit procedure for small estates	Value of entire estate subject to probate, less liens and encumbrances, is $50,000 or less. 30-day waiting period. N.D. Cent. Code § 30.1-23-01
Summary probate for small estates	Value of the entire estate, less liens and encumbrances, does not exceed the homestead, plus exempt property, family allowance, costs of administration, funeral expenses, and medical expenses of the last illness. N.D. Cent. Code § 30.1-23-03
Uniform Probate Code	Yes
Trustee must send notice after change of trustee	Yes. N.D. Cent. Code § 59-16-13
Trustee must send notice after grantor dies	Yes. N.D. Cent. Code § 59-16-13
Trust registration	No
Uniform Prudent Investor Act	N.D. Cent. Code §§ 59-17.01 and following
Statutory requirement for annual accounting to beneficiaries	Yes. N.D. Cent. Code § 59-16-13

Ohio

Topic	State Rule
Creditor's claims procedure for trusts	No
Uniform Trust Code	Yes. Ohio Rev. Code Ann. §§ 5801 and following
Nonjudicial settlement procedure	Yes. Provides for private settlement agreements. Ohio Rev. Code Ann. § 5801.10
Do beneficiaries have statutory right to see trust?	Yes. Trustee must provide current beneficiary with a copy of the trust. Ohio Rev. Code Ann. § 5808.13
State inheritance tax	No
State estate tax	No
State taxing authority website	www.tax.ohio.gov
Community property	No
Affidavit procedure for small estates	No
Summary probate for small estates	Available if either: • value of the estate is $35,000 or less, or • surviving spouse inherits everything, either under a will or by law, and value of the estate is $100,000 or less. Ohio Rev. Code Ann. § 2113.03
Uniform Probate Code	No
Trustee must send notice after change of trustee	Yes. Ohio Rev. Code Ann. § 5808.13
Trustee must send notice after grantor dies	Yes. Ohio Rev. Code Ann. § 5808.13
Trust registration	No. But see Ohio Rev. Code Ann. § 5301.255
Uniform Prudent Investor Act	Ohio Rev. Code Ann. §§ 5809.01 and following
Statutory requirement for annual accounting to beneficiaries	Yes. Ohio Rev. Code Ann. § 5808.13

Oklahoma

Topic	State Rule
Creditor's claims procedure for trusts	No
Uniform Trust Code	No
Nonjudicial settlement procedure	No
Do beneficiaries have statutory right to see trust?	No
State inheritance tax	No
State estate tax	No
State taxing authority website	www.ok.gov/tax
Community property	No
Affidavit procedure for small estates	Available if fair market value of estate in Oklahoma, less liens and encumbrances, is $50,000 or less. Ten-day waiting period. Okla. Stat. Ann. tit. 58, § 393
Summary probate for small estates	Available if value of estate is $200,000 or less, or the person has been dead for more than five years, or the person resided in another state at the time of death. Okla. Stat. Ann. tit. 58, § 245
Uniform Probate Code	No
Trustee must send notice after change of trustee	No
Trustee must send notice after grantor dies	No
Trust registration	No
Uniform Prudent Investor Act	Okla. Stat. Ann. tit. 60, §§ 175.60 and following
Statutory requirement for annual accounting to beneficiaries	No

Oregon

Topic	State Rule
Creditor's claims procedure for trusts	No
Uniform Trust Code	Yes. Or. Rev. Stat. §§ 130.001 and following
Nonjudicial settlement procedure	Yes. Or. Rev. Stat. § 130.045
Do beneficiaries have statutory right to see trust?	Yes. Trustee must give qualified beneficiary copy of trust upon request. Or. Rev. Stat. § 130.710
State inheritance tax	No
State estate tax	Yes for estates over $1 million. Or. Rev. Stat. § 118.160
State taxing authority website	oregon.gov/dor
Community property	No
Affidavit procedure for small estates	No
Summary probate for small estates	Fair market value of the estate is $275,000 or less, and not more than $75,000 of the estate is personal property and not more than $200,000 is real estate. Or. Rev. Stat. §§ 114.515 and following
Uniform Probate Code	No
Trustee must send notice after change of trustee	Yes, Or. Rev. Stat. § 130.710
Trustee must send notice after grantor dies	Yes, Or. Rev. Stat. § 130.710
Trust registration	No
Uniform Prudent Investor Act	Or. Rev. Stat. §§ 130.750 and following
Statutory requirement for annual accounting to beneficiaries	Yes. Or. Rev. Stat. § 130.710

Pennsylvania

Topic	State Rule
Creditor's claims procedure for trusts	No
Uniform Trust Code	Yes. 20 Pa. Cons. Stat. Ann. §§ 7701 and following
Nonjudicial settlement procedure	Yes. 20 Pa. Cons. Stat. Ann. § 7710.1
Do beneficiaries have statutory right to see trust?	Yes. Pa. Cons. Stat. Ann. § 7780.3
State inheritance tax	72 Pa. Cons. Stat. Ann. §§ 9101 and following
State estate tax	No
State taxing authority website	revenue.pa.gov
Community property	No
Affidavit procedure for small estates	No
Summary probate for small estates	Property (not counting real estate, certain vehicles, certain payments the family is entitled to, and funeral costs) is worth $50,000 or less. 20 Pa. Cons. Stat. Ann. § 3102
Uniform Probate Code	No
Trustee must send notice after change of trustee	Yes. 20 Pa. Cons. Stat. Ann. § 7780.3
Trustee must send notice after grantor dies	Yes. Pa. Cons. Stat. Ann. § 7780.3
Trust registration	No
Uniform Prudent Investor Act	20 Pa. Cons. Stat. Ann. §§ 7201 and following
Statutory requirement for annual accounting to beneficiaries	Yes. 20 Pa. Cons. Stat. Ann. § 7780.3

Rhode Island

Topic	State Rule
Creditor's claims procedure for trusts	No
Uniform Trust Code	No
Nonjudicial settlement procedure	No
Do beneficiaries have statutory right to see trust?	No
State inheritance tax	No
State estate tax	Yes, for estates of more than $1.538 million in 2018. (Amount is indexed for inflation.) R.I. Gen. Laws §§ 44-22-1 and following
State taxing authority website	tax.state.ri.us
Community property	No
Affidavit procedure for small estates	No
Summary probate for small estates	No real estate, and value of property that would be subject to probate (not counting tangible personal property) doesn't exceed $15,000. R.I. Gen. Laws § 33-24-1
Uniform Probate Code	No
Trustee must send notice after change of trustee	No
Trustee must send notice after grantor dies	No
Trust registration	No
Uniform Prudent Investor Act	R.I. Gen. Laws §§ 18-15-1 and following
Statutory requirement for annual accounting to beneficiaries	Yes. R.I. Gen. Laws § 18 -13-15

South Carolina

Topic	State Rule
Creditor's claims procedure for trusts	No
Uniform Trust Code	Yes. S.C. Code Ann. §§ 62-7-101 and following
Nonjudicial settlement procedure	Yes. S.C. Code Ann. § 62-7-111
Do beneficiaries have statutory right to see trust?	Yes, qualified beneficiaries can request a copy, but the trustee can redact the trust to show only what's relevant to the beneficiary. S.C. Code Ann. § 62-7-813
State inheritance tax	No
State estate tax	No
State taxing authority website	dor.sc.gov
Community property	No
Affidavit procedure for small estates	Value of property passing by will or under law, less liens and encumbrances, is $25,000 or less. Probate judge must approve affidavit. 30-day waiting period. S.C. Code Ann. § 62-3-1201
Summary probate for small estates	Value of property passing by will or under law, less liens and encumbrances, is $25,000 or less (not counting exempt property, funeral expenses, and medical expenses of last illness). S.C. Code Ann. § 62-3-1203
Uniform Probate Code	Yes
Trustee must send notice after change of trustee	Yes. S.C. Code Ann. § 62-7-813
Trustee must send notice after grantor dies	Yes. S.C. Code Ann. § 62-7-813
Trust registration	No
Uniform Prudent Investor Act	S.C. Code Ann. § 62-7-933
Statutory requirement for annual accounting to beneficiaries	Yes. S.C. Code Ann. § 62-7-813

South Dakota

Topic	State Rule
Creditor's claims procedure for trusts	No
Uniform Trust Code	No
Nonjudicial settlement procedure	No
Do beneficiaries have statutory right to see trust?	No. S.D. Codified Laws Ann. § 55-2-13. Trustee shall furnish qualified beneficiaries copy of trust instrument pertaining to the beneficiary's interest in the trust, unless otherwise provided in trust instrument.
State inheritance tax	No
State estate tax	No
State taxing authority website	dor.sd.gov
Community property	No
Affidavit procedure for small estates	Value of entire estate, less liens and encumbrances, is $50,000 or less. S.D. Codified Laws §§ 29A-3-1201 and following
Summary probate for small estates	"Informal probate" available regardless of value of estate. S.D. Codified Laws Ann. §§ 29A-3-301 and following
Uniform Probate Code	Yes
Trustee must send notice after change of trustee	Yes. S.D. Codified Laws Ann. § 55-2-13, unless otherwise provided in trust instrument.
Trustee must send notice after grantor dies	Yes. S.D. Codified Laws Ann. § 55-2-13, unless otherwise provided in trust instrument.
Trust registration	No
Uniform Prudent Investor Act or Rule	S.D. Codified Laws Ann. §§ 55-5-7 and following
Statutory requirement for annual accounting to beneficiaries	No

Tennessee

Topic	State Rule
Creditor's claims procedure for trusts	No
Uniform Trust Code	Yes. Tenn. Code Ann. §§ 35-15-101 and following
Nonjudicial settlement procedure	Yes. Tenn. Code Ann. § 35-15-111
Do beneficiaries have statutory right to see trust?	Yes. Trustee must provide a copy of the trust, or an abstract of the trust along with the required statutory notice, to qualified beneficiaries. Tenn. Code Ann. § 35-15-813
State inheritance tax	No
State estate tax	No
State taxing authority website	tn.gov/revenue
Community property	No
Affidavit procedure for small estates	No
Summary probate for small estates	Value of property, not counting property held jointly with right of survivorship or real estate, is $50,000 or less. Tenn. Code Ann. §§ 30-4-102 and following
Uniform Probate Code	No
Trustee must send notice after change of trustee	No
Trustee must send notice after grantor dies	Tenn. Code Ann. § 35-15-813
Trust registration	No
Uniform Prudent Investor Act	Tenn. Code Ann. §§ 35-14-101 and following
Statutory requirement for annual accounting to beneficiaries	No

Texas

Topic	State Rule
Creditor's claims procedure for trusts	No
Uniform Trust Code	No
Nonjudicial settlement procedure	No
Do beneficiaries have statutory right to see trust?	No
State inheritance tax	No
State estate tax	No
State taxing authority website	comptroller.texas.gov/taxes
Community property	Yes
Affidavit procedure for small estates	There is no will, and value of entire estate, not including homestead and exempt property, is $75,000 or less. Probate judge must approve affidavit. Can be used to transfer homestead, but no other real estate. 30-day waiting period. Tex. Est. Code §§ 205.001 and following
Summary probate for small estates	1. Value of property doesn't exceed that needed to pay family allowance and certain creditors. Tex. Est. Code §§ 354.001 and following 2. "Independent administration" available, regardless of value of estate, if requested in the will or all inheritors agree to it. Tex. Est. Code §§ 401.001 and following
Uniform Probate Code	No
Trustee must send notice after change of trustee	No
Trustee must send notice after grantor dies	No
Trust registration	No
Uniform Prudent Investor Act	Tex. Prop. Code Ann. §§ 117.001 and following
Statutory requirement for annual accounting to beneficiaries	No. Beneficiary can demand an accounting once a year. Tex. Prop. Code. Ann. § 113.151

Utah

Topic	State Rule
Creditor's claims procedure for trusts	No
Uniform Trust Code	Yes. Utah Code Ann. §§ 75-7-101 and following
Nonjudicial settlement procedure	Yes. Utah Code Ann. § 75-7-110
Do beneficiaries have statutory right to see trust?	No. Trustee must give qualified beneficiaries a copy of the portions of the trust that affect their interests. Utah Code Ann. § 75-7-811
State inheritance tax	No
State estate tax	No
State taxing authority website	tax.utah.gov
Community property	No
Affidavit procedure for small estates	Value of entire estate subject to probate, less liens and encumbrances, is $100,000 or less. May also transfer up to four boats, motor vehicles, trailers or semitrailers if value of estate subject to probate, excluding the value of the vehicles, is $100,000 or less. 30-day waiting period. Utah Code Ann. § 75-3-1201
Summary probate for small estates	Value of entire estate, less liens and encumbrances, does not exceed the homestead allowance, exempt property, family allowance, costs of administration, funeral expenses, and medical expenses of the last illness. Utah Code Ann. § 75-3-1203
Uniform Probate Code	Yes
Trustee must send notice after change of trustee	Yes. Utah Code Ann. § 75-7-811
Trustee must send notice after grantor dies	Yes. Utah Code Ann. § 75-7-811
Trust registration	No
Uniform Prudent Investor Act	Utah Code Ann. §§ 75-7-901 and following
Statutory requirement for annual accounting to beneficiaries	Yes. Utah Code Ann. § 75-7-811

Vermont

Topic	State Rule
Creditor's claims procedure for trusts	No
Uniform Trust Code	Yes. Vt. Stat. Ann. tit. 14A, §§ 101 and following
Nonjudicial settlement procedure	Yes. Vt. Stat. Ann. 14A § 111
Do beneficiaries have statutory right to see trust?	Yes. Trustee must give qualified beneficiaries a copy of the the trust upon request. Vt. Stat. Ann. 14A § 813
State inheritance tax	No
State estate tax	Yes, for estates of more than $2.75 million. Vt. Stat. Ann. tit. 32, §§ 7442a and following
State taxing authority website	tax.vermont.gov
Community property	No
Affidavit procedure for small estates	No
Summary probate for small estates	Deceased is survived by a spouse, civil union partner, or children and owned no real estate, and value of personal property is $10,000 or less. Vt. Stat. Ann. tit. 14, § 1902
Uniform Probate Code	No
Trustee must send notice after change of trustee	Yes. Vt. Stat. Ann. tit. 14A, § 813
Trustee must send notice after grantor dies	Yes. Vt. Stat. Ann. tit. 14A, § 813
Trust registration	No
Uniform Prudent Investor Act	Vt. Stat. Ann. tit. 14A, §§ 901 and following
Statutory requirement for annual accounting to beneficiaries	Yes. Vt. Stat. Ann. tit. 14A, § 813

Virginia

Topic	State Rule
Creditor's claims procedure for trusts	No
Uniform Trust Code	Yes. Va. Code Ann. §§ 64.2-700 and following
Nonjudicial settlement procedure	Yes. Va. Code Ann. § 64.2-709
Do beneficiaries have statutory right to see trust?	Yes. Trustee must provide qualified beneficiaries with a copy of the the trust upon request. Va. Code Ann. § 64.2-775
State inheritance tax	No
State estate tax	No
State taxing authority website	tax.virginia.gov
Community property	No
Affidavit procedure for small estates	Entire personal probate estate $50,000 or less. Will, if any, must be filed with probate court. 60-day waiting period. Va. Code Ann. § 64.2-601 For real estate, if there's no will, the heirs or personal representative can record affidavit setting out names of heirs; clerk will send abstract of affidavit to the revenue commissioner, and then real estate can be transferred. Va. Code Ann. § 64.2-510
Summary probate for small estates	No
Uniform Probate Code	No
Trustee must send notice after change of trustee	Yes. Va. Code Ann. § 64.2-775
Trustee must send notice after grantor dies	Yes. Va. Code Ann. § 64.2-775
Trust registration	No
Uniform Prudent Investor Act	Va. Code Ann. §§ 64.2-781 and following
Statutory requirement for annual accounting to beneficiaries	Yes. Va. Code Ann. § 64.2-775

Washington

Topic	State Rule
Creditor's claims procedure for trusts	No
Uniform Trust Code	No
Nonjudicial settlement procedure	No
Do beneficiaries have statutory right to see trust?	Yes. Trustee must provide qualified beneficiaries with a copy of trust upon request. Wash. Rev. Code Ann. § 11.98.072
State inheritance tax	No
State estate tax	Yes, for estates over $2,193,000 (in 2018), indexed for inflation. Wash. Rev. Code Ann. §§ 83.100.010 and following
State taxing authority website	dor.wa.gov
Community property	Yes
Affidavit procedure for small estates	Value of assets subject to probate, not counting surviving spouse's or domestic partner's community property interest, less liens and encumbrances, is $100,000 or less. 40-day waiting period. Wash. Rev. Code §§ 11.62.010 and following
Summary probate for small estates	If there is a will, the personal representative named in the will makes the request. If there is no will, process is available to surviving spouse or registered domestic partner if the estate is composed of community property only, and the deceased person left no children or grandchildren from another relationship. Wash. Rev. Code Ann. §§ 11.68.011 and following
Uniform Probate Code	No
Trustee must send notice after change of trustee	Yes. Wash. Rev. Code Ann. § 11.98.072, unless otherwise provided in trust or separate writing
Trustee must send notice after grantor dies	Yes. Wash. Rev. Code Ann. § 11.98.072, unless otherwise provided in trust or separate writing
Trust registration	No
Uniform Prudent Investor Act	Wash. Rev. Code Ann. §§ 11.100.010 and following
Statutory requirement for annual accounting to beneficiaries	Yes. Wash. Rev. Code Ann. § 11.106.020

West Virginia

Topic	State Rule
Creditor's claims procedure for trusts	No
Uniform Trust Code	Yes. W.Va. Code §§ 44D-1-101 and following
Nonjudicial settlement procedure	Yes. W.Va. Code § 44D-1-111
Do beneficiaries have statutory right to see trust?	Yes. W.Va. Code § 44D-8-813
State inheritance tax	No
State estate tax	No
State taxing authority website	revenue.wv.gov
Community property	No
Affidavit procedure for small estates	No
Summary probate for small estates	Value of estate, not counting real estate, is $100,000 or less; or if the personal representative is the sole beneficiary of the estate; or if surviving spouse is the sole beneficiary of the estate; or if all the beneficiaries state that no disputes are likely, there are enough assets to pay debts and taxes, and the executor agrees. W.Va. Code § 44-3A-5
Uniform Probate Code	No
Trustee must send notice after change of trustee	Yes. W.Va. Code § 44D-8-813
Trustee must send notice after grantor dies	Yes. W.Va. Code § 44D-8-813
Trust registration	No
Uniform Prudent Investor Act	W.Va. Code §§ 44-6C-1 and following
Statutory requirement for annual accounting to beneficiaries	Yes. W.Va. Code § 44D-8-813

Wisconsin

Topic	State Rule
Creditor's claims procedure for trusts	No
Uniform Trust Code	Yes. Wis. Stat. Ann. § 701.0101
Nonjudicial settlement procedure	Yes. Wis. Stat. Ann. § 701.0111
Do beneficiaries have statutory right to see trust?	Yes. Wis. Stat. Ann. § 701.0813 Beneficiaries may see either a copy of the portion of the trust instrument relating to the interest of the qualified beneficiary, or a copy of the trust instrument.
State inheritance tax	No
State estate tax	No
State taxing authority website	revenue.wi.gov
Community property	Yes (marital property)
Affidavit procedure for small estates	Decedent's solely owned property in Wisconsin is worth $50,000 or less. Wis. Stat. Ann. § 867.03
Summary probate for small estates	Value of estate, less mortgages and encumbrances, is $50,000 or less and decedent is survived by a spouse, domestic partner, or minor children. Also available if value of estate, less mortgages and encumbrances, does not exceed costs, expenses, allowances, and claims. Wis. Stat. Ann. § 867.01
Uniform Probate Code	No, but has an informal probate procedure similar to that used in UPC states
Trustee must send notice after change of trustee	Yes. Wis. Stat. Ann. § 701.0813
Trustee must send notice after grantor dies	Yes. Wis. Stat. Ann. § 701.0813
Trust registration	No
Uniform Prudent Investor Act	Wis. Stat. Ann. §§ 881.01 and following
Statutory requirement for annual accounting to beneficiaries	Yes. Wis. Stat. Ann. § 701.0813

Wyoming

Topic	State Rule
Creditor's claims procedure for trusts	No
Uniform Trust Code	Yes. Wyo. Stat. §§ 4-10-101 and following
Nonjudicial settlement procedure	Yes. Wyo. Stat. § 4-10-111
Do beneficiaries have statutory right to see trust?	Yes. Trustee must give qualified beneficiaries copy of the trust upon request. Wyo. Stat. § 4-10-813.
State inheritance tax	No
State estate tax	No
State taxing authority website	revenue.wyo.gov
Community property	No
Affidavit procedure for small estates	Value of entire estate, less liens and encumbrances, is $200,000 or less. Must file affidavit with county clerk. 30-day waiting period. Wyo. Stat. § 2-1-201
Summary probate for small estates	Value of entire estate, including real estate and mineral interests, is $200,000 or less. Wyo. Stat. § 2-1-205
Uniform Probate Code	No
Trustee must send notice after change of trustee	Yes. Wyo. Stat. § 4-10-813
Trustee must send notice after grantor dies	Yes. Wyo. Stat. § 4-10-813
Trust registration	No
Uniform Prudent Investor Act	Wyo. Stat. Ann. §§ 4-10-901 and following
Statutory requirement for annual accounting to beneficiaries	Yes. Wyo. Stat. § 4-10-813

Sample Trust

Here is an edited version of a typical simple couple's trust, created in a community property state. We included sections we think will help you understand your job as trustee, and left out some to keep the document shorter. At least parts of it will probably look similar to the trust you're working with—though there's no such thing as a standard trust form.

The Blackforth Family Trust

ARTICLE ONE

1.1. The settlors are identified. Both settlors are also the trustees.

1.1. Declaration. Thomas Blackforth and Peggy Blackforth, husband and wife, of _____ County, _____ , (called "the settlors" or "the trustees," depending on the context) declare that they hold certain property in trust, to be held, administered, and distributed according to the terms of this instrument.

1.2. This names the trust and tells how to name any subtrusts that might be created.

1.2. Name of the Trust. The trusts created by this instrument shall be named the Blackforth Family Trust ("the trust"). Each separate trust created by this instrument shall be referred to by adding the name of that separate trust to the name of the trust.

1.3. The trust is effective on the date husband and wife sign it.

1.3. Effective Date. This declaration shall be effective immediately on execution by all the parties.

1.4. The settlors' children are identified.

1.4. Names of Children. The settlors' only living children are Jonathan Blackforth (born on January 1, 1995) and Emma Blackforth (born on August 10, 2000). The settlors have no deceased children who left living descendants.

ARTICLE TWO

Trust Property

2.1 Trust property includes what has been titled in the name of the trust (such as real estate and brokerage accounts), and property that is listed on Schedule A, attached to the trust.

2.1. Definition of Trust Estate. All property subject to this instrument from time to time is referred to as the "trust estate" and shall be held, administered, and distributed as provided in this instrument. The trustee shall hold, administer, and distribute the property described in any schedules of property (which are attached hereto and made a part of this trust instrument), any other property that may be hereafter subject to this trust, and the income and proceeds attributable to all such property, in accordance with the provisions of this instrument.

ARTICLE THREE

Rights and Powers of Settlors

3.1. Power of Revocation While Both Settlors Are Living. During the joint lifetimes of the settlors, any trust created by this instrument may be revoked or terminated, in whole or in part, by either settlor as to any separate and quasi-community property of that settlor and any community property of the settlors.

3.2. Power of Revocation and Amendment After Death of Deceased Settlor. After the death of the first settlor to die (the "deceased settlor"), the survivor of the settlors (the "surviving settlor") may at any time amend, revoke, or terminate, in whole or in part, this entire trust. After the death of the surviving settlor, none of the trusts created by this instrument may be amended, revoked, or terminated.

3.3. Method of Revocation or Amendment. Any amendment, revocation, or termination of any trust created by this instrument shall be made by written instrument signed by both settlors or by the settlor making the revocation, amendment, or termination, and delivered to the trustee.

ARTICLE FOUR

Distributions During Settlors' Joint Lives

4.1. Payment of Income During Settlors' Joint Lives. So long as both settlors are living, the trustee shall pay to or apply for the benefit of the settlors, or either of them, all of the net income from the trust in monthly or other convenient installments (but not less often than annually) as the settlors, or either of them, and the trustee may agree on from time to time.

4.2. Distributions of Principal During Settlors' Joint Lives. So long as both settlors are living, the trustee shall distribute to or apply for the benefit of the settlors, or either of them, as much of the principal of the trust as the trustee, in the trustee's discretion, deems necessary for the comfort, welfare, and happiness of the settlors, or either of them.

3.1. Either settlor can revoke the trust while both are alive.

3.2. After one settlor dies, the surviving settlor has the right to amend or revoke the trust.

3.3. A revocation or amendment must be in writing, signed by the settlor(s), and delivered to the trustee.

How settlors may spend trust assets during their lifetimes.

4.1. During their joint lifetimes, both settlors are entitled to all income from the trust.

4.2. Both can use trust principal for their comfort, welfare, and happiness. This means unrestricted use. If someone other than the settlors serves as trustee, that person must pay to the settlors whatever they need or want.

ARTICLE FIVE

Distributions After Deceased Settlor's Death

5.1. Payment of Death Taxes, Debts, and Expenses on Statement From Personal Representative. After the deceased settlor's death, on receipt by the trustee of a written statement from the personal representative of the deceased settlor's estate requesting that the trustee pay death taxes, debts, and expenses with respect to any property in the deceased settlor's estate, the trustee shall pay, either directly or to the personal representative, any amounts requested by the personal representative for those purposes. If there is no personal representative, the trustee shall make the payments directly. Payments of debts and expenses shall be made by the trustee from the trust estate. All death taxes payable by reason of the death of the deceased settlor shall also be paid by the trustee from the trust estate.

5.2. Trustee's Power to Defer Division or Distribution. Whenever the trustee is directed to divide any part of the trust estate or distribute trust assets on the death of either settlor, the trustee may, in the trustee's discretion, defer actual division or distribution for such reasonable period of time as is needed to effectively identify, take possession of, value, divide, and distribute the assets of the trust.

5.3. Trust for the Benefit of the Surviving Settlor. On the deceased settlor's death, the balance of the Trust Estate shall be held, administered, and distributed for the benefit of the surviving settlor as set forth in Article Six.

ARTICLE SIX

Dispositive Provisions of Trusts Created After Deceased Settlor's Death

6.1. Survivor's Trust. The trustee shall hold, administer, and distribute the Trust Estate as follows:

(a) Payment of Income. The trustee shall pay to or apply for the benefit of the surviving settlor the entire net income of the trust, in monthly or other convenient installments, but not less often than annually.

(b) Discretionary Payment of Principal by Trustee. At any time or times during the trust term, the trustee shall pay to or apply for the benefit of the surviving settlor so much of the principal of the trust as the trustee deems proper for the comfort, welfare, and happiness of the surviving settlor. In exercising discretion, the trustee shall give the consideration that the trustee deems proper to all other income and resources that are then known to the trustee and that are readily available to the surviving settlor. All decisions of the trustee regarding payments under this subsection, if any, are within the trustee's discretion and shall be final and incontestable by anyone.

(c) Right of Surviving Settlor to Withdraw Principal. The trustee shall pay to the surviving settlor as much of the trust principal as the surviving settlor may from time to time demand in a signed writing delivered to the trustee.

(d) General Power of Appointment. On the death of the surviving settlor, the trustee shall distribute all property subject to the trust (including the trust principal, all net income then held by the trustee, and all income then accrued but not collected by the trustee) to any entity or entities, person or persons, and on any trust terms and conditions, or to or in favor of the estate of the surviving settlor, as the surviving settlor may direct by will, but only if that will expressly refers to and indicates an intention to exercise this power of appointment.

(e) Payment of Taxes, Debts, and Expenses. On the death of the surviving settlor and subject to any power of appointment exercised by him or her, the trustee, in the trustee's discretion, may pay out of the income or principal (or partly from each) of this trust the taxes, debts and expenses (as defined in Article Eight) arising on the death of the surviving settlor unless the trustee determines that other adequate provisions have been made for the payment of these taxes, debts, and expenses.

(c) The surviving settlor can withdraw all of the trust principal if he or she chooses.

(d) The general power of appointment gives the surviving settlor power to leave trust assets to anyone, but it must be done by including a provision in the surviving settlor's will. (See the discussion in Chapter 4.) It is usually easier for a settlor who wants to change beneficiaries to amend the trust.

(e) The successor trustee will pay taxes, debts, and expenses from this trust upon the surviving settlor's death.

(f) Most estates don't owe federal estate tax, but this directs the trustee to pay it if it is due.

(f) Payment of Federal Estate Taxes. The trustee shall determine from the personal representative of the estate of the surviving settlor the amount of the federal estate tax allocable to the property of the trust by reason of Internal Revenue Code Section 2207 and shall set aside a portion of the trust principal for the purpose of paying that tax upon written demand of the personal representative.

(g) The surviving settlor may make gifts in a separate signed writing.

(g) Specific Gifts. The surviving settlor may, by a separate signed and dated instrument, list certain items of the surviving settlor's tangible personal property or pecuniary gifts to be given to individuals or charities identified in that writing.

(h) Assets that are not given away under section 6.1(g) are to go to the settlors' children in equal shares.

(h) Personal Effects. Upon the death of the surviving settlor, the trustee shall distribute all of the settlors' jewelry, clothing, household furniture and furnishings, personal automobiles, and any other tangible articles of a personal nature, or the settlors' interest in any such property, not otherwise specifically disposed of by this trust, by will, or in any other manner, together with any insurance on the property, to the settlors' children who survive the surviving settlor for ten (10) days, in equal shares as they shall agree, or as the trustee in the trustee's discretion shall determine if the children do not agree. The trustee shall pay all packing and shipping charges as costs of administration.

(i) If the surviving settlor did not exercise the power of appointment, trust property is to be distributed as stated in section 6.2.

(i) Default Provision. If any of the property subject to the power of appointment of the surviving settlor is not effectively appointed by him or her, that property, after payment of any taxes, debts, and expenses pursuant to the applicable provisions of this instrument, shall be distributed as provided in Section 6.2, below.

6.2. Rules for distribution of the shares to the children.

6.2. Disposition of Residuary Estate. On the death of the surviving settlor, the trustee shall hold, administer, and distribute the balance of the Trust Estate as follows:

(a) The trustee is directed to create an equal share for each of the settlors' children. If a child is deceased, that child's children will inherit the share that belonged to the deceased child.

(a) The trustee shall divide the trust property into as many shares of equal market value as are necessary to create one (1) share for each of the settlors' children who survive the surviving settlor and one (1) share for each of the settlors' children then deceased who leave issue then living.

(b) Each share created for a then-living child shall be distributed outright to that child if that child has reached the age of thirty (30) years. If the child has not reached the age of thirty (30) years at that time, the share created for the child shall be held, administered, and distributed by the trustee in a separate trust according to the terms set forth in this Article Six applicable to the Trusts for Children.

(b) Children who are at least 30 get their share outright. The share of any child under 30 is placed into a trust.

(c) The trustee shall distribute each share created for a then-deceased child outright to the then-living issue of that then-deceased child, with those issue to take that share by right of representation. However, if any individual issue of a deceased child has not reached the age of thirty (30) years at the death of the surviving settlor, the trustee shall continue to hold, administer, and distribute the share created for the issue of that deceased child in a separate trust according to the terms set forth in this Article Six applicable to the Trusts for Children.

(c) A share created for a deceased child goes to that child's descendants (issue) in equal shares. For example, if a son died and left two children, they would split the father's share. If those grandchildren were under 30, their shares would be held in trust as well.

(d) If none of the settlors' issue survive the surviving settlor, the trustee shall distribute the property outright as follows: one half (1/2) to the heirs of the deceased settlor and one half (1/2) to the heirs of the surviving settlor.

(d) If there are no surviving children or issue, the trust assets are distributed in equal shares to the settlors' living heirs, as determined by state law. (Some settlors name specific relatives or charities to inherit instead.)

6.3. Trusts for Children. Those assets added to and made part of a trust for the benefit of any of the issue of the settlors (hereinafter "child") shall be held, administered, and distributed as follows:

6.3. Here are the terms of any trusts created for children.

(a) Discretionary Payments. At any time or times during the trust term, the trustee shall pay to or apply for the benefit of the child as much, or all, of the net income and principal of the child's trust as the trustee deems proper for the child's health, education, support, and maintenance. In exercising discretion, the trustee shall give the consideration that the trustee deems proper to all other income and resources that are known to the trustee and that are readily available to the child for use for these purposes. All decisions of the trustee regarding payments under this subsection, if any, are within the

(a) The trustee may spend the trust money for anything that the trustee deems proper for health, education, maintenance, and support. The trustee is directed to take beneficiaries' other income and resources into account.

trustee's discretion and shall be final and incontestable by anyone. The trustee shall accumulate and add to principal any net income not distributed.

(b) Termination of Trust. The trust shall terminate when the child reaches the age of thirty (30) years or on the death of the child, whichever occurs first.

(c) Distribution in Three Stages When Child Living. When the child reaches the age of twenty-three (23) years, the trustee shall distribute to the child one-third (1/3) of the principal of the child's trust. When the child reaches the age of twenty-eight (28) years, the trustee shall distribute to the child one-half (1/2) of the remaining principal of the child's trust. When the child reaches the age of thirty (30) years, the trustee shall distribute the remaining property of the child's trust to the child. If the child has already reached the age of twenty-three (23) years or twenty-eight (28) years when the child's share is first allocated to the child's trust, then on making the allocation, the trustee shall distribute to the child one-third (1/3) or two-thirds (2/3), as the case may be, of the child's trust, and the balance shall be retained pursuant to this section.

(d) Distribution on Death of Child Before Age of Thirty. If the trust terminates on the death of the child, the trustee shall allocate the remaining trust property to the then-living issue of the child by right of representation, subject to the provisions of this Article Six; or if the child leaves no then-living issue, to the settlors' then-living issue, subject to the provisions of this Article Six; and if there are none, then as provided in Section 6.2(d).

6.4. Spendthrift Clause. The interests of the beneficiaries under this instrument are not transferable by voluntary or involuntary assignment or by operation of law, and shall be free from the claims of creditors and from attachment, execution, bankruptcy, and other legal process, to the maximum extent permitted by law.

(b) The trust ends when a child reaches 30.

(c) The trustee is directed to distribute a child's trust in three stages: at 23, 28, and 30. If a child is already older than 23 when the trust is created, the trustee is to distribute the amount they would already have received.

(d) If a child died before age 30, his or her share would go to his or her children in equal shares. If a child left no children or other descendants, the share would go to the other siblings, or to the descendants of any deceased siblings.

6.4. This prevents beneficiaries from gambling away or borrowing against their inheritance, or losing it to creditors while the funds are held in the trust.

ARTICLE SEVEN

Trustees

7.1. Remaining Settlor to Act as Sole Trustee on Death or Incapacity of Other Settlor. The settlors shall be the initial cotrustees of the trust. If, while both settlors are acting as cotrustees, either settlor dies, becomes incapacitated, or is otherwise unable or unwilling to continue to act as a cotrustee, the other settlor shall become the sole trustee, with full power to continue the trust administration.

> 7.1. The settlors are the initial trustees. Upon the death of one, the surviving settlor is trustee.

7.2. Successor Trustees. If the office of trustee of any trust created in this instrument becomes vacant by reason of death, incapacity, or any other reason, and no successor trustee or cotrustees have been designated under any other provision of this trust instrument, the following, in the order of priority indicated, shall be trustee:

John Barnes

Jane Boffet

Helen Gregg

If those named above are unwilling or unable to serve as successor trustee, and no additional successor trustee has been designated by the settlors, a new trustee or cotrustees shall be appointed by the last serving trustee. If those named above are unwilling or unable to serve as successor trustee, a new trustee or cotrustees shall be appointed by the court.

> 7.2. This lists the three people next in line to serve as trustee. If none of them could serve, the last one could appoint a trustee. If no one were appointed, a court could appoint a trustee.

7.3. Definition of Trustee. Reference in this instrument to "the trustee" shall be deemed a reference to whomever is serving as trustee or cotrustees, and shall include cotrustees and alternate or successor trustees, as the context requires.

7.4. Removal and Replacement of Trustee by Settlors. While both settlors are alive, the settlors shall have the power, at any time and for any reason, with or without cause, to remove any trustee acting under this instrument, and notwithstanding any other provision of this instrument, designate another trustee to replace the removed trustee.

> 7.4. While they are both alive, the settlors can remove a trustee for any reason and designate another.

Removal shall be effected by giving a written notice of removal to the trustee to be removed and to the designated successor. The removal shall become effective on the delivery to the settlors of a written acceptance of the trust by the successor trustee, and the settlors shall promptly notify the trustee being removed of the receipt of that acceptance.

7.5. Waiver of Bond. No bond or undertaking shall be required of any individual who serves as a trustee under this instrument.

7.6. Compensation of Trustees. The trustee shall be entitled to reasonable compensation for services rendered, payable without court order.

7.7. Procedure for Resignation. Any trustee may resign at any time, without giving a reason for the resignation, by giving written notice, at least thirty (30) days before the time the resignation is to take effect, to the settlors, if living, to any other trustee then acting, to any persons authorized to designate a successor trustee, to all trust beneficiaries known to the trustee (or, in the case of a minor beneficiary, to the parent or guardian of that beneficiary), and to the successor trustee. A resignation shall be effective on written acceptance of the trust by the successor trustee.

7.8. Death or Incapacity of Trustee. An individual trustee shall cease to be a trustee upon his or her death or incapacity.

(a) Death of a trustee shall be evidenced by a certified copy of the death certificate delivered to the successor trustee.

(b) Incapacity shall be determined in the manner set forth in Article Eight.

7.9. General Powers of Trustee. To carry out the purposes of the trusts created under this instrument, the trustee shall have all of the powers enumerated in this trust instrument and all powers now or hereafter conferred on the trustees under California law, subject to any limitations stated elsewhere in this trust instrument. The powers shall include, without limitation, the following:

Sidebar notes:

7.5. Trustees don't have to post a bond to serve.

7.6. Trustees are entitled to reasonable compensation.

7.7. A trustee may resign, in writing, by giving 30 days' notice.

7.8. A trustee who dies or becomes incapacitated ceases to act as trustee.

7.9. This is a long list of powers that the trust grants to the trustee, in addition to those granted under state law. Most trustees won't need all of them.

(a) Power to Sell. The trustee may, with or without court authorization, sell (for cash or on deferred payments, and with or without security), convey, exchange, partition, and divide trust property; grant options for the sale or exchange of trust property for any purpose, whether the contract is to be performed or the option is to be exercised within or beyond the term of the trust; and lease trust property for any purpose, for terms within or extending beyond the expiration of the trust, regardless of whether the leased property is commercial or residential and regardless of the number of units leased.

(b) Power to Deal With Personal Representative. The trustee may engage in any transactions with the personal representative of the estate of either settlor that are in the best interest of any trusts created in this instrument.

(c) Management Powers. The trustee may manage, control, improve, and maintain all real and personal trust property.

(d) Land Development. The trustee may subdivide or develop land; make or obtain the vacation of plats and adjust boundaries, or adjust differences in valuation on exchange or partition by giving or receiving consideration; and dedicate land or easements to public use with or without consideration.

(e) Real Property Improvement. The trustee may make ordinary or extraordinary repairs or alterations in buildings or other trust property, demolish any improvements, raze existing party walls or buildings, and erect new party walls or buildings, as the trustee deems advisable.

(f) Retention of Experts. The trustee may employ and discharge agents and employees, including but not limited to attorneys, accountants, investment and other advisers, custodians of assets, property managers, real estate agents and brokers and appraisers, to advise and assist the trustee in the management of any trusts created under this trust instrument, and compensate them from the trust property.

(g) Stock Powers. With respect to securities held in trust, the trustee may exercise all the rights, powers, and privileges of an owner, including, but not limited to, the power to vote, give proxies, and pay assessments and other sums deemed by the trustee necessary for the protection of the trust property; participate in voting trusts, pooling agreements, foreclosures, reorganizations, consolidations, mergers, and liquidations, and, in connection therewith, deposit securities with and transfer title to any protective or other committee under such terms as the trustee deems advisable; exercise or sell stock subscription or conversion rights; and accept and retain as investments of the trust any securities or other property received through the exercise of any of the foregoing powers.

(h) Holding Powers. The trustee may hold securities or other trust property in the trustee's name as trustee or in the name of a nominee, with or without disclosure of the trust, or in unregistered form, so that title may pass by delivery.

(i) Deposit of Securities. The trustee may deposit securities in a securities depository that is either licensed or exempt from licensing.

(j) Power to Borrow. The trustee may borrow money for any trust purpose from any person or entity, including one acting as trustee hereunder, on such terms and conditions as the trustee deems advisable, and obligate the trust for repayment; guarantee the obligations of others; encumber or hypothecate any trust property by mortgage, deed of trust, pledge, guarantee, or otherwise, whether for terms within or extending beyond the term of the trust, as the trustee deems advisable, to secure repayment of any such loan; replace, renew, and extend any such loan or encumbrance; and pay loans or other obligations of the trust deemed advisable by the trustee.

(k) Power to Insure. The trustee may procure and carry, at the expense of the trust, insurance in such forms and in such amounts as the trustee deems advisable to protect the trust property against damage or loss, and to protect the trustee against liability with respect to third persons.

(l) Power to Enforce. The trustee may enforce any obligation owing to the trust, including any obligation secured by a deed of trust, mortgage, or pledge held as trust property, and purchase any property subject to a security instrument held as trust property at any sale under the instrument.

(m) Power to Extend Payment. The trustee may extend the time for payment of any note or other obligation held as an asset of, and owing to, the trust, including accrued or future interest, and extend the time for repayment beyond the term of the trust.

(n) Power to Settle and Compromise. The trustee may pay or contest any claim against the trust; release or prosecute any claim in favor of the trust; or, in lieu of payment, contest, release, or prosecution, adjust, compromise, or settle any such claim, in whole or in part, and with or without consideration.

(o) Power to Protect Trust Against Claims. The trustee may, at trust expense, prosecute or defend actions, claims, or proceedings of whatever kind for the protection of the trust property and of the trustee in the performance of the trustee's duties, and employ and compensate attorneys, advisers, and other agents as the trustee deems advisable.

7.10. Power to Retain Trust Property. The trustee shall have the power to retain property received into the trust at its inception or later added to the trust, as long as the trustee considers that retention in the best interests of the trust or in furtherance of the goals of the settlors in creating the trust, as determined from this trust instrument, but subject to the standards of the prudent investor rule as set forth in the California Uniform Prudent Investor Act, as amended from time to time.

> 7.10. The trustee can keep trust property as long as that's in the best interest of the trust and allowed under the prudent investor act.

7.11. Trustee's Power to Invest Property. Subject to the standards of the prudent investor rule as set forth in the California Uniform Prudent Investor Act, as amended from time to time, the trustee shall have the power to invest and manage the trust assets as a prudent

> 7.11. The trustee must follow the prudent investor rule, as set out in state law.

investor would, by considering the purposes, terms, distribution requirements, and other circumstances of the trust.

7.12. Early Termination of Trust. If any trust created herein has a total value at the end of any calendar year of less than sixty thousand dollars ($60,000) or becomes so small in relation to the costs of administration as to make continuing administration uneconomical, the trustee may, in the trustee's discretion, terminate the trust and distribute it to the beneficiaries.

> 7.12. If the trust (or a child's subtrust) is worth less than $60,000 or simply isn't worth maintaining due to administrative costs, the trustee can terminate it.

7.13. Division or Distribution in Cash or Kind. In order to satisfy a pecuniary gift or to distribute or divide trust assets into shares or partial shares, the trustee may distribute or divide those assets in kind, or divide undivided interests in those assets, or sell all or any part of those assets and distribute or divide the property in cash, in kind, or partly in cash and partly in kind.

> 7.13. This lets the trustee distribute assets in cash or in kind (in stocks or real estate, for example).

7.14. Payments to Legally Incapacitated Persons. If at any time any trust beneficiary is a minor, or it appears to the trustee that any trust beneficiary is incapacitated, incompetent, or for any other reason not able to receive payments or make intelligent or responsible use of the payments, then the trustee, in lieu of making direct payments to the trust beneficiary, may make payments to the beneficiary's conservator or guardian; to the beneficiary's custodian under the Uniform Gifts to Minors Act or Uniform Transfers to Minors Act of any state; or to one or more suitable persons as the trustee deems proper.

> 7.14. If a beneficiary other than a descendant of the settlors (who are subject to Section 6.3) is a minor, or is incapacitated, the trustee may distribute the share to a parent, conservator, or guardian, or the custodian of any other funds held for the child.

7.15. Trustee's Liability. No trustee shall be liable to any interested party for acts or omissions of that trustee, except those resulting from that trustee's willful misconduct or gross negligence. A successor trustee shall have no liability with respect to a predecessor trustee's acts or omissions or the acts or omissions of a predecessor trustee's agent.

> 7.15. A trustee is liable for willful misconduct or gross negligence, but not for unintentional miscalculations or mistakes of judgment made in good faith.

7.16. Duty to Account. The trustee shall render accounts at least annually, at the termination of a trust, and on a change of trustees, to the persons and in the manner required by law. Upon receipt of an account from the trustee, a beneficiary has one hundred eighty (180) days to make any objection to such account or to make any claim against the trustee for matters adequately disclosed in such account.

7.16. The trustee must give beneficiaries an accounting annually, when the trust terminates, and when there's a new trustee.

ARTICLE EIGHT
Concluding Provisions

8.1. Perpetuities Savings Clause. Notwithstanding any other provision of this instrument, every trust created by this instrument or by the exercise of any power of appointment created by this instrument shall terminate no later than twenty-one (21) years after the death of the last survivor of the settlors and their issue who are alive at the time the trust became irrevocable.

8.1. The trust must end 21 years after the death of the last of the settlors' descendants who are alive when the surviving settlor dies. This prohibits trusts that benefit descendants who could inherit in the very distant future.

8.2. Definitions of Death Taxes, Debts, and Expenses. As used in this instrument, the following definitions apply:

(a) The term "death taxes" shall mean all inheritance, estate, succession, and other similar taxes that are payable by any person on account of that person's interest in the estate of a settlor or by reason of that settlor's death, including penalties and interest, but excluding the following: (i) any additional tax that may be assessed under Internal Revenue Code Section 2032A; and (ii) any federal or state tax imposed on any generation-skipping transfer, as that term is defined in the federal tax laws, unless that generation-skipping transfer tax is payable directly out of the assets of a trust created by this instrument.

8.2. Death taxes are defined as any taxes arising as a result of a person's death. Excluded are certain taxes arising out of special farm-use valuations and generation-skipping transfer taxes (an additional tax on transfers between those two or more generations apart).

(b) The term "debts and expenses" shall include the following: (i) all costs, expenses of litigation, counsel fees, or other charges that the trustee incurs in connection with the determination of the amount of the death taxes, interest, or penalties referred to in subsection (a) of this section; and (ii) legally enforceable debts, funeral expenses, expenses of last illness, and administration and property expenses.

8.3. Definition of Incapacity. As used in this instrument, "incapacity" or "incapacitated" means a person operating under a legal disability such as a duly established conservatorship, or a person who is unable to do either of the following:

(a) Provide properly for that person's own needs for physical health, food, clothing, or shelter; or

(b) Manage substantially that person's own financial resources, or resist fraud or undue influence.

The determination of incapacity shall be made by the physician of the person whose capacity is at issue.

8.4. Definition of Education. As used in this instrument, the term "education" refers to the following:

(a) Education at public or private elementary, junior high, middle, or high schools, including boarding schools;

(b) Undergraduate, graduate, and postgraduate study in any field, whether or not of a professional character, in colleges, universities, or other institutions of higher learning;

(c) Specialized formal or informal training in music, the stage, the handicrafts, or the arts, whether by private instruction or otherwise; and

(d) Formal or informal vocational or technical training, whether through programs or institutions devoted solely to vocational or technical training, or otherwise.

8.5. California Law to Apply. All questions concerning the validity, interpretation, and administration of this instrument, including any trusts created under this instrument, shall be governed by the laws of the State of California, regardless of the domicile of any trustee or beneficiary.

8.3. Incapacity is defined here. A person who can't provide for daily needs or manage finances is incapacitated. This determination is to be made by the person's primary doctor. An incapacitated person can no longer act as trustee (see Section 7.8).

8.5. This trust is to be interpreted under California state law.

8.6. Definition of Child, Children, and Issue. As used in this instrument, the terms "child" and "children" refer to all of the children listed in Article One and any other children hereafter born to or adopted by both of the settlors. The term "issue" refers to the adopted as well as the natural child, children, or issue of the settlors and the respective issue of the settlors' children. This definition may be modified by the provisions of Article One.

8.6. Children are defined as the children listed in Article One, plus any children born to or adopted by the settlors. Stepchildren are not included.

8.7. No-Contest Clause. If any beneficiary under this trust in any manner files, without probable cause, a direct contest of this trust or any of its provisions, including any trust amendment, or a direct contest of any existing will or codicil executed by either settlor, then any share or interest in this trust given to that contesting beneficiary is revoked and shall be disposed of as if the contesting beneficiary had predeceased the settlors without issue. Any legal or other expense incurred by the trustee with relation to a specific beneficiary of the trust may, in the trustee's absolute discretion, be charged to that beneficiary's share of the trust estate.

8.7. This is designed to stop beneficiaries from suing to try to get a larger inheritance. A beneficiary who files a contest to the trust could lose his or her share.

ARTICLE NINE

Signature and Execution

9.1. Execution. We certify that we have read the foregoing declaration of trust and that it correctly states the terms and conditions under which the trust estate is to be held, administered, and distributed. As trustees of the trusts created by this declaration of trust, we approve this declaration of trust in all particulars and agree to be bound by its terms and conditions. As settlors of the trusts created by this declaration of trust, we approve this declaration of trust in all particulars and agree to be bound by its terms and conditions.

9.1. The settlors approve the trust as stated.

Executed on _____ , at _____ , California.

_____
Thomas Blackforth, Settlor and Trustee

_____
Peggy Blackforth, Settlor and Trustee

Index

Let Us Go On to Maturity

BY THE SAME AUTHOR . . .

Knowing God's Secrets

Limiting God

LET US GO ON
TO MATURITY

by
JOHN E. HUNTER

ZONDERVAN PUBLISHING HOUSE
GRAND RAPIDS, MICHIGAN

Library of Congress Catalog Card Number: 67-17226

Printed in the United States of America

"Therefore leaving the principles of the doctrine
of Christ, *let us go on to maturity*."
(Hebrews 6:1)

CONTENTS

Let Us Go On to Maturity

CHAPTER 1

THE RISEN CHRIST

THE WEEK I ARRIVED in America during the summer of 1966 I received an urgent phone call from a Christian leader in a nearby town. He said there was a state college in their area and just two weeks before, one of the professors had spoken at a luncheon meeting for all interested students. He had taken as his theme "God is Dead." He had brought all manner of forceful philosophy to prove his point. The following week the college newspaper had given his message a big write-up on the front page. The entire experience had caused much unpleasantness in the surrounding community. This college had begun upon a Christian foundation and this attack on the faith from one of the faculty seemed too much for the townspeople to take. There was also a small, struggling Christian group among the students and this open attack had proved demoralizing to their witness.

So it was that the Christian leader asked me if I could go to the college one lunch hour that week and speak in answer to such an open attack. I was both free and willing to stand alongside those who were fighting this battle on their own campus. We arrived to find a large gathering of students plus some townspeople. The professor himself was also in the audience.

I began by saying that, although I had been invited to speak as a result of the "God is Dead" lecture, I had no intention of arguing the case or even discussing the idea. I was not interested in considering a God who was dead — I had come to speak about a Christ who was alive, One who said, "I am

11

he that liveth, and was dead; and, behold, I am alive for evermore" (Revelation 1:18).

We then considered logically and factually the tremendous
truth of the resurrection of Christ. I read for them I Corinthians
15:1-11 and showed them the detailed list of witnesses who had
seen the risen Christ. We saw how, in verse 6, it is recorded
that, at that time, there were about five hundred people who
had seen the Lord — all at the same time. It would have been
possible, when the letter was written, to have checked with witness after witness regarding the personal appearance and behavior of the risen Lord — the entire incident was a historical
fact.

In the early part of this present century a group of lawyers
and legal men in London, England, met together to discuss the
evidence for the actual resurrection of the Lord Jesus. They
wished to see if there was sufficient evidence which would be
acceptable in an English court of law. When all their delibera-
tions were ended they came up with this considered opinion,
that there was sufficient evidence to make the resurrection of
Christ one of the best accepted facts of ancient history.

We followed with a discussion of the fact that the resurrection of Christ was not just an isolated incident with nothing
else to support it. I showed them a small book called *Count-
down* by G. B. Hardy, published by the Moody Press.* (I hoped
that many might purchase a copy for themselves.) Mr. Hardy
is really communicating with the college age when he writes
in such a pointed, acceptable manner. On page 25, speaking
of a definition of religion, he writes: "There are but two essential requirements:

1. Has any one cheated death and proved it?
2. Is it available to me?

Here is the complete record:
    Confucius' tomb — occupied
    Buddha's tomb — occupied
    Mohammed's tomb — occupied
    Jesus' tomb — EMPTY

Argue as you will . . . THERE IS NO POINT IN FOLLOWING A
LOSER." Mr. Hardy then goes on to present a wonderful fact

* Used by permission of Moody Press, Moody Bible Institute, Chicago.

which has thrilled the hearts of true Christians through the ages. In the Old Testament there are approximately three hundred passages where we can read incidents and details pertaining to the Christ, the Messiah who was to come. This is historical foreknowledge, where God has guided the writers to record the names of places and actions and incidents hundreds of years before they ever happened. This is a not a matter of philosophy or clever human speculation or supposition, but a plain statement of fact, clear and logical and capable of no human explanation. All three hundred items of prophecy, or historical foreknowledge came true in the life of the Lord Jesus Christ.

Some critics, in their attempts to find an explanation, suggest that the Lord Jesus deliberately arranged to fulfill these incidents. In suggesting this they most surely prove the deity of Christ, because no one but God could have fulfilled such "arrangements."

Consider the following items of historical foreknowledge with the Old Testament references and the New Testament fulfillment:

Born of a virgin — Isaiah 7:14; Matthew 1:22, 23
In the family of David — Isaiah 11:1; Luke 1:32
Born at Bethlehem — Micah 5:2; Matthew 2:4-6
The massacre of the children — Jeremiah 31:15; Matthew
   2:16-18
Carried to Egypt and the return — Hosea 11:1; Matthew
   2:15
Anointed of the Spirit — Isaiah 61:1, 2; Luke 4:17-21
Entry into Jerusalem on an ass — Zechariah 9:9; Matthew
   21:4, 5
Betrayed by His intimate friend — Psalm 41:9 — John 13:18
Forsaken by His disciples — Zechariah 13:6; Matthew 26:31
Sold for thirty pieces of silver — Zechariah 11:12, 13; and the
   story of the Potters' field — Matthew 26:15; 27:3-10
The spitting and the buffeting—Isaiah 50:6; Matthew 27:30
The gall and the vinegar — Psalm 69:21; Matthew 27:34, 48
Not one bone broken — Exodus 12:46; John 19:33, 36
His feet and hands pierced — Psalm 22:16; John 20:25

His garments divided by lot — Psalm 22:18; John 19:23, 24
Malefactors and rich men — Isaiah 53:9; Matthew 27:38;
57-60.

Consider for a moment, as an example, the prophecy in
Zechariah 11:12, 13 — "They weighed for my price thirty pieces
of silver . . . And I took the thirty pieces of silver, and cast them
to the potter in the house of the LORD." The first half we can
see fulfilled in Matthew 26:15 — "What will ye give me, and I
will deliver him unto you? And they covenanted with him for
thirty pieces of silver." But whoever could conceive of a situation where a man would take thirty pieces of silver and throw
them to the floor in the house of the Lord! Imagine throwing
a handful of silver along the floor of the temple! Yet Matthew
27:5 says — "and he cast down the pieces of silver in the temple,"
an amazing literal fulfillment of what was foretold hundreds
of years before.

The most remarkable fulfillment of prophecy was the literal
resurrection of Christ from the dead. Each of the three hundred foretellings in the Old Testament became facts in the New
Testament. Professor W. Stoner, M.S., with the endorsement of
the American Scientific Affiliation, has estimated that for the
Lord Jesus to have fulfilled these prophecies purely by chance
could be expressed mathematically as one chance in 10^{181} or
10 with a hundred and eighty more zeros added on. What a
number — what a chance — what a Saviour!

The resurrection of the Lord Jesus is not only an accepted
historical fact, but a fact proved so by the culminating fulfillment of the historical foreknowledge of God.

When that luncheon meeting had ended many of the
students were impressed by the logic of the Word of God com-
pared to the "inspired" philosophy of a defeated generation.
The local radio station had taped the entire message and this
was played back several times that week over the air.

But, may I ask, What does the resurrection of Christ mean
to you? What impact does it have on your daily life? Is it just
a historical event, an item of your faith — or is it such that your
entire life begins anew with this glorious fact? What part does

the risen Christ play in your daily confrontation with the mounting pressures experienced on every hand? The tragedy today is that many Christians live as if the Lord never rose from the dead. They know their sins are forgiven, that they are going to heaven when they die because He died on the cross, but, in the meantime, they face the hopeless struggle of trying to cope with events and circumstances that reduce them to hopeless failures. The resurrection of Christ is an item present in their belief but absent in their behavior.

The wonderful fact we can go on to share in this chapter is that the resurrection achieved two dramatic ends. First, the resurrection of Christ *fulfilled all the prophecies of God.* Second, the resurrection of Christ *released all the promises of God.* This risen Lord is the One who makes possible our utter and complete enjoyment of the glorious promises of God hidden away in the Word of God. It is the enjoyment of these promises that makes possible a life where sin is restrained, temptation is resisted, fear is neutralized, and anxiety and depression lose their power.

Take, as an example, the precious words of God in Isaiah 26:3, "Thou wilt keep him in perfect peace, whose mind is stayed on thee: because he trusteth in thee." Put these words alongside verses 12 and 13 of the same chapter and see the greatest missing experience in the world today—a sense of deep, abiding, inward, personal peace. The generation in which we live is lashing itself into a crazy turmoil of passion, excitement, fear and hostility coupled with a senseless infatuation with pleasure and noiseful living.

Yet, there continues to be a deep, deep, longing for peace; for that inner peace that soothes away the hurt and brings a restful calm to the tired personality. The risen Christ has made all this possible in our experience. He is utterly relevant to the crying needs of young and old. He has released all God's promises. This peace can be ours when His presence is real in our hearts and lives.

There are two glorious promises in Isaiah 42:1-3 that could bring wondrous blessing today to any person hungry enough to receive all that God gives — in Christ, the risen Christ. See how it begins — "Behold my servant, whom I uphold; mine elect, in whom my soul delighteth; I have put my spirit upon him: he shall bring forth judgment to the Gentiles." This last phrase is better translated — "he shall reveal truth to the nations" — something the Lord Jesus can do for us. In verse 3 we find a twofold promise that can be experienced through the risen Lord. The first phrase reads — "A bruised reed shall he not break." This is a lovely word picture of the relationship of the Lord Jesus to a poor, helpless, lost sinner.

I lived for fifteen years in a farming community in the midst of rich fertile fields. I came to realize that the presence of reeds in a field was a sign of damp, acid soil. Such an area of ground would be useless for raising crops. It was wasteland until time and money had been spent dealing with the soil condition. Therefore, a reed is really a useless plant and it grows in a waste place. Now put this information into verse 3 and you find that "a bruised reed" is a useless plant, in a waste place, in a damaged condition. What a vivid description this is of many lives today— useless — in a wasted area — bruised and damaged by sin and circumstance.

Now notice what is the reaction of the risen Lord to such a case of abject want — "A bruised reed shall he not break." The world will ignore or reject or destroy such a pathetic failure, but not so the risen Christ. He can make the waste place to blossom like the rose. He can bring forgiveness of sin, cleansing from guilt, and through His own indwelling Spirit, the peace of God that irons out all the wrinkles of a creased and crushed personality. This is how the risen Lord makes true the promise of God for the needy sinner who is "without Christ . . . having no hope . . . without God in the world" (Ephesians 2:12).

The first promise in verse 3 was for a poor tired sinner. The second promise is for a poor tired saint — "the smoking flax shall he not quench." This is another word picture that takes for its example the simple oil lamp used in the Middle East, even to this day. The container is a small boat-shaped vessel made of clay or metal. The front of the lamp is pinched together leaving a small hole into which a piece of twisted flax is inserted. This then acts as the wick. The lamp is filled with oil, into which the twisted flax reaches. The oil is then drawn up the flax so that the wick becomes saturated with the oil. When a flame is applied to the protruding section of the flax it ignites and continues to burn with a soft warm glow. This is the simple principle under which the eastern lamp operates. It is easy to see that the lamp can function only as long as there is oil either in the vessel or saturating the flax. It is necessary to make sure that such oil is always present.

However, the time could arise when the oil had not been replenished. If this should happen the vessel would go dry and the flax would go dry as the saturating oil was gradually consumed. There would thus be a flame, but no oil to burn. What would happen next is the word picture in this verse — there would be a "smoking flax." The oil would burn with a warm soft light, but the flax would burn with an acrid smoke. The lamp, instead of giving comfort and illumination, would simply give off a smoke screen offensive to the nose, hurtful to the eyes and useless in, its performance.

The immediate reaction would be to quench the flax, to stop it from causing discomfort to those around. But — "a smoking flax shall he not quench." The risen Christ is God's answer not only for the tired sinner, but also for the tired saint. There are many sincere and earnest Christians who today are struggling hard to live for Jesus. They want to be a true answer to the word of Christ — "Ye are the light of the world" (Matthew 5:14). There they are, each one a twist of flax, each one in his own appointed place, but each one trying to burn for Jesus. How simple is the lesson of the lamp — it isn't the flax that burns but the oil!

The flax can only smoke, giving off a witness of its own ability to cause discomfort and distress. All that is needed is "Give me oil in my lamp, keep me burning." Oil throughout the Bible is a type and picture of the Holy Spirit, thus the illustration of the lamp completely demonstrates the basic truth in living the Christian life — my Christian life is not what I can do for Jesus but what He can do through me.

All I can do as a sincere, hard-working twist of flax is to smoke, whereby I consume my own potentiality and throw no light on the surrounding darkness — I simply add to and become part of that darkness! But when I realize that "the smoking flax shall he not quench," the entire situation can change immediately. Other people may wish to quench me. Quite rightly so, for I would be a constant offense and embarrassment, but not so the risen Lord.

As I recognize the truth of His Holy Spirit indwelling me and learn once again that He is the light of the world, then, as I allow the risen Lord to fill me and possess me and control me, the capacity to shine is fully restored. It would be good to realize that a smoking flax would need to be trimmed before it could give a clear light once more. Trimming is simply the removal of a burned-out self so that the oil can flow freely through the twist of flax. Incidentally, an oil lamp, when it is functioning perfectly, still needs to be trimmed at regular intervals so that no burned-out self will interfere with the work of the oil.

As we move on now into this book we will be thinking constantly of these wonderful truths — that the risen Christ is God's answer to all our needs — that He not only fulfilled the prophecies of God but He also made real all the glorious promises of God — that the quality of our Christian life is our response to these facts.

A Prayer for Meditation

Thank You, Heavenly Father, for such a wonderful salvation.

Thank You that the Lord Jesus in all His risen power is the answer to all my need.

Thank You for His precious blood shed for me on Calvary's cross, so that my sins might be completely dealt with.

As I have appropriated His death FOR *me, so may I appropriate His risen life* IN *me.*

May the desert blossom as a rose and may the light shine clear and true as I yield my heart and life to be filled, possessed and controlled by His Holy Spirit. In Jesus' name. Amen.

CHAPTER 2

THE PROBLEM OF CHRISTIAN MATURITY

As WE READ AND STUDY the books in the Bible we can often assume that these are books of a bygone age written to people long since dead and buried. But, if we turn to I Corinthians 1:2, we find that not only is this letter addressed to people who lived in Corinth hundreds of years ago, it is also for "all that in every place call upon the name of Jesus Christ our Lord, both theirs and ours." We thus find ourselves intimately involved in this powerful letter. What it had to say to the Corinthians, it says to us today — in comfort, challenge and rebuke.

A closer examination of verse 2 gives us a threefold picture of these Corinthians of long ago. They were . . . *the church of God . . . sanctified in Christ Jesus . . . called saints.* This is indeed a wonderful appellation and brings to our imagination a group of people who were holy, dedicated, living strong, triumphant Christian lives. Our first reaction is to hesitate before moving any closer. These are special people, super-saints, and we are not worthy to associate with them, even though the same verse unites us in "Jesus Christ our Lord, both theirs and ours."

However, it is good to realize that this threefold designation is what they were in the presence of God. Positionally, this was their standing, and it was all through the infinite grace of God. They were the Church, the called-out ones. They were sanctified in Christ Jesus, but this was not anything they had achieved, this was the work of the Holy Spirit. They were also saints. This is no reference to holy statues or stained glass windows; to somber individuals with halos around their heads. The teaching is that they had been made holy in the sight of God.

In like manner we, too, are the Church of God; we, too, have been sanctified in Christ Jesus and, by the boundless mercy of God we are saints — not because of the quality of the lives we live, but because of the quality of the death that Jesus died.

This then was their standing in the sight of God, but what was their standing in the sight of the people among whom they lived and worked and moved? If we turn to I Corinthians 3: 1-3 we find quite a different picture. Verse 1 says: "And I, brethren, could not speak unto you as unto spiritual, but as unto carnal, even as unto babes in Christ." They were still . . . sanctified in Christ Jesus . . . called saints, in the sight of God, but what a different situation this chapter reveals. Paul could address them as brethren, but they were not spiritual. They were carnal, which means they were living the old life where self was in complete control.

Verse 3 describes how this carnal life was showing itself, "there is among you envying, and strife, and divisions." Their beliefs were one thing, but their behavior was quite something else. Notice the progression from envying, which is thoughts in operation, to strife, which is words in operation, to end up in divisions, which are deeds in operation. The entire development of thought, word and deed is here revealed in these Corinthian Christians.

Verse 1 designates them as *babes in Christ*. From this we gather that they had been born again. They had life with all the potential of glorious future development for Christ. They possessed the capacity to be all that God wanted them to be — but they were still babes in Christ. They had been saved by the blood of Christ through the infinite grace of God — but then they had stopped in their Christian experience.

They were "saved and stuck." Possessing everything from God, they had achieved nothing for God. They were living the same kind of miserable defeated lives that they had lived before they ever came to Christ — even though they were . . . *the church of God . . . sanctified in Christ Jesus . . . called saints*. Now, see the point of this letter which is addressed not only to them, but also to us! We need to search our hearts and see if we have this ungodly progression of envy, strife and division operating through thought, word and deed. Have we been born again only to remain as babes in Christ?

Babies are sweet and precious when God sends them into our families. How helpless they are! They are dependent upon us for every item of daily living, every moment of every day. But this we gladly undertake because we know that, in God's good time, the helpless babe will not only cry, but creep and crawl and then go on into those fascinating ages of three, four and five. Then on into youth and older years when all the baby helplessness is past and gone. This is our hope, and when it is fulfilled we praise God for His great goodness.

But sometimes, just sometimes, the baby does not go on to develop as the rest do. Some unseen, unknown mental limitation causes development to slow down or even to stop. What a heartache this can be to the parents who find that their baby is always going to be a baby — whatever age or size may develop. What was precious now becomes a problem, and, although God by His great mercy can provide strength sufficient for the task, there is a sense of pathetic loneliness and a lack of fulfillment. When babies stay babies someone has to undertake in new and heartsearching ways.

This, in a measure, was the problem in Corinth. The Corinthian Christians had been born again, they had received life through Christ Jesus, but something had entered to arrest the development of these young Christians. This was a resurgence of the old way of life, the carnal nature was demonstrating itself in their envy and strife and division.

I Corinthians 5:1, 2 reveals another area where their complete failure was shown. "It is reported commonly that there is fornication [sexual looseness] among you." Notice the word *commonly*. This was an open sin for all the world to gaze at, but no one in the church had been moved to judge it and put a stop to the moral cancer in their midst. The pagans had been shocked by such sexual depravity, but not the church. These people were still *the church of God . . . sanctified in Christ Jesus . . . called saints,* but what a mockery they were making of their faith.

It hardly seems possible that people can be Christians and

still be engaged in any form of sexual looseness — until we look around us today and see how low the moral standards are falling not only in the world but in the Church itself. This is not only so among those of high school or college age, but also among older Christians. Areas of sexual looseness are reported and find their way to the newspaper, unless influence is brought to bear to keep such a "scandal" out of the court of the social conscience.

Why is this so? Why do people today become involved in such wretched and miserable practices? One of the answers is that they have never grown up in the faith? They have been content to be saved and to know they are going to heaven when they die. They miss the glorious experience of going on with Christ. They somehow assume that God's salvation consists only of having forgiveness of sins and an assurance of heaven.

This is sad because no one benefits by their ignorance — except the devil. They themselves are irresponsible, unsatisfied and so useless in the faith. They, being babes in Christ, make so much work for other people. Not only can they not assume places of leadership and responsibility, but they display all the emotional instability of a babe and need special care and additional patience as they limp through life — a constant casualty on the hands of pastor and people.

Chapter 6 has one more thing to say about these people who were "saved and stuck." A further example of their carnal ways and of their baby-like behavior is seen in verses 1-8. Here Paul is reproving them for failing to settle their quarrels in the sight of God. In verse 5 he says, "I speak to your shame"; in verse 7, "Now therefore there is utterly a fault among you, because ye go to law one with another." These Christians had been taking cases into the pagan law courts which should have been settled in humility in the presence of God. They had been accusing one another, defaming and dragging one another before the spotlight of pagan power — just to prove a point to get even.

These three chapters make sad reading as we measure up the emptiness and the fruitless lives in the Corinthian church of those days — and all because they were babes in Christ. They had enough faith to come to the cross and trust Christ for salvation, but not enough to realize that, "he which hath begun a good work in you will finish it" (Philippians 1:6).

Let us remember that this letter is also written to us today. God began the good work in our lives. Is it continuing? If so, who is in charge of "Operation Completion"? There is one thing we can say regarding the background of the Corinthian Christians — they lived in one of the most wicked cities that ever existed. Corinth was one of the sin centers of the ancient world. On every hand they would see sin and sex and violence.

The Corinthians had also been raised in the darkness of this paganism. This was to them the only life they had ever known. But what was true for them is also true of many young Christians today, who, having been raised in a culture based on sin, sex and violence, have now to live a Christian life against such a background of pressure on every hand. The challenge in this letter is — Am I still a babe in Christ? Do I need to grow up in my faith?

There is a world of contrast between the epistles to the Corinthians and the epistle to the Hebrews. As we have seen, the Corinthians had a pagan background, steeped in all the vice and impurity of that wicked city. The letter to the Hebrews was written to people of another "world," another culture, whose moral fiber was based on the majestic glory of the Law and whose one aim was to keep themselves unspotted from Gentile contamination. Jehovah was their God and they were His people, and the rest of the world was a thing apart.

We saw that the Corinthians were addressed as, "*sanctified in Christ Jesus . . . called saints.*" If we turn to Hebrews 3:1 we see how the writer there greets them as, "*holy brethren, partakers of the heavenly calling.*" Notice again the dignity of these words. They were holy brethren — consecrated and set apart for God. They were partakers of the heavenly calling — they had a share in all the glorious promises and wondrous potential of the outreaching plan of God.

Here were a people truly prepared by race and relationship to God, to go out and do exploits for God. But when we turn to Hebrews 5:10 - 6:3 we find an unusual comment on their reaction to this glorious relationship. In verse 10 the writer was beginning a Bible study on the Lord Jesus as, "an high priest after the order of Melchisedec." He interrupts this study to say, in verse 11, "Of whom we have many things to say, and hard to be uttered, seeing ye are dull of hearing!" What an abrupt statement — *ye are dull of hearing!* Who were dull of hearing? *The holy brethren, partakers of the heavenly calling.*

He goes on in verse 12, "For when for the time ye ought to be teachers, ye have need that one teach you again." Not only were they dull of hearing, they were dull of doing, dull of teaching, dull of witnessing, dull of serving and being out on the job for the Lord. Verse 12 continues this penetrating analysis by asserting that they had become so needy and helpless in their lives, they needed milk and only milk. Strong meat, the implications and teaching of the fuller Word of God, was too much for them. Verse 13 says that because they were at the milk stage they were mere babes in Christ. The *Amplified Bible* gives, "For **every** one who continues to feed on milk is obviously inexperienced *and* unskilled in the doctrine of righteousness, [that is, of conformity to the divine will in purpose, thought and action,] for he is a mere infant — not able to talk yet!"

The Holy Spirit uses stronger words still in verse 14, indicating that they were not full-grown, because those who were really adult in their faith were those, "who by reason of use have their senses exercised to discern both good and evil." This is certainly a penetrating analysis by God's Holy Spirit into a people who were *holy brethren, partakers of the heavenly calling.*

See how it begins with their dullness of hearing. They had not allowed the Word of God to enter their personal lives. It was so satisfying, outwardly, to be known as holy brethren and to take pride in their heavenly calling — but it led nowhere.

Their behavior reflected their lack of involvement with God's Word. There was no dynamic for service and no discernment between good and evil. Once again, as with the Corinthians, the same charge is leveled at them — they were babes in Christ. They had been born again, they had Life, but they, too, were "saved and stuck."

Notice the comparison with the Corinthians. The ex-pagan believers were babes because of the things they *did* — the envy, strife and divisions — the sexual immorality — the vindictiveness in the law courts. These Hebrew Christians were babes because of the things they did *not* do. This is indicated especially in 6:1 — "Therefore leaving the principles [the A.B.C.'s] of the doctrine of Christ, let us go on unto perfection."

The one cure for their problem is here stated so clearly — *let us go on unto perfection.* It is good at this point to make sure that we fully understand the meaning of the word *perfection.* This is no idealistic dream impossible of attainment — the better translation of the word *perfection* is "maturity." *Let us go on to maturity.*

What these Hebrew Christians needed more than all else was to grow up, to allow the Word of God to challenge them, teach them, possess them until they were mature. We thus see that although the Corinthian Christians and Hebrew Christians were different in many ways — the same spiritual complaint was made about them — they were babes in Christ.

This period of prolonged babyhood had been the result of different backgrounds, situations and circumstances — but one remedy was prescribed for both, they needed to go on to maturity. Living in a world full of opposition and persecution they needed muscles on their faith and strength to stand and withstand the pressures of a pagan world.

Having challenged them severely in Hebrews 5, the writer goes on in 6:9-12 to comfort them. He says, "But, beloved, we are persuaded better things of you, and things that accompany salvation, though we thus speak." Notice that intriguing phrase — *things that accompany salvation.*

My salvation is not only an end in itself, there are also many wonderful things that should accompany my salvation. These had been absent so far in the experience of these Hebrew Christians. Verses 11 and 12 present a precious admonition from the Lord, "and we desire that every one of you do shew the same diligence to the full assurance of hope unto the end: That ye be not slothful, but followers of them who through faith and patience inherit the promises."

There had been laziness in their lives, dullness and a lack of fruitfulness for God, but now things were going to change. They were going on to maturity. There would be many exciting things accompanying their salvation. Best of all they were going on through faith and patience to inherit the promises of God, here and now, in their daily experience.

This thought links us with the first chapter of our book — the risen Christ not only fulfilled all the prophecies of God, He released and made possible all the promises of God. So the promises they were going to inherit would all find their fulfillment in an increasing knowledge and a deeper relationship with the risen Lord Jesus.

Such was the Word of God for the Hebrews as well as for the Corinthians. And, of course, the whole point of this challenge is that it comes to us with the same authority as it came to them. So many Christians today are "saved and stuck." They have been born again, their sins are forgiven, they are on their way to heaven — but they are still babes in Christ, they have never grown in the faith.

They may be babes because of the things they do — as in Corinth. They may be babes because of what they do not do — as with the Hebrews. Whatever the cause, the result is the same —an experience of prolonged babyhood with all its attendant limitations, frustrations and utter uselessness in the things of God.

If only Christian men and women would go on to maturity, and experience power in their daily lives and a robust quality of vigorous endurance, what a change would come over our churches. The pagan world around us would be challenged by lives inexplicable, but so desirable in their capacity to handle sin and sorrow, temptation and turmoil.

The need is present in all our hearts and lives, and the answer to that need is available to all who will go on to maturity. How wonderful it would be if, as we read this book, God should unlock to us the door that leads to Christian maturity.

A Prayer for Meditation

Thank You, Heavenly Father, that there is an answer to fear and failure and frustration.

Thank You that I do not need to go on as a babe in Christ. How wonderful to realize that through Your Word I can grow and find a new quality of Christian maturity.

Create in me a new desire to go on into the truth of Your Word.

As I read this book may the Lord Jesus become increasingly real to me in thought and word and deed.

May I be ready to hear and quick to obey — for Jesus' sake. Amen.

CHAPTER 3

JOSHUA — GOD'S PLAN

WE SAW IN OUR first chapter that the resurrection of Christ achieved two dramatic ends. First, the resurrection of Christ fulfilled all the prophecies of God. Second, the resurrection of Christ released and made possible all the promises of God. This is seen especially in II Corinthians 1:20 where we read, "For all the promises of God in him are yea, and in him Amen, unto the glory of God." The *Amplified Bible* gives this, "For as many as are the promises of God, they all find their Yes (answer) in Him (Christ)."

Consider the lovely and simple meaning of this truth. Wherever we find a precious promise of God in the Bible, one that holds out blessing, encouragement and guidance, we can say to ourselves, "Is this true for me, really true today?" The answer comes back every time, "Yes, indeed it is true, for all God's promises find their Yes in Christ."

We sometimes sing a chorus, "Christ is the answer to my every need," and how blessedly true this is. But more than being the answer to my need, He is also the answer to God's eternal promises. When we realize that most of these promises are safely hidden in the Old Testament, this gives us a further incentive to look therein to discover the treasury of God.

Another reason for turning to the Old Testament is found in the passage, I Corinthians 10:1-12. Here we have it clearly stated that we are to look back to the events surrounding the story of the adventures of the children of Israel on their journey from Egypt to the Promised Land of Canaan.

Their reactions to the promises of God are to be, to us, a source of warning and clear instruction. Verse 6 says, "Now these things were our examples [our warnings and admonitions]." Verse 11 says, "Now all these things happened unto them for ensamples: and they are written for our admonition." The word "ensamples" means — as types or figures — as examples and warnings to us. "For our admonition" means to fit us for right action by good instruction.

God gave the Israelites many promises. The land of Canaan was called the Promised Land. Their reaction to the promises of God was their very history. Everything depended upon whether they accepted or rejected the promises of God. In like manner my Christian life, the quality of life that I live, is dependent to a large extent upon my response to the promises of God.

God's Word has taught us that our Lord Jesus is God's eternal "Yes" to every promise, so that all we have to do is to turn the potential of promise into the power of experience. This we do every time we experience the sufficiency of Christ in any situation or need or crisis.

We can be helped along this line of thinking if we do exactly what I Corinthians 10:1-12 tells us. Let us turn back to the Book of Joshua and see this very subject being demonstrated in the life and experience of this one man.

Notice the title of this book, it is "The Book of Joshua" — the story of a man's life shown in his response to the promises of God. In like manner you are writing "The Book of You" — whatever your name may be. Your life story is being most surely recorded in the secretariat of heaven, and the daily report is not so much the problems and situations that arise, but the way you respond to such events.

The promises of God are the powerhouse of blessing, the eternal tools of God whereby victories are won and character is carved out of the bedrock of human experience. And remember, every promise is available, nothing is withheld, because the Lord Jesus Christ is God's "Yes" to every question arising from the promises of His Word.

In this day, with its great emphasis on young people, we are inclined to think that youth has almost a prerogative to the opportunities of service for God. "Too old at forty" is more than a catch phrase, and some Christians can be tempted to make increasing age an excuse for holding back in their involvement for God.

The Book of Joshua comes as an immediate challenge to such an idea. Joshua was a man who lived in Egypt in the days of bondage and who was old enough, when the Israelites came out, to be sent as a member of the search party to spy out the Promised Land. Then for forty years he lived in the wilderness before he became the hero of the Book of Joshua.

Joshua 24:29 tells us that he was a hundred and ten when he died, so we can see quite clearly that when his real life story began he was well over forty years old. Possibly he was between sixty and seventy.

Joshua 1 begins with quite an abrupt statement. The first words God said to Joshua were, "Moses my servant is dead." In a way, this would come as a blow. Deuteronomy 34:7 says, "And Moses was an hundred and twenty years old when he died: his eye was not dim, nor his natural force abated."

Moses had not been ill, he was not suffering in any way. Deuteronomy 34:1 records that Moses went up from the plains of Moab to the top of Pisgah and while he was there he died and the Lord buried him, "but no man knoweth of his sepulchre unto this day" (verse 6). Moses had made many ascents of mountains before to meet with God, and in God's time he had returned to his people. The children of Israel were used to this behavior, but this time he never came back.

They were waiting, but nothing happened. Then we read in Joshua 1, "Now after the death of Moses the servant of the Lord it came to pass that the Lord spake unto Joshua the son of Nun, Moses' minister, saying, Moses my servant is dead." He wasn't coming back any more, and this is where the Book of Joshua begins, with one man's reaction to responsibility.

This was going to mean a totally new life for Joshua. For the last forty years he had been Moses' minister — Moses' servant — taking orders and assisting his master in the colossal task of guiding this great crowd of wanderers. Moses was called the servant of God and Joshua was the servant of Moses. We can see from verses 6, 7 and 9 that the first reaction of Joshua was one of fear, and of utter inability to face up to, and cope with, such a situation.

Joshua had not made a decision for forty years; he had simply done as Moses commanded, and now he was being called upon to assume the leadeship of several millions of people. No wonder his heart was filled with fear! It was not that he was a coward, far from it. His was the natural reaction to the office of leadership after so many years of quiet obedience.

He would also be apprehensive concerning the children of Israel. No one would know more than Joshua about the heartaches and sorrows of Moses. There must have been many occasions when Moses returned to his tent with a broken heart over the wretched treatment he had received from the people whom he was seeking to lead and serve. Deuteronomy 31:27 records some searching words spoken by Moses to this same people, "For I know thy rebellion, and thy stiff neck: behold, while I am yet alive with you this day, ye have been rebellious against the LORD; and how much more after my death?"

These words would rise again in the memory of Joshua — *how much more after my death?* They would break Joshua's heart as they had broken the heart of Moses. The people would murmur and complain and be completely ungrateful for whatever was done for them. No wonder Joshua faced the news of Moses' death with fear, anxiety, and real trepidation.

Now notice that this is how the Book of Joshua begins — with a man caught up in circumstances that frighten him and baffle him. This may be how the "Book of You" is beginning. Perhaps you, too, are frightened, frustrated and baffled by what appears to lie before you. See then the great value of this book to your own heart, especially in the first nine verses.

God's reaction to Joshua's fear was to give him a threefold plan on which he would step out to experience victory and blessing. God gave Joshua — A Promise — A Program — A Power — and his response to this threefold gift is the story of the Book of Joshua.

In like manner, as we realize that every promise of God finds its answer in Christ, we too can write the book of our own life against the same threefold plans of God. As we see our experience and enjoyment of Christ as God's "Promise" and "Program" and "Power" for us, then the way to a new life swings open for each one of us.

The "Promise" God gave to Joshua was a wonderful twofold promise seen in 1:3 and 5. In verse 3 we read, "Every place that the sole of your foot shall tread upon, that have I given unto you as I said unto Moses." Notice, first, the two tenses in the verse, *your foot shall tread upon.* This is a reference to every future experience. Then comes, *that have I given unto you.* This is a guarantee of past assurance — I have already given it to you.

In other words, God was giving Joshua a promise of certain victory in every future circumstance, on one simple condition. It is possible to read this verse and miss the condition of blessing laid before Joshua. God said, *Every place that the sole of your foot shall tread upon.* Notice it was the sole of his "foot," not the sole of his "shoe" or "sandal."

This may seem to be a minor detail, but actually it involves a great basic condition. There are several places in the Bible where men were told to remove their shoes from off their feet, because they were standing upon holy ground. The ground was holy because God was there in a special and unique way. Therefore, when they removed their shoes they were recognizing the presence of God.

This is what is implied in verse 3. If Joshua would humbly and reverently recognize the presence of God and act in relation to that presence, then God promised that he would possess every such place.

In verse 3 the promise is — *every place.* In verse 5 we read, "There shall not a man be able to stand before thee all the days of thy life," so the promise here is for "every day." This makes the twofold promise one of tremendous potential — *every place, every day.* This was how God began "The Book of Joshua." To a man full of fear and frustration came this glorious offer of God.

I Corinthians 10 reminds us that this is for us, this can be our warning to fit us for right action by good instruction. Pause for a moment and consider that this is one of the promises of God that finds its answer in Christ, and realize that what God was saying to Joshua long ago He is saying to you and to me today.

The "Program" God gave to Joshua is found in verse 8. This is a long verse of forty-eight words but every word is packed with powerful instruction from God. It concerns "This book of the Law." This is a reference to Joshua's Bible. Certainly it would be much shorter than ours, but it was to be the center of his daily program for God.

The directions were that Joshua had to *meditate therein day and night*. This called for a special time to be set aside morning and evening during which he could meditate on the Word of God. If we consider that Joshua was probably one of the busiest men who ever lived, this command comes to us with special force.

Many of us are so busy keeping up with our daily program that somehow it becomes increasingly difficult to find time and space for the Word of God. But when we consider that Joshua was busy in the things of God all day long, not in the things of the world, and yet he needed these special times of meditation, then how much more is this true for us.

Notice, also, that God's program was not "reading" the Word of God, but "meditating" therein. Meditation is fast becoming a lost art. The emphasis today is on speed reading whereby the student is able to "devour" an increasing number of words each minute — but this wasn't so for Joshua. Reading is one-way traffic whereby my eyes go to the script and sweep by hurriedly to the end. Meditation is two-way traffic whereby my eyes go to the words and the words return to my conscious area of thought. Psalm 119 uses the word "meditate" in verses 15, 23, 48, 78, 97, 99 and 148. The purpose of meditation is seen in verse 11 of this same Psalm, "Thy word have I hid in my heart, that I might not sin against thee."

Meditation provides food for thought, a background to life, material for good works and weapons with which to attack and resist the world, the flesh and the devil. As a cow chews the cud, thereby extracting additional food value from what was eaten, so the magic of meditation blesses again and again the one who meditates. This was how God made sure that Joshua's soul would be fed so that he could grow and cope with the inrush of the demands of those needy people.

The whole purpose of Joshua 1:8 is seen in the last two phrases, "for then thou shalt make thy way prosperous, and then thou shalt have good success." God's program had a definite purpose in the life of Joshua, just as it would have in your life and mine. There is not a reader who would not desire this same promise of success and prosperity. This is what we long for in all our Christian lives.

But there may be some who say, "Well, I've done all this — I've meditated on God's Word and learned many Scriptures, but it hasn't made my way prosperous nor given me much success!" To such I would say, this verse does not promise success or prosperity to all who meditate in the Bible. This is where so many people can be misguided in their program, and become disillusioned in their practice of it.

The increase of Bible study groups and fellowships is a most blessed thing. Under the hand of God tremendous blessing can come thereby. But Bible study groups are no guarantee of success and prosperity. Attendance at such does not equip one with infallible blessing.

The whole "punch" of verse 8 is found in the center, *that thou mayest observe to do according to all that is written therein.* Obedience is the key to success! Meditation will lead me to the door of blessing, but obedience is the key that opens the door and sends me through.

We must realize that when God was speaking to Joshua He was referring not only to the spiritual blessings to be enjoyed. In a special way this was to be worked out in the practical things of life. Joshua had to apply the knowledge he had gained by meditation to making the choices and decisions in the days ahead.

This is where many of us fail. We somehow assume that the Bible is specifically spiritual and nothing else. I have met many Christians whose spiritual life and church life is acted out in accordance with the Book of Rules, but whose life and behavior in the world around them is conducted under a different pattern. No wonder such people have so little peace and joy and blessing in their hearts. God's program has to be my program for every walk of my life — church, domestic, cultural, business, social and any other area that involves decisions and choices.

Finally, God gave to Joshua the "power" with which this program could be carried through. In verse 6 God had said, *Be strong and of a good courage.* In verse 7 the words were, *Only be thou strong and very courageous.* It is good to learn here that God never calls one of His children to do a task without giving them the means to fulfill that work. If God is calling you to go, or do, or be, for Him, then you can be sure if the call is from God that the power will also come from God.

God was calling on Joshua for an increased demonstration of strength and courage. In your life, at this present moment, there may be conditions and areas that frighten and baffle you, and you feel it is impossible to face up to the situation. Joshua's courage and strength was very low at that moment, then God suddenly called for extra strength and "good courage" and to be "very courageous."

God went further in verse 9 to issue a command. "Have not I commanded thee? Be strong and of a good courage; be not afraid, neither be thou dismayed: for the LORD thy God is with thee whithersoever thou goest." But everything God demanded, God provided. The entire problem was solved in the last ten words of verse 9: *the Lord thy God is with thee whithersoever thou goest.*

Joshua had no strength — but he had to be strong. Joshua had no courage — but he had to be courageous. How was this going to be possible? There was only one answer — Joshua was going to be strong in the strength of another! The One who made the promise of *every place* in verse 3 and *every day* in verse 5 now supplied the power to make the promise a living reality.

The verse we must continue to remember is that with which we began, "For as many as are the promises of God, they all find their Yes (answer) in Him (Christ)" (II Corinthians 1:20,

Amplified Bible). This, together with the admonition in I Corinthians 10, is how "The Book of Joshua" can lead to "The Book of You."

If you will identify yourself in every way possible, with this man — his age, his fear, his panic, his inability to cope, then, the more you see yourself *in* the story the more blessing you will receive *out* of the story.

The last three verses of this chapter provide a happy sequel to the entire story. Joshua, having been commanded of God in verse 9, then goes out to command the people in verse 10. He claimed the promise, fulfilled the program, exercised the power and stepped out in obedience to the will of God. The last three verses give us the reaction of the people to the action of Joshua, "All that thou commandest us we will do, and whithersoever thou sendest us we will go" (verse 16).

His obedience to God was reflected in the obedience of the people. In verse 17 they said, "According as we hearkened unto Moses in all things, so will we hearken unto thee: only the LORD thy God be with thee." The chapter ends with these rousing words from the people, "only be strong and of a good courage." All that God said to Joshua was re-echoed in the hearts of the people. His step of simple obedience had won their hearts and they were prepared to commit their lives into the hands of a man whose life was truly committed to God.

This is how this thrilling "Book of Joshua" begins, this is how "The Book of You" could begin. Joshua began anew, so can you. He had wandered for forty years in the wilderness but he got out — by a "promise" and a "program" and a "power."

It matters not how long you have experienced wandering and a wilderness experience. There can be an end to it all. There can be a new life as a child of God. There can be a new and wonderful "Book of You" if you will also accept the "promise," the "program" and the "power," and realize in all this that, all this is true in Christ.

A PRAYER FOR MEDITATION

Thank You Heavenly Father, for the Book of Joshua.
Thank You for this man whose need was so great but who found a full satisfaction in his God.

Father, I would see myself in this story.

I confess my fears, my weaknesses, my utter inability to cope with the pressures of life.

Oh, may I receive this promise for every place and every day — in Christ Jesus.

May I become obedient to Thy Word, day and night, so that I may share Thy success — in Christ Jesus.

May I experience the reality of being strong in the strength of another — even Christ Jesus. Amen.

Chapter 4

THE PERIL OF IMMATURITY

In chapter two we considered the church at Corinth. We saw how the Corinthians were addressed as, *the church of God . . . sanctified in Christ Jesus . . . called saints.* But we found that what they were by the grace of God, and how they lived in the power of the flesh, were two different things. We saw their envying and strife and divisions. We were amazed at their sexual looseness, and distressed by their treatment of one another in the law courts. We saw that all this came because they were babes in Christ — they had never gone on to real maturity.

We reflected that this was a challenge to us to examine the quality of our lives. We need to do this still further in the light of the deeper challenge that Paul brought to these people at Corinth.

In I Corinthians 3:9-16 the Holy Spirit reveals a new line of teaching which should make every one of us stop in our tracks and measure up to the peril of continuing to live a life of insipid immaturity. The entire section is concerned with the works done by the Christian.

Beginning with verse 11 we read,

> For other foundation can no man lay than that is laid, which is Jesus Christ.
> 12 Now if any man build upon this foundation gold, silver, precious stones, wood, hay, stubble;
> 13 Every man's work shall be made manifest: for the day shall declare it, because it shall be revealed by fire; and the fire shall try every man's work of what sort it is.
> 14 If any man's work abide which he hath built thereupon, he shall receive a reward.

15 If any man's work shall be burned, he shall suffer loss: but he himself shall be saved; yet so as by fire.

16 Know ye not that ye are the temple of God, and that the Spirit of God dwelleth in you?

These are words of tremendous importance and they become increasingly so when we put them alongside II Corinthians 5:9-11, words which were written to the same people,

9 Wherefore we labour, that, whether present or absent, we may be accepted of him.

10 For we must all appear before the judgment seat of Christ; that every one may receive the things done in his body, according to that he hath done, whether it be good or bad.

11 Knowing therefore the terror of the Lord, we persuade men; but we are made manifest unto God.

Notice that these Corinthian Christians were being told to be ready *for the day . . . for the judgment seat of Christ.* This latter phrase is also to be found in Romans 14:10, so that we have here a threefold witness to a coming day in the life of every believer.

The Judgment Seat of Christ must not be confused with the Great White Throne. The only similarity between the two is the fact that the Lord Jesus Christ is the Judge in each case. We need to see that Revelation 20:12 is specific when it says, "And I saw the dead, small and great, stand before God." Again in verse 13 we are assured that those who appear before the Great White Throne are *the dead.*

Every one who has been born again has ceased to be numbered among the dead. They have become the living ones and their names are in the Lamb's Book of Life. That is why in this same verse 12 we read, "I saw the dead, small and great, stand before God; and the books were opened: and another book was opened, which is the book of life: and the dead were judged out of those things which were written in the books, according to their works."

The dead have their names and their deeds recorded in the many books of the dead and they will be judged out of those things which are written in the books. There is no sign or reference whatever to the presence of the living ones on this terrible occasion. The fact that the Book of Life is there is a double check in case any one should claim that a mistake had been made.

We see this in detail in the words of our Lord in Matthew 7:21-23. He indicated that, "Not every one that saith unto me, Lord, Lord, shall enter into the kingdom of heaven." He explained that, "Many will say to me in that day, Lord, Lord, have we not prophesied in thy name? and in thy name have cast our devils? and in thy name done many wonderful works?" These were people seeking to justify themselves on the grounds of what they had done. Then the Lord gave His final and awful answer to all such, "And then will I profess unto them, I never knew you: depart from me, ye that work iniquity."

The one simple test was this: *I never knew you.* How this issues forth into strong relief the words of Christ in John 10:27, 28, "My sheep hear my voice, and I know them, and they follow me: And I give unto them eternal life; and they shall never perish, neither shall any pluck them out of my hand."

Those whom He knows have eternal life. Because they have this quality of life they have been born again. Because they have been born again and have life, their names are in the Lamb's Book of Life. Because their names are in the Book of Life they will never stand before the Great White Throne.

Those whom He knows not are still spiritually dead. They may be church members, holding office and doing many wonderful works. But, as the Lord taught in Matthew 7, if He knows them not, they have no place in His kingdom.

This should cause every reader to pause and be sure in his own heart that he has been born again — that he has reality and not religion. The need for this double check is so necessary when we hear the Lord Jesus saying, *Many will say to me!*

The Judgment Seat of Christ is therefore quite different from the Great White Throne. The Great White Throne is concerned with eternal judgment. The Judgment Seat of Christ is concerned with rewards, not punishments. This fact needs to be fully understood at the outset.

I Corinthians 3:14 says, "If any man's work abide . . . he

shall receive a reward." The next verse goes on to state, "If any man's work shall be burned, he shall suffer loss: but he himself shall be saved; yet so as by fire." The entire purpose of this Judgment Seat is the giving or the withholding of rewards.

Anyone who gets to this Seat is already saved, born again, sure of eternal life and blessing.

This teaching was vitally necessary to the Corinthian church. They were unconcerned about the quality of life they were living. They were satisfied to know they were babes in Christ, saved by the blood of Christ and that they were going to heaven when they died. The Holy Spirit was opening to them the tremendous truth that their lives were going to be examined and tested in a coming day.

This teaching is equally necessary today. We need to be aware of the peril of immaturity. Every one of us needs to be jolted into a conscious and positive realization that he will have to stand before the Lord to give an account of his life.

The phrase, The Judgment Seat of Christ, is a picture word, taken from the customs and behavior of the people of New Testament times. The picture is that of a lord, or a ruler, who has been away from his kingdom, returning and making a critical survey of what each of his servants has done in his absence. Each one would come before him and give an account of what he had done, showing whether his time had been spent profitably in his master's service. The ruler would carefully consider the efforts of each of his servants and, as he evaluated their work, he would give them rewards commensurate with their value.

Some of the servants would receive worthy and honorable rewards, some would receive a nominal gift, while others, because of their laziness or lack of effort, would receive nothing. The entire ceremony was concerned with the giving, or the withholding, of rewards.

This is what our passages teach us concerning our own lives and their value to the Lord Jesus Christ.

Check back in our passages and see how personal this Judgment Seat of Christ is. In I Corinthians 3 there is a constant emphasis on the words *every man* and *any man*. Verses 10, 12,

13 (twice), 14, 15 indicate this truth. II Corinthians 5:10 emphasizes that, "we must all appear before the judgment seat of Christ; that every one may receive."

Notice, too, in I Corinthians 3:9, that "we are laborers together with God" and in II Corinthians 5:9 we read, "Wherefore we labour, that, whether present or absent, we may be accepted of him." The emphasis is on the word "labor." We are not seated in secluded splendor apart from the rush and turmoil of a busy world. We are out in the midst of it, experiencing weariness and exhaustion for the Lord's sake.

The Judgment Seat of Christ is concerned with things that are both personal and practical. The picture we have is of the Lord seated, and each one of us appearing before Him individually. If anyone should wonder how long such a procedure would take, the answer is very simple — time has ceased to be when this event takes place. Time is of no consequence.

If we were to stop and consider that at one specific moment in the economy of God we would each stand before the Lord Jesus, what a difference this would make in our lives. So much of what we are occupied with is just froth and bubble which has absolutely no significance when viewed against the background of the Judgment Seat of Christ.

Consider the deliberate and serious language of Paul in II Corinthians 5:9-11, "Wherefore we labor . . . we may be accepted of him . . . we must all appear . . . knowing therefore the terror of the Lord . . . we persuade men." This was the biggest thing in Paul's life. Notice the phrase, *Knowing therefore the terror of the Lord.* This in no way implies that Paul was being scared into serving God. On the contrary, its shows Paul full of a sense of reverence and awe. He was enveloped with a tremendous sense of the greatness of God. He was conscious that he was to be held accountable to this Holy One for his deeds and desires in this life. Paul had an appointment with Christ in eternity at which time he would give an account of his stewardship in this life.

If this same thought could grip us, what stupendous results might be seen in our lives. Everything we thought, or said, or did, would be seen against a new background. We would rearrange our priorities, and our sense of values would be drastically revised. The words of the Lord in Luke 12:15 need to sound again and again in so many of our hearts and lives.

Consider what Christ said, "Take heed, and beware of covetousness: for a man's life consisteth not in the abundance of the things which he possesseth." Let us be absolutely honest and say that in many of our lives we do not, *Take heed or beware*. Abundance of things plays a great part in so many Christian lives today. We line up our philosophy with the way of the world, and gather things and more things. When we do so we imply that this is what life is meant to be in our eyes. Poverty has never been detrimental to the power of the Church, but wealth has often weakened, and destroyed, and diverted, the main thrust of the Christian life.

Paul was gripped with this overruling sense of utter reverence and responsibility. He knew that some day the Lord would go through his life page by page. This would be the divine demonstration of "This Is Your Life." This realization in no way destroyed his appetite for living or his joy in life — it was the overruling pattern by which his life moved on from day to day.

This was what the Holy Spirit was bringing as a challenge to those spiritual babes in Corinth. They needed to beware of the peril of immaturity. They needed to take stock of the quality of living flowing out from their daily experience.

I Corinthians 3:10 tells us that what is under review at the Judgment Seat of Christ is the work that we have done for the Lord. This is not our sin being judged, this is our work being reviewed. Our sin is dealt with through the precious, shed blood of Christ. There is no question here of my sin and my own deliberate failure and shame. Thank God for the forgiveness and cleansing that follows the confession and sorrow.

All of us, in one way or another, are building on the foundation described in verse 11. Some of the works we do may be excellent, some may be satisfactory. With so many of us, we are completely unaware that we are building day by day in thought, word, or deed. We are always witnesses for Christ, but our heedless, careless, selfish lives so often make a witness which is anything but to His glory.

So it is that verse 12 divides the quality of our work into six separate categories — gold, silver, precious stones, wood, hay and stubble. Your Christian life so far will be a mixture of the six components. Notice, here, there is a descending order of values, beginning with the costliness of the pure gold and ending with the empty, spent, uselessness of dry, brittle stubble.

But while there are six different groups there are only two classes of works — those that remain, and those that are consumed. Verse 13 describes how these six groups are tested — they are tried by fire. Notice that it is the works that are tried by fire, not the Christian.

Gold, silver, and precious stones will remain untouched by the fire, but the wood, hay and stubble will disappear in a cloud of smoke. It is a beautiful thought to consider that gold and silver can withstand the fire because that is how they are produced. They have already passed through the refiner's fire and therefore they are pure. Precious stones are produced in the earth by pressure and intense heat, so they, too, can withstand the testing of the Lord. This gives us a true indication of the quality of the works that please God and which meet with His approval at the Judgment Seat of Christ. They are essentially pure — refined as in gold and silver. They are the result of pressure and testing and fire, and each one had to be dug out of the earth by labor and toil.

This same passage in I Corinthians 3 gives us the two essential standards against which our works are to be judged. Verse 13 says, *the fire shall try every man's work of what sort it is.* Notice that last phrase, *of what sort it is.* This is the standard by which your Christian life will be judged. It is not "how big it is," or "how much it is," but simply *what sort it is.*

Basically, there are two sorts possible, and your work for Christ will be one or the other. When the Lord Jesus was speaking to Nicodemus in John 3:6 He uttered a most profound saying which has unlimited application, "That which is born of the flesh is flesh; and that which is born of the Spirit is spirit." There are two sorts of work possible — that which is born of the flesh and that which is born of the Spirit.

Do not be misled into thinking that the term "flesh" is

either a physical reference, denoting only the flesh upon our bones, or that it is a spiritual reference denoting only evil, lust, impurity and godlessness. The term "the flesh" in the Bible means, "all that a man is, without Christ." It may mean evil and sin and impurity. It can also mean all those characteristics of human goodness — graciousness, elegance, and charm. These are also the marks of the flesh. Some people are naturally gracious and tenderhearted, just as others seem to be born to cause trouble.

When a sinner receives Christ as his personal Saviour he is born again. He receives a new quality of life. The Lord Jesus comes to dwell in his heart and life in the person of His Holy Spirit (Revelation 3:20). The sinner began by being only in the flesh, but salvation brings him the indwelling Spirit also. So a Christian has both the flesh and the Spirit — he is a partaker of the divine nature (II Peter 1:4).

When verse 13 of I Corinthians 3 says, *of what sort it is,* this is how there can be two sorts. There can be that which I have done for Christ, that which I have originated, the product of my own fleshly activity. Or there can be that which has come through the outworking of the indwelling Christ.

That which is born of the flesh is flesh, and Romans 8:8 teaches, *they that are in the flesh cannot please God.* The flesh always wants to have its own way, whether bad or good. It is not subject to God, it is an open demonstration of independence put out in defiance of the Lord Himself.

That which is born of the Spirit is what has come in my life as I have yielded and continued to yield my life to Christ. He has been in control. His will has been done through me, so that the works that come as a result are truly the works of the Spirit. These are the works that bring glory to Christ, that fulfill His will and that stand the test of the fire at the Judgment Seat of Christ.

So when verse 13 says, *of what sort it is,* we know now what is implied. There are two sorts — "my sort" and "His sort." "My sort" are the wood, hay and stubble. "His sort" are the gold, silver and precious stones.

There is one other essential standard we need to see in I

Corinthians 3. Verse 10 says, "But let every man take heed how he buildeth thereupon." In verse 13 it was *what sort it is,* now in verse 10 it is *how he builds.* Notice that this is simply "how" you do the work, it is not "how much" or "how big," but simply the manner in which you set about your work for Christ.

If we think about this word "how" it becomes quite an important challenge. I can serve the Lord and be involved in my church or my group simply because I am expected to do this. If I did not join in, then hints would be given, criticisms implied, and questions asked, so I do it just because of others.

I can also serve the Lord in order to draw attention to myself. I get myself in the limelight and win for myself a good name, so I'm happy to do it to win praise.

I can also serve as a means of promoting myself, my job, my family. It will be good for business and people will be able to learn about me and what I can do.

There are endless reasons for "how" we do our work for Christ, but only a few are going to count at the Judgment Seat of Christ. First and foremost it should be out of deep responsive love to Christ. How do I do it? Willingly, gladly, with all my heart, with no reserve or holding back.

The "how" and the "what sort it is" will decide whether we hear those wonderful words, "Well done, thou good and faithful servant: thou hast been faithful over a few things . . . enter thou into the joy of thy lord" (Matthew 25:21, 23).

As to what the rewards are, we have no real indication. It says in I Corinthians 3:14, *he shall receive a reward.* Revelation 22:12 — the last chapter in the Bible — states, "And, behold, I come quickly; and my reward is with me, to give every man according as his work shall be." Therefore we see a definite teaching of rewards for work done. Many of us would say that we want no reward, that just to be with Jesus will be our blessing and our greatest joy. This is good and a most commendable attitude, but the reward is connected with the Judgment Seat, and this will be a place of real heart searching. Some will lose their reward, whatever that may be.

Many of us may feel that this is something we can quietly leave until we get to glory, but Paul didn't agree with this. He

had that deep earnestness of desire that filled his whole being —
For me to live is Christ! He challenged the heedless, careless
Corinthians who were content to be babes in Christ.

Remember that I Corinthians is also written to us (see 1:2).
This is something we have to face and something on which we
have to act and react. The peril of immaturity in your life could
blight your witness, paralyze your work and send you to the
Judgment Seat with emptiness and shame.

> Only one life,
> 'Twill soon be past.
> Only what's done for Christ
> Will last.

A PRAYER FOR MEDITATION

*Father, as I search my heart and life I see the empty wasted
days, weeks, months and years.*

*Forgive me that I have been content to be spiritually im-
mature.*

*I have never thought of "what sort it is," or "how" my life
has progressed in relationship to the Judgment Seat of Christ.
So much has been "my sort" carelessly and heedlessly done.*

*Teach me, good Lord, to serve Thee as Thou deservest — to
give and not to count the cost.*

To fight and not to heed the wounds.

To toil and not to seek for rest.

*To labor and not to ask for any reward, save that of know-
ing that I do Thy will. In Jesus' name do I pray. Amen.*

CHAPTER 5

JOSHUA —
THE ONE CONDITION OF ALL BLESSING

As our book continues we will see, more clearly, the great similarity there is between the teaching in the New Testament concerning the need for going on to maturity, and the progressive experiences set forth in the life of Joshua. Each one is complementary to the other.

In chapter two we considered our great need as set forth in the Corinthian and Hebrew epistles. In chapter three we discussed how the need in Joshua's life was going to be met by God. Chapter four emphasized the need for a determined response to God. Now this chapter, dealing with Joshua's life once more, is going to show us how that determined response can be accomplished.

In chapter three we noticed that God gave Joshua a "promise," a "program," and a "power." The entire Book of Joshua was to be the record of that man's response to this threefold approach from God.

Let us pick up the story once more as we find it in Joshua 1:3, "Every place that the sole of your foot shall tread upon, that have I given unto you, as I said unto Moses." This was part of the twofold promise of God — every place — every day.

In this way God began to deal with Joshua. The words, *Every place that the sole of your foot shall tread upon,* mark the commencement of God's reasoning with him. Everything else that God had to say was consequent upon this initial approach. In one sense everything else that God had for Joshua was dependent upon his response to this first great condition.

48

We have already considered the significance of the words, *The sole of your foot.* This was not the sole of his shoe or his sandal, but his bare foot placed on the ground. In doing this Joshua would demonstrate the presence of God. He would show that he was standing on holy ground. And it was this acceptance of God's presence which was to be the guarantee of all future victory.

If we look back to Exodus 3 we see the same detail being worked out in the life of Moses. Verse 1 tells us that Moses was at *the backside of the desert* when God came into his life. What a potent phrase this is. He was not just in the desert, he was in the backside of the desert — the ultimate in failure and barrenness!

Exodus 7:7 tells us that Moses was eighty years old when this happened. He had already lived forty years in the glamor and glory of Egypt as the son of Pharaoh's daughter. Acts 7:22 says, "Moses was learned in all the wisdom of the Egyptians, and was mighty in words and deeds." This is a tremendous statement, because the Egyptians possessed unique qualities of wisdom covering many fields of knowledge, and yet Moses was learned in *all* this wisdom. In our language today we would say that he had several Ph.D. degrees. He was also *mighty in words and deeds.* Not only was he supremely learned, but he also had a tremendous capacity for communicating his knowledge. He was a man of action.

Such a combination of gifts and talents marks Moses as one of the greatest men of all ages. This was proved to be so in his later exploits as the leader of God's people.

But, Exodus 3 begins with this amazing man in the backside of the desert. All his wisdom, his words and his works were devoted to shepherding a flock of sheep or goats. What an utter waste of time and ability! Acts 7:30 tells us that he did this work for forty years. For forty years he was a nobleman, then for forty years he was a nobody. After that God spoke to him.

Exodus 3:2 goes on to describe the incident of the burning bush. Notice Moses' first words, "I will now turn aside, and see." God made the approach but Moses had to turn aside and see. Everything began when Moses turned aside — what a significant challenge to us.

Verse 4 tells of God's response when Moses did turn aside, "God called unto him out of the midst of the bush." God called his name twice and Moses replied, *Here am I.*

Then comes the importance of verse 5. God said, "Draw not nigh hither: put off thy shoes from off thy feet, for the place whereon thou standest is holy ground." As it was with Joshua, so it was with Moses. God's first approach was the challenge to recognize the presence of deity by standing with the sole of the foot on bare ground.

All that happened from then on in the life of Moses came because he recognized the presence of a Holy God in his life. This is something we need to experience in our own hearts and lives. Some of us may be, today, *in the backside of the desert,* wasting our potential in lonely areas. What we need is this face to face confrontation with God, with the reality of a holy God, so that our immediate response is to recognize His holiness by standing in the presence of deity.

An interesting thought here is that shoes were worn by free men but slaves walked barefooted. Therefore, when a man removed his shoes in the presence of God he was resigning his freedom and recognizing himself as a slave in God's sight. *Not my will, but Thine be done.*

We can now go on to see Joshua's response to the promise of God. In Joshua 3 are recorded the preparations that Joshua made to cross the river Jordan into the land of Canaan. So far Joshua had done no miracle, nor had there been any demonstration of God's authority vested in him. But in verse 7 we read, "The LORD said unto Joshua, This day will I begin to magnify thee in the sight of all Israel, that they may know that, as I was with Moses, so I will be with thee."

Joshua was going to magnify God and God was going to magnify Joshua.

Then in verse 8 God told Joshua to command the priests that bore the ark saying, "When ye are come to the brink of the water of Jordan, ye shall stand still in Jordan." Here was a tremendous challenge of faith. Verse 15 tells us that the Jordan was overflowing all its banks, so that it was not a tiny trickle but a full-flowing river, capable of damage and destruction. Yet Joshua had to proclaim by faith that when the priests came to the water's edge they would be able to *stand still in Jordan.*

Consider Joshua making the utterly impossible announcement that this thing would happen. He had no rod of Moses that parted the Red Sea, nor had he a cloak of Elijah to separate the waters. All he had was a promise from God, *Every place that the sole of your foot shall tread upon, that have I given unto you.* The way to victory was the recognition of deity!

See now what happened as recorded in verse 13, "And it shall come to pass, as soon as the feet of the priests that bear the ark of the LORD, the Lord of all the earth, shall rest in the waters of Jordan, that the waters of Jordan shall be cut off from the waters that come down from above; and they shall stand upon an heap." These are the words spoken by Joshua to the people. Joshua was taking this great step of faith, but notice what he said, *as soon as the feet of the priests.* He was going to claim the promise of God.

Verse 15 describes what happened next. It says, "The feet of the priests that bore the ark were dipped in the brim of water," and the river parted so that they were able to *stand still in Jordan.*

Joshua 4:3 tells of Joshua commanding that twelve memorial stones be taken out of Jordan, "out of the place where the priests' feet stood firm." In verse 9 he places twelve more stones "in the midst of Jordan, in the place where the feet of the priests stood."

Verse 18 tells how this miraculous crossing was ended. It states specifically that when *the soles of the priests' feet were lifted up unto the dry land,* the Jordan flowed in full force once more.

Thus it was that Joshua was magnified in the presence of all the people, but only because he had the people standing with bare feet. A simple act of obedience brought the blessing he so much needed.

You will remember that I Corinthians 10 told us to look at these stories, and see ourselves in the incidents recorded —

to see if there is a lesson that we need to learn, or a warning we need to take.

Here then is one definite lesson every one of us must learn — so simple yet so vital — as I recognize the presence of God, so I experience the power of God.

But Joshua had to learn not only to "recognize the presence of God," but he also had to discover the tremendous importance of "practicing the presence of God." This is shown in a story which begins in Joshua 5.

In chapter 5 the people are safely across the Jordan. They have established themselves in the Promised Land, and Joshua is now planning to move on to the next item on their schedule — the capture and destruction of the city of Jericho.

In verse 13 we have a picture of Joshua, by himself, standing and viewing the city of Jericho from a distance. He had probably seen this city once before, forty years ago when he, along with Caleb and the other spies, had made a reconnaissance of the land of Canaan. Of those who had seen Jericho before, only Joshua and Caleb remained alive. None of the children of Israel had ever seen a walled city — they knew nothing but life in the wilderness. Therefore Joshua would be viewing this strong strategic city. This was to be no easy task, for Jericho was built especially strong to withstand the attacks of a well-organized army.

As Joshua looked and pondered the entire situation he was suddenly aware of another man standing not too far away. This other man was armed and he stood with a drawn sword in his hand. Obviously the man was prepared to fight — he was no man of peace.

Joshua's response was immediate. He approached the armed stranger, probably with his own sword drawn in case of sudden attack. He challenged the newcomer, "Art thou for us, or for our adversaries?" (5:13). Here was no wasting of words. Joshua didn't trouble to ask for the man's name. All he wanted to know was, "Whose side are you on — our side or their side?"

There was a slight pause, and then the unknown stranger spoke. He first answered Joshua's question with one word "Neither!" — "I am not here to take sides." Then he told Joshua who he was, "as captain of the host of the LORD am I now come" (verse 14). This One had not come to take sides, He had come to take over. He was to be in charge of the whole of "Operation Jericho." He had command of the entire army of God and, as such, was in complete control of the situation.

Joshua's response was immediate. He fell on his face to the earth. He worshiped this Holy One and said, "What saith my Lord unto his servant?" He quickly handed over the entire problem to the Holy One, called Him Lord, and asked for orders as a servant would do.

Notice in verse 15 the one command that Joshua received, "And the captain of the LORD's host said unto Joshua, Loose thy shoe from off thy foot; for the place whereon thou standest is holy. And Joshua did so." There was only one thing needed from Joshua — not only to recognize the presence of God, but also to practice the presence of God.

Joshua had stood there alone, in his own strength, facing a problem he could never have solved. All the while the answer was his in the promise of God found in chapter 1, *Every place that the sole of your foot shall tread upon, that have I given unto you.* Knowing the promise was one thing, but practicing that promise was another.

So it was that here again God taught Joshua the reality of the promises of God. Joshua actually saw, for the first and last time, the Prince of the army of God. What he had heard with his ears he saw now with his own eyes. God's promises came true in a Person.

This Person could be none other than the Lord Jesus Christ. He was Deity and He demanded worship, yet He stood before Joshua in the body of a man. What an amazing thought that Joshua, in his day, was going to be able to say — as Paul wrote later — "I can do all things through Christ which strengtheneth me" (Philippians 4:13).

God had given Joshua a "promise," a "program" and a "power." The power we saw in Joshua 1:9, *the Lord thy God is with thee whithersoever thou goest.* Now the presence of the Prince of God was the answer to the power he needed. Both the promise and the power came true in the Person of Christ.

I Corinthians 10 asks — Is there any thing you can learn from this? Do you have a Jericho next on your schedule? Is there some problem, some situation, which is continuing to baffle you? Why don't you not only recognize the presence of God in Christ but also practice His presence, moment by moment. He has said, "I will never leave thee, nor forsake thee" (Hebrews 13:5).

It is interesting here, for a moment, to consider the Lord Jesus as the Captain or Prince of the army of God. In Matthew 26:51-53, Peter stood in the Garden of Gethsemane with a sword drawn in his hand. He was prepared to defend the Son of God! But Jesus said, "Thinkest thou that I cannot now pray to my Father, and he shall presently give me more than twelve legions of angels?" (verse 53). A legion was 6,000 men, so that the Lord Jesus was stating that more than 72,000 angels were ready to move at His request. Still He did not call for help. Once again He was in control of the entire situation.

We see Joshua's twofold truth, "recognizing the presence of God" and "practicing the presence of God," in Paul's beautiful prayer in Ephesians 3:14-19,

> 14 For this cause I bow my knees unto the Father of our Lord Jesus Christ,
> 15 Of whom the whole family in heaven and earth is named,
> 16 That he would grant you, according to the riches of his glory, to be strengthened with might by his Spirit in the inner man;
> 17 That Christ may dwell in your hearts by faith . . .
> 19 . . . that ye might be filled with all the fulness of God.

This is a tremendous passage. It is not only a wonderful prayer of faith, but also a clear and definite statement of truth set forth in logical sequence.

To understand the sequence better we need to turn to I Thessalonians 5:23 and see there another prayer of Paul which again reveals glorious truth, "And the very God of peace sanctify you wholly; and I pray God your whole spirit and soul and body be preserved blameless unto the coming of our Lord Jesus Christ."

Notice the spelling of the word "wholly." Some people say the word and think it is spelled "holy." It is not "sanctified holy," but *sanctified wholly*. In other words, the power of the Spirit of God is to be seen in every part of my life.

This verse teaches that there are three parts to my humanity. In Genesis 1:26 God had said, "Let us make man in our image, after our likeness." This does not imply that man was going to look like God for *God is a Spirit,* but that man in his humanity in some way was to be like God in His deity. Notice that God said, *Let us* — this was the voice of the Triune God; the Holy Trinity; Father, Son and Holy Spirit. What God was in His essential being — a Trinity — man was going to be in his essential being.

Thus it is we have the trinity of man — spirit, soul and body. Man is not just a body and a soul — that is, a physical body plus a human personality — but spirit, soul and body (trichotomy).

The soul of man in the Bible is often called the heart of man — what we would today call his personality. People remember us, not so much because of our body — our beauty or lack of beauty — but because of the impact of our human personality.

This is a tremendous blessing, because many of us are not initially physically attractive. We all have our significant areas of physical deficiency! But a gracious, loving personality can completely overshadow and hide the physical failures.

The soul of man — or the heart of man — or the personality — is itself a trinity. Modern psychology and the Bible agree in defining three areas in the personality. The names used for the areas may differ, but the significance is the same. These areas are — the emotions — the mind, or intellect — the will.

We can find Scriptures to show each of these areas.

The emotions are clearly indicated in Matthew 15:19 where the Lord Jesus said, "For out of the heart proceed evil thoughts, murders, adulteries, fornications, thefts, false witness, blasphemies." This is the display of intense emotional disturbance.

Again in Luke 1:51 we read, "he hath scattered the proud in the imagination of their hearts." This is the emotional seat of all pride and vanity.

In John 14:1 the Lord Jesus said, "Let not your heart be troubled." The emotion of fear is evident in the human heart.

The fact that the mind is also a part of the human heart is seen clearly in Matthew 9:4 where we read, "And Jesus knowing their thoughts said, Wherefore think ye evil in your hearts?"

Again in Mark 2:8 we read, "Immediately . . . Jesus . . . said unto them, Why reason ye these things in your heart?" The heart was thus the place where the mind and the intellect could function.

In Daniel 1:8 we read these words, "But Daniel purposed in his heart." He was determined, his will was in evidence. Thus we can see from the Bible the clear threefold teaching concerning the soul, or heart, or personality of man.

It was this threefold concept of man that Paul was concerned with in his prayer, already referred to, in Ephesians 3. Paul was praying for a total involvement of the whole man.

We can understand Paul's sequence of thought if we get a simple visual aid in our mind. Consider a circle — an inner circle. Then, see this inner circle surrounded by another circle — thus giving two concentric circles. Then, put one more circle around that picture and you have something like a target as used in archery — an inner circle plus two more concentric circles.

The inner circle we can call the spirit. The circle surrounding that we can call the soul — or personality. The outer circle then becomes, of course, the body.

We are now in a position to line up the two truths that Joshua learned with the great prayer that Paul prayed.

Joshua had to learn, first, to "recognize the presence of God" — then, to keep on "practicing the presence of God."

Paul prayed first in Ephesians 3:16 that they might be "strengthened with might by his Spirit in the inner man." The inner man is that inner circle — the human spirit. Paul thus wanted the Ephesians to realize first of all that becoming a Christian was not just having my sins forgiven, but also having a real, conscious sense of the Spirit in my human spirit.

This is seen again in Romans 8:16 where Paul says, "The Spirit himself beareth witness with our spirit, that we are the children of God." I become a child of my parents when I am born the first time. I become a child of God when I am born again. This is *how* I am born again — by the Spirit Himself coming to dwell in my human spirit. This is also *where* I am born again, and *when* I am born again.

Remember, the Lord Jesus said in John 3:3, "Except a man be born again, he cannot see the kingdom of God." If I have not received the Spirit, then I am not born again, I am not a child of God.

Romans 8:9 says, "But ye are not in the flesh, but in the Spirit, if so be that the Spirit of God dwell in you. Now if any man have not the Spirit of Christ, he is none of his." Notice the tremendous significance of this verse — the Holy Spirit is the Spirit of Christ. The Lord Jesus dwells within us in the presence of His Spirit. If He is not there, then I am not a Christian.

So Paul's first request was that these Christians might *be strengthened with might by his Spirit in the inner man — the human spirit.* As with Joshua, so they were to recognize the presence of God.

This is something so many Christians have never truly realized by conscious personal application. They know they have been saved by the blood of Christ. They know, like the Israelites, they have been redeemed from Egypt — from the bondage of sin: that their sins are forgiven by the death of Christ.

What they fail to realize is this very thing for which Paul prayed, that, because they were saved, they might be strengthened with might by His Spirit in their human spirit.

God's salvation is not only Christ *for* me on the cross, but Christ *in* me through His Spirit. And the fact of Christ *in* me is the realization of the presence of God.

The presence of Christ brings the power of Christ. That is why Paul prayed *strengthened with might.* The Greek word which is translated "might" is *dunamis.* This word is expressive of intense power. It is from this word that the word dynamite was coined — an explosive and eruptive force.

In other words, when I become a Christian, the Lord Jesus comes to dwell in my inner man, my human spirit, and because He is there I have within me the explosive, eruptive power of God.

When I realize this, then I recognize the presence of God. But Joshua also had to practice the presence of God. For me this means the application of this indwelling power day by day in my human life.

Paul indicated this when he went on to pray in Ephesians 3:17, "That Christ may dwell in your hearts by faith." To understand this more clearly, think once again of those three concentric circles. First was the inner one — the human spirit. Second was the middle one — the heart or the human personality.

Recognizing the presence of God is realizing that the Lord Jesus dwells in my inner man — practicing His presence is allowing Christ to move into the area of my human personality.

Notice the words, "allowing Christ." This is the test of "practicing the presence of Christ." There are many Christians who have been born again, but who are content to rest on the knowledge of sins forgiven and a home in heaven. They choose to run their own lives their own way. Their emotions, minds and wills are entirely at their own disposal. What they want, or what they say, is the experience of their daily life.

Paul's prayer becomes fulfilled when I, first of all, recognize that the Lord Jesus dwells within my human spirit. Then, when I open my personality to Christ, *He is able to dwell in my heart by faith.* My Lord Jesus moves out of the inner circle into the middle circle of my personality.

This means that He moves into the area of my emotions, my mind or intellect, and my will. The words *dwell in your heart* are more clearly defined in the *Amplified Bible*, "May Christ through your faith [actually] dwell — settle down, abide, make His permanent home — in your hearts!"

This is not a temporary visit but a permanent residency. It is not calling in Christ, as one would call in a doctor to make a house visit. The doctor comes, diagnoses and departs, and in one sense we hope we will never need him again. Conversely, if things go wrong, we can always call him in once more.

This is not the way to practice the presence of Christ. I practice His presence when I invite Him to *settle down, abide, make His permanent home.* This He will do in every area of my personality. It will be Christ dwelling in my emotions, Christ dwelling in my mind, and Christ dwelling in my will.

Remember, also, that when Christ comes in, the power comes in. He comes in to control. This is what it means to be filled with the Spirit. This is not me having more of the Spirit, but the Spirit having more of me. Being filled with the Spirit is being controlled by the Spirit.

Being filled with the Spirit will not result in my going into a wild ecstatic orbit of spiritual aberration. As I am filled, so I will be controlled and my new Christian experience will be the demonstration of the life of Christ through my emotions, my mind and my will.

One immediate result will be the explosive and eruptive power of Christ within the confines of my personality. Notice how the Lord Jesus can often change a human personality — by controlling it and by cleansing it — as He did the Temple.

Not only will the presence of Christ in my human personality be controlling and cleansing, but it will also be costly. This is why so many of us are not prepared to practice the presence of Christ day by day. It becomes too costly and probably too embarrassing.

It is much easier to recognize the presence of Christ and then run things my own way. I seem to be getting the best of both worlds. In truth, I am experiencing the poverty of two situations.

Paul continued his prayer by adding, in verse 19, "that ye might be filled with all the fulness of God." If we think once more of our three concentric circles this final request is really the extension of the entire outreach of Christ. Beginning in my spirit, the fullness of God will control my human personality, and my own body will be the area where the impact is seen in the world around.

This is clearly set forth in II Corinthians 4:10, 11, where Paul states his own desire, "that the life also of Jesus might be made manifest in our body . . . that the life also of Jesus might be made manifest in our mortal flesh."

This is the most practical application of truth we can ever meet. This is when my faith gets to my fingers and my truth to my toes. This is what the world is waiting to see — not the indwelling Christ — but the outworking of the indwelling Christ, through me. This is the practice of the presence of Christ.

One natural reaction to this teaching of Paul is the thought that, though it may be wonderful in theory, it is impossible to carry through. Humanly speaking this is true, but Paul gives the secret of success in Ephesians 3:20, "Now, unto him that is able to do exceeding abundantly above all that we ask or think, according to the power that worketh in us."

Not only can this be true, but it will become abundantly true, *above all that we ask or think*. It comes true through the power that worketh in us. The power that comes within the inner man is the same power that will be seen through the outer man, but only inasmuch as we are prepared to yield our personalities to the complete control of Christ.

This chapter is called "The One Condition of All Blessing," and this is it. As it was with Joshua, so it is with us. First, we must recognize the presence of Christ, then practice that presence — just living as if it were true — day by day.

A Prayer for Meditation

Heavenly Father, this is a tremendous challenge to my soul.

Thank You that my sins are forgiven — this is so wonderful to me.

Thank You for the indwelling Christ — not only Christ for *me, but also Christ* in *me.*

Give me a quiet willingness to cooperate and yield my entire being to You, so that the Lord Jesus can make His permanent home in my redeemed personality.

May the results be that I am more Christlike — because more of me is open to His explosive power. This I pray in the name of my Saviour. Amen.

CHAPTER 6

THE PLAN FOR MATURITY — FOR ME

THERE IS AN OLD SAYING which goes, "Some people eat to live — while others live to eat." In one sense this divides the world into two camps these days — those who go to bed hungry and those who retire, full and sufficed.

But one of the problems of our modern civilization — especially here in America — is that not all the food we eat is food. It may fill and fatten, but it does not all nourish. Thus it is that there has grown up in America the great vitamin industry.

Rightly or wrongly, this is an attempt to give to people the opportunity to make modern food nourishing. Food research scientists have made many wonderful discoveries in the areas of food deficiencies. The results of their studies are seen in the many colored multi-shaped pills which bear intriguing names and which carry amazing promises of blessing to come.

There is no doubt that many people today owe their health and strength — even their very lives — to the work of the vitamin scientists.

Now what is true in the world of physical food is equally true in the realm of spiritual food. As not all physical food is nourishing, so not all spiritual food is nourishing. It may fill and fatten, but it does not bring that excellency of well-being to the blood stream.

There needs to be, in the spiritual food I eat, that unique quality of nourishment that enriches my spiritual blood stream, that puts a sparkle into my spiritual eyes and adds real strength to my spiritual muscles.

61

The plan for Christian maturity involves the daily absorption of spiritual vitamins. There must be a daily intake so that my spiritual strength is renewed and revitalized.

Maturity is growth in action, and if I am to grow I need a definite vitamin content to my diet — whether it is physical or spiritual growth.

Vitamins, too, are essential to withstand disease and the attacks of germs and viruses. This is true on the physical and spiritual level. There are many Christians who are becoming sick these days — spiritually sick — with diseases and infections brought by germs and viruses. If they had the correct spiritual vitamins in their blood stream they would be able to resist and repel such intrusions.

Deficiency in spiritual vitamins is the cause of much of the sickness in the Church today. So, in this chapter, we will consider the plan for Christian maturity which is based on a simple knowledge of spiritual vitamins.

To make the study easy and understandable we will take the seven separate letters in the word "vitamin" and use each letter to introduce an essential truth, thought or concept, which *must* be in our spiritual blood stream if we are to grow to maturity. The very succession of the letters will bring also a logical progression of truth and teaching.

In this chapter we will consider the four letters V-I-T-A. This will give us teaching on "The Plan for Maturity — *For* Me." In a later chapter we will consider the three letters M-I-N. In that chapter we will consider teaching on, "The Plan for Maturity — *Through* Me."

VICTORY

Our first vitamin then begins with the letter V. There must be a daily realization of the spiritual vitamin of "Victory" in my life. This is where I begin. The presence, or absence, of victory in my life will color the whole of my daily living. Everything I think, or say, or do, will demonstrate to the world the measure of my victory, or the reality of my defeat.

There can be no peace, until there is victory. This is true in every sphere of human experience. Compromise may prevent war, but it will never produce peace. There has to be the reality of victory before there can be the release of peace.

It is this way in the Christian life. There are many Christians today whose lives are characterized by an absence of peace. They live in a world of trouble, toil and turmoil. They long for peace, they pray for peace, they may even agonize for peace, but they fail to grasp the simple truth that there can be no peace until there is victory.

Let us pursue this thought several stages further by searching in the Word of God.

1. *The Christian faith begins with victory.* In Philippians 2:5-11 we have the complete story of the work of the Lord Jesus Christ. It begins with the poverty of Bethlehem, but it ends with the exaltation of the Lord. He has already been exalted. He already has "a name which is above every name: that at the name of Jesus every knee should bow . . . And that every tongue should confess that Jesus Christ is Lord, to the glory of God the Father."

The whole of my faith is based upon the glorious victory of Christ. Colossians 1:20 says, "having made peace through the blood of his cross." Because the peace has been made, we know the victory has been won.

2. *God's salvation is victory.* Psalm 98:1, 2 has a rich truth to tell, "O sing unto the LORD a new song; for he hath done marvellous things: his right hand, and his holy arm, hath gotten him the victory.

"The LORD hath made known his salvation: his righteousness hath he openly shewed in the sight of the heathen."

We learned in chapter 1 that all the prophecies of God were fulfilled in the Lord Jesus, and that all the promises of God are true in Him (see II Corinthians 1:20), "For all the promises of God in him are yea, and in him Amen."

See both these truths illustrated in this Psalm. God has made known His salvation—and His salvation is victory—through Christ.

3. *God's victory is to be shared.* I Chronicles 29:11, 12 records David's great words of praise and prayer to Almighty God. Some of the richest conceptions of truth and worship are

seen here. "Thine, O Lord, is the greatness, and the power, and the glory, and the victory . . . Both riches and honour come of thee . . . and in thine hand it is to make great, and to give strength unto all."

We see here that this great victory of God is to be shared. It can be known in terms of riches and honor. It can be experienced in greatness and strength — to all.

4. *Victory is a gift to be received.* I Corinthians 15:57 contains one of the greatest encouragements in the Bible, "But thanks be to God, which giveth us the victory through our Lord Jesus Christ."

There may be some who are reading these words with avid interest, because this is what you are seeking — victory over sin — over temptation — over sorrow — fear — anxiety — loneliness — and a thousand other things.

This is what you are working at — seeking, reading, praying, struggling — hoping that some day you will win the victory over this enemy in your life.

Let me give you one amazing word of encouragement — you will never, never win the victory. It matters not how hard you struggle in "blood, toil, tears and sweat," you will never win the victory. Never, because victory is not something you win, it is something you receive! *Thanks be to God, which giveth us the victory.*

All that God has for us, in every area, comes as a gift. "God so loved the world, that he gave his only begotten Son" (John 3:16). "The gift of God is eternal life through Jesus Christ our Lord" (Romans 6:23). "Every good gift and every perfect gift is from above, and cometh down from the Father of lights" (James 1:17). So it is with the experience of victory — it is a gift from God.

The complementary act to giving is not asking, but receiving. I don't ask for a gift that is being offered to me — I take it, and say thank you. I don't earn it, or achieve it, nor am I worthy of the gift of God. I simply come with my need and take what is offered.

Just as I came to the cross and accepted Jesus as my Saviour, so I come to the Christ and accept Him as my Victory. I am saved by faith, I walk by faith — even so I have victory by faith.

I don't have to understand it nor be able to explain it — I simply take the victory that God offers in the person of the Lord Jesus Christ.

He dwells in my heart and life through His Holy Spirit. I accept this fact, and on the basis of His presence with me, I accept all the implications of His presence — most of all, His victory lived out through my yielded life.

5. *This is the victory.* I John 5:4 makes this possible to us today, "this is the victory that overcometh the world, even our faith." This is the victory . . . even our faith.

Faith is spelled out F-A-I-T-H. This can be developed as — Forsaking All I Take Him. This is what faith really is — turning my back on all my failure and taking "all that He is, for all that I need."

At the cross I needed a Saviour from sin, so I turned from my sin and took Christ as my Saviour — taking that which God so freely gave.

Now in the crisis of daily living, I need victory over those things and experiences that drag me down or turn me aside. The same faith I used at the cross I now use in the crisis. I turn from my petty struggles of failure and I take "all that He is, for all that I need." I take Him as my victory. I commit to my Lord the issues of the problem. I relate to Him the entire situation. Then, with my life fully yielded to Him I go forward in faith, believing that "God is able to make all grace abound toward you; that ye, always having all sufficiency in all things, may abound to every good work" (II Corinthians 9:8).

This then is the vitamin of victory. I need it every day if my life is to count for God and Christ.

I need it and I can experience it. The entire question is — will I take what God offers? There is no alternative to Christ.

INDWELLING HOLY SPIRIT

The first essential vitamin is the reality of victory in my life. This is made possible by the second essential vitamin, an assurance of the indwelling Holy Spirit. Observe that it is the indwelling Spirit who guarantees my victory.

It is not enough to know about the Holy Spirit or to believe in Him — there must be the conscious experience of the indwelling Spirit.

The Holy Spirit dwells within our hearts and lives to represent all that the Lord Jesus Christ is. The Lord said in John 14:26, "But the Comforter (Counselor, Helper, Intercessor, Advocate, Strengthener, Standby), the Holy Spirit, Whom the Father will send in My name [in My place, to represent Me and act on My behalf] He will teach you all things. And He will cause you to recall — will remind you of, bring to your remembrance — everything I have told you" (*Amplified Bible*). His work is to glorify Christ in and through the life of the believer.

I Corinthians 2:9 has a wonderful word for us in this respect, "Eye hath not seen, nor ear heard, neither hath entered into the heart of man, the things which God hath prepared for them that love him."

This is so often used as a means of encouraging Christians to endure present trouble so that all these blessings may be theirs when they get to heaven. But how wrong is such an application. The next verse gives us the true interpretation, "But God hath revealed them unto us by his Spirit."

These blessings are for us now, as we allow the indwelling Holy Spirit to control our lives. We can enjoy heaven on the way to heaven — through the same Spirit.

Verse 12 in the same context says, "Now we have received, not the spirit of the world, but the Spirit which is of God; that we might know the things that are freely given to us of God." Observe the impact of truth — *we have received . . . that we might know.*

In chapter 2 of this book we saw the intriguing phrase in Hebrews 6:9, *things that accompany salvation.* The Hebrew Christians had a salvation which had made them babes in Christ, but which had left them dull of hearing and dull of doing. They were short of the *things that accompany salvation.*

What they needed was a conscious sense of the indwelling Holy Spirit, so controlling in their daily lives that they might know the things that were freely given to them of God.

The things freely given were those that could accompany their salvation, that would, in turn, deal with the dullness in their hearing and doing.

In Hebrews 3:12, 14 the writer is still addressing "the holy brethren, partakers of the heavenly calling." He says, "Take heed, brethren, lest there be in any of you an evil heart of unbelief, in departing from the living God. . . . For we are made partakers of Christ, if we hold the beginning of our confidence stedfast unto the end."

He is reminding them of the tremendous potential there is in Christ, if we will only continue in steadfast confidence. It is not only Christ for me on the cross, but the outworking of the indwelling Holy Spirit of Christ in my life day by day.

THANKFULNESS

One of the evidences of our deteriorating society is the growing abandonment of the use of good manners. It is sad to see pleasant, kindly and comforting words and ways being discarded in the desire to be "with it." They cost so little, yet they pay such high dividends and bring unknown rewards to all who use them.

One of these simple customs is the demonstration of an appreciative attitude in saying "thank you."

This is important in the social world around us, but it is much more important in our relationship to our Heavenly Father.

The third great spiritual vitamin essential to a robust and effective Christian life is this continual attitude of thankfulness toward God. A deficiency in this area is clearly seen in a lack of joyous living.

Thankfulness, in a sense, is the button which, when pressed, releases the indwelling Holy Spirit who, in turn brings the victory and the blessing.

I Thessalonians 5:16-18 has significant words to say in this respect. "Rejoice evermore. Pray without ceasing. In every thing give thanks: for this is the will of God in Christ Jesus concerning you."

I am often asked questions concerning the will of God — "How can I know the will of God?" — "What is the will of God for me?" I would say to all who ask that there is a twofold aspect of the will of God. There is the general will of God — this applies to all believers. Then there is the specific will of God — this applies to the individual believer.

There is not much point in pursuing the specific will of God for my life until I have lined up my daily living against the general will of God.

The general will of God is seen in verse 18 of this passage, "In every thing give thanks: for this is the will of God in Christ Jesus concerning you." Does this mean that I have to thank God for everything, for the times when things go wrong and when trouble and disaster flood my life? It hardly seems sensible to thank God for the disasters and tragedies of life.

Notice the preposition at the beginning of this verse. It is not *for* everything but *in* everything. I don't thank God *for* the tragedy, I thank God *in* the tragedy. I thank Him, in the situation, that I have the means to handle the problem, the tragedy, or whatever it may be.

This is where the third vitamin follows so perfectly after the second.

We have just considered the tremendous basic fact that, because I am a born-again believer, the Lord Jesus dwells within my heart and life through the indwelling Holy Spirit. He is there always and in all ways.

Consider the *Amplified Bible* translation of Hebrews 13:5, "for He (God) Himself has said, I will not in any way fail you *nor* give you up *nor* leave you without support. [I will] not, [I will] not, [I will] not in any degree leave you helpless, *nor* forsake *nor* let [you] down, [relax My hold on you]. — Assuredly not!"

This is what we are promised. It is the simple acceptance of this promise that fills our hearts with a quiet confidence.

When my daily life is lived against the background of such blessing it is then I can, *In every thing give thanks*. I don't thank God because I'm in trouble, but I do thank God that, even though I am in trouble, I have the resources to deal with the entire situation.

I remember again that a situation only becomes a problem

if I do not have sufficient resources with which to meet it. If I do have the resources, then the situation becomes an incident!

There are thousands of Christians who have never learned to say "thank you" to God. Their prayers abound with desires and demands, for help and strength and blessing.

They miss the whole point of Philippians 4:4-7. Can you see, at a glance, what is wrong with this quotation?

> Rejoice in the Lord alway: and again I say, Rejoice.
> Let your moderation be known unto all men. The Lord is at hand.
> Be careful for nothing; but in every thing by prayer and supplication let your requests be made known unto God.
> And the peace of God, which passeth all understanding, shall keep your hearts and minds through Christ Jesus.

Does this seem correct to you? Is this what you do — you come in everything by prayer and supplication? But do you complain that the peace of God does not keep your heart and mind?

If this is so, you have missed out of your quotation two vital words. You can find them in verse 6, "Be careful for nothing; but in every thing by prayer and supplication *with thanksgiving* let your requests be made known unto God."

The two vital words here are, *with thanksgiving*. I bring my prayers and my supplications, but I bring them all *with thanksgiving*. The vitamin of "thankfulness" must be present in all my petitions and prayers.

When I pray with thankfulness, I pray from the position of strength. I know the glory of God's salvation. I rejoice in the forgiveness of sins and a home in heaven. But more than these, I am ever conscious that the blessed Lord is with me, dwelling in my heart and life through His Holy Spirit.

His presence guarantees His power — I know this. I rejoice in this and it is this for which I am eternally thankful.

If my prayers are only a constant round of asking, a cold barren emptiness of asking with no awareness of this vitamin of thankfulness, then I pray from a position of weakness and uncertainty.

The fact that I continue to ask denotes that I do not possess. It also indicates a condition of uncertainty — there is a doubt as to whether I will ever receive that for which I have asked so often.

Truly, so much of our prayers should be a calm, joyous, blessed profession of thankfulness. They should contain a confession in which we acknowledge the presence of our blessed Lord and in which we thank Him for His presence and His power.

Then, against the background of the sure presence of Christ, we line up our petitions and our requests. If we do this, we find a transformation taking place. We find that incidents and problems and pressures that seem so overwhelmingly large to us somehow slip into their proper proportion. Viewed against the sure presence of Christ and the eternal promises of God, our prayers take on a freshness of confidence inspired by all that is ours in Christ.

This is why in verse 7 we read, "And the peace of God, which passeth all understanding, shall keep your hearts and minds through Christ Jesus." We cannot experience the blessing of verse 7 until we fulfill the conditions of verse 6 — *with thanksgiving*.

Notice what it is that keeps our hearts and minds — it is *the peace of God*. Therefore even though we may be in circumstances fraught with pressures and problems and difficulties, the peace of God can be our true tangible possession as we thank Him for all that is available and claim what is ours in the Lord Jesus.

Ability

"Victory" through the "Indwelling Christ" brought about by our "Thankfulness" in prayer should find an immediate demonstration of the vitamin of "Ability" in our daily living. But does it?

I have listened, over the years, to hundreds of testimonies from the lips of teenagers. I have seen young people rise to their feet with an earnest determination and then tell of what Christ has done for them. So often they have ended their testimony with a verse of Scripture in which they have affirmed their desire to go on and live for Christ.

The two Scriptures most frequently used are Galatians 2:20,

"I am crucified with Christ," and Philippians 4:13, "I can do all things through Christ." Notice that these Scriptures say, *I am . . . I can.*

But, how abused these Scriptures become. The regular repetition of *I am* and *I can* produces a travesty of truth when one looks at the lives these same young people live. This is true of all of us.

The one thing missing is the vitamin of "Ability" — the ability to live up to this level and to experience this truth in daily living.

The vitamin of ability becomes real in our individual experience when we know and understand the "secret of the two laws." Campus Crusade has been used to bring the blessings of salvation to many hearts through the simple teaching of "The Four Spiritual Laws." Now, here are two more Spiritual Laws that can turn belief into behavior, and apathy into ability.

Romans 7:14-24 contains some of the saddest words in the Bible,

> For that which I do I allow not: for what I would, that do I not; but what I hate, that do I. . . . For I know that in me (that is, in my flesh), dwelleth no good thing: for to will is present with me; but how to perform that which is good I find not. For the good that I would I do not: but the evil which I would not, that I do . . . O wretched man that I am! who shall deliver me from the body of this death?

Is this the language of your life? Do you experience the wretched frustration of knowing how you ought to act, but of being continually unable to put it into practice? Do you find yourself doing that which you have earnestly repudiated, fought against, and condemned? This, in one way or another, is the daily experience of many Christians.

It is a help to view this behavior against the truth of verse 23. Here we read that there is "another law in my members, warring against the law of my mind, and bringing me into captivity to the law of sin which is in my members."

Notice the teaching that declares there is a *law of sin which is in my members.* Romans 8:2 calls it also, *the law of sin and death.* This is a "natural" law in every sense of the word.

It is "natural" for people to tell lies, to behave deceitfully, to have impure minds and to go into sin. When I was a principal of a school I never had to teach children to lie, to steal or to tell dirty stories. All these things came naturally.

In a similar way I Corinthians 2:14 says, "But the natural man receiveth not the things of the Spirit of God: for they are foolishness unto him: neither can he know them, because they are spiritually discerned." He cannot know them because he is spiritually dead.

This is where the law of sin and death operates. Just as there is a physical law of gravity, so there is a spiritual law of sin and death. The law of gravity is known to all of us, by continual daily experience. It is that force which pulls an object down to earth when it is released in space.

If I hold a book in my hand, then release my hold, the book falls to the floor. We are not surprised when this happens. We expect it to do so. We would be more amazed if it stayed there suspended in the air. This is the continual downward pull of gravity. This is why we and all other solid bodies stay on the ground.

What this downward pull of gravity does in the physical world, the law of sin and death effects in the moral and spiritual world. This is why lovely children become teenagers whose lives become filled with sin, lust and failure. There is a constant downward drag in every human heart and the civilization in which we now live offers increasing opportunities for this law to manifest itself.

So many young people are surrounded by a society which is geared to fasten on to the weaknesses of human nature, and then to drag them downward in a blinding mist of pleasure.

If this law of sin and death were the only force operating in the world today there would be no hope, no possibility of recovery, no chance of peace and joy and love. But the glory of the message of salvation is that there *is* a hope, and a blessed opportunity to defeat this downward pull.

Romans 8:2 tells of the other law which can overcome the sin and failure in the human heart, "For the law of the Spirit of life in Christ Jesus hath made me free from the law of sin and death."

The law of the *Spirit of life in Christ Jesus* is God's sure answer to the natural failure of the human heart.

Because the Lord Jesus indwells me through His Holy Spirit I am made *a partaker of the divine nature* (II Peter 1:4). My natural human nature can do nothing but fail — it is constantly subject to the law of sin and death. But now, because I have been born again and have received the Lord Jesus into my heart and life, I have the answer to sin and failure.

I can do nothing but fail; He can do nothing but succeed. He is always the victor over sin and death. Inasmuch as I commit my way, day by day, to Christ — in that much I can experience the upward pull of His victory.

This is where the vitamin of ability is known and experienced. See how the progession develops. First there is the "Victory" of Christ, then the "Indwelling Holy Spirit" to bring that victory into my heart and life. My "Thankfulness" is my daily acknowledgment of the One who never leaves me. Now the vitamin of "Ability" is the demonstration, in my own life, that these things are true, that *I am . . . I can.*

The Christian life is, in effect, the daily struggle between the downward pull of the law of sin and death and the upward thrust of the spirit of life in Christ Jesus. We can understand this more clearly if we consider the battle that is fought on every runway every time a plane takes off.

I experience this frequently when I fly to various places around the world. As the jet stands on the runway it will weigh altogether over 150 tons. The force of gravity will be holding it firmly on the ground. There will be no thought that it might float or blow over!

But at a given time the pilot will switch on the four jet engines — monsters of tremendous power. When he is ready he will taxi to the end of the long runway and the battle will begin. The force of gravity will fight hard to hold the huge plane on the ground. But the power put forth from the four jets will bring into operation the new law of aerodynamics. This new law is the truth that under certain conditions a heavy object can rise against the pull of gravity. This is the one and only way to defeat gravity.

As the plane rushes down the runway the battle is on — gravity versus aerodynamics — the downward pull versus the upward thrust. Suddenly the pilot has his moment of victory. He "pulls back his stick" and the plane leaps into the air. Gravity has been defeated by the power of aerodynamics.

I do not understand the mysterious law of aerodynamics — but I don't have to. All I have to do is to commit myself to the plane, to enter, sit down, relax and enjoy the wonders of modern flight.

In an amazing way the plane's victory becomes my victory. Because it overcame gravity, so can I — as long as I stay in the plane, committed to the plan and program of the plane.

I do not have to understand how the jet can fly this way. I do not have to help the plane in any way. Only two things are necessary from me — first, that I believe the plane is capable of making the flight, and second, that I commit myself to the plane. Remember, committing myself is not only believing that the plane can make it, but also climbing inside and yielding my whole life to its plan and purpose.

In a way, this is the story of "the two laws" in the experience of every true Christian. There is a downward pull of the law of sin and death — always at work in our human nature, ever ready to drag us down and hold us down in sin and failure, fear and frustration.

But God has provided for us the blessed wonderful law of the Spirit of life in Christ Jesus. I don't need to understand how such a glorious experience could be mine. All I need to do is to "climb into the plane," to commit my whole life to Christ. As I yield my whole being — thought, word and deed — to His power, plan and purpose, then His victory becomes my victory.

There needs to be a constant realization of this fact. I need to walk every step of the way committed to Christ. If I choose to go on my own way, to step out of the purpose and plan of Christ, then I also step out of His power. Instead of the upward thrust controlling my life, the downward pull takes over, and I become liable to all the failure and frustration that is "natural" to my human nature.

If this truth is to be worked out in my life, then I need to come to the place where I "climb into the plane." I need to make an act of committal in which I not only express my belief in the ability of Christ to give me success and victory, but I also actually make His ability my ability, His power my power, His victory my victory.

Having begun with an act of committal, I need from then on to "stay in the plane" — to practice the activity of committal. In every situation and decision I need to affirm my dependence and to prove my affirmation by walking in humble obedience before Him. I need to remember that obedience is the proof of dependence.

When I fly I will be utterly obedient to that plane. If the plane wants to climb to six miles high — so will I. If it wants to travel at 600 mph — so will I. If the plane wants to descend and land — so will I. My committal to the plane will be complete.

These four wonderful spiritual vitamins are the basis for "The Plan for Maturity — For Me." I can be as mature as I want, as long as I nourish my soul on the vitamins of God.

A PRAYER FOR MEDITATION

My Father, I am hungry for spiritual nourishment. I need vigor and vitality in my life and witness,

May I read, mark, learn and inwardly digest all that Thou hast for me.

Teach me to commit myself to the Lord Jesus Christ, then teach me to stay committed.

Encourage me to be obedient in all things.

As I go down the runway of life, may the victory of Christ become my victory — lifting me up against the downward pull of the world, the flesh and the devil.

May my life, as a result, be lived to His glory as the "life of Christ is made manifest in my mortal flesh," through Jesus Christ. Amen.

CHAPTER 7

JOSHUA — INCOMPLETE OBEDIENCE

IN CHAPTER 5 we considered God's dealings with Joshua. We saw the one condition of all blessing — that Joshua had, first, to recognize the presence of God in each situation, then, to practice the presence of God as the events crowded in.

In our last chapter we learned that obedience is the proof of dependence, and dependence is the secret of victory.

We can now move on to see the development of these two chapters spelled out in the experience of Joshua.

God had given Joshua — a "promise," a "program" and a "power." This was to be the background against which his new life of leadership was to be lived. Joshua would have all the power he needed, as he looked to God for guidance and wisdom.

If we turn to Joshua 11:16-23 we see the results of that dependence. It is the list of battle honors won through the presence and power of God. Verse 16 begins, "So Joshua took all that land." Verse 17 ends with, "all their kings he took, and smote them, and slew them." Verse 18 reports that, "Joshua made war a long time with all those kings."

In verses 21 and 22 we read about the Anakims, who were the "giants" of the land. These are the people who were described by the ten spies on their return from the mission to spy out the land of Canaan. In Numbers 13:33 they had said, "There we saw the giants, the sons of Anak, which come of the giants: and we were in our own sight as grasshoppers, and so we were in their sight."

In Joshua 11:21 we read, "And at that time came Joshua, and cut off the Anakims from the mountains . . . Joshua destroyed them utterly with their cities."

Verse 22 continues, "There was none of the Anakims left in the land of the children of Israel: only in Gaza, in Gath, and in Ashdod, there remained."

"So Joshua took the whole land. . . . And the land rested from war."

At first sight, verses 16-23 seem to present a glowing account of the victories won. This is especially so when we read the last six words, *and the land rested from war.* We get the impression that everything was a great success, the whole mission was successfully accomplished . . . and they all lived happily ever after! But they did not, and if we examine verse 22 we will find out why they did not.

The land rested from war, but the peace they enjoyed was the peace before the storm. Verse 22 can teach us much on the subject of incomplete obedience when we remember the commands given to Joshua, the power at his disposal, and then we read this, "There was none of the Anakims left in the land of the children of Israel: only in Gaza, in Gath, and in Ashdod, there remained."

The verse begins with the words, *There was none of the Anakims left* — but this was not so. There were some of these deadly enemies left. It says so in the same verse, *only in Gaza, in Gath, and in Ashdod, there remained.*

This is the one blot on the perfect page of performance. Joshua did not deal with those three cities — Gaza, Gath and Ashdod. For some reason, unknown and unstated, he chose to allow these cities to stand, even though they were occupied with deadly enemies.

Were they too hard to conquer? No, because God had promised Joshua . . . every place . . . every day, victory could be his as he recognized the presence and power of God. We can find no apparent reason for this failure to wipe out the enemy. The only answer we can suggest is that this is a perfect example of the way we, today, yield our lives to Christ.

There are many of us who promise to yield our lives to

Christ. We are moved with deep sincerity. We commit all that we are to Christ. We deal with all the enemies in our lives, and gladly we drive them out so that our lives will be completely for our Saviour and Lord. We take action against the habits, friendships, associations and other areas that would hold us back from full surrender.

Of us it could be said, *There was none of the Anakims left—* then we add, with a tiny whisper . . . *only in Gaza, in Gath, and in Ashdod, there remained.* Like Joshua, we choose to allow unconquered areas to remain in our lives.

The great tragedy was that these three areas became the seeds of future sorrow and disaster. In Joshua's day they may have been small and insignificant, because, even though they were unconquered, the land rested from war. But the days came when the names Gaza, Gath and Ashdod brought fear and suffering to the children of Israel. The small neglected seeds grew to be monsters of overwhelming power.

As we continue our story and see what happened to unconquered Gaza, Gath and Ashdod, the tragedy will be brought home to us. None of these events and calamities need ever have happened. If only Joshua had taken time to deal effectively with all the Anakims, the people would have been spared the many days of shame and defeat.

And, of course, this is the lesson for us today. Our incomplete obedience to God, our holding back of special areas in our lives, brings a repetition of the story we are considering. The pet sins we retain can become the monsters that will bind us with chains.

The first city Joshua left unconquered was Gaza. If Joshua had done his job properly we would never have heard of the place again. The name Gaza means "The strong place."

We meet this city again in the Book of Judges. Chapters 14–16 of this book tell us the story of the man called Samson. The name Samson means the "Strong Man." Samson was a judge and judged Israel for twenty years. By his physical strength, and through the special guiding of God, he was able to preserve Israel from their enemies, the Philistines.

Judges 13:5 tells us what the angel of the Lord said to

Samson's mother before he was conceived, "For, lo, thou shalt conceive, and bear a son; and no razor shall come on his head: for the child shall be a Nazarite unto God from the womb: and he shall begin to deliver Israel out of the hand of the Philistines." A Nazarite was a person especially set apart for God—in thought and word and deed.

Numbers 6:1-21 gives instructions for the life of a Nazarite. Three things were essential. First, the Nazarite could eat nothing that came from the vine — either grapes or juice (verse 3). Then the hair of his head was to be neither cut nor shaven (verse 5). Last, he could never come near a dead body, under any circumstances (verse 6). Notice how the angel emphasized to his mother that no razor was to be used on his head!

Samson's life recorded in Judges 14–16 is the pathetic story of a strong man who was able to overcome every enemy — except his own lusts. One by one the special marks of the Nazarite were pushed aside by Samson's natural desires. In Judges 14:5-9 he deliberately approached the carcass of a lion. Verse 10 of the same chapter describes the beginning of a seven day feast that Samson made for his own wedding, *for so used the young men to do,* a feast full of drinking and merriment.

Often he broke these same two distinguishing marks of a Nazarite, but he always remained true to the special command of the angel, *no razor shall come to his head.* He was God's strong man, God's chosen man, God's holy man, but the tragedy of his life was that Gaza, the strong place, was to prove too strong for him in the end.

Chapter 16 begins, "Then went Samson to Gaza, and saw there an harlot, and went in unto her. And it was told the Gazites, saying, Samson is come hither."

His lust finally took him to the "Strong Place." Here his enemies planned to kill him in the morning, but Samson escaped at midnight. However, this was the beginning of the end. The lords of the Philistines took action to accomplish his destruction.

Samson became involved with Delilah, and through her the lords of the Philistines sought his downfall. Each lord promised Delilah eleven hundred pieces of silver for the capture of Samson (Judges 16:5). Their bribes, acting on her deceit, finally led Samson to give away the secret of his strength — his uncut hair. This was the one remaining sign of a Nazarite, the visible sign of his complete allegiance and dedication to God.

So the "Strong Place" plotted against the "Strong Man" and won. Samson's hair was shaved off. When he was attacked by the enemy, "he awoke out of his sleep, and said, I will go out as at other times before, and shake myself. And he wist not that the LORD was departed from him" (verse 20).

He knew not that the Lord was departed from him! Oh, the empty loneliness, the awful tragedy of Samson! He had finally turned his back on God by repudiating his allegiance to God — and God had turned away from him.

Verse 21 describes the utter humiliation of Samson, "But the Philistines took him, and put out his eyes, and brought him down to Gaza, and bound him with fetters of brass; and he did grind in the prison house." Thus Samson lost his strength, his sight, his liberty and his standing as a Nazarite of God.

When Samson was captured and humbled, Israel lost their leader. They as a people were overcome and overthrown and, worst of all, the name of the LORD was dragged in the dust. The Philistines sacrificed unto Dagon their god, they rejoiced and said, "Our god hath delivered Samson our enemy into our hand" (verse 23). In their eyes, Dagon had defeated Jehovah and the LORD was despised.

This then, is part of the story of Gaza. It is a story of humiliation and degradation which has so many side effects — and all because of one man's unfaithfulness to God.

But, of course, the most important part of this story is that it need never have happened. If Joshua had done what God told him to do, Gaza would have disappeared from the pages of history for ever.

Remember, I Corinthians 10:6, 11 tells us that these stories are written for our warning, that we should take note and see whether any of us are behaving in the same way. How necessary is this warning of incomplete obedience from the lives of both Joshua and Samson!

Gath was another Anakim community that Joshua did not destroy. As you will remember, Gath along with Gaza and

Ashdod, should have been wiped out. This was the second seed that was left to grow into a monster of oppression, and in this case it was a physical monster.

I Samuel 17 begins with Israel utterly frustrated and fearful of the Philistine champion — Goliath. Verse 4 gives this significant information, "And there went out a champion out of the camp of the Philistines, named Goliath, of Gath, whose height was six cubits and a span." Observe that this man came from Gath — the city that should have disappeared.

Because Joshua allowed Gath to stand, Goliath, several generations later, stood in open defiance and challenged the whole of Israel. In Joshua's day one man—strong in the strength of God — could have dealt with the entire city. Now in Goliath's day one man of Gath was able to deal with the entire nation. What a reversal of power!

Verses 8-10 give us the vaunting words of Goliath. He was so sure of himself. He could cry with fullest confidence, "I defy the armies of Israel this day; give me a man, that we may fight together." He knew he was invincible, and so did Saul and the men of Israel. "When Saul and all Israel heard those words of the Philistine, they were dismayed, and greatly afraid" (verse 11).

Verse 16 tells us, "And the Philistine drew near morning and evening, and presented himself forty days." The Israelites were brainwashed into defeat. They were at their wit's end to know how to deal with such a situation. King Saul should have been their champion. He was the tallest man they had (I Samuel 10:23), so that by size and sovereignty Saul should have faced the taunting Goliath. But Saul was dispirited and discouraged. Through his own disobedience to God he had willfully turned his back on Him. As a result, like Samson, he was left to stand in his own weakness.

Thus it was that when Israel's hopes were at their lowest God answered the challenge of Goliath. The giant had cried, *give me a man, that we may fight together.* God answered him, not by sending a full-grown man, but by sending a teenager.

Beginning at verse 20 we read of the coming of David. The important thing to realize is that he came fresh from the presence of God, "And David rose up early in the morning, and left the sheep with a keeper." We read in Luke 2:8, "And there were in the same country shepherds abiding in the fields, keeping watch over their flocks by night." These men saw the glory of the Lord in the Babe of Bethlehem on that first Christmas night. It is good to remember that David, hundreds of years before, had been abiding in those same fields, keeping watch over his flock by night. He was called from the presence of God to reveal the glory of the Lord to a broken, dispirited people.

David lived close to God. He had been anointed secretly by Samuel, and was aware of his divine calling. His heart and lips were filled with praises toward God, with words that found expression in the glorious Psalms of David. God was relevant to David, and day by day as he watched his sheep, he would commune with and draw closer to the Lord who was his Shepherd.

It was this young man, with his knowledge of the nearness of God, who was sent to deal with the man from Gath.

David arrived just in time to see the eightieth appearance of Goliath. He heard the proud boasting and saw the result, "And all the men of Israel, when they saw the man, fled from him, and were sore afraid" (verse 24).

As David spoke to the shattered Israelites he heard the full details of the failure of Saul's army. He heard also of the rewards that Saul was offering to anyone who would stand up to Goliath. Verse 25 gives details of the threefold reward — "riches, relationship and redemption."

David, coming from the presence of God, saw things differently than the frightened soldiers. They could only point to the towering monster and complain, "Look at him! Look how big he is! Look how much bigger he is than we are!" But David could say, "Yes, but look how much smaller he is than God!"

They were both viewing the same problem, but David, with his firm faith in God, was standing as Joshua had stood — with the "promise," the "program" and the "power."

David's confident words were reported to Saul, who sent for him immediately (verse 31). Saul again underlined the human impossibility of David fighting Goliath. But David spoke of God's help on previous occasions — against a lion and a bear — and his faith was sure. "This uncircumcised Philistine shall be as one of them, seeing he hath defied the armies of the living God. . . . The LORD that delivered me out of the paw . . . he will deliver me out of the hand of this Philistine" (verse 37).

Saul was so impressed with David's assurance that he sent him to the battle. He tried to gird David in his armor but his offer was refused. David said, "I cannot go with these; for I have not proved them" (verse 39).

David went against Goliath armed with that which had given him victory before — a sure sense of the "promise," the "program" and the "power." His material weapons were the simplicity of five smooth stones. They were in his hand, but he was safe in the hands of God.

When Goliath, the man of Gath, saw David, the man of God, he despised and disdained him. Goliath saw only "a youth, and ruddy, and of a fair countenance." But David said, "I come . . . in the name of the LORD of hosts, the God of the armies of Israel, whom thou hast defied" (verse 45). David had the invisible weapon of "the name of the LORD of hosts."

David's words in verses 46 and 47 represent the highest quality of faith. He who had the promise and the power told his enemy what would soon follow.

The Philistine drew near, but David hastened and ran to meet him. What quiet confidence! With the utmost assurance David stated, "the battle is the LORD's, and he will give you into our hands" (verse 47). Notice the words *our hands*, not "my hands." David was not claiming anything for himself. He was God's man, representing Israel.

One of the most beautiful aspects of this story is the demonstration of the quiet intimacy between God and David. God was completely relevant to David.

The rest of the story is so well-known — the defeat of Goliath — the sudden renewed enthusiasm of the army of Israel and the glorious deliverance that came that day. It was all because of David, God's man.

We have been considering this story as an example of the result of incomplete obedience. We have seen the boasting pride of Goliath as the result of Joshua's failure to deal with Gath.

This failure is seen in greater depth if we turn to II Samuel

21:18-22. This chapter records the further battles of David when, as the king, he sought to subdue all his enemies. It tells how Goliath had four brothers, all of whom were of great stature. One in particular had "on every hand six fingers, and on every foot six toes, four and twenty in number" (v. 20).

Referring to Goliath's other brothers verse 22 says, "These four were born to the giant in Gath, and fell by the hand of David, and by the hand of his servants." This shows us two things. First, that there was a breed of giants living in Gath. Second, that when David faced Goliath on that fateful day there were four more brothers in the Philistine ranks.

This is surely David's reason for taking the five smooth stones. He only needed one, but, if the other brothers had attempted to avenge the death of Goliath, David was equipped to deal with them. When God sent David to the battle, He gave him sufficient resources to deal with any eventuality.

This can also be true of us, as shown in I Corinthians 15:57, *But thanks be to God, which giveth us the victory through our Lord Jesus Christ.* All of our resources are in Christ, but our failure to appropriate all that "He is" puts us in the same position as Saul and his army. We are God's people, but are unable to cope with the situation.

The third Anakim center that Joshua left standing was Ashdod. As we re-examine these three places we find that Gaza was the place of defeat, Gath the place of defiance, and Ashdod the place of defilement.

I Samuel 4 recounts the miserable attempt of the Israelites to overcome the Philistines at Ebenezer. The first attack was a failure in which Israel lost about four thousand men (verse 2).

At that time Eli was the priest at Shiloh, and his sons, Hophni and Phinehas, were the officiating priests.

These sons were utter failures in every sense of the word. I Samuel 2:12 says, "Now the sons of Eli were sons of Belial; they knew not the Lord." What an amazing condemnation! They wore the priestly garments, and performed the priestly functions, but they did not know the Lord. Their behavior, as recorded in verses 13-17 and 22-25, made mockery of anything holy.

The tragic result of the ministry of these ungodly sons is seen in the behavior of the elders of Israel in I Samuel 4:3. After the first defeat by the Philistines these elders said, "Let us fetch the ark of the covenant of the LORD out of Shiloh unto us, that, when it cometh among us, it may save us out of the hand of our enemies." What a crazy idea this was, but how it demonstrated the absence of true worship and the absence of God's presence.

David, in our previous story, could speak of the Lord being with him. These men spoke about an "it" — *when it cometh . . . it may save us.* They became "it-ites" and perished.

Verse 4 tells how Hophni and Phinehas joined the "it-ites," and verse 5 records the excitement in the Israelite camp when the Ark appeared in their midst, "all Israel shouted with a great shout, so that the earth rang again." The presence of "it" brought them courage.

But notice the reaction of the Philistines as recorded in verse 7. When they heard the noise, "the Philistines were afraid, for they said, God is come into the camp." What an amazing situation! The pagan Philistines recognized the Ark as the presence of God, while the Israelites were getting excited over "it."

The result of the next attack was an utter and complete disaster. Israel was crushed, "for there fell of Israel thirty thousand footmen" (verse 10). Hophni and Phinehas perished as did Eli. But the supreme tragedy was the capture, by the Philistines, of the holy Ark of God.

Chapter 5 begins with these awful words, "And the Philistines took the ark of God, and brought it from Ebenezer unto Ashdod." That place which Joshua overlooked in his initial conquest grew so powerful that it could capture the Holiest of all — the Ark of God, the mercy seat of Jehovah — and this is the irony of it all.

Ebenezer means "Hitherto hath the Lord helped us," but these wicked men had turned their backs on God. All they wanted was a religion that would make them respectable and sucessful. All they found was bitter sorrow!

The name Ashdod means "fortress," and to this seat of the enemy the Ark was taken. The Ark was placed in the temple of Dagon, a vile, filthy heathen idol. Later, Dagon fell because of the judgment of God, but not before the LORD was subjected to defilement and disgrace.

The theme continues to remain the same — this need never have happened if only, at the beginning, Joshua had dealt with all the Anakims.

We meet the name Ashdod in strange circumstances later on in the Book of Nehemiah. The earlier chapters of this book record the faithful work of Nehemiah as he strove to rebuild the walls of Jerusalem. We read of the enemies he met — Sanballat and Tobiah the Ammonite. As his work prospered, we read these words in Nehemiah 4:7, 8, "But it came to pass, that when Sanballat, and Tobiah . . . and the Ashdodites, heard that the walls of Jerusalem were made up . . . then they were very wroth. And conspired all of them together to come and to fight against Jerusalem."

Here we find the neglected Ashdod preparing openly to fight against Jerusalem from the outside. But worse was to come.

Nehemiah had to leave his work at Jerusalem for some time, but when he returned he was horrified to see the infiltration of the enemy within the city of Jerusalem.

Nehemiah 13:4 records that, "Eliashib the priest, having the oversight of the chamber of the house of our God, was allied unto Tobiah: And he had prepared for him a great chamber."

Verses 23, 24 tell us that, "In those days also saw I Jews that had married wives of Ashdod . . . . And their children spake half in the speech of Ashdod, and could not speak in the Jews' language."

Imagine this fantastic infiltration of Ashdod right into the holy city of Jerusalem. Some Jewish men had married pagan women, but the pagan women had brought their cultures and their language with them. Therefore, within the walls of Jerusalem a generation of young people was growing up who could not speak the Jews' language. All they knew was the speech of Ashdod, the place of defilement, with all its unholy, ungodly associations.

This is a true picture of what is happening today in many

churches and homes in our land. The impurity of Ashdod finds its way everywhere, even into the speech of the people.

This study is not a blast against joy and happiness and the many things that can make our faith attractive and wholesome. But, as I Corinthians 10 reminds us, it is a challenge to all of us to see how far the "promise," the "program" and the "power" have been put into effect in our own immediate context. Failure to deal with a known area of sin will surely lead to a harvest of hopeless struggling.

Gaza produced a generation of wealthy lords of the Philistines. Gath produced a generation of giants. Ashdod brought secret defilement reaching like a cancer into all areas of holy living. But none of it need ever have arisen, if only Joshua had done what God told him to do.

In like manner, many of the trials and difficulties and problems we face today are of our own begetting. It is easy to blame the world and the pressures of our modern society for the failure within the church and within our own lives. Not only is it easy, it is also a comfortable excuse by which I can absolve myself and rationalize my fruitlessness and failure.

But, when all is said and done, it is still true in many cases that, as it was with Joshua, so it is with us. If we would only get on our knees and claim the promise, carry out the program, and experience the power in every area of our personality — emotions, mind or intellect, and will — then we would be spared the hurt and bitter sorrow of incomplete obedience.

A Prayer for Meditation

O Heavenly Father, I stand appalled at the record of history. I see the uselessness of trying without trusting, and the stupidity of complaining without committing.

Teach me to recognize more and more the holiness of God. Then teach me to relate my daily living to that same holiness.

May the words of David be my prayer: Search me, O God, and know my heart: try me, and know my thoughts: And see if there be any wicked way in me, and lead me in the way everlasting. For Jesus' sake. Amen.

Chapter 8

THE PLAN FOR MATURITY — THROUGH ME

In Chapter 6, as we considered "The Plan for Me," we opened up the idea of spiritual vitamins. We realized the need for those special items in our spiritual diet that would put a crispness into our living, and a boldness into our witnessing.

We considered "Victory" as the basis on which our life is to be lived; the "Indwelling Holy Spirit" as the One who would make that victory possible. "Thanksgiving," we found, was the means whereby the indwelling Christ was recognized and released in our daily living. "Ability" in our lives was seen when the downward pull of spiritual gravity was counteracted by the upward thrust of "the law of the Spirit of life in Christ Jesus."

All these truths were specifically *for* me. I was the one in whom the victory was made manifest. We can now go on to consider the remaining three letters in the word, M-I-N, and see how they, in turn, are essentially to operate *through* me.

The failures we considered in the last chapter can only be prevented by the continual application of the positive aspect of these "vitamins" — through me.

MERCY

This is a simple word we know so well — but use so little. There are quite a number of such simple, Scriptural words which somehow get left out of daily conversation. There is little evidence of mercy in the busy world in which we live. Few people want mercy these days. We are much more concerned in getting our rights, in being equal, and in demonstrating our personal attitudes and aspirations.

Mercy is really love in operation. Because God is love, then mercy is the way in which that love is made manifest to us.

This world knows little of "love" — that basic quality of real Christian love — and as a result it is not interested in mercy. This vitamin of mercy is an essential in the plan for Christian maturity, especially for a maturity that is going to be evidenced through me.

The fact that my approach to life is one full of mercy, will, of itself, make an unusual impact on all around me. It is sometimes said of evangelical Christians that there is a lack of tender compassion in their outlook to the world around them. They are so busy witnessing and winning souls for Christ that they have little time for showing simple acts of loving-kindness — just for the sake of being gracious. Kindness might even be mistaken for compromise.

Mercy, too, seems to be considered unnecessary between some Christians — inasmuch as it is seldom demonstrated. It is taken for granted that we all love each other — with a very small "l." But, somehow we feel we should not have to show mercy to our brothers and sisters in Christ. No one says as much in so many words, but "actions speak louder than words."

I have counseled with several Christians who have been deeply hurt and wounded, simply because someone did not show mercy. Mercy certainly is the prerogative of God, but it should also be the plan for every true believer.

Let us think first of *The Reality of Mercy* and see how important this is in the Word of God.

II Corinthians 1:3 says, "Blessed be God, even the Father of our Lord Jesus Christ, the Father of mercies, and the God of all comfort." What a blessed concept that is! God is the *Father of mercies.*

Ephesians 2:4, speaking of our salvation, says, "But God, who is rich in mercy." The *Amplified Bible* brings out the exalting sense of the words, "But God! So rich is He in His mercy!"

Titus 3:5 emphasizes that, "Not by works of righteousness

which we have done, but according to his mercy he saved us." Observe how, in each case, it is truly love in operation.

Peter was a man who experienced much of the mercy of God and of Christ. He could say in I Peter 1:3, "Blessed be the God and Father of our Lord Jesus Christ, which according to his abundant mercy hath begotten us again unto a lively hope by the resurrection of Jesus Christ from the dead." No wonder he speaks of the *abundant mercy.*

A lovely picture of the reality of mercy in the Old Testament is found in II Samuel 9. David is firmly and safely on the throne of Israel. All his enemies have been subdued and he is now in a position to exercise his power as king of Israel. Verse 1 tells of the quality of tender compassion in his heart, "And David said, Is there yet any that is left of the house of Saul, that I may shew him kindness for Jonathan's sake?"

There was one, a son of Jonathan named Mephibosheth, who dwelt in Lo-debar. Lo-debar means "no pasture" — a desolate place. Mephibosheth had been lame since the age of five, but David sought him out, raised him up and restored to him the possessions of Saul. He also made him to eat at his table "as one of the King's sons" (verse 11).

This is mercy of the highest order. It exalts the giver and brings nothing but blessing to the recipient. This is a true picture of God's mercy to us who were also in a desolate place and powerless to help ourselves.

The *Reality of Mercy* is the expression of God's love toward us. The *Result of Mercy* is our response to God. In Romans 15 the Holy Spirit is moving Paul to encourage Christian behavior. He writes in verse 1, "We then that are strong ought to bear the infirmities of the weak, and not to please ourselves." He goes on in verse 5 to speak of "the God of patience and consolation."

Verse 9 has a special challenge to all of us. Having written of the grace and kindness of God Paul continues, "And that the Gentiles might glorify God for his mercy." This is where we become involved in the story. The *Result of Mercy* is our response to God and this should be a determined attitude on our part to *glorify God for His mercy.*

How is this to be carried out? This is seen in our third

thought concerning mercy. First the *Reality of Mercy,* then the *Result of Mercy* which leads us to the *Response to Mercy.*

My response to God's mercy is described in Romans 12:1, 2, "I beseech you therefore, brethren, by the mercies of God, that ye present your bodies a living sacrifice, holy, acceptable unto God, which is your reasonable service. And be not conformed to this world: but be ye transformed by the renewing of your mind, that ye may prove what is that good, and acceptable, and perfect, will of God."

This precious vitamin of mercy is going to be seen in a two-fold way, in my response to God, and in my reaction to those around me, whoever they may be.

My response to God will be seen in this revolutionary act of *presenting my body a living sacrifice, holy, acceptable unto God.* This is something often talked about, discussed and dissected, but is not often done. If I am conscious of the mercy of God, and if this mercy really touches the depths of my being, then I will have only one response — to present my body a living sacrifice.

The lack of response to presenting our bodies to the Lord is surely our lack of appreciation of the mercy of God. The reality of that mercy and the result of that mercy sends us in worship and humble adoration to present all that we are — with no reservations.

We can pick out a central theme in these two verses as follows, *present . . . that ye may prove.* This is something many young people need to appreciate. I have counseled with many concerning the "will of God" for their lives. They have a sincere interest in knowing God's will, but they have reversed the order of this theme. They want to know what God's will might be. Then, if it appeals to them, they will present their bodies. There is almost a sense of bargaining with God.

The only way to prove the will of God to be always good, always acceptable, and always perfect is to seek to appreciate more and more the mercies of God, and then in glad response, to yield my body a living sacrifice. The consequences, whatever they may be, can never add up to the infinite mercies of God so freely bestowed upon me.

Thus it is I need this precious vitamin of "Mercy" — to glorify God and to gladden the hearts of all whom I contact. Without it there will be a lack of sweet tenderness in my daily life. I may be absolutely correct in all my ways, but it will be a cold correctness, devoid of that warm glow that characterized the Lord Jesus when He was here on earth.

INHERITANCE

If tomorrow's mail brought you a letter from an attorney telling you that some unknown relative had left you an inheritance of $100,000, many things would surely happen. After you had recovered from the shock, your new resources would permit you to move into a new quality of living, because you would have a new capacity for living. Wouldn't that be marvelous? — or would it?

The strange thing about our next vitamin, "our daily Inheritance," is that these new things have come to pass in our lives. They do so daily. We *can* experience a new quality of living, because we *do* now have a new capacity for living, due to our new resources. Yet so many of us go on living the same spiritual preinheritance lives. We live in the same spiritual shack, wear the same spiritual rags and engage in the same drudgery of daily survival — and all the while we are spiritual millionaires.

Ephesians 1:11 reminds us of our spiritual heritage. Paul was speaking of the wonder and the glory of Christ, then he added, "In whom also we have obtained an inheritance." We have this amazing declaration, that Jesus Christ, in all His riches of power, wisdom and blessing, is our inheritance — day by day, and moment by moment. Verse 14 confirms this by stating that the Holy Spirit Himself is "the earnest of our inheritance." The word *earnest* here means "the first installment."

The Holy Spirit is the One who represents Christ in our daily experience (John 14:26). Christ indwells us in the Person of His Holy Spirit (Romans 8:9).

Paul lived up to the inheritance he possessed. We read in Philippians 1:21, "For to me to live is Christ" and in 4:13, "I can do all things through Christ which strengtheneth me." Paul drew heavily on his spiritual resources, but he was never overdrawn. What the Lord Jesus Christ was in the experience of Paul He can be also in our experience, as by faith we continue to realize the infinite riches we have through the indwelling Christ.

In Ephesians 1:7 Paul speaks of the Lord Jesus, "In whom we have redemption through his blood, the forgiveness of sins, according to the riches of his grace." This is the wonder of our redemption. It is all through Christ, and it is all truly and sincerely appreciated by every born-again believer. This is what Christ did *for* me when He died on the cross, and for this I praise His holy Name and bow in worship and thankful adoration.

The blessed wonder of our "Inheritance" is all that the Lord Jesus can be *in* me — not only *for* me on the cross, but *in* me through His Holy Spirit. The appropriation and application of this "spiritual vitamin" is sure to lead to a robust and purposeful Christian life. A realization of my untold resources in Christ brings the rest of life into a truer perspective. My sense of values becomes much more honest and sincere as I evaluate my daily life against the glory of my inheritance in Christ.

But, not only does the vitamin of inheritance put me into the good of a new relationship with Christ, it also challenges me into a growing awareness of the relationship the Lord Jesus has with me. Ephesians 1:15 gives us the beginning of a precious prayer of Paul. In this prayer Paul is asking *the God and Father of our Lord Jesus Christ* to do something special for these Ephesian Christians. What he asked for them is what is so much needed in our hearts and lives.

In verse 18 he asked, "The eyes of your understanding being enlightened; that ye may know what is the hope of his calling, and what the riches of the glory of his inheritance in the saints."

Notice this second use of the word "inheritance," but see how different it is from that in verse 11. In verse 11 it was "my inheritance in Christ"; in verse 18 it is "his inheritance in me." The vitamin of inheritance has a two-way effect. First, it exposes all the resources of Christ to me. Second, it presents all that I am to Him.

The full benefit of this vitamin is only seen when I live in the good of this double thrust. The fact is that many of us are prepared, after we are made aware of the truth, to recognize the intimate blessing of the indwelling Christ, and, as a result, we draw upon our inheritance in Him. However, few of us are prepared to go the entire length of this teaching and respond to the simple fact that the Lord Jesus also has an inheritance — in us. To do so could be a costly business — it could hurt, it may harm our pet plans and ambitions.

We saw, as we began this chapter, that these next three "vitamins" would lead us to "The Plan for Maturity — Through Me." It is not just what God would do *for* me, but what He could do *through* me.

The vitamin of "Mercy," we saw, would be seen in a twofold way — in my response to God and in my reaction to those around me, whoever they may be. In a similar way, the powerful vitamin of "Inheritance" will only be evident in all its fullness in my life when I am drawing on all the potential of Christ, and when my humanity is placed unreservedly at His disposal.

The Story of the Lost Inheritance

The Old Testament is God's Picture Book in which He shows and teaches many of the lessons we need to learn in our daily Christian experience.

One such lesson is the story of the lost inheritance. In Genesis 15 God is dealing specifically with Abram whom He had called out of Ur of the Chaldees. In verse 1 God said, "Fear not, Abram: I am thy shield, and thy exceeding great reward." In verse 7 God disclosed His purpose to Abram, "And he said unto him, I am the LORD that brought thee out of Ur of the Chaldees, to give thee this land to inherit it." Notice that God was here promising an inheritance to Abram.

In Genesis 28 Isaac blessed Jacob before he departed to visit Laban. In doing so, in verse 4, he said, "And give thee the blessing of Abraham, to thee, and to thy seed with thee; that thou mayest inherit the land wherein thou art a stranger, which God gave unto Abraham." Here the promise of the inheritance was passed on from Abraham to Jacob and to his descendants.

In Leviticus 20 God was speaking unto the people through His servant Moses. In verse 24 we read, "But I have said unto you, Ye shall inherit their land, and I will give it unto you to possess it, a land that floweth with milk and honey: I am the LORD your God, which have separated you from other people." Here again is the unconditional promise of God. First it was to a man, then it was to a family, now it is to a nation. The promise was an inheritance from God.

The story of the deliverance of the children of Israel from Egypt was all part of the story of the lost inheritance. Their inheritance was Canaan, a land flowing with milk and honey. But the tragedy of their deliverance was the way in which they fell short of God's plan.

They were delivered *from* Egypt, but they were never delivered *into* Canaan. Deuteronomy 6:20-25 tells what a Jewish father had to say to his son, "Then thou shalt say unto thy son, We were Pharaoh's bondmen in Egypt; and the LORD brought us out of Egypt with a mighty hand: . . . And he brought us out from thence, that he might bring us in, to give us the land which he sware unto our fathers."

The purpose of their redemption was to bring them out of bondage into their inheritance. The resultant tragedy of their deliverance was that they had enough faith to get out of Egypt — but not enough to enter Canaan and claim their inheritance.

The Book of Deuteronomy was written *in the wilderness* (1:1) at the end of forty wasted years of wandering. Moses could say in 12:9, "For ye are not as yet come to the rest and to the inheritance, which the LORD your God giveth you." They had the deliverance — but not the inheritance. Because they had not the inheritance, they did not enjoy the rest of God.

I Corinthians 10 tells us to examine this story carefully and see if it depicts our own experience. Are we sure of our redemption from sin and of our deliverance from guilt? But more so, have we entered into our own special inheritance — the fullness of the boundless resources of Christ? Israel's inheritance was *a land flowing with milk and honey*. Our inheritance is *a Land flowing with might and happiness*.

The story of the lost inheritance is simply that Israel chose to wander in a wilderness of want, instead of entering into all that God had for them. How true this is in many Christian lives today! Many people are wandering in their private wilderness of want, instead of entering into the sufficiency of Christ.

But this story had an unhappy sequel in the history of the children of Israel. Because they did not enter into their inheritance, God was not able to enter into His inheritance. Deuteronomy 4:20 says, "But the LORD hath taken you, and brought you forth out of the iron furnace, even out of Egypt, to be unto him a people of inheritance, as ye are this day." In Deuteronomy 9:29, Moses, when speaking to God said, "Yet they are thy people and thine inheritance." In Deuteronomy 32:9 Moses stated, "For the LORD's portion is his people; Jacob is the lot of his inheritance."

Just as Israel had an inheritance — so had God. The children of Israel were God's peculiar inheritance. *For* them He wrought all the miracles of Egypt as He effected their deliverance. *Through* them He was going to work out all His counsels and purposes. But when Israel refused to enter Canaan and claim their inheritance, God was denied the possibility of using them as His inheritance.

The story of the lost inheritance is the story of a double loss, and this is what Ephesians 1:11 and 18 is telling us. If I exclude the vitamin of inheritance from my daily spiritual diet I lose out — and so does God!

Inasmuch as I recognize all that the Lord Jesus can be *in* me through His indwelling Holy Spirit, and, also, inasmuch as I realize that I am the vehicle through whom He is going to fulfill His purposes — then, in that much do I appropriate my inheritance in Him, and in that much is Christ able to operate through my yielded life.

New Creature

Much of the successful sale of physical vitamins comes because of the approach used in advertising. People find it hard to resist the offer of a new capacity for daily living. The harried housewife is eager to gain that lasting quality of physical strength that will enable her to cope with family, friends and frustrations.

The overworked, overstrained businessman is interested in a product that promises to restore his peace of mind, and which also offers increased abilities to think fast, plan wisely and remain buoyant throughout the day.

In saying this, we thank God for all the skills of medical research which have enabled scientists to unlock new secrets and release to us those precious vitamins which do so much for so many people.

It is good to know that God has for us a spiritual vitamin which does all this and much more. II Corinthians 5:17 contains these wonderful words, "Therefore if any man be in Christ, he is a new creature: old things are passed away; behold, all things are become new." Other translations say, "he is a new creation."

This is the culminating glory of being a true Christian. I am "in Christ" and Christ is "in me" and, as a result, I am a new creation. Notice the tenses used in this verse. It is not a promise of things to come, but is a proclamation of that which is true, here and now: *he is . . . old things are . . . all things are.*

This is in keeping with the words of the Lord Jesus in John 5:24, "Verily, verily, I say unto you, He that heareth my word, and believeth on him that sent me, hath everlasting life, and shall not come into condemnation; but is passed from death unto life." *He hath everlasting life . . . he is passed.* This passing from spiritual death into everlasting life is the act and process of becoming a new creation.

I remember seeing an effective TV commercial which sought to illustrate the amazing effects of a certain vitamin on a tired mother. The mother was seen in an exhausted condition, collapsed in a chair. She then took the vitamin and, a few moments later, we saw the dramatic effects of its mysterious power. The tired body had been slumped in the chair, but out of this abject weariness there stepped the same woman full of life and abounding with energy. The success of the advertisement lay in showing the same woman, at the same time, in the two conditions — one still an exhausted wreck (what she had been) — the other a miracle of dynamic energy (what she had become).

This precious spiritual vitamin of experiencing and demonstrating "being a new creation" is the culminating wonder and joy of being a born-again believer. What the scientists offer as a physical experience is multiplied a thousand times in every area of the human personality. Unless a person has experienced the sheer joy of being a new creature in Christ, words would fail to convey the multiplicity of blessings that come, seen and unseen, moment by moment, and day by day.

All the previous spiritual vitamins, the "Victory," the realization of the "Indwelling Holy Spirit," the "Thanksgiving," the "Ability," the "Mercy" and the "Inheritance," all lead to, and from, this wondrous fact — that I am a new creation even while living in this same body and in these same circumstances.

It is satisfying to know that God is not interested in "patching up" people. Humanism and other similar philosophies are dedicated to "making the best of a bad situation," to patching up broken personalities and stopping the holes through which the sea is pouring in. This is not God's way of doing things.

The God of redemption is the God of creation, and His hand is seen at work in both areas. God never gathers the old leaves that have fallen from the trees, to wash them and press them so that they look fresh and clean. God never puts old leaves back on the trees. His springtime is the demonstration of "a new creation" in the world of nature, in every area of living things.

As the life flows again within the heart of the tree, so the evidences of the new life appear in the new buds and the new leaves. The tree becomes a demonstration of new life, and God is glorified in His creation.

In a much more wonderful manner, when I have been born again through believing in the shed blood of Christ on Calvary's cross, then I, too, receive a new quality of life. I John 5:11, 12 assures me that, "this is the record, that God hath given to us eternal life, and this life is in his Son. He that hath the Son hath life; and he that hath not the Son of God hath not life."

This is why, and how, I am a new creation in Christ. I am

a new creation because I now possess a new quality of life — nothing less than the indwelling Christ.

The fact and the experience of the incoming Christ is so completely revolutionary that, as II Corinthians 5:17 says, *old things are passed away.* The "old things" — the old desires, the old ambitions, the old approach to life and living, the old capacity to act and react to situations and circumstances — all these, and a thousand others are passed away. This is not the proof of a new negative approach to life — full of don'ts and can'ts — but it is the laying aside of a tired weariness that was slumped in the chair of hopelessness.

The same verse goes on to add, "behold, all things are become new." Notice the word *behold* and remember how it was used by the angel to Joseph, "Behold, a virgin shall be with child" (Matthew 1:23); by the angel to Mary, "behold, thou shalt conceive in thy womb" (Luke 1:31); and by the angel to the shepherds, "behold, I bring you good tidings of great joy" (Luke 2:10). Could you *behold and see* that *the Lord hath done great things for thee?* Not only are you born again, but in the very experiencing of this *all things are become new.*

Notice the simple comparison, the *old things* are passed away, however many or few they were, but *all things* are become new. As a new creation in Christ I have, here and now, not only the desires for new things but the capacity to experience them and carry them out.

Whether this becomes true in my actual experience depends upon my reaction to this precious vitamin of being a new creation. If I put it to work in my daily Christian life, by the faith of a simple committal to Christ every step of the way, then gradually and surely will this new life become apparent.

It does not come about by my putting on an act, trying to copy Jesus or live like Him — that would be just the works of the flesh. Romans 8:8 tells us, "So then they that are in the flesh cannot please God" — whether the "flesh" be "bad" or "good."

The resulting experience in my daily life would be such as Paul describes in II Corinthians 4:10, 11, "that the life also of Jesus might be made manifest in our body . . . that the life also of Jesus might be made manifest in our mortal flesh." Notice the life of Jesus is *made manifest*. I do not manifest it, or try to make it manifest — the life is made manifest. The trees do not try to grow leaves. The rising sap, which is the new life of the tree, makes itself evident through the display of new leaves.

Remember also that there is no Spring for a dead tree. If I am still spiritually dead, never having been born again, then I can never demonstrate the evidences of a new creation. I am still a dead tree, however beautifully the sun may shine.

We have already established in our thinking the truth that we are new creatures, here and now, that we are passed from death unto life. In this respect it is interesting to turn to Revelation 21 and to read of the new heaven and the new earth. Verse 5 says, "And he that sat upon the throne said, Behold, I make all things new." Notice the phrase, *I make all things new*. It is the *things* that will be made new, not the people. Observe also II Peter 3:13, 14, "Nevertheless we, according to his promise, look for new heavens and a new earth, wherein dwelleth righteousness. Wherefore, beloved, seeing that ye look for such things."

God is making the people new, here and now, through the wonder of the new creation. God will make all things new in His own good time.

Here then is "The Plan for Maturity — Through Me." We have spoken of the "vitamins" that can make spiritual babies grow into men and women of God who, in their turn, can be warriors for God and living testimonies to the value of a faith that can cope with everything — every place — every day.

A Prayer for Meditation

Dear Father, how refreshing it is to know that the Christian faith is not a boring experience, but a blessed example of all that Christ can be for me, and in me.

May these "vitamins" become an essential part of my spiritual diet.

As they move within my spiritual blood stream may the evidences of a new creation be seen in me.

May I manifest mercy in a world that has forgotten to care.
May I live in all the wealth of my inheritance in Christ.
May I respond equally, as I see myself as His inheritance.
    May the "old things" continue to pass and fade away, and may the "all things new" be, all for Jesus, in whose name I pray. Amen.

CHAPTER 9

THE BOOK OF RAHAB — SAVED TO LIVE

THUS FAR WE HAVE BEEN considering the twofold work of the Lord Jesus Christ for the believer. We have considered the work of Christ *for* me, when He died on the cross in my place and paid the price of my sins. We read of this in I Peter 2:24, "Who his own self bare our sins in his own body on the tree, that we, being dead to sins, should live unto righteousness: by whose stripes ye were healed."

Then we have considered the work of Christ *in* me, through His indwelling Holy Spirit. This is spoken of in Colossians 1:26, 27, "the mystery which hath been hid from ages and from generations, but now is made manifest to his saints: to whom God would make known what is the riches of the glory of this mystery among the Gentiles; which is Christ in you, the hope of glory."

Observe that the death of Christ *for* me on the cross qualifies me to die, and go to heaven as a forgiven sinner, saved by the blood of His cross.

Observe also that the life of the risen Christ *in* me, indwelling me through His Holy Spirit, qualifies me, as a forgiven sinner, to live here and now, in this hostile, evil world system. The Lord Jesus said in John 14:19, "because I live, ye shall live also." Because He died, I die; because He lives, I live.

We have seen, also, that Christian maturity is a growing experience and demonstration of the life of Christ at work in the heart and life of the believer. This is especially seen in Colossians 1:28 where Paul says, "Whom we preach, warning every man, and teaching every man in all wisdom; that we may present every man perfect in Christ Jesus." Notice that verse 28 begins with a "Whom" not with a "what."

Paul did not preach a "what," or an "ethic," or a "program," or even "religion" — he preached a "whom." The "whom" of verse 28 is found in verse 27 — that is *Christ in you.*

So the message Paul preached concerned not only Christ *for* me, but Christ *in* me. Notice the progression of preaching in verse 28 — *warning every man — teaching every man — presenting every man perfect.* The word "perfect" is better translated "mature." This is the very word we have been considering in our own Christian experience.

We see that Paul had a threefold use of the word *every man.* He warned everyone, taught everyone and expected everyone to grow up into maturity. But notice that maturity is based on the "whom" — "Christ in you." This is so important, and yet so often overlooked by Christians.

It is possible to live my Christian life knowing only Christ for me, on the cross. When this is so I am a saved soul. I go to heaven when I die, but I am not equipped to face a world which is hostile to God and to His Christ.

It is only when I go on, to grow on to maturity — that maturity which is based on the work of Christ in me day by day — that I can be all that God would have me to be.

We have considered this in depth in our previous chapter when we thought of the spiritual vitamins that can charge our complete Christian concept.

We now turn to the Old Testament and find the same teaching set forth in story form. The story we will consider we have entitled "The Book of Rahab."

We have already looked into the "Book of Joshua" in chapters 3, 5 and 7 of this book. Notice the hidden emphasis in the title of the book. It is the "Book of Joshua" — the story of what God did with his life. In one sense your present life is "The Book of You," and we have already seen, in chapter 4, that at the Judgment Seat of Christ this personal "Book of You" will be the subject of discussion and examination by Christ Himself.

With this idea of the "Book of You" in mind, let us go on to consider the story we have of Rahab — the story of her life — "The Book of Rahab." We will find this to be a tremendous illustration of the very things we have been considering thus far.

We first read of Rahab in the Bible in Joshua 2. As we read these twenty-four verses she emerges as a most remarkable person. Verse 1 speaks of the two spies who were sent to spy out Jericho, "they went, and came into an harlot's house, named Rahab, and lodged there." Bible scholars tell us that Rahab's home was the local inn at which all travelers could stay. This may be so, but the fact remains that she is known throughout the Bible as Rahab the harlot, or Rahab the prostitute.

Wherever we meet her she is stuck with this awful name. Rahab was the lowest of the low in the eyes of the Jews — a woman — a pagan — a prostitute. But it was this woman in whose life God choose to do marvelous things as He revealed Himself to her, and then through her.

Verse 3 of this chapter tells us how the king of Jericho sent a note to Rahab and told her to hand over the spies. Instead of betraying them however, she hid them under stalks of flax. She lied about them and saved their lives by sheer trickery.

Having saved them, she shared with them the feelings and fears of the entire city of Jericho, "your terror is fallen upon us . . . all the inhabitants of the land faint because of you" (verse 9).

Having disclosed the feelings of her people, she then went on to declare her own faith in God. Verses 9 and 11 contain these amazing words from a poor, pagan prostitute, "I know that the LORD hath given you the land . . . for the LORD your God, he is God in heaven above, and in earth beneath." Notice how unusual is this woman's faith. It seems to have come from nowhere and with no sense of preparation.

On the basis of this faith she then went on to ask for mercy. She wanted the spies to "swear unto me by the LORD . . . that ye will save alive my father, and my mother, and my brethren, and my sisters, and all that they have, and deliver our lives from death" (verses 12, 13). We notice that there is no mention of a husband or children. It appears as though she was thinking only of others.

The two Israelite spies agreed to her request on two conditions. The first was that she should be silent on what had been done, and the second, that "when we come into the land, thou shalt bind this line of scarlet thread in the window which thou didst let us down by" (verse 18).

This remarkable woman then outlined a plan of escape and return to camp for the two men. Finally, when they had departed, she demonstrated the quality of her faith by binding the scarlet line in her window immediately.

Rahab confessed her faith in verse 11, but she demonstrated her faith in verse 21. The spies had said, *when we come into the land,* but her faith was such that she expected them at any time.

We meet Rahab again in Joshua 6. In this chapter we read of the complete destruction of Jericho. Verse 21 says, "And they utterly destroyed all that was in the city, both man and woman, young and old, and ox, and sheep, and ass, with the edge of the sword." The entire city was destined for annihilation. Rahab, along with her family, should have met the same fate. She was, in one sense, as good as dead. However, verse 22 tells how Joshua sent the same two men saying, "Go into the harlot's house, and bring out thence the woman, and all that she hath, as ye sware unto her."

Verse 23 tells how the young men went and brought out Rahab and her kindred and all that she had and, "left them without the camp of Israel." We can't help but notice that Rahab's testimony was better than Lot's was at Sodom. Genesis 19:12 tells how the angels "said unto Lot, Hast thou here any besides? son in law, and thy sons, and thy daughters, and whatsoever thou hast in the city, bring them out of this place."

Verse 14 tells how "Lot went out, and spake unto his sons in law . . . and said, Up, get you out of this place; for the LORD will destroy this city. But he seemed as one that mocked unto his sons in law."

Whatever it was that Rahab said, her family all believed her and so they shared her deliverance.

Verse 25 of Joshua 6 contains two important facts concerning Rahab, "And Joshua saved Rahab the harlot alive . . . and she dwelleth in Israel even unto this day." She might have been saved to continue as a poor, pagan prostitute, to be a creature of no importance, never to be heard of again. But the outstanding fact here is that she was *saved alive.* She was saved to live — not saved so as by fire, but saved from the dead and then saved to continue a new and more wonderful life — *and she dwelleth in Israel even unto this day.*

Now let us observe an amazing thing that happened to her when she began this new quality of life and what the Bible has to say concerning her.

Matthew 1:1-16 is "The book of the generation of Jesus Christ." It is the list of those from whom, and through whom, the Lord Jesus Christ was born in the flesh. In one sense it is the Royal Line and these names are those in the Royal Family. Verse 5 reads, "And Salmon begat Booz of Rachab; and Booz begat Obed of Ruth; and Obed begat Jesse; And Jesse begat David the king."

The spellings are slightly changed in two of the names, but the characters are the same. It should read, "And Salmon begat Boaz of Rahab; and Boaz begat Obed of Ruth."

We thus find that Rahab didn't disappear when she was saved. She was saved to live — and what a life she had! She married Salmon. Just think what a remarkable woman she must have been! She was a pagan, she was penniless, and she was a known prostitute, yet something about her drew her to Salmon and he married her. It is possible that Salmon was a wealthy man for his son Boaz was.

Rahab had a son, and his name was Boaz. It is this same Boaz we meet in the Book of Ruth. As we consider how kindly Boaz dealt with this poor pagan girl named Ruth, who was already a widow, we remember that his mother had also been a poor, pagan girl without a husband to care for her.

Remember also how kind Rahab had been to the spies when they were in need in Jericho. The man Boaz was gracious and kind because he had that kind of a mother. Rahab still lived on through Boaz.

It is also a lovely thought to consider Rahab in relationship to Ruth. Ruth had one mother-in-law whom she loved called

Naomi. She got another mother-in-law when she married Boaz, and this was Rahab.

We read in Ruth 4:16 how, when Ruth had her son, called Obed, "Naomi took the child, and laid it in her bosom, and became nurse unto it." It is a happy thought to consider that Rahab was the other grandmother, that she, too, may have held little Obed in her arms. She who should have perished in the flames at Jericho lived on in Boaz and Obed. Later she lived on in Jesse and then in David.

The greatest miracle of all is to realize that through her was descended both Joseph and Mary, "of whom was born Jesus, who is called Christ" (Matthew 1:16). The thought is so immense, so challenging, so completely beyond human understanding, that when Rahab was saved to live, she was saved so that one day there might be a Mary, *of whom was born Jesus, who is called Christ.*

This is indeed the highest point of Rahab's history, but it is not the end of her story in the Bible. The "Book of Rahab" begins in the Old Testament and reaches into the New Testament. In the New Testament it reaches into the gospels, and into the epistles also.

Hebrews 11 is the great chapter on faith. "Now faith is the substance of things hoped for, the evidence of things not seen." In its forty verses are gathered the heroes of faith, the men and women, chosen from all history, as the finest representatives of faith in action. We meet such heroes as Enoch, Abraham, Isaac, Jacob and other giants of the Old Testament.

But verse 31 reads, "By faith the harlot Rahab perished not with them that believed not, when she had received the spies in peace." Here we find this amazing woman again, still linked with the word harlot. This time she is set forth as one of the heroes of faith — chosen from the ranks of Jewish history.

There is only one other woman in this eleventh chapter mentioned as a special example of faith. Verse 11 records, "Through faith also Sara herself received strength." What a comparison these two make — Sara and Rahab! Rahab was a prostitute, and the name Sara means "princess." So we have the princess and the prostitute chosen to represent faith that honored God and magnified Him in all His purposes.

If we stop and consider that this epistle was written to the Hebrews, of all people, we can realize in a new way the dignity that must have been attached to the name Rahab. What a far cry it was from the fires of blazing Jericho to the fame of God's holy Word!

But even this is not the end of Rahab in the New Testament. We meet her again in the epistle of James. This becomes increasingly fascinating when we remember that James was the one who emphasized the need of works, as well as faith. James 2:20 so challenges us, "But wilt thou know, O vain man, that faith without works is dead?" James sets out to prove the absolute necessity of works to vindicate and substantiate the profession of faith.

To illustrate his point he chooses two great characters from Jewish history. In James 2:21-24 he speaks of Abraham as a man justified by works *and not by faith only*. Then in verse 25 he writes, "Likewise also was not Rahab the harlot justified by works, when she received the messengers, and had sent them out another way?" Fancy putting Rahab alongside Abraham, as the two chosen ones! What a woman! What a testimony she had! The former pagan prostitute becomes the example for all people to follow — not only because of her faith but also because of her works. No wonder Joshua 6:25 says, "she dwelleth in Israel even unto this day." She does so, in many different ways.

We have noted as we have read the Scriptures that this wonderful woman is constantly referred to as Rahab the harlot. The name goes with her everywhere — except in one place. It is such a delightful gesture and such a blessed comfort to look in Matthew 1:1-16 and find that when it comes to the Royal Line she is noted without that title. In verse 5 she is just Rahab, the lady who was the wife of Salmon, the lady whose son became the grandfather of the great King David. There she stands in all her honor and dignity — and how truly she deserved it.

This then is "The Book of Rahab" which illustrates for us, in a unique way, the twofold work of God for the believer.

Rahab was due to perish in Jericho, but she was saved. However, her salvation didn't end with her escape from death — she was saved to live. The wonder of her life was that God's purposes were fully accomplished through her.

This should mean something to us when we remember that I Corinthians 10 is telling us to work at these stories and learn lessons for today.

Are you saved? Were you also saved to live? Is your life so yielded to Christ that by your faith and through your works the purposes of God are being fully accomplished through you? How is the "Book of You" developing?

A Prayer for Meditation

Dear Father, this story challenges my heart.

Rahab had so little and I have so much. Yet she did so much and I do so little.

Forgive me, Father, for my selfishness and lack of vision.

May I be bold in my faith and step out fearlessly into a future unknown to me but perfectly clear to my Saviour.

May my works be such that people will take knowledge of me, that I have been with Jesus — and, best of all, that Jesus is always with me. In His name. Amen.

CHAPTER 10

THE POWER OF CHRISTIAN MATURITY

WE HAVE BEEN THINKING much, thus far, around the theme of growing up in the Christian faith. We have seen the many areas of need in the Church today where there is an overdisplay of spiritual babyhood. We have considered the peril of immaturity, and then we have gone on to see, in the Old and New Testaments, what is involved in being a mature Christian.

We have read in Hebrews 6:1, "let us go on to perfection [maturity]" and in Colossians 1:28, "warning every man, and teaching every man in all wisdom; that we may present every man perfect [mature] in Christ Jesus."

Our minds have been examining the teaching of the Bible so that we can face up to our responsibility in this matter.

What we need now is some basic thinking on the mechanics of Christian maturity. The previous nine chapters have presented us with the truth. How then can this truth become real in my daily experience?

This is the purpose of this chapter with its title, "The Power of Christian Maturity."

We will begin by reading Ephesians 4:1-13 and considering it in the light of our present theme — maturity made real in my own experience.

Verse 1 opens with an immediate challenge, "I therefore, the prisoner of the Lord, beseech you that ye walk worthy of the vocation wherewith ye are called." Notice the phrase *walk worthy*. This is an apt description of maturity in action. Another translation for *walk worthy* is, *that ye walk perfectly balanced*.

This phrase *perfectly balanced* is most descriptive. We can understand the full meaning of it if we consider one of the expensive watches that are available today. Some of these watches are almost miracles of minute engineering. The quality of the precision craftsmanship is such that the movement is practically "perfectly balanced," which means that wherever the watch goes — high in space, or down in the depths of the sea — it keeps perfect time. Whatever the temperature, from blazing heat to arctic cold, its behavior is always the same. As long as it is worn it needs no winding, no attention of any kind. It is made to do a special job and it does it in any, and all, circumstances.

If these descriptions are translated into terms of human experiences — pressures and tensions — the high, the low, the heat and the cold — then the personality which is "perfectly balanced," and continues so to be, is exhibiting all the marks of a mature Christian. This is what the Church needs so much in these days of spiritual irresponsibility.

Verses 2 and 3 give a simple description of what this maturity looks like in terms of human relationships, "Living as becomes you — with complete lowliness of mind (humility) and meekness (unselfishness, gentleness, mildness), with patience, bearing with one another *and* making allowances because you love one another. Be eager *and* strive earnestly to guard *and* keep the harmony *and* oneness of [produced by] the Spirit in the binding power of peace" (*Amplified Bible*).

The verses which follow dwell on the oneness of our faith which comes from the "One God and Father of all, who is above all, and through all, and in you all" (verse 6).

Verses 7-12 speak of the gifts that have come to us through Christ. Verse 11 teaches us that some of these gifts were men, doing specific ministries, "apostles; . . . prophets; . . . evangelists; . . . pastors and teachers; For the perfecting of the saints." The word *perfecting* here means the *complete adjusting*.

Verse 13 is the key verse which tells us why all this was done and all these were given, "Till we all come in the unity of the faith, and of the knowledge of the Son of God, unto a perfect man, unto the measure of the stature of the fulness of Christ."

Notice the words *a perfect man.* This is the same word again denoting *a mature man.*

We notice also that it is the *knowledge of the Son of God* that will bring us to maturity.

The *Amplified Bible* gives added insight into this tremendous verse, "until we all attain oneness in the faith and in the comprehension of the full and accurate knowledge of the Son of God; that [we might arrive] at really mature manhood — the completeness of personality which is nothing less than the standard height of Christ's own perfection — the measure of the stature of the fullness of the Christ, *and* the completeness found in Him."

This is something we can dig into, something we can make our own, *really mature manhood . . . completeness of personality . . . the measure of the stature of the fullness of Christ.*

This verse is teaching us a new way to spell out the meaning of Christian maturity. It speaks of a *completeness of personality* and the *fullness of Christ.* We can put these two thoughts together now and see what they mean in terms of our own personal experience.

The word personality is a term well understood by us. It denotes what a person really is. It is that impression we remember as we think of our friends and associates. We do not usually bring to mind the physical features of those remembered; we think in terms of their disposition, their attractiveness, their wholesomeness — all the characteristics which draw us to one another.

This is good, in many respects, because some, who can make no claims to physical beauty, have such a sweet radiance of personality that the light that shines from within dissolves the shadow that shows without.

But our verse here is speaking about completeness of personality, thus teaching that it is possible to have an incompleteness of personality. It is in this area that the mechanics of Christian maturity operate, and it is here that immaturity is evident.

The human personality is that which is called, in the Bible, the *heart of man.* There are many verses in the Old and New

Testaments where the writer or speaker refers to the *heart of man* or the *heart*. When this is done the object is to indicate the human personality — the man who lives within the human body.

The Bible also uses the word *soul* to denote the *heart* or the personality. I Thessalonians 5:23 says, "I pray God your whole spirit and soul and body be preserved blameless unto the coming of our Lord Jesus Christ." Here is direct teaching concerning the trinity of man. In Genesis 1:26 we read, "And God said, Let us make man in our image, after our likeness." Verse 27 continues, "So God created man in his own image, in the image of God created he him."

This does not mean that man resembled God physically because *God is a Spirit*. But the God who said *Let us*, was the triune God, the One whom we worship as the Trinity. Man was made in the image and after the likeness of the triune God — the Trinity, so he was created as a "human trinity" — spirit, soul and body.

Man has a human spirit whereby he is able to have fellowship and union with God. He has a human soul, or heart, or personality by which he can have fellowship and union with those around him. He has a human body which is the vehicle through which these fellowships can be demonstrated, enjoyed and fulfilled.

Our verse in Ephesians 4:13 is thus pointing us to *really mature manhood — the completeness of personality which is nothing less than the standard height of Christ's own perfection,* a maturity based on completeness.

The author of Psalm 119 also had this thought in mind. In verse 2 he says, "Blessed are they that keep his testimonies, and that seek him with the whole heart." Notice that the *blessedness* comes when the *whole heart* is involved — the completeness of personality.

In verse 10 we read, "With my whole heart have I sought thee." In verse 34 the longing for maturity is shown, "Give me understanding, and I shall keep thy law; yea, I shall observe it with my whole heart." His sincerity is seen in verse 58, "I intreated thy favour with my whole heart." His determination is in evidence in verse 69, "I will keep thy precepts with my whole heart." Verse 145 reveals the depth of his hunger for God, "I cried with my whole heart."

What we need, therefore, is a *whole heart* experience, a *completeness of personality* that will lead us to *really mature manhood*.

The Bible also teaches that the human heart — or the personality — can be divided into three areas — the emotions, the mind or intellect, and the will. In Matthew 15:19 the Lord Jesus said, "For out of the heart proceed evil thoughts, murders, adulteries, fornications, thefts, false witness, blasphemies." All the sordid emotional actions and reactions come from the human heart — or personality.

In John 14:1 and 27 the Lord said, "Let not your heart be troubled." Emotional fear and distress are experienced in the human heart — or personality.

In Matthew 9:4 we read, "And Jesus knowing their thoughts said, Wherefore think ye evil in your hearts?" Mark 2:8 records, "And immediately when Jesus perceived in his spirit that they so reasoned within themselves, he said unto them, Why reason ye these things in your hearts?" The human heart, or personality, is thus shown as the center also of the mind or the intellect.

The whole of the Book of Daniel became possible because of 1:8, "But Daniel purposed in his heart." Daniel made a decision, and by his act of will he demonstrated the quality of his maturity, even though he was a young man. Notice that the decision was made *in his heart*. The human heart is thus the place where the will is exercised.

We can now begin to see that the phrase *completeness of personality* has a depth of meaning which can come as an immediate challenge to our hearts and lives. Ephesians 4:13 speaks of *the measure of the stature of the fullness of the Christ*. This signifies that *really mature manhood* and *completeness of personality* result from the *fullness of Christ*. Inasmuch as Christ is allowed to *fill me*, in that much do I experience a growing completeness of personality.

This is something akin to the phrase we read in Ephesians 5:18, "And be not drunk with wine, wherein is excess; but be filled with the Spirit." To be filled with the Spirit does not mean or imply that I get more of the Spirit for I already have the Spirit. But it does mean that the indwelling Spirit gets more of me. As I open up my heart, or personality, to His entrance — as I yield myself to His will — then He can fill more of me. As He fills more of me, then I have more of Him.

Remember always that to be filled with the Spirit is to be controlled by the Spirit. What I yield He fills. What He fills He controls. Therefore, being filled with the Spirit leads to discipline and control — as Ephesians 5:18 indicates — and not to *excess*.

Remember, also, that the Lord Jesus said in John 16:13, 14, "Howbeit when he, the Spirit of truth, is come, he will guide you into all truth: for he shall not speak of himself . . . He shall glorify me." The proof of a Spirit-filled life is the fact that Christ is uplifted and glorified in the life of the believer.

Any claim to *being filled with the Holy Spirit* which is not backed up by a Christ-centered and Christ-exalting life is something different from the teaching of the Word of God.

We are considering in this chapter the mechanics of Christian maturity. What is the power, and how does it operate? How can I be a mature Christian? What does it involve when it is spelled out letter by letter?

At this stage we can begin to answer the questions we have been asking. Christian maturity does not come naturally — by age, experience, education or church office. I do not become mature by praying for it and agonizing for it. Nor do I reach this position by extended Bible study, or by reading books on victorious Christian living, or by attending "Deeper Life Conferences," or "Keswick Conventions."

Christian maturity comes from completeness of personality which itself is the result of the fullness of Christ. My heart, or personality, consists of the three areas that make up "me" — my emotions, my mind or intellect, and my will. As the Lord Jesus Christ, through His Holy Spirit, is allowed to move into these three areas and fill them, so I experience a growing sense of His fullness. The measure of His fullness is the measure of my maturity, regardless of my age, race, education or experience.

Remember always that the evidence of His filling is the evidence of His control. Where He fills, He controls. Where I control, He cannot fill. Where He cannot fill or control, then I cannot experience real maturity.

Many Christians are incomplete in their own life by their lack of knowledge concerning these three areas — the emotions, the mind or intellect, and the will.

My relationship to Christ must begin through the emotional side of my personality. This is so because every relationship I have, or experience, or make, begins on an emotional basis. There is nothing wrong with being emotionally moved in my response to Christ — it is both natural and to be expected.

Some people miss so much by being against the Gospel, because they say it is emotional. I have seen some of these same people watching an exciting football game. Their emotional response and involvement was magnificent to behold. In fact their enjoyment of the game could be measured by the emotions they displayed. There is nothing wrong with this — this is the way we are made.

These same people insist that our relationship to God should be on the intellectual level and, in this, they are perfectly correct. But to insist on the intellectual only, to the exclusion of the emotional is unfair and unnatural. I need to know the rules to understand the football game, but mere intellectual appreciation does not make a respectable citizen stand and cheer in response to a brilliant play.

The difficulty arises when the emotional side of the personality is stressed and encouraged to the exclusion of the mind or intellect and the will. The *whole heart* is the unity of the three areas. The *completeness of personality* is only achieved when each of the three areas is filled with the fullness of Christ.

I have worked with young people for many years. I have enjoyed the sincerity of their singing and the honesty of their words of testimony. I have listened to many a high school and college student telling of their love for the Lord Jesus. I have seen tears flow, as promises were made to love Him and serve Him.

All that was said was absolutely sincere, and an interested

listener might be moved to feel that this was the beginning of a wonderful life for Christ. But history proves that this is not always so. There are many disillusioned, disappointed and dissatisfied Christians today in our churches. Yet, at one time they spoke brave, sincere words for Jesus.

The answer is basically simple. Sincerity is not enough. An emotional response is necessary, but, if that is all there is, then there can never be a growth to maturity. The whole heart means every area yielded to Christ.

It is often easy to be emotionally moved. Emotions cost nothing. In fact, a good emotional response to Christ can often draw special attention to the one involved. My exalting of my love for Christ could even result in my exalting of myself.

I start to grow when I sit down and count the cost of allowing the Lord Jesus to move into the area of my mind and my intellect. When the Lord Jesus moves into a life He brings His own standards of values and His own orders of priority. He said in Luke 12:15, "A man's life consisteth not in the abundance of the things which he possesseth." The Lord Jesus taught and lived this truth while here on earth. He will still want to live this truth in any heart He indwells. But the world in which we live does not teach this truth. We live in the most materialistic society that has ever existed. We do business against this background. We are taught to think and live without this truth as our guiding star.

Mature Christianity shows itself when new standards emerge and new priorities take over in every area of life. To many Christians this will mean new standards of honesty in school, college, business and home. And, let us be honest, some of us are not willing to allow Christ's standards to be evident in our lives. It may cost me my job, or my career, or my character.

To other Christians, allowing Christ to fill and control the mind or intellect will mean new standards of purity in thought and word and deed. This is where the high school and college student has to count the cost. "Shall I be 'with it,' or 'with Him'?" The test here is really going to hurt. This may cost me my popularity, my girl friend, my boy friend. I may lose the "office" I have been working for in the school organization, or my place on the team.

These new standards of purity will challenge my tastes in clothing, literature, music, art and every other aspect where cultural tastes are evidenced. And, it may cost too much to allow Christ's standards to control me. It may be much easier to let things stay as they are — and just get by with the rest. I don't *have* to yield full control to Christ, but I will never begin to move into maturity unless I do.

It is good at this point to emphasize that allowing Christ to control is not something to be "endured." I do not have to lose so many "things" that I find myself lonely and bereft of all joy and delight — because God will never be any man's debtor. When Christ comes with His new standards He brings His new satisfaction. I exchange my paltry pleasures for the sheer joyous delight of His presence in my life. It pays a thousand times in this life to love and serve the Lord Jesus, but I may prefer the coinage of this world to the companionship of Christ.

The third area of my personality that Christ wants to fill is the volitional aspect or the will. Incidentally, modern psychology and psychiatry also teach that the human personality consists of these three divisions. Various schools and thinkers use differing names for the three areas, but their teaching is basically that set forth in the Bible — a personality composed of emotions, mind and will.

The will is that decisive part which puts into orbit the reasoning of the mind fired by the enthusiasm of the emotions. It is the finger on the trigger which, when squeezed, commits the owner to a definite line of action. It turns reasoning into reality.

The tragedy is that many Christians can be fired up with emotional enthusiasm; they can reason the thing through and work out a plan of action. However, when it comes to making the final decision they hesitate and finally draw back. As a result, nothing is crystallized. The cause of Christ suffers and in many instances the Christian who draws back soon slips back. Instead of maturity and progress there is the sense of failure that clouds the vision and weakens the witness.

Until Christ fills and controls my will, little of lasting value will emerge from my heart and life. There are Christians at home today who once felt the pull of the mission field. They sensed and were moved by the need and the urgency. They considered, and, led by Christ, they planned how this moving of the Spirit in their lives could lead to missionary training and service. In some cases they even went on to actual training and preparation. But, somewhere along the line, the "will" never fitted into the program. The final thrust was never given, and what could have been so precious and powerful became so pointless and useless.

We have been basing our thinking on Ephesians 4:13 with its vision of *really mature manhood* and *completeness of personality*. Verse 14 goes on to enjoin us, "That we henceforth be no more children, tossed to and fro." Here again is the warning against remaining as a babe in Christ. How true are these words today — *tossed to and fro!*

Verse 17 challenges us to measure ourselves against the world around us, "that ye henceforth walk not as other Gentiles (heathen) walk, in the vanity of their minds." The word *vanity* here means "the folly, the emptiness and the futility of their lives." Spiritual immaturity leads to this very thing — "emptiness and futility."

Verses 18 and 19 present a remarkable picture of the world around us with its darkness, willful blindness, spiritual apathy and utter impurity.

Then verse 20 says, "But ye have not so learned Christ." This is a short, simple verse, but it pulls us up fast. How have you learned Christ? Not learned what He has done, but come to learn Him — face to face, moment by moment?

In one way, many of us do not know Christ as He is. We know what He has done, and what He has said, and what He will do when He comes again, but we do not have a close intimate knowledge of Him. This can only come as we open up our *whole hearts* to His control.

The rest of Ephesians 4 becomes a wonderful setting forth of what truly happens when there is completeness of personality through the filling of emotions, mind and will. Verse 21 says, "If so be that ye have heard him, and have been taught by him, as the truth is in Jesus." If this is so, then the results in the Christian experience will be as follows: Verse 23 says there will be a "new mind." Verse 24 adds: "that ye put on the 'new man.'" Verse 25 speaks of a "new membership," *for we are members one of another.*

Verse 27 tells of a "new master," and verse 28 of a "new method." Verse 29 speaks of the "new ministry" we will have — *minister grace unto the hearers.* Verse 31 describes the "new manners" that will be seen when the old life is *put away.*

This is so wonderful and so needed in every church, but it can only come true when Christians see their need, the answer to that need, then act upon it!

The need for Christian maturity is evident. The power to meet that need is present in the person of the indwelling Christ. All that God is waiting for is our willingness to come as the writer in Psalm 119:2 and, "seek him with the whole heart."

A Prayer for Meditation

I thank Thee, Heavenly Father, that spiritual maturity is something I can know and experience.

Teach me more about completeness of personality in my own experience.

May my faith go deeper than mere emotionalism and further than excited enthusiasm.

May my mind, intellect and will be involved in my relationship with the Lord Jesus.

Grant me wisdom to see the implications of being filled with Christ, and courage to count the cost.

May I exercise that childlike faith that sees the need, recognizes the provision to meet that need, then acts with humble simplicity to make it real in my own experience. This I pray in the name of my Saviour, the Lord Jesus Christ. Amen.

CHAPTER 11

THE BOOK OF ACHAN — SAVED TO PERISH

WE HAVE BEEN CONSIDERING, in the previous chapters, the glorious possibility of becoming so involved with the Lord Jesus that the complete personality is open to experience His infilling.

Such a step is the sure way to knowing the power of Christian maturity. In one sense, going on with Christ is the natural thing to do. If our hearts desire greater things and better things, then this is the answer, a deeper involvement with the Lord Jesus Christ.

But history and human experience show that a Christian can have this desire, be all set to yield his life to His fullness, and then one utterly stupid, unnecessary act or decision can smash the entire wonderful possibility.

This present chapter, "The Book of Achan," is the awful story of such a foolish act — so stupid and senseless in its doing but so terrible and devastating in its consequences.

We have thought already on the significance of the title, "The Book of Joshua" — what God could do with one man's yielded life. The same thought is seen also in "The Book of Ruth" and "The Book of Daniel," as well as in other such titles. God used men and women to change the course of history. Race and respectability did not count in these operations. All that was necessary was a willingness to be involved with God.

The "Book of Achan" is also the life of Achan. It began so full of promise, it ended suddenly, so full of judgment.

The "Book of Achan" makes a searching contrast to the "Book of Rahab." Rahab was a pagan, outside the family of

God, condemned to perish in the judgment of Jericho — but she was saved. What is more, she was saved to live, and "she dwelleth in Israel even unto this day" (Joshua 6:25). She deserved nothing but condemnation, yet she received only blessing.

Achan was one of God's chosen people. He had been redeemed and preserved and blessed. His days of wandering in the wilderness were over. He had crossed the Jordan. He had shared in the victory at Jericho. He was all set to move into his own inheritance. He had sons and daughters who would live on to perpetuate his memory, so that Achan, too, could continue to dwell in Israel *even unto this day*.

The dark days were over. There was nothing but sunshine and blessing ahead. Then — one stupid, senseless act shattered all that might have been his. His whole world fell to pieces and, in a horrible moment of judgment, he and all that he had vanished forever.

Rahab was saved to live. Achan was saved — only to die and perish. Rahab dwelleth in Israel even to this day, but Achan perished with his whole family and possessions. He remains only as an awful warning and an ugly memory. There was nothing left but a heap of stones and the wisps of smoke rising from the burning.

What a wasted life, when all could have been so different! What challenge and a warning to every child of God! We have been saved to live, but we, too, can be saved to "perish." Not that we lose our eternal salvation purchased by the blood of Christ at Calvary. That is ours. But, all that we might be in wholesome witness, and all that might come from our yielded lives, can be utterly crushed and swept away through a stupid, useless, senseless act or decision. The warning is clear and plain.

We have considered, elsewhere, that names in the Bible can have a special significance, indicating in a way the character of the one so named. This becomes apparent when we consider the names given in Joshua 7:1. Here are shown for us the four generations that ended with Achan. First we have his great-grandfather whose name was Zerah. This name means "a sprout," or "a shoot," indicating the development of a new life and a new beginning.

Next comes Achan's grandfather whose name is given as Zabdi. This name means "God is endower," or "God is the giver." This comes as a natural progression from the new beginning.

The father's name was Carmi, meaning "fruitful and noble," thus showing how "the shoot" was fulfilling the promise.

Then comes Achan, and here the name sequence ends, for Achan means "trouble." This was the name given to him at his birth, and how significant it was for the days ahead.

Thus we have four generations leading on from blessing to blessing and then an abrupt stop — all that might have been, failed to mature. Achan had sons, but their names are not known. There was no need to know who they were for they perished with their father. The shoot that held such hopes for the future was suddenly cut off.

The purpose of the story of Achan is to see the extent of the repercussions that came from his one stupid act. Not only did Achan and his entire family suffer as a result, but also the entire nation. Such a thing can still happen today when a man's stupid folly affects not only his family, but also his church and the witness of God's people in that place.

We see this illustrated in Joshua 7:1, "But the children of Israel committed a trespass in the accursed thing." In one way this does not seem fair, for only Achan was the offender — the rest of his family were completely innocent. But a little research into the story reveals several significant statements.

In Deuteronomy 7 Moses was telling the people God's plans for the entry into Canaan. Remember that the Book of Deuteronomy was the "post mortem" on the wilderness failure. In 1:1 we read, "These be the words which Moses spake unto all Israel on this side Jordan in the wilderness." These words would be fresh in the ears of all the Israelites.

In Deuteronomy 7:23 we read, "But the Lord thy God shall deliver them unto thee . . . he shall deliver their kings into thine hand. . . . The graven images of their gods shall ye burn with fire: thou shalt not desire the silver or gold that is on them . . . Neither shalt thou bring an abomination into thine house, lest thou be a cursed thing like it: but thou shalt utterly detest it, and thou shalt utterly abhor it; for it is a cursed thing."

The word "accursed" which is used here and later on, means "destined and dedicated for destruction." See the significance of this in verse 26, "lest thou be a cursed thing like it." The teaching was clear — anyone who identified himself with an unholy, evil thing condemned to destruction would also be identified in that destruction.

Note also the words in verse 25 whereby the children of Israel had not "to desire the silver or gold" that was on the images of the pagan gods.

Achan deliberately went against this teaching that he himself had heard from the lips of Moses.

Then in Joshua 6:17-19 Joshua gave strict instructions regarding Jericho, "The city shall be accursed, even it, and all that are therein, to the LORD . . . And ye, in any wise keep yourselves from the accursed thing, lest ye make yourselves accursed, when ye take of the accursed thing, and make the camp of Israel a curse, and trouble it. But all the silver, and gold . . . are consecrated unto the LORD."

These words were heard by Achan hours before his foolish heart rebelled. There was the warning — everything in Jericho was accursed and to be burned — if a man took anything, then the curse would fall on him and he would be burned. In taking the accursed thing he would bring a curse on the whole camp and everyone would suffer. Nothing could be plainer or more simple to understand. In spite of this, Achan took a Babylonish garment, two hundred shekels of silver, and a wedge of gold (Joshua 7:21).

Why did he do it? Why do Christians do stupid things today that bring shame on their families and the stain of dishonor on their church? Undoubtedly Achan fell a victim once more to the wiles of Satan. We read in I John 2:16, "For all that is in the world, the lust of the flesh, and the lust of the eyes, and the pride of life, is not of the Father, but is of the world." This is the devil's trinity of temptation, his one means of attack on the children of men.

We see the Satanic attack first in Genesis 3:6, "And when the woman saw that the tree was good for food, and that it was pleasant to the eyes, and a tree to be desired to make one wise, she took of the fruit thereof" — the lust of the flesh, the lust of the eyes, the pride of life.

Here the enemy scored the first of his many victories in human hearts. He was able to do this with the woman because she had previously listened to the insinuation of Satan. She had said in verse 3, "God hath said, Ye shall not eat of it, neither shall ye touch it, lest ye die." To which Satan had added his denial, "Ye shall not surely die" (verse 4).

Satan had made his greatest lie in saying, "Sin — and you can get away with it." This is what he has been saying all down the ages — "Go on, sin! You won't die, you can get away with it!" Both the man and woman listened to the devil in Genesis 3 and this became the fall of man, when man openly rebelled against his Creator and believed the lie of the devil.

This is what Achan did. He heard all the warnings. He knew what would happen. He walked into the situation with his eyes wide open. He knew his family would perish, and that Israel would suffer. He knew it — but he did not believe it! He thought he could get away with it — just this once.

This is the story behind so much failure in so many Christian lives. We know what the Bible says, but we think we can get away with it. We read in Galatians 6:7, "Be not deceived; God is not mocked: for whatsoever a man soweth, that shall he also reap," but we rationalize ourselves out of the verse and out of the verdict.

This is why the story of Achan is so important at this stage of our study in this book. Remember always, that I Corinthians 10:1-12 directs us to measure our own lives against these specific stories in the Old Testament, "wherefore let him that thinketh he standeth take heed lest he fall" (verse 12). In spite of our longings and desires for Christian maturity there is always the awful possibility of failure such as Achan experienced. Sincerity is no protection against sin.

Joshua 7 makes miserable reading. The shadow of Achan falls across the words as we read them. The amazing thing is to see how quickly the words of Joshua 6:18 came true, "And ye, in any wise keep yourselves from the accursed thing, lest ye make yourselves accursed, when ye take of the accursed thing, and make the camp of Israel a curse, and trouble it." The camp of Israel did become a curse and there was trouble, but no one knew why, except Achan.

Joshua had been greatly encouraged by the initial victory at Jericho. Israel had won their first great battle, and the hearts of the people were rejoicing with growing confidence. Verses 2-4 of chapter 7 tell of this confidence as the men prepared to attack Ai.

They had viewed the situation. They made their plans for using two or three thousand men. They moved in to attack, expecting nothing but victory — and then came utter tragedy, "and they fled before the men of Ai. And the men of Ai smote of them about thirty and six men: for they chased them . . . wherefore the hearts of the people melted, and became as water" (verse 5). How descriptive is that phrase, their hearts *became as water*.

In a moment all their confidence vanished. When their hearts melted, their courage evaporated and their hopes vanished. Verse 6 tells us how, "Joshua rent his clothes, and fell to the earth upon his face before the ark of the Lord until the eventide, he and the elders of Israel."

Here was God's man to whom had been given "the promise, the program and the power." He had been promised, "Every place . . . every day," and now he was stunned into silence.

As Joshua and the people of Israel agonized concerning this awful tragedy, bewildered and crushed with defeat, only one man knew the cause. Achan waited in trembling suspense.

Joshua's first reaction was to blame God. In verse 7 his words pour out in accusing admonition, "Alas, O Lord God, wherefore hast thou at all brought this people over Jordan, to deliver us into the hands of the Amorites, to destroy us?" He almost accuses God of treachery. Then Joshua spoke the familiar language of defeat, so often heard in the wilderness, "would to God we had been content, and dwelt on the other side of Jordan." What vain words — who could be content in the wilderness?

In verse 8 the blame is put on Israel. In verse 9 Joshua considered the possibility of all the inhabitants of Canaan surrounding Israel and destroying them to "cut off our name from the earth." Then, in a moment of panic, he cries to God, "and what wilt thou do unto thy great name?" Joshua in his own moment of extreme weakness and failure suddenly imagines the panic there must be in heaven. God, as well as Israel, was suddenly in trouble. How was God going to get Himself out of this predicament?

Then God spoke, "Get thee up; wherefore liest thou thus upon thy face?" (verse 10). This was not a time for panic, but for purging out the sin and evil. As we have seen, only Achan was involved in this tragedy, but notice the words of God in verse 11, "Israel hath sinned, and they have also transgressed my covenant . . . for they have even taken of the accursed thing, and have also stolen, and dissembled also, and they have put it even among their own stuff."

The words of Joshua had come true — one man's sin had blighted the nation and caused suffering and loss to thirty-six men. The men who died would leave widows and orphans. This defeat was only the beginning of other tragedies that might follow, unless the problem was dealt with and the trouble stamped out.

Notice the fourfold accusation that God made against the people. First, *they have taken of the accursed thing*, then, *they have stolen*. Third, *they have dissembled also* (dissembled means to lie or deceive), and last, *they have put it even among their own stuff*.

This last point is not unimportant. Remember Moses had said in Deuteronomy 7:26, "Neither shalt thou bring an abomination into thine house, lest thou be a cursed thing like it." By hiding the loot among his own goods, Achan had brought the cursed thing into his tent and into the camp.

Observe how the whole nation was guilty — "they have taken . . . they have stolen" — and yet it was the action of just one man.

Notice how Achan had committed this fourfold offense. The articles taken and hidden were, "a goodly Babylonish garment, and two hundred shekels of silver, and a wedge of gold" (Joshua 7:21). Joshua 6:19 says, "but all the silver, and gold . . . shall come into the treasury of the LORD." So Achan had taken the accursed thing — *a goodly Babylonish garment;* he had also stolen the silver and gold, because that belonged to God. He had lied and deceived, because after the failure at Ai he remained silent, though he was aware of the cause of the defeat. He could have confessed and spared the entire camp the agony of anxious fear. Finally he had brought the cursed thing within the camp of Israel.

The rest of the chapter is the story of the inevitable consequences of sin. How the heart of Achan must have melted as he saw the relentless selection of God at work, as told in verses 16-18. First, the tribe of Judah, then the family of the Zarhites, then the men of Zabdi, then the father of Achan, Carmi, then, finally, the man himself. What a wretched picture Achan must have made that awful morning as he stood there alone in all his failure!

Joshua's words in verse 19 are wonderful, "And Joshua said unto Achan, My son, give I pray thee, glory to the Lord GOD of Israel, and make confession unto him; and tell me now what thou hast done." Achan had one last chance to give glory to God — and he took it!

How miserable it must have seemed in the cold light of day. The messenger ran to Achan's tent, discovered the garment, the silver and the gold and "they took them out of the midst of the tent, and brought them unto Joshua, and unto all the children of Israel, and laid them out before the LORD" (verse 23). What a pitiful sight they must have made — one garment, some silver and a piece of gold. For these a man had gambled away his life, his loved ones, the honor of Israel and the glory of God.

And so Achan died, and all his family and all his cattle. Everything identified with Achan was burned and the funeral pyre was buried under a pile of stones. Verse 26 says, "And they raised over him a great heap of stones unto this day." Notice those pathetic words, *unto this day!*

The same words appear in Joshua 6:25 concerning Rahab, "she dwelleth in Israel even unto this day." Rahab dwells even unto this day, but Achan was destroyed even unto this day. What a comparison! What a catastrophe! Nothing in Achan's experience with God reached maturity. We have only the madness of a stupid moment when Satan tempted and Achan fell.

I Corinthians 10:6 says, "Now these things were our examples, to the intent we should not lust after evil things, as they also lusted." Remember when Paul wrote "we," he included himself. Paul was capable of such failure — so are we.

How near can you get to Christian maturity and yet lose the lot? Ask Achan!

A Prayer for Meditation

Heavenly Father, this is a terrible story — and it is true. Rahab was saved to live — grant that this may be my experience as I go on with God.

Achan was saved to perish — deliver me, O God, from such an awful tragedy.

May I see "sin" as it really is. Preserve me from seeking loot in the spoil of this world.

Keep me close to "the promise — the program — and the power." Keep me close to Thee, through Jesus Christ my Lord. Amen.

CHAPTER 12

THE PURPOSE OF CHRISTIAN MATURITY

As WE COME to this last chapter in the book we will take time to put ourselves once more under the microscope of God.

The previous chapter challenged us with the awful failure of Achan — something which was personal and individual. It was one man alone who caused the tragedy and the heartache.

We saw in chapter 10 that the power for maturity was a completeness of personality where emotions, mind and will were filled with Christ. When the whole heart is "in gear" with Christ, then the power of the risen Lord is experienced in every area of human living — then it is that maturity is seen and known.

We can see the personal aspect of maturity when we examine Paul's letter to the Philippians 3:7-15. Here is a letter written by the most mature Christian who ever lived, a man who demonstrated constantly a unique ability to handle every situation, whether in suffering or in satisfaction.

These nine verses are his personal testimony to his relationship with the risen Lord Jesus. In Philippians 1:21 he wrote, "For to me to live is Christ, and to die is gain." In the verses we are considering he expands that concept and spells out for us the details involved in such a dedication.

These nine verses are essentially personal. Thirteen times he uses the personal pronoun "I" as he tells what his desires are toward the Lord Jesus:

> 7 But what things were gain to me, those I counted loss for Christ.
> 8 Yea, doubtless, and I count all things but loss for the excellency of the knowledge of Christ Jesus my Lord: for whom I have suffered

the loss of all things, and do count them but dung, that I may win Christ,

9 And be found in him, not having mine own righteousness, which is of the law, but that which is through the faith of Christ, the righteousness which is of God by faith:

10 That I may know him, and the power of his resurrection, and the fellowship of his sufferings, being made conformable unto his death;

11 If by any means I might attain unto the resurrection of the dead.

12 Not as though I had already attained, either were already perfect: but I follow after, if that I may apprehend that for which I am apprehended of Christ Jesus.

13 Brethren, I count not myself to have apprehended: but this one thing I do, forgetting those things which are behind, and reaching forth unto those things which are before,

14 I press toward the mark for the prize of the high calling of God in Christ Jesus.

15 Let us therefore, as many as be perfect, be thus minded.

The important thing here is to read verses 7-14, realize what is involved, and then let verse 15 hit home, "Let us therefore, as many as be perfect, be thus minded." (The word *perfect* is the word "mature," which is the basis of our study in this book).

We must grasp the fact that this testimony of Paul is not just something we gaze at with holy admiration. We are not to be spectators applauding the mighty deeds of a popular hero. We are to be involved in the same attitudes and aspirations, *let us be thus minded.*

These verses give us the entire purpose of Paul's living, and Paul's purpose must be our purpose, if we want to go on to maturity.

There is tremendous truth, especially in verses 10, 11 and 12. This truth is more fully revealed in the *Amplified Bible:*

10 [For my determined purpose is] that I may know Him — that I may progressively become more deeply and intimately acquainted with Him, perceiving and recognizing and understanding [the wonders of His Person] more strongly and more clearly. And that I may in that same way come to know the power outflowing from His resurrection [which it exerts over believers]; and that I may so share His sufferings as to be continually transformed [in spirit into His likeness even] to His death, [in the hope]

11 That if possible I may attain to the [spiritual and moral] resurrection [that lifts me] out from among the dead [even while in the body].

12 Not that I have now attained [this ideal] or am already made perfect, but I press on to lay hold of (grasp) *and* make my own, that for which Christ Jesus, the Messiah, has laid hold of me *and* made me His own.

What magnificent words these are. The entire passage radiates a boldness and an outlook which puts to shame the tawdry ambitions of many Christian hearts.

We can understand these verses more clearly if we see that Paul was pressing for a threefold appreciation of the Lord Jesus. His burning desire was to know "the Person — the Power — the Purpose" involved in his relationship with Christ.

If we can make this our own earnest desire then we, too, will be on the pathway of maturity.

Paul's first longing was *that I may know Him.* He was attracted to and fascinated by the "Person" of the Lord Jesus. Ever since that wonderful day — recorded in Acts 9:4, 5, when Paul had heard the amazing question, "Saul, Saul, why persecutest thou me?" to which he had stammered out his own question, "Who art thou, Lord?" — he had been filled with an eager desire to know more, so that he could give more.

It is possible to be so taken up with the work of Christ that we discover little of the Person of Christ. I can be meticulously accurate in my doctrine, and yet be vague and uncertain in my personal devotion to my blessed Saviour. To know Him, I must live with Him. There must be a wonderful intimacy between my soul and my Saviour.

This sense of breathless wonder is seen in many of the great hymns of our faith, hymns we love to sing because they touch the chords of our hearts. How much more satisfying when the heart can play its own responsive melody of love and adoration.

This fact of "knowing Him" is something every one of us must pursue if we are to go on, like Paul, to be involved with Him. There is only one way in which we can achieve this experience. It is by spending time with Christ in worship and adoration. The method of spending that time may differ according to our abilities and opportunities, but the necessity is essential. Always remember that worship and adoration are not the same as asking for favors or presenting petitions. Love is often most effective in its silence.

Paul's desire was *to perceive and recognize and understand the wonders of His Person.* Remember that the One whom Paul met on the Damascus Road was the risen Christ in all His power and glory. The One of whom he desired to know more was that same risen Christ, who said in Matthew 28:18, 20, "All power is given unto me in heaven and in earth . . . and, lo, I am with you alway, even unto the end of the world." The Lord had promised His presence; Paul sought to prove His presence.

But there was a purpose in Paul's fervent desire to know the Person of Christ. As he proved His presence so he would experience His power. This is the second great thrust in Philippians 3:10, "And that I may in that same way come to know the power outflowing from His resurrection [which it exerts over believers]" (*Amplified Bible*). The more Paul knew of the Person of Christ, the more he would experience the power of Christ.

The greatest need in the Church today is that those who have been redeemed by the blood of Christ should go on to experience the presence of the risen Christ so that they can demonstrate the power of the indwelling Christ — *the power outflowing from His resurrection.*

A knowledge of this will make possible an understanding of verse 11. The King James' version reads, *If by any means I might attain unto the resurrection of the dead.* This is both uncertain and ambiguous in communicating the real meaning. The *Amplified Bible* reads, *That if possible I may attain to the [spiritual and moral] resurrection [that lifts me] out from among the dead [even while in the body].* The reference to the resurrection in this verse is not pointing to the dramatic experience of a coming day, but to the outworking day by day of the fact of being born again.

Ephesians 2:1 says, "And you hath he quickened, who were dead in trespasses and sins." We were dead, but now we are alive from the dead. John 5:24 has come true in our experience,

"Verily, verily, I say unto you, He that heareth my word, and believeth on him that sent me, hath everlasting life, and shall not come into condemnation; but is passed from death unto life."

When we passed from death unto life we experienced the resurrection referred to in Philippians 3:11. But, notice carefully what Paul is saying in this same verse. He speaks of *a spiritual and moral resurrection.* All Christians have experienced the spiritual resurrection when they were born again. What is so vital now is that the power of the risen Christ that brought the spiritual life should be released, and become operative in the moral life.

It was for this that Paul yearned and pressed forward. It is this that is so much needed in the Church today — the application of the power of Christ to the moral life of the believer. The Lord Jesus said in Matthew 7:20, "Wherefore by their fruits ye shall know them." This is eternal truth applicable to all ages and situations. What a blessed thing it would be if we as believers opened our moral lives more and more to the infusion of the risen Life of Christ.

Such an act would take care of so much of the spiritual junk that clutters up the free-flowing of the Gospel — the pride, the gossip, the backbiting, the jealousy, the impurity in thought, word and deed. All these and the other attendant works of the flesh would be swept away if a moral resurrection took place in our lives.

The aspirations of Paul in II Corinthians 4:10, 11 would then become real in us, "that the life also of Jesus might be made manifest in our body . . . that the life also of Jesus might be made manifest in our mortal flesh." The life of Jesus will be made manifest in our mortal flesh when the power of the risen Christ is made manifest in our moral life.

This can only become true when we, first of all, "know Him" in increasing intimacy, and then know His power at work in our fragile flesh. The moral resurrection will be seen in the growth in Christian maturity as the fragrance of His presence, and power, permeate the complete personality — emotions, mind and will.

The third thing Paul wanted to know is expressed in verse

12, "I press on to lay hold of (grasp) *and* make my own, that for which Christ Jesus, the Messiah, has laid hold of me *and* made me His own" (*Amplified Bible*). When Christ saved Paul, He had a purpose and a plan in mind for Paul's life. Now, what Paul is seeking is that he might be identified with that purpose and that plan.

Knowing "the Person" leads to experiencing "His Power." Yielding my entire life to that "Power" sets in motion the "Purposes" of Christ in my life.

Paul was on the move, he was always "going" — even when he was locked in a prison cell. Remember that the Philippian letter was written in prison, but even there he was "pressing on" and "reaching forth."

Paul saw himself always in relation to the purpose of God. This could be an encouragement to many of us if we went on, so to know the "Purpose" of the "Power" of the "Person" indwelling our hearts and lives, that we saw ourselves caught up in the plans and purposes of God.

If we could see ourselves "in gear" with Christ, then we would know His power "meshed" with the whole of our yielded personality. We could then go on to appreciate that as His "driving power" was experienced in our day by day living, then His plans and purposes would be both set forth and fulfilled through us.

This is what Paul is proclaiming in this personal testimony— something so practical and down to earth, yet something which simply must be experienced if ever the believer is to go on to maturity.

Remember always that "going on" with Christ is not necessarily finding success and "going up" in the world. With Paul, the experience of "going on" with Christ was, in reality "going down" — but always, with Christ.

Then, of course, the point of this passage comes in verse 15, "Let us therefore, as many as be perfect [mature], be thus minded." What Paul said of himself, he says to you and me. His desires must be our desires. His experience must be our experience. We, too, must be able to say, *For my determined pur-*

pose is that I may know Him — the Person — the Power — the Purpose for my life.

Inasmuch as I bow my heart in humble acceptance of this fact, and yield my life to Christ for His outliving, then, in that much, I "grow up" from day to day and Christian maturity becomes my most cherished experience.

A Prayer for Meditation

Heavenly Father, I thank Thee for this testimony of Paul. Help me to know more and more of the glorious Person of my Lord Jesus Christ.

As I know Him, may I understand so much more of His amazing power.

I, too, would desire a moral resurrection within my own personality. Teach me how this can come true in my own experience.

As I grow in grace and maturity may I know more fully Your purposes for my life.

As I understand this plan give me such love in my heart that most gladly will I yield myself in fullest cooperation.

May all this be done for the honor and glory of the Lord Jesus Christ. Amen.

THE ZONDERVAN PAPERBACK SERIES
Each 95¢

THE REBELLIOUS PLANET — Lon Woodrum	No. 12292s
YOU CAN WITNESS WITH CONFIDENCE — Rosalind Rinker	No. 10714s
APOSTLE TO THE ILLITERATES (Frank C. Laubach) — David Mason	No. 10141s
THE GOSPEL BLIMP — Joe Bayly	No. 12288s
FREEDOM FROM THE SEVEN DEADLY SINS — Billy Graham	No. 9716s
THE YEARS THAT COUNT — Rosalind Rinker	No. 10715s
PLAY BALL! — James Hefley	No. 9797s
PRAYER—CONVERSING WITH GOD—Rosalind Rinker	No. 10716s
HOW TO ENJOY THE CHRISTIAN LIFE—Don Mainprize	No. 10106s
THESE MY PEOPLE — Lillian Dickson	No. 9524s
LIFE IS FOR LIVING — Betty Carlson	No. 9384s
SCIENCE RETURNS TO GOD — James H. Jauncey	No. 9927s
NEVER A DULL MOMENT — Eugenia Price	No. 10584s
SO YOU'RE A TEENAGE GIRL — Jill Renich	No. 10706s
ABOVE OURSELVES — James H. Jauncey	No. 9950s
BECOMING A CHRISTIAN — Rosalind Rinker	No. 10718s
BUT GOD! — V. Raymond Edman	No. 9555s
FIND OUT FOR YOURSELF — Eugenia Price	No. 10603s
THE SAVING LIFE OF CHRIST — W. Ian Thomas	No. 10908s
YOUR CHILD — Anna B. Mow	No. 12256s
SAY 'YES' TO LIFE — Anna B. Mow	No. 10383s
KNOWING GOD'S SECRETS — John Hunter	No. 9883s
THEY FOUND THE SECRET — V. Raymond Edman	No. 9564s
WE'RE NEVER ALONE — Eileen Guder	No. 9710s
MAN TO MAN — Richard C. Halverson	No. 6818s
A WOMAN'S WORLD — Clyde M. Narramore	No. 12230s
HELLBENT FOR ELECTION — P. Speshock	No. 10830s
LIFE AND LOVE — Clyde M. Narramore	No. 10412s
YOUNG ONLY ONCE — Clyde M. Narramore	No. 10414s
LIMITING GOD — John Hunter	No. 9884s
GAMES FOR ALL OCCASIONS—Carlson and Anderson	No. 9051s
WOMAN TO WOMAN — Eugenia Price	No. 10589s
PILGRIM'S PROGRESS — John Bunyan	No. 6610s
BILLY GRAHAM — John Pollock	No. 10571p
5500 QUESTIONS AND ANSWERS ON THE WHOLE BIBLE	No. 9624p
LIVING CAN BE EXCITING — Aaron N. Meckel	No. 12280s